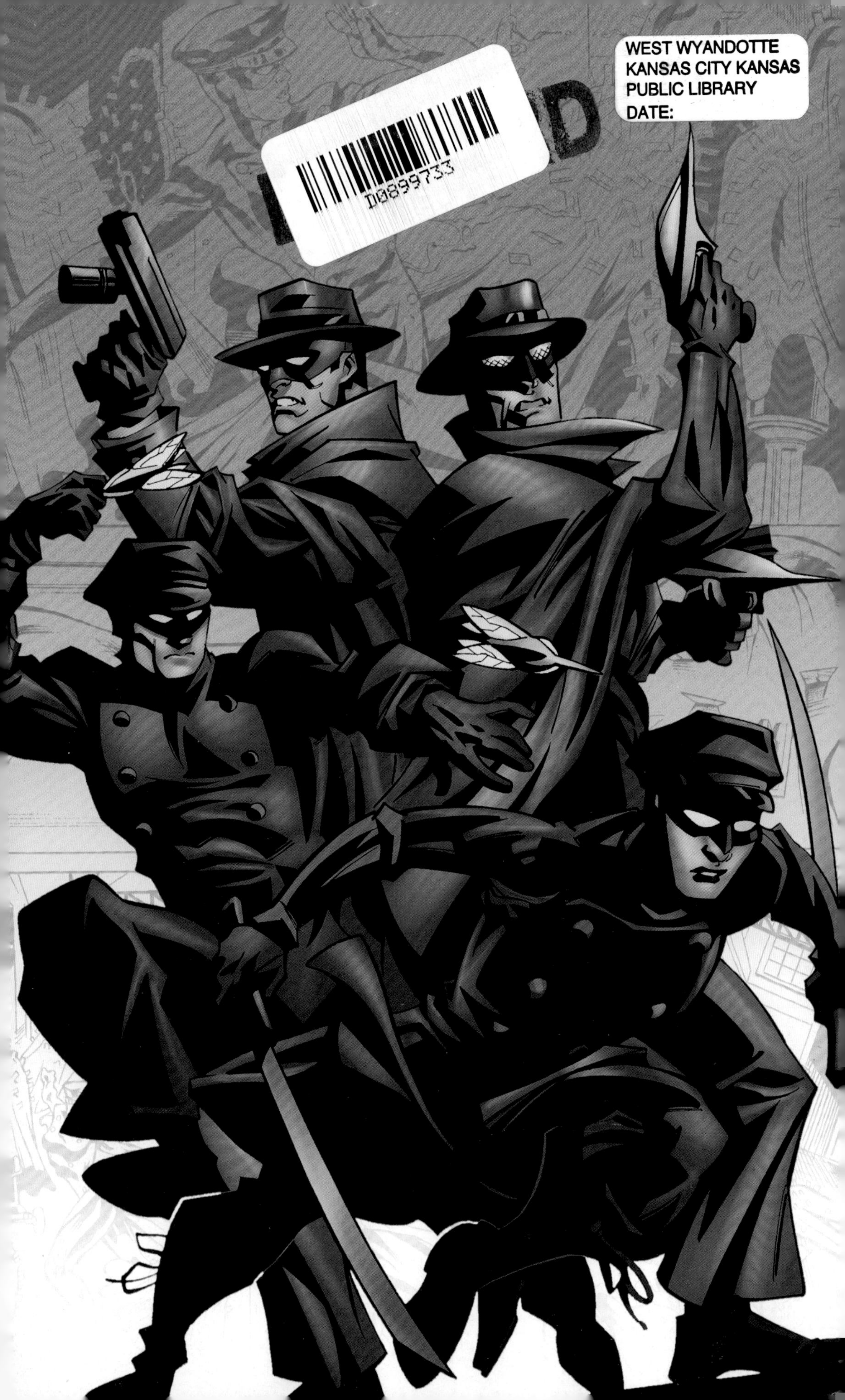

GREEN HORNET

VOLUME FOUR: RED HAND

plotted by
PHIL HESTER (issues 16-19)

written by
ANDE PARKS

illustrated by
IGOR VITORINO (issues 16-20)
RONAN CLIQUET (issue 21)

colored by
IVAN NUNES

lettered by
TROY PETERI (issues 16-17)
MARSHALL DILLON (issues 18-21)

collection cover by
JONATHAN LAU

collection design by JASON ULLMEYER

special thanks to DAVID GRACE at Green Hornet Inc.

DYNAMITE®
ENTERTAINMENT
WWW.DYNAMITE.NET

NICK BARRUCCI	• PRESIDENT
JUAN COLLADO	• CHIEF OPERATING OFFICER
JOSEPH RYBANDT	• EDITOR
JOSH JOHNSON	• CREATIVE DIRECTOR
RICH YOUNG	• DIRECTOR OF BUSINESS DEVELOPMENT
JASON ULLMEYER	• SENIOR DESIGNER
JOSH GREEN	• TRAFFIC COORDINATOR
CHRIS CANIANO	• PRODUCTION ASSISTANT

ISBN-10: 1-60690-315-2   ISBN-13: 978-1-60690-315-5   First Printing   10 9 8 7 6 5 4 3 2 1

GREEN HORNET™ VOLUME FOUR: RED HAND. First printing. Contains materials originally published in Green Hornet #16-21. Published by Dynamite Entertainment. 155 Ninth Ave. Suite B,
Runnemede, NJ 08078. Copyright © 2012 The Green Hornet, Inc. All rights reserved. The Green
Hornet, Black Beauty, Kato, and the hornet logos are trademarks of The Green Hornet, Inc. www.the-
greenhornet.com. Dynamite, Dynamite Entertainment & The Dynamite Entertainment colophon ®
2012 DFI. All Rights Reserved. All names, characters, events, and locales in this publication are
entirely fictional. Any resemblance to actual persons (living or dead), events or places, without
satiric intent, is coincidental. No portion of this book may be reproduced by any means (digital or
print) without the written permission of Dynamite Entertainment except for review purposes. The
scanning, uploading and distribution of this book via the Internet or via any other means without the
permission of the publisher is illegal and punishable by law. Please purchase only authorized electronic editions, and do not participate in or encourage electronic piracy of copyrighted materials.
Printed in China.

For media rights, foreign rights, promotions, licensing, and advertising: marketing@dynamite.net

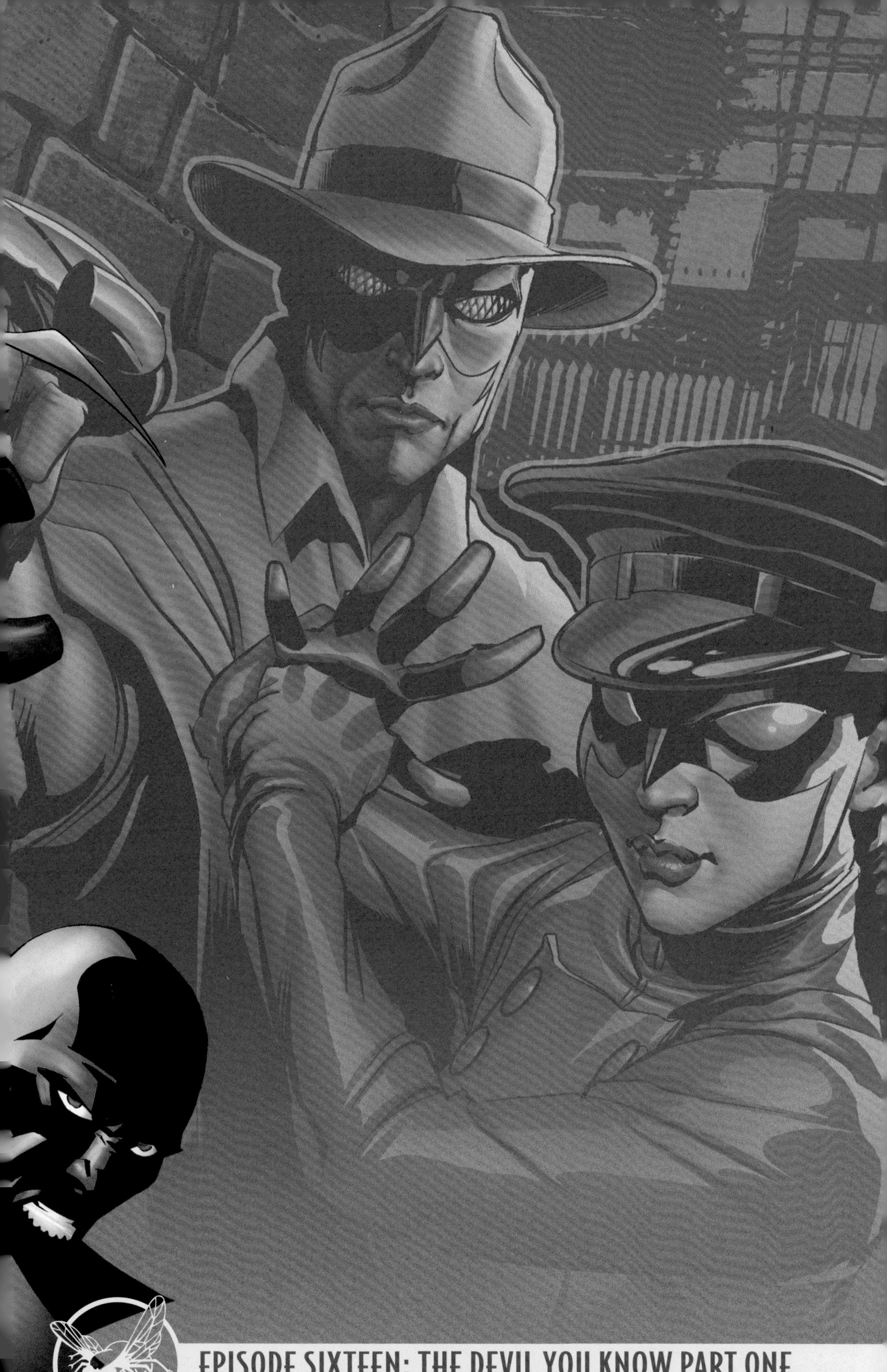

EPISODE SIXTEEN: THE DEVIL YOU KNOW PART ONE

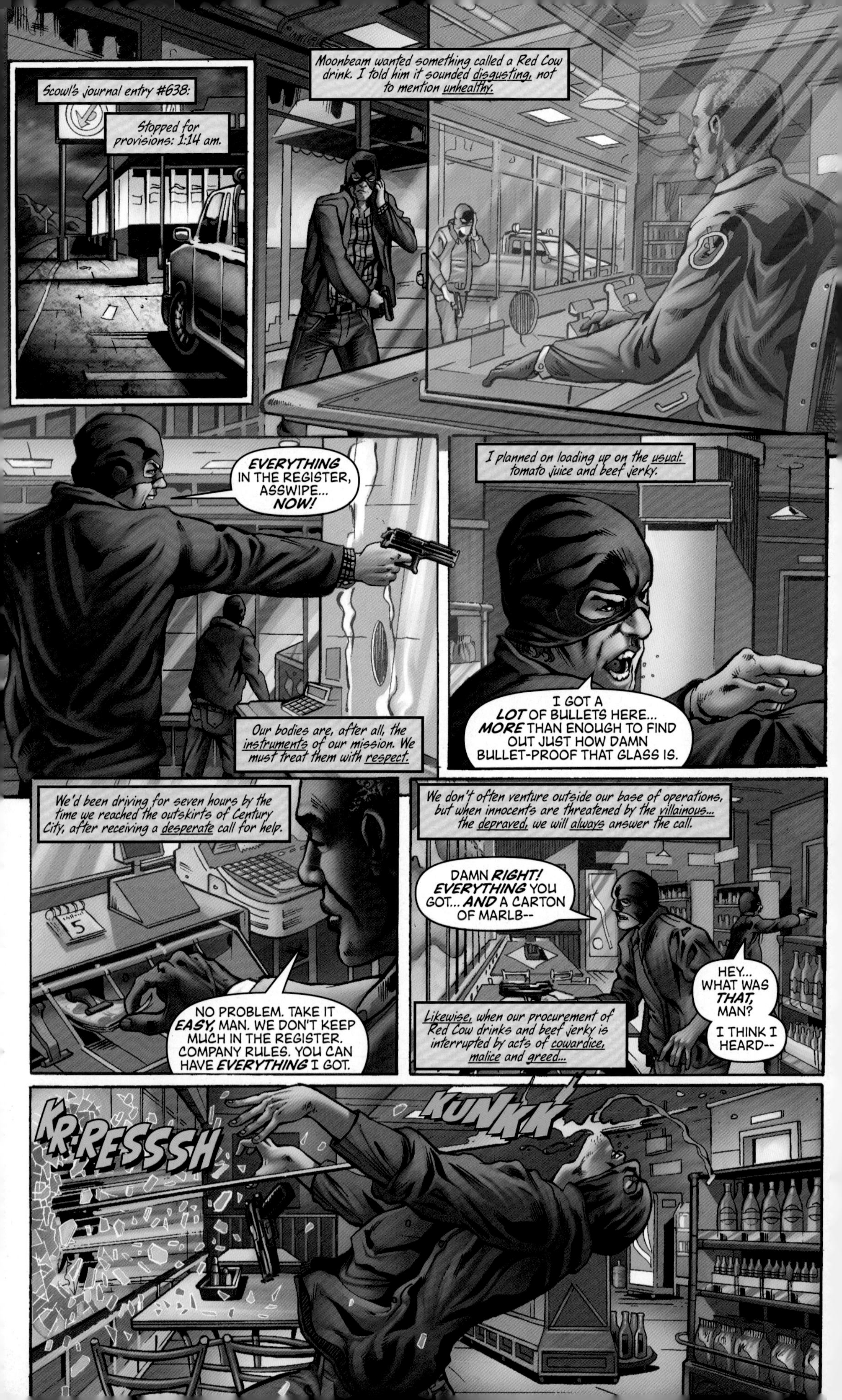

Scowl's journal entry #638:
Stopped for provisions: 1:14 am.
Moonbeam wanted something called a Red Cow drink. I told him it sounded disgusting, not to mention unhealthy.
EVERYTHING IN THE REGISTER, ASSWIPE... NOW!
Our bodies are, after all, the instruments of our mission. We must treat them with respect.
I planned on loading up on the usual: tomato juice and beef jerky.
I GOT A LOT OF BULLETS HERE... MORE THAN ENOUGH TO FIND OUT JUST HOW DAMN BULLET-PROOF THAT GLASS IS.
We'd been driving for seven hours by the time we reached the outskirts of Century City, after receiving a desperate call for help.
NO PROBLEM. TAKE IT EASY, MAN. WE DON'T KEEP MUCH IN THE REGISTER. COMPANY RULES. YOU CAN HAVE EVERYTHING I GOT.
We don't often venture outside our base of operations, but when innocents are threatened by the villainous... the depraved, we will always answer the call.
DAMN RIGHT! EVERYTHING YOU GOT... AND A CARTON OF MARLB--
Likewise, when our procurement of Red Cow drinks and beef jerky is interrupted by acts of cowardice, malice and greed...
HEY... WHAT WAS THAT, MAN?
I THINK I HEARD--
KR-RESSSH
KUNKK

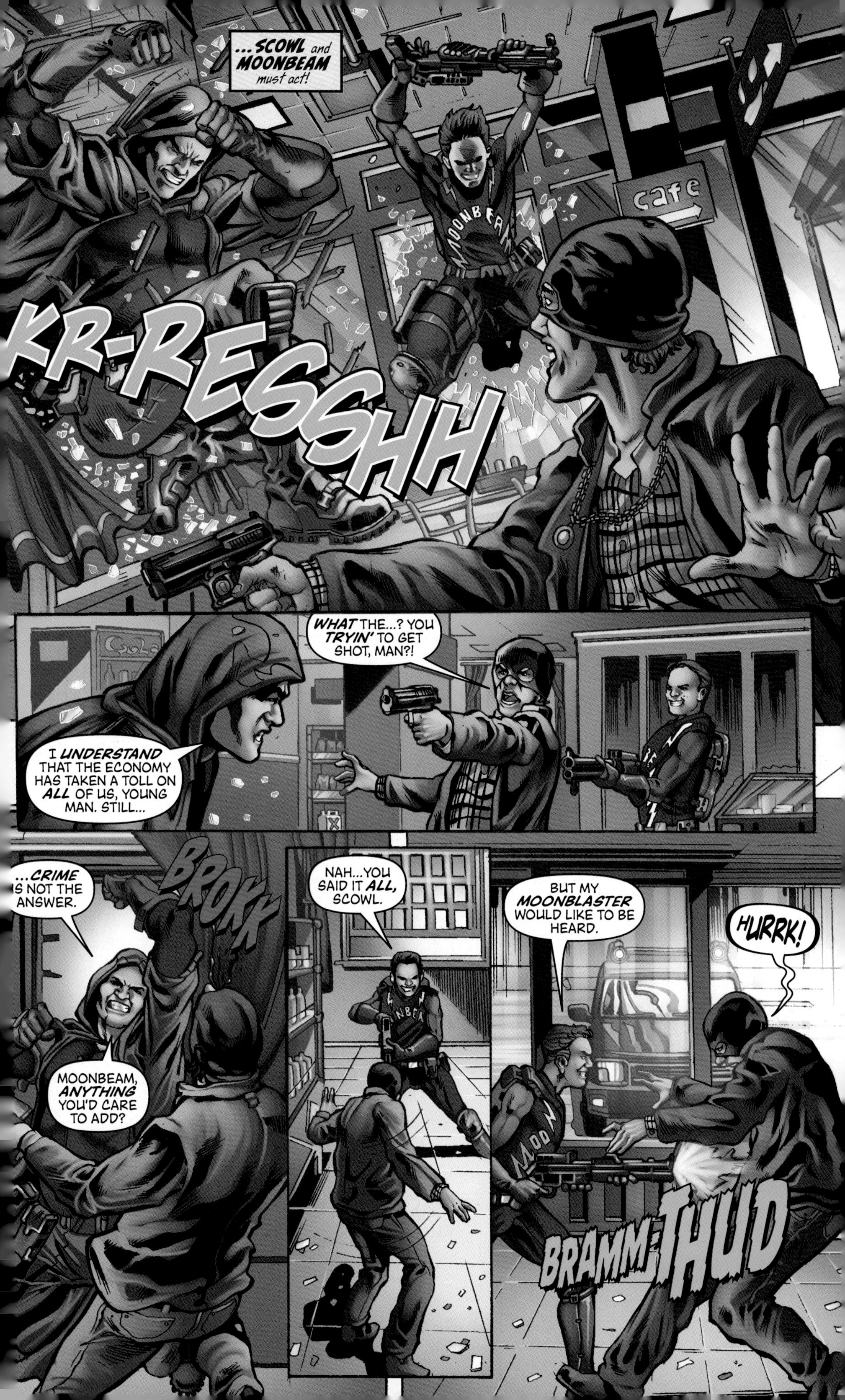
...SCOWL and MOONBEAM must act!
KR-RESSHH
WHAT THE...? YOU TRYIN' TO GET SHOT, MAN?!
I UNDERSTAND THAT THE ECONOMY HAS TAKEN A TOLL ON ALL OF US, YOUNG MAN. STILL...
...CRIME IS NOT THE ANSWER.
BROKK
MOONBEAM, ANYTHING YOU'D CARE TO ADD?
NAH...YOU SAID IT ALL, SCOWL.
BUT MY MOONBLASTER WOULD LIKE TO BE HEARD.
HURRK!
BRAMM-THUD

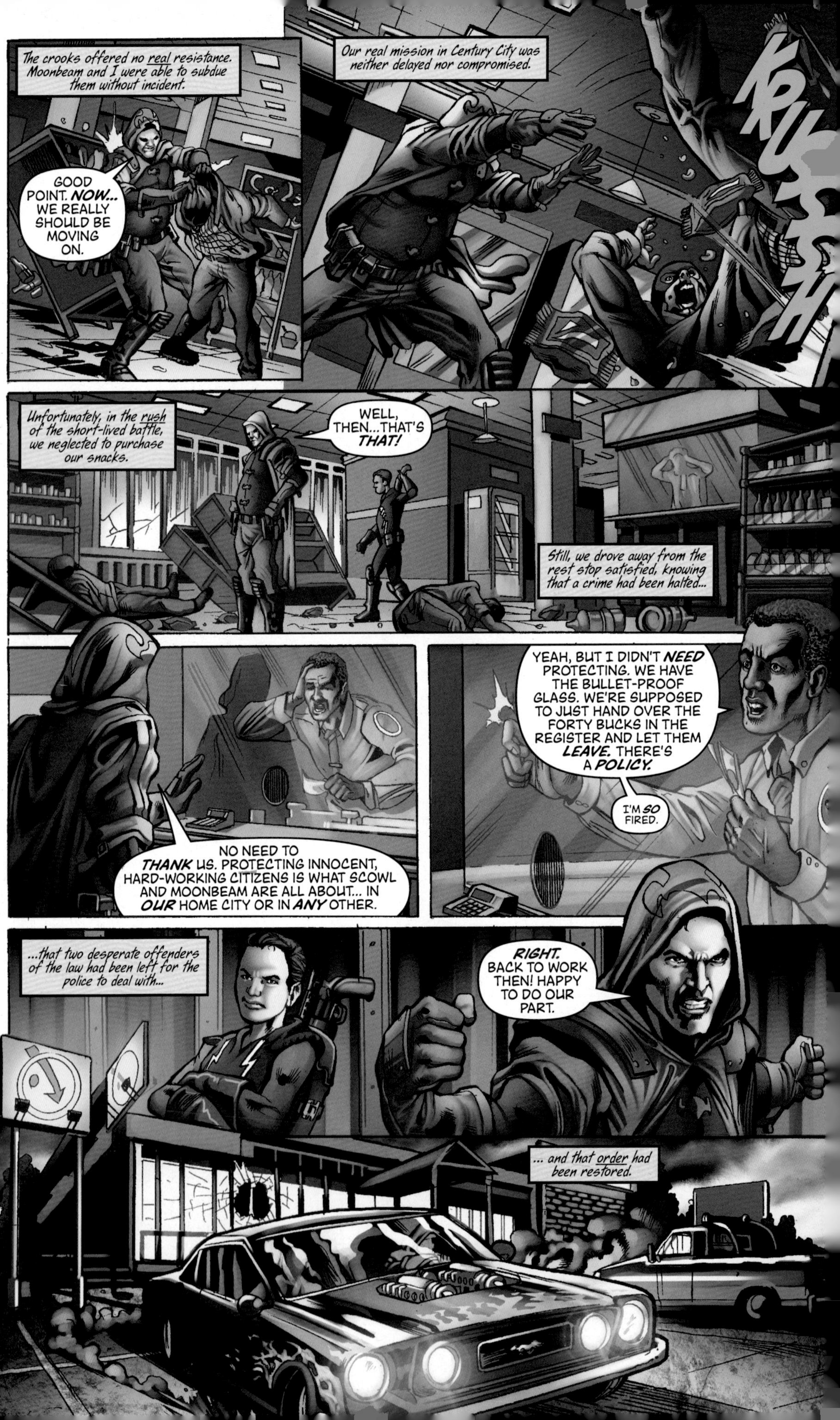
The crooks offered no real resistance. Moonbeam and I were able to subdue them without incident.
GOOD POINT. NOW... WE REALLY SHOULD BE MOVING ON.
Our real mission in Century City was neither delayed nor compromised.
KRUSSH
Unfortunately, in the rush of the short-lived battle, we neglected to purchase our snacks.
WELL, THEN...THAT'S THAT!
Still, we drove away from the rest stop satisfied, knowing that a crime had been halted...
NO NEED TO THANK US. PROTECTING INNOCENT, HARD-WORKING CITIZENS IS WHAT SCOWL AND MOONBEAM ARE ALL ABOUT... IN OUR HOME CITY OR IN ANY OTHER.
YEAH, BUT I DIDN'T NEED PROTECTING. WE HAVE THE BULLET-PROOF GLASS. WE'RE SUPPOSED TO JUST HAND OVER THE FORTY BUCKS IN THE REGISTER AND LET THEM LEAVE. THERE'S A POLICY.
I'M SO FIRED.
...that two desperate offenders of the law had been left for the police to deal with...
RIGHT. BACK TO WORK THEN! HAPPY TO DO OUR PART.
... and that order had been restored.

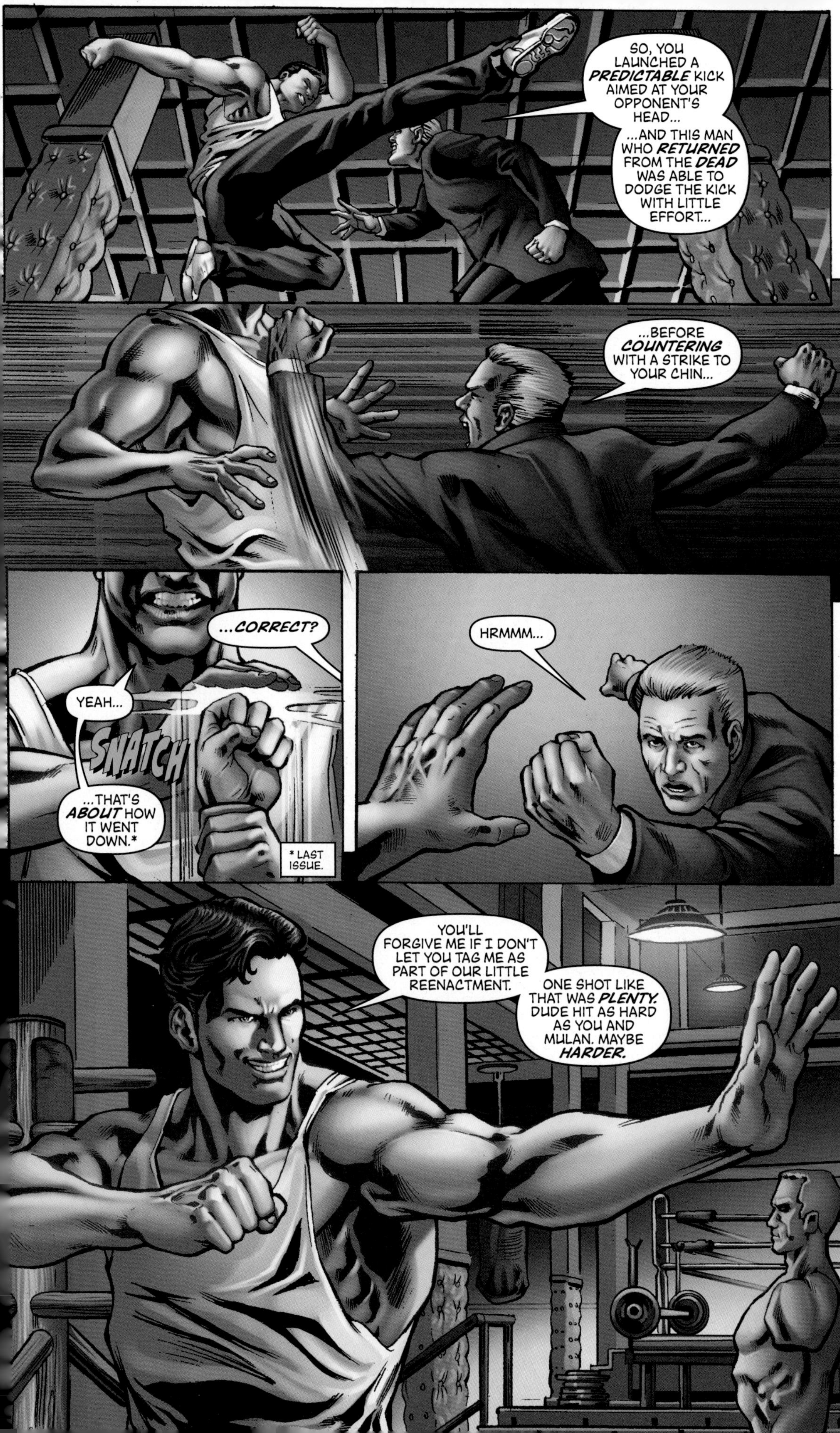

SO, YOU LAUNCHED A ***PREDICTABLE*** KICK AIMED AT YOUR OPPONENT'S HEAD...
...AND THIS MAN WHO ***RETURNED*** FROM THE ***DEAD*** WAS ABLE TO DODGE THE KICK WITH LITTLE EFFORT...
...BEFORE ***COUNTERING*** WITH A STRIKE TO YOUR CHIN...
...***CORRECT?***
YEAH...
SNATCH
...THAT'S ***ABOUT*** HOW IT WENT DOWN.*
* LAST ISSUE.
HRMMM...
YOU'LL FORGIVE ME IF I DON'T LET YOU TAG ME AS PART OF OUR LITTLE REENACTMENT.
ONE SHOT LIKE THAT WAS ***PLENTY.*** DUDE HIT AS HARD AS YOU AND MULAN. MAYBE ***HARDER.***

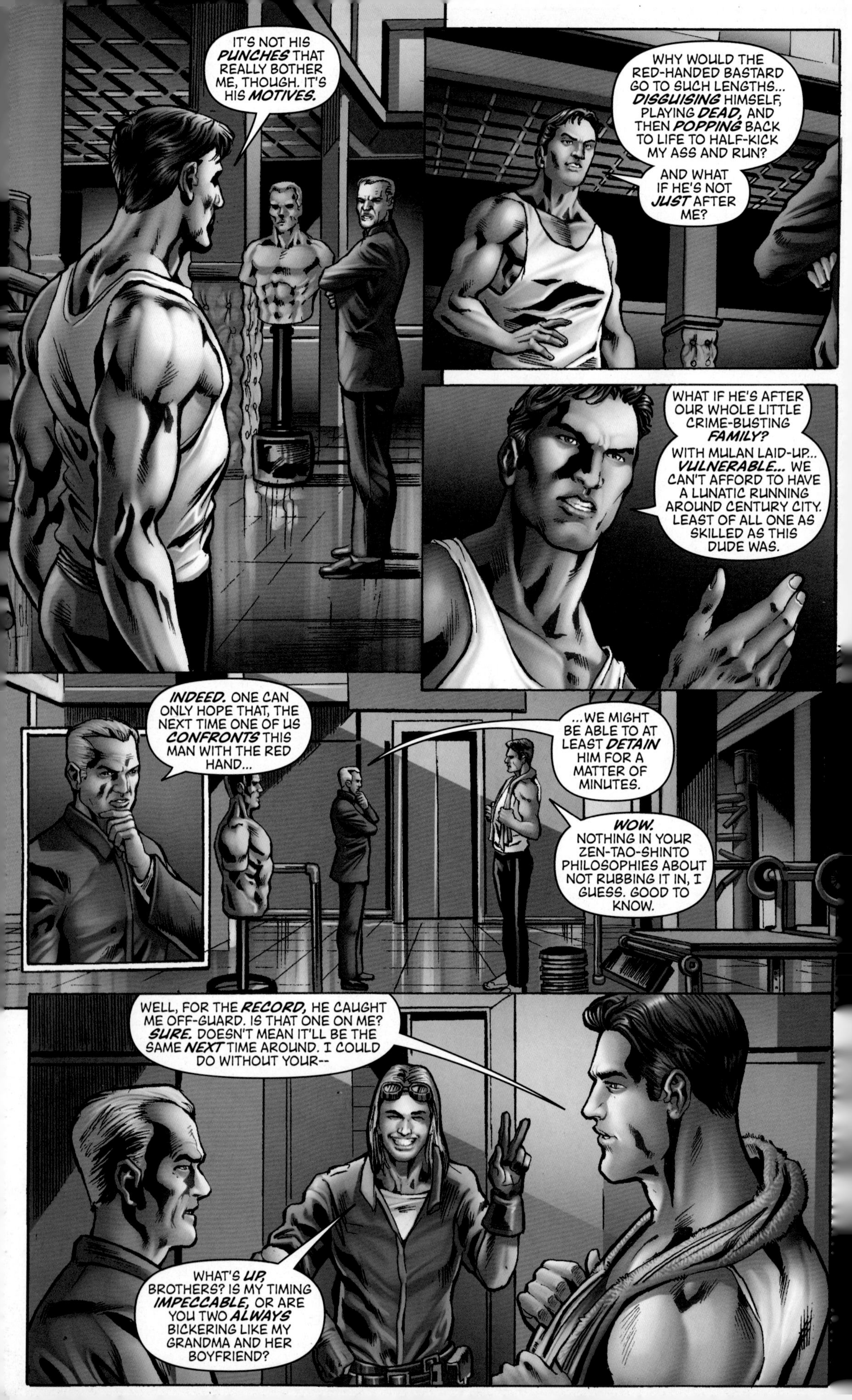
IT'S NOT HIS PUNCHES THAT REALLY BOTHER ME, THOUGH. IT'S HIS MOTIVES.
WHY WOULD THE RED-HANDED BASTARD GO TO SUCH LENGTHS... DISGUISING HIMSELF, PLAYING DEAD, AND THEN POPPING BACK TO LIFE TO HALF-KICK MY ASS AND RUN?
AND WHAT IF HE'S NOT JUST AFTER ME?
WHAT IF HE'S AFTER OUR WHOLE LITTLE CRIME-BUSTING FAMILY?
WITH MULAN LAID-UP... VULNERABLE... WE CAN'T AFFORD TO HAVE A LUNATIC RUNNING AROUND CENTURY CITY. LEAST OF ALL ONE AS SKILLED AS THIS DUDE WAS.
INDEED. ONE CAN ONLY HOPE THAT, THE NEXT TIME ONE OF US CONFRONTS THIS MAN WITH THE RED HAND...
...WE MIGHT BE ABLE TO AT LEAST DETAIN HIM FOR A MATTER OF MINUTES.
WOW. NOTHING IN YOUR ZEN-TAO-SHINTO PHILOSOPHIES ABOUT NOT RUBBING IT IN, I GUESS. GOOD TO KNOW.
WELL, FOR THE RECORD, HE CAUGHT ME OFF-GUARD. IS THAT ONE ON ME? SURE. DOESN'T MEAN IT'LL BE THE SAME NEXT TIME AROUND. I COULD DO WITHOUT YOUR--
WHAT'S UP, BROTHERS? IS MY TIMING IMPECCABLE, OR ARE YOU TWO ALWAYS BICKERING LIKE MY GRANDMA AND HER BOYFRIEND?

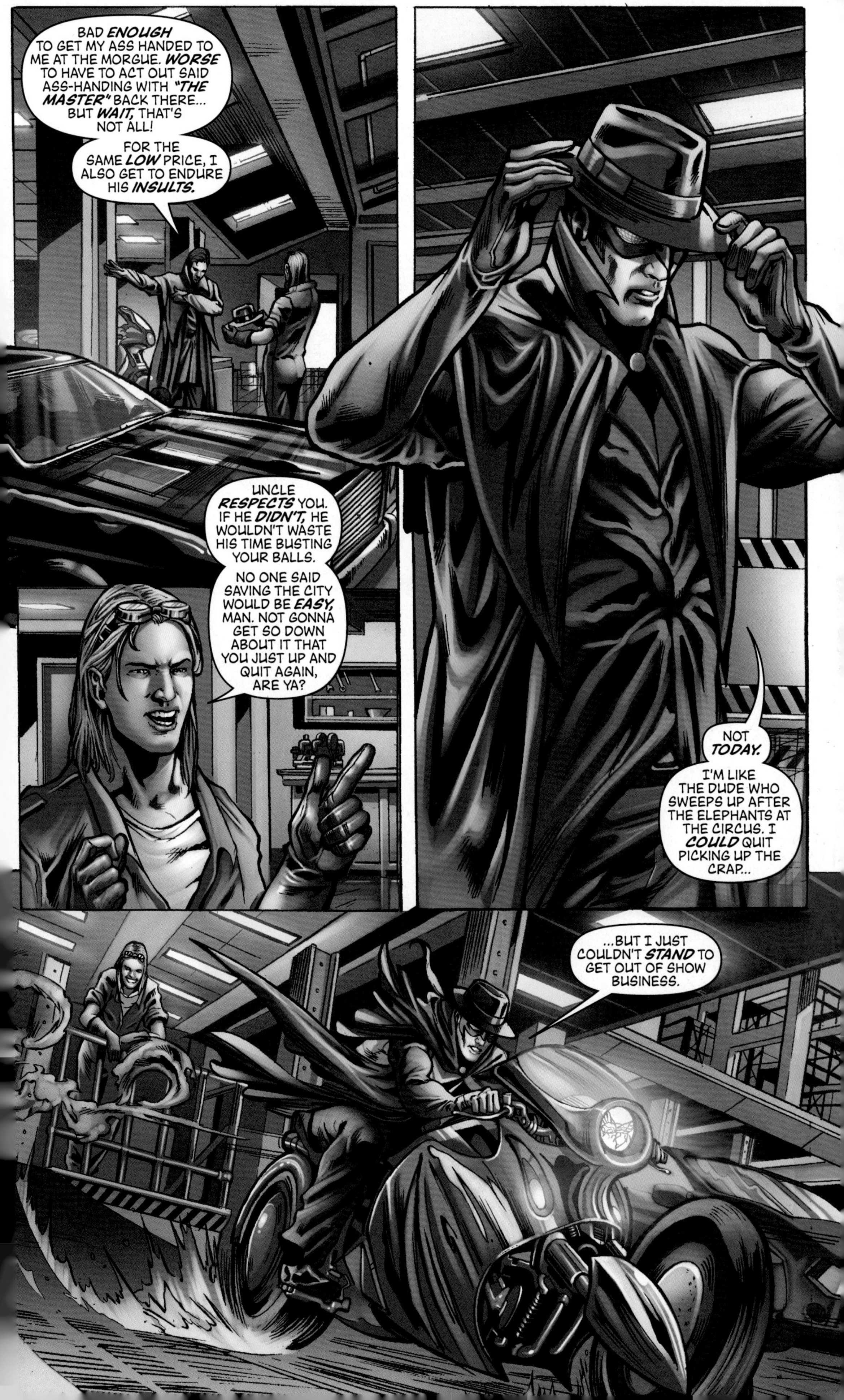
BAD ENOUGH TO GET MY ASS HANDED TO ME AT THE MORGUE. WORSE TO HAVE TO ACT OUT SAID ASS-HANDING WITH "THE MASTER" BACK THERE... BUT WAIT, THAT'S NOT ALL!
FOR THE SAME LOW PRICE, I ALSO GET TO ENDURE HIS INSULTS.
UNCLE RESPECTS YOU. IF HE DIDN'T, HE WOULDN'T WASTE HIS TIME BUSTING YOUR BALLS.
NO ONE SAID SAVING THE CITY WOULD BE EASY, MAN. NOT GONNA GET SO DOWN ABOUT IT THAT YOU JUST UP AND QUIT AGAIN, ARE YA?
NOT TODAY.
I'M LIKE THE DUDE WHO SWEEPS UP AFTER THE ELEPHANTS AT THE CIRCUS. I COULD QUIT PICKING UP THE CRAP...
...BUT I JUST COULDN'T STAND TO GET OUT OF SHOW BUSINESS.

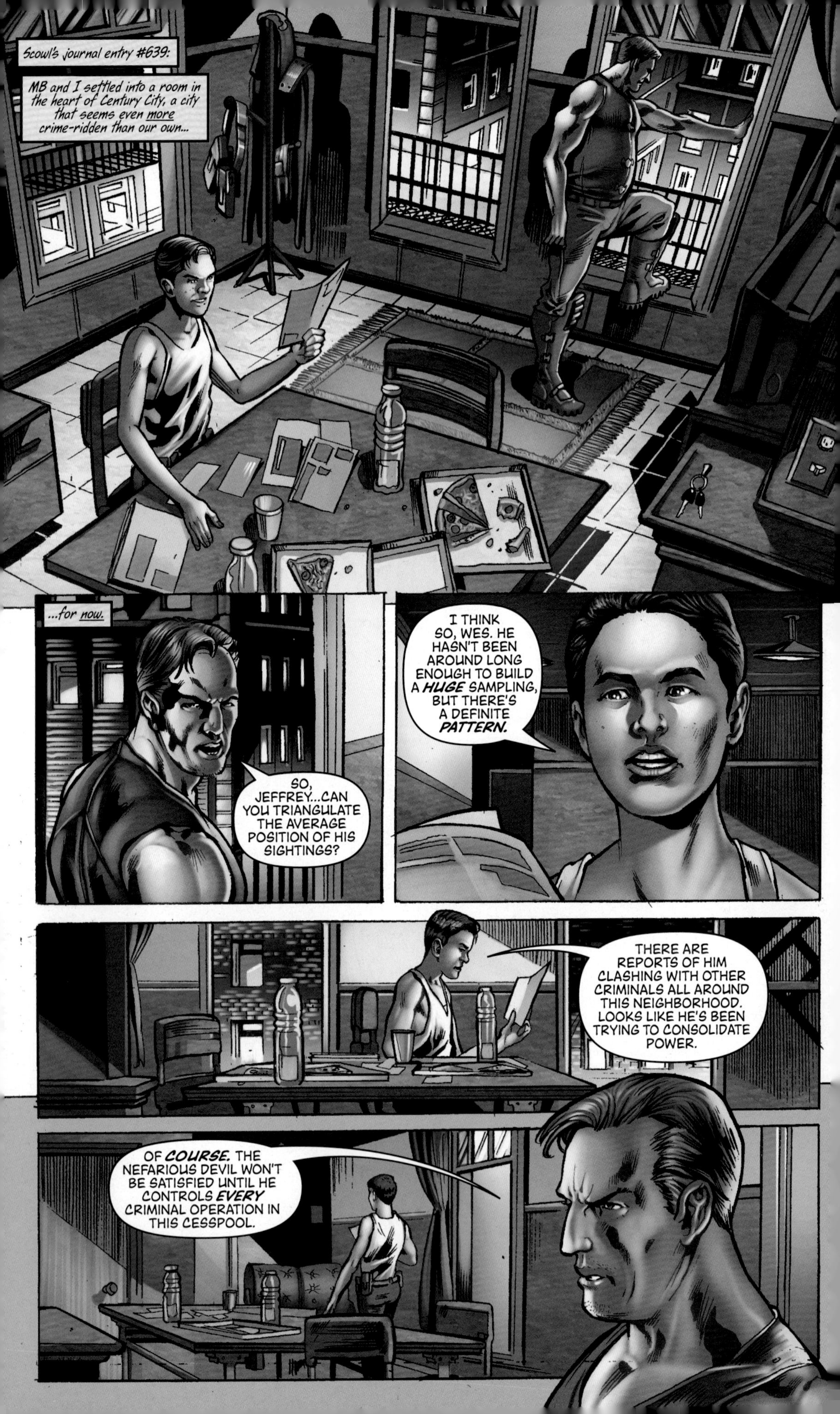
Scowl's journal entry #639:
MB and I settled into a room in the heart of Century City, a city that seems even more crime-ridden than our own...
...for now.
SO, JEFFREY...CAN YOU TRIANGULATE THE AVERAGE POSITION OF HIS SIGHTINGS?
I THINK SO, WES. HE HASN'T BEEN AROUND LONG ENOUGH TO BUILD A *HUGE* SAMPLING, BUT THERE'S A DEFINITE *PATTERN.*
THERE ARE REPORTS OF HIM CLASHING WITH OTHER CRIMINALS ALL AROUND THIS NEIGHBORHOOD. LOOKS LIKE HE'S BEEN TRYING TO CONSOLIDATE POWER.
OF *COURSE.* THE NEFARIOUS DEVIL WON'T BE SATISFIED UNTIL HE CONTROLS *EVERY* CRIMINAL OPERATION IN THIS CESSPOOL.

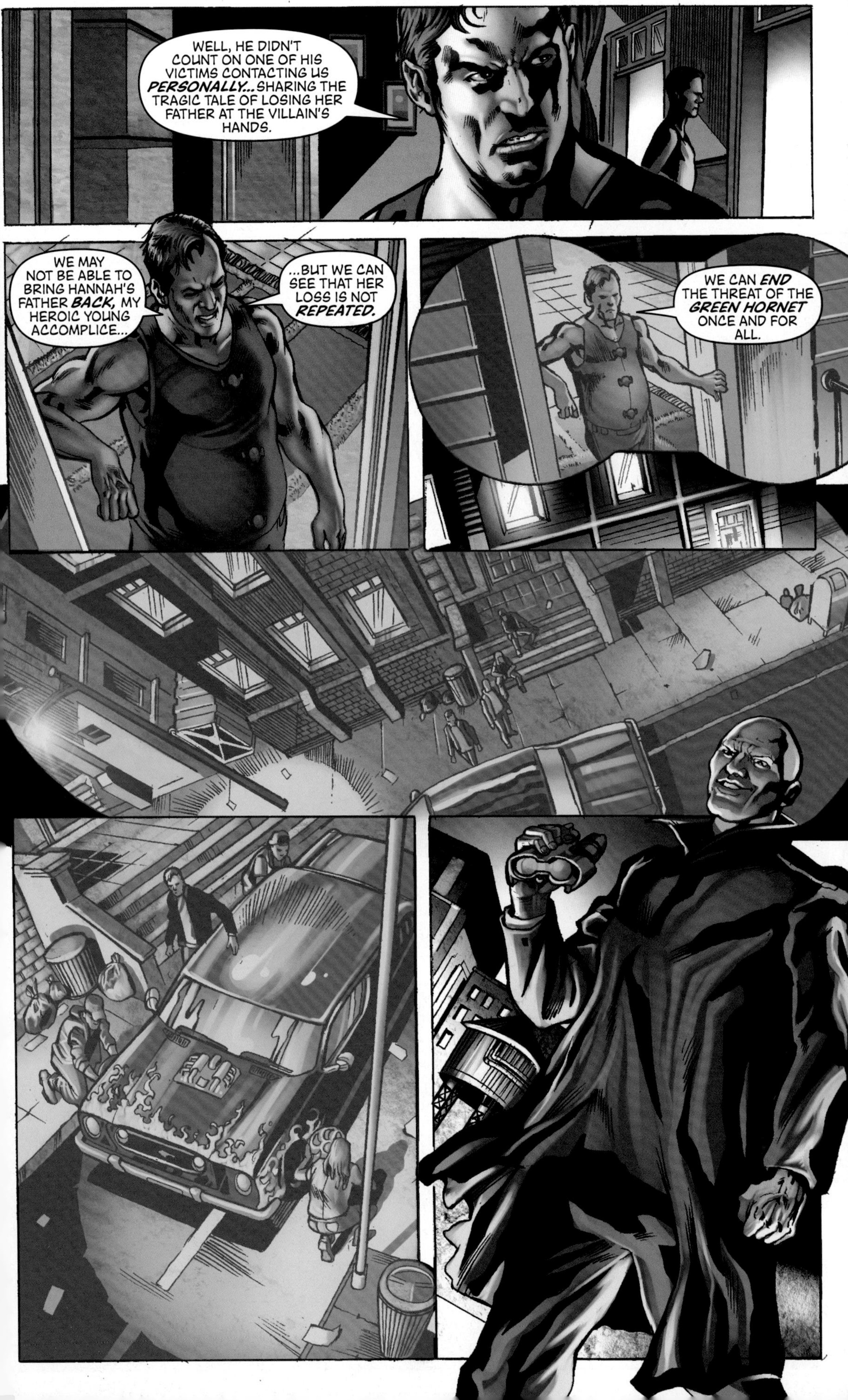
WELL, HE DIDN'T COUNT ON ONE OF HIS VICTIMS CONTACTING US PERSONALLY... SHARING THE TRAGIC TALE OF LOSING HER FATHER AT THE VILLAIN'S HANDS.
WE MAY NOT BE ABLE TO BRING HANNAH'S FATHER BACK, MY HEROIC YOUNG ACCOMPLICE...
...BUT WE CAN SEE THAT HER LOSS IS NOT REPEATED.
WE CAN END THE THREAT OF THE GREEN HORNET ONCE AND FOR ALL.

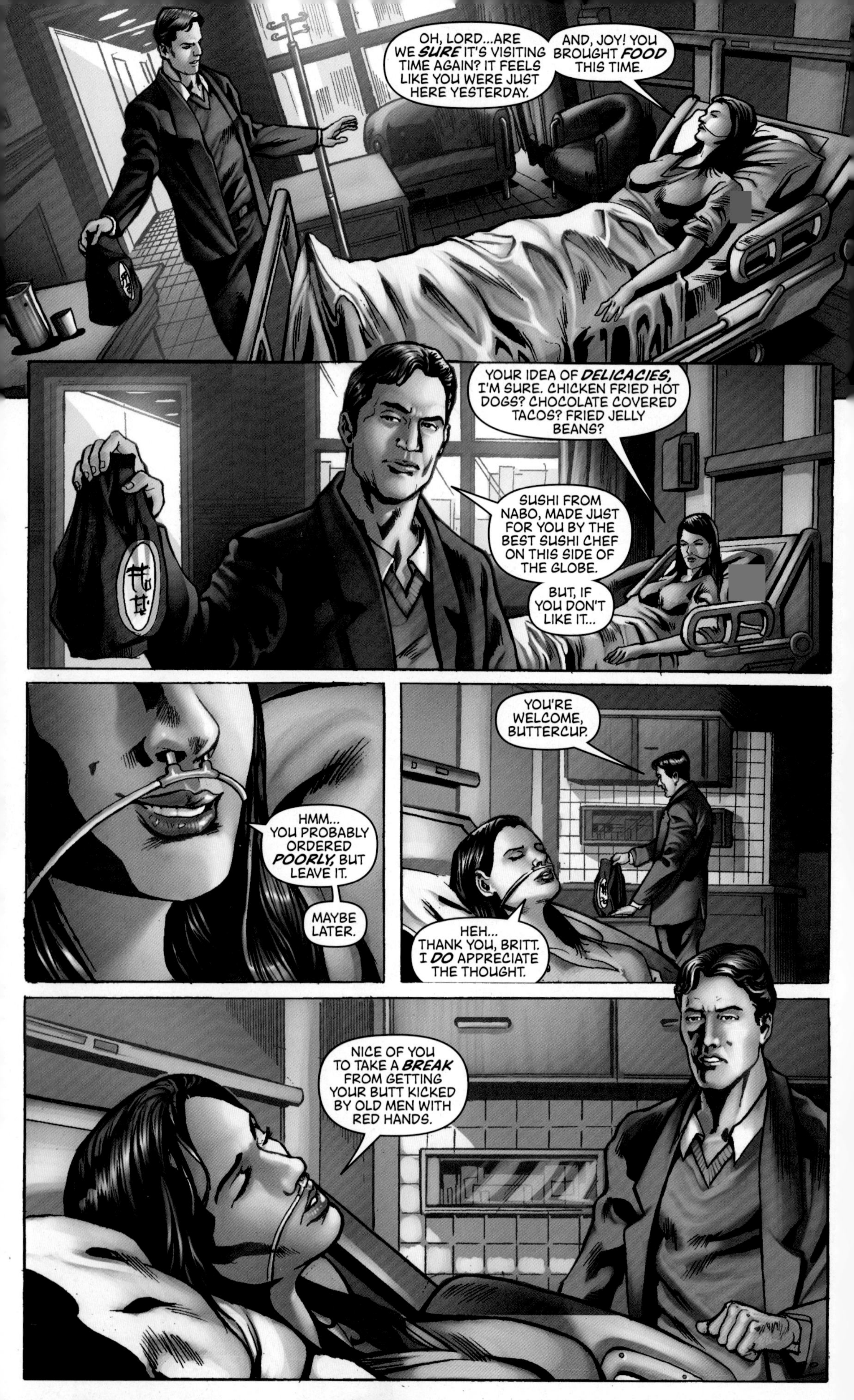
OH, LORD...ARE WE SURE IT'S VISITING TIME AGAIN? IT FEELS LIKE YOU WERE JUST HERE YESTERDAY.
AND, JOY! YOU BROUGHT FOOD THIS TIME.
YOUR IDEA OF DELICACIES, I'M SURE. CHICKEN FRIED HOT DOGS? CHOCOLATE COVERED TACOS? FRIED JELLY BEANS?
SUSHI FROM NABO, MADE JUST FOR YOU BY THE BEST SUSHI CHEF ON THIS SIDE OF THE GLOBE.
BUT, IF YOU DON'T LIKE IT...
HMM... YOU PROBABLY ORDERED POORLY, BUT LEAVE IT.
MAYBE LATER.
HEH... THANK YOU, BRITT. I DO APPRECIATE THE THOUGHT.
YOU'RE WELCOME, BUTTERCUP.
NICE OF YOU TO TAKE A BREAK FROM GETTING YOUR BUTT KICKED BY OLD MEN WITH RED HANDS.

THE PAIN MEDICATION MAKES IT HARDER TO REMEMBER THE *DETAILS*. DID YOU MANAGE TO LAND A *SINGLE* BLOW?

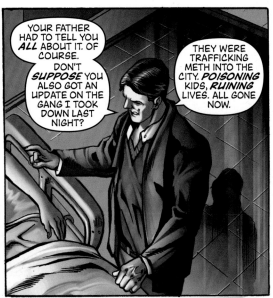

YOUR FATHER HAD TO TELL YOU *ALL* ABOUT IT. OF COURSE. DON'T *SUPPOSE* YOU ALSO GOT AN UPDATE ON THE GANG I TOOK DOWN LAST NIGHT?

THEY WERE TRAFFICKING METH INTO THE CITY. *POISONING* KIDS, *RUINING* LIVES. ALL GONE NOW.

STILL, WHAT IS THAT COMPARED TO A FREAK WITH A BAD TATTOO GETTING IN A *LUCKY* SHOT?

IF I WERE YOU, LITTLE MISS BED-RIDDEN, I WOULD *WATCH* WHAT I SAID. FOR *ONCE* IN OUR TIME TOGETHER, I'M PRETTY SURE I COULD WHUP YOUR LITTLE--

PSSABLADAHH-PSSSHH

WHAT? MULAN...YOU OKAY?

KRIEGGAGUMM-ERHHGGA

I CAN'T MAKE THAT OUT. YOU NEED ME TO CALL THE NURSES? I CAN--

YOW!

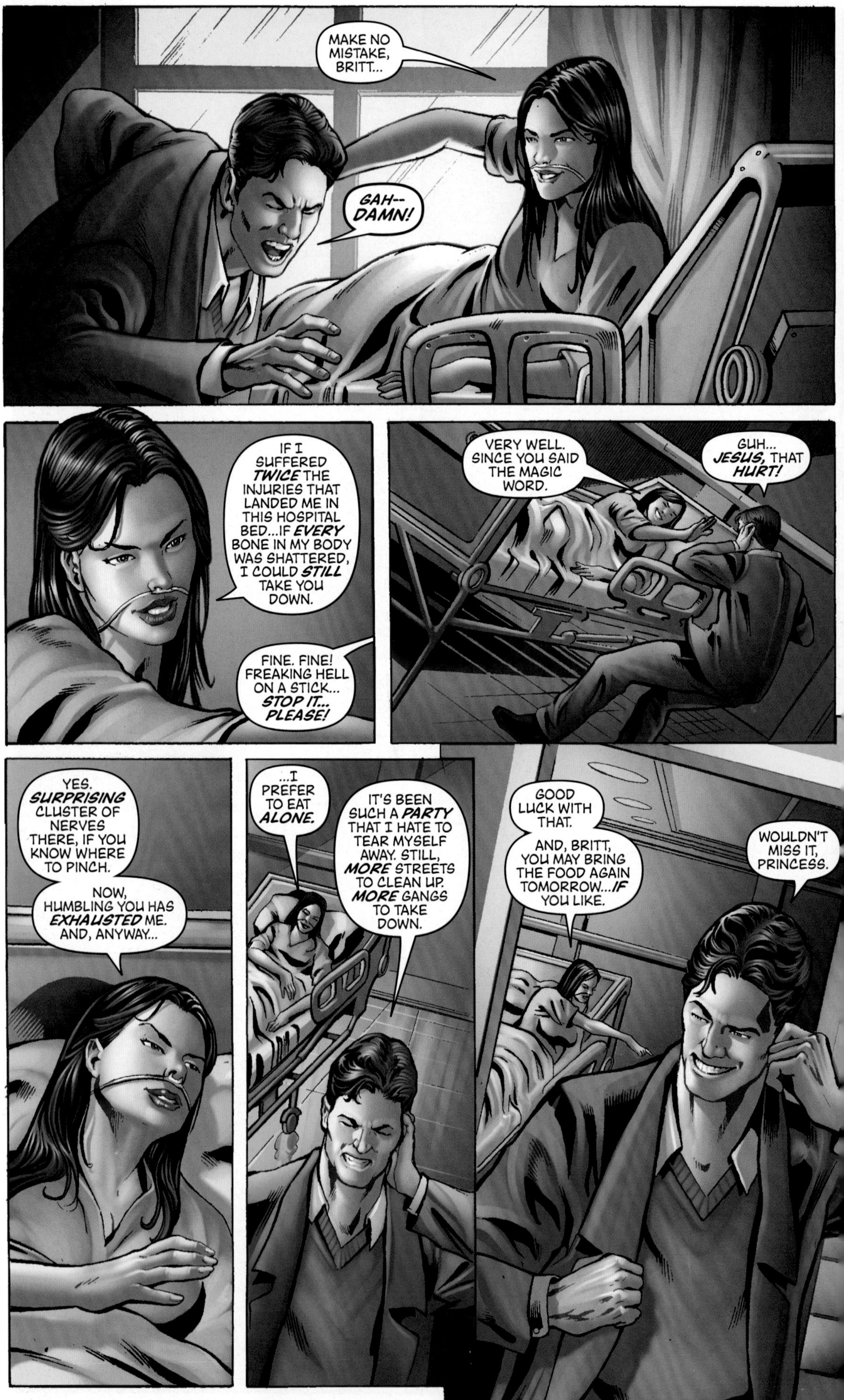
MAKE NO MISTAKE, BRITT...
GAH-- DAMN!
IF I SUFFERED TWICE THE INJURIES THAT LANDED ME IN THIS HOSPITAL BED...IF EVERY BONE IN MY BODY WAS SHATTERED, I COULD STILL TAKE YOU DOWN.
FINE. FINE! FREAKING HELL ON A STICK... STOP IT... PLEASE!
VERY WELL. SINCE YOU SAID THE MAGIC WORD.
GUH... JESUS, THAT HURT!
YES. SURPRISING CLUSTER OF NERVES THERE, IF YOU KNOW WHERE TO PINCH.
NOW, HUMBLING YOU HAS EXHAUSTED ME. AND, ANYWAY...
...I PREFER TO EAT ALONE.
IT'S BEEN SUCH A PARTY THAT I HATE TO TEAR MYSELF AWAY. STILL, MORE STREETS TO CLEAN UP. MORE GANGS TO TAKE DOWN.
GOOD LUCK WITH THAT.
AND, BRITT, YOU MAY BRING THE FOOD AGAIN TOMORROW...IF YOU LIKE.
WOULDN'T MISS IT, PRINCESS.

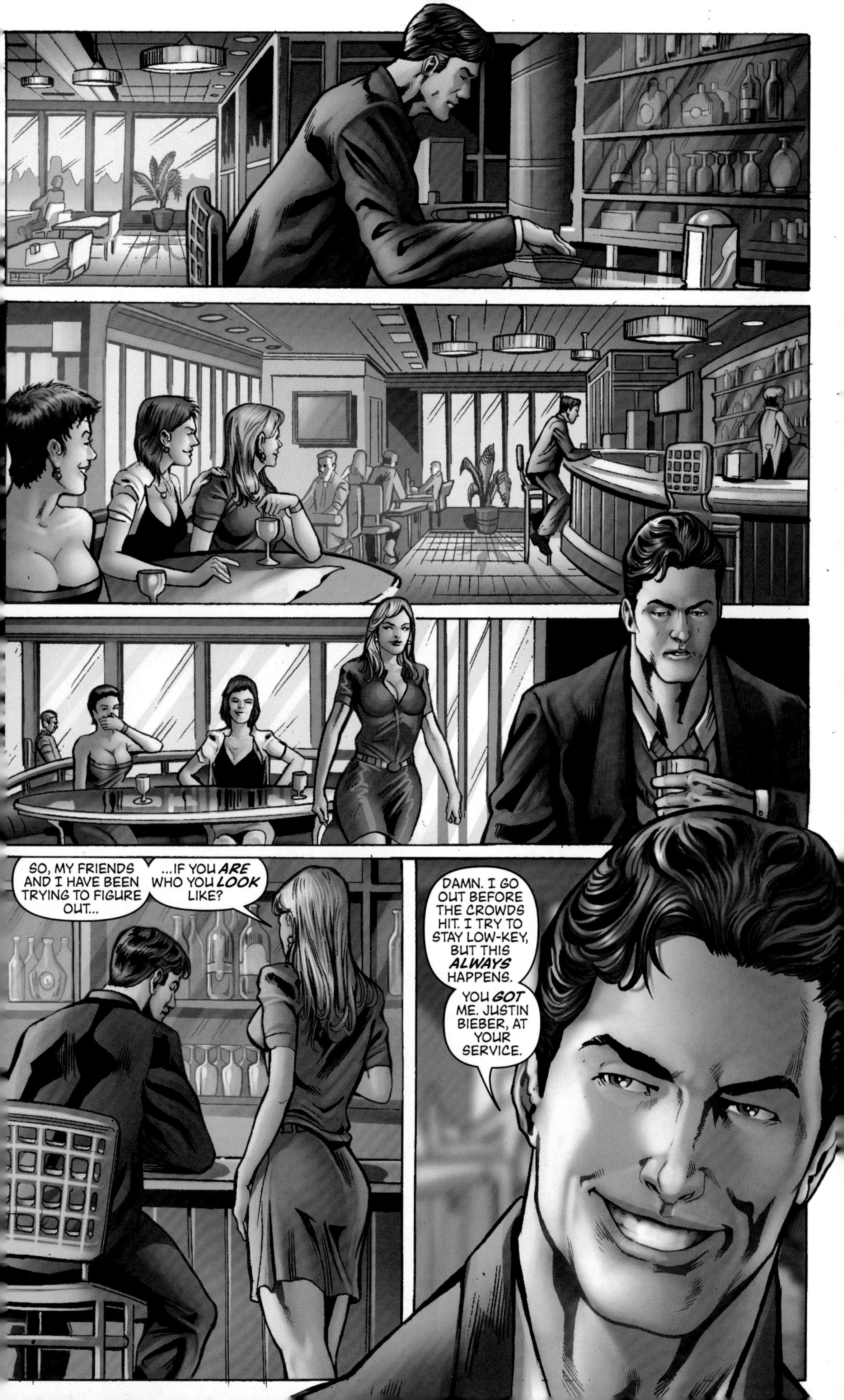

SO, MY FRIENDS AND I HAVE BEEN TRYING TO FIGURE OUT...
...IF YOU ARE WHO YOU LOOK LIKE?
DAMN. I GO OUT BEFORE THE CROWDS HIT. I TRY TO STAY LOW-KEY, BUT THIS ALWAYS HAPPENS.
YOU GOT ME. JUSTIN BIEBER, AT YOUR SERVICE.

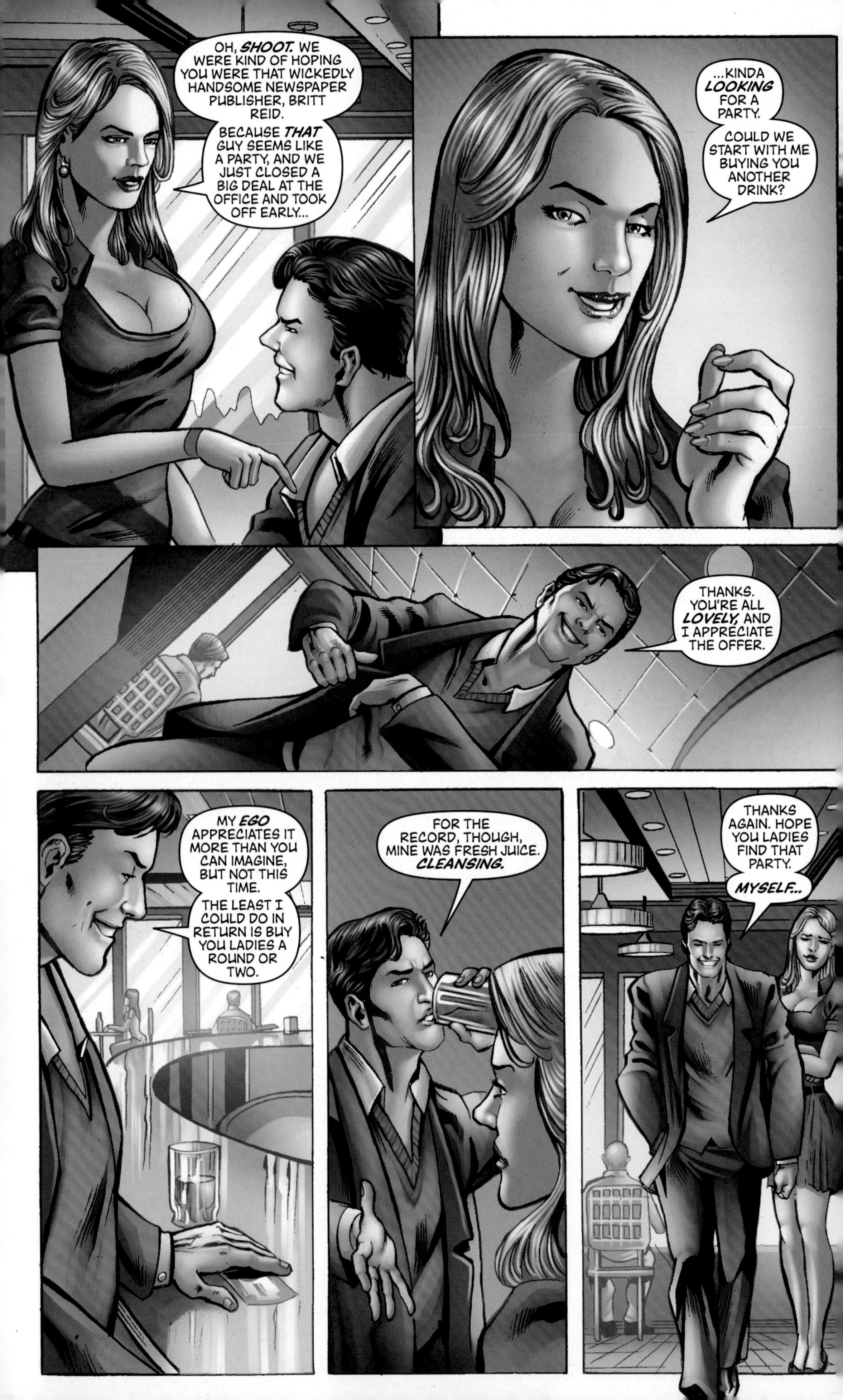
OH, *SHOOT.* WE WERE KIND OF HOPING YOU WERE THAT WICKEDLY HANDSOME NEWSPAPER PUBLISHER, BRITT REID.
BECAUSE *THAT* GUY SEEMS LIKE A PARTY, AND WE JUST CLOSED A BIG DEAL AT THE OFFICE AND TOOK OFF EARLY...
...KINDA *LOOKING* FOR A PARTY.
COULD WE START WITH ME BUYING YOU ANOTHER DRINK?
THANKS. YOU'RE ALL *LOVELY,* AND I APPRECIATE THE OFFER.
MY *EGO* APPRECIATES IT MORE THAN YOU CAN IMAGINE, BUT NOT THIS TIME.
THE LEAST I COULD DO IN RETURN IS BUY YOU LADIES A ROUND OR TWO.
FOR THE RECORD, THOUGH, MINE WAS FRESH JUICE. *CLEANSING.*
THANKS AGAIN. HOPE YOU LADIES FIND THAT PARTY.
MYSELF...

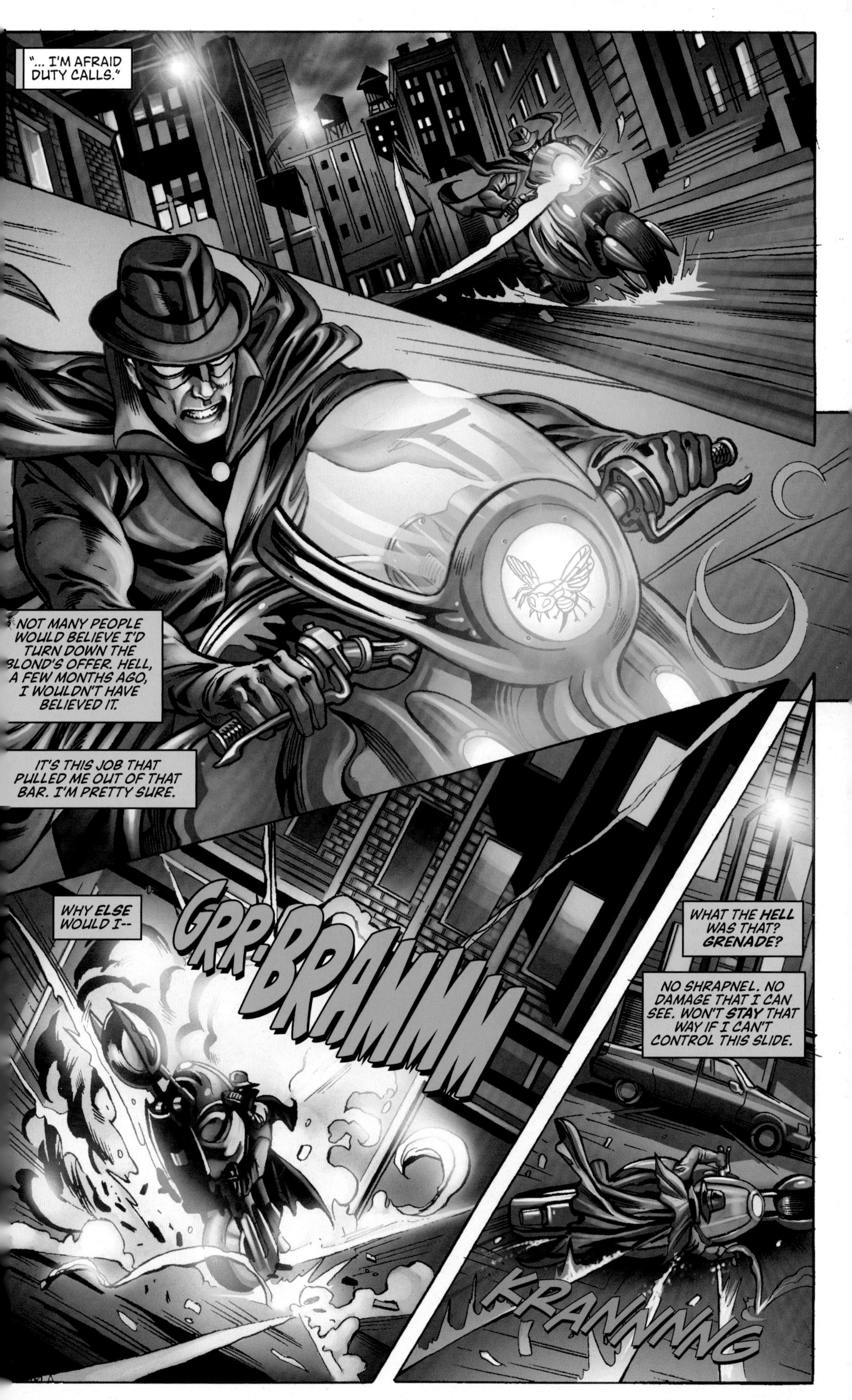
"... I'M AFRAID DUTY CALLS."
NOT MANY PEOPLE WOULD BELIEVE I'D TURN DOWN THE BLOND'S OFFER. HELL, A FEW MONTHS AGO, I WOULDN'T HAVE BELIEVED IT.
IT'S THIS JOB THAT PULLED ME OUT OF THAT BAR. I'M PRETTY SURE.
WHY ELSE WOULD I--
GRR-BRAMMMM
WHAT THE HELL WAS THAT? GRENADE?
NO SHRAPNEL. NO DAMAGE THAT I CAN SEE. WON'T STAY THAT WAY IF I CAN'T CONTROL THIS SLIDE.
KRANNNNG

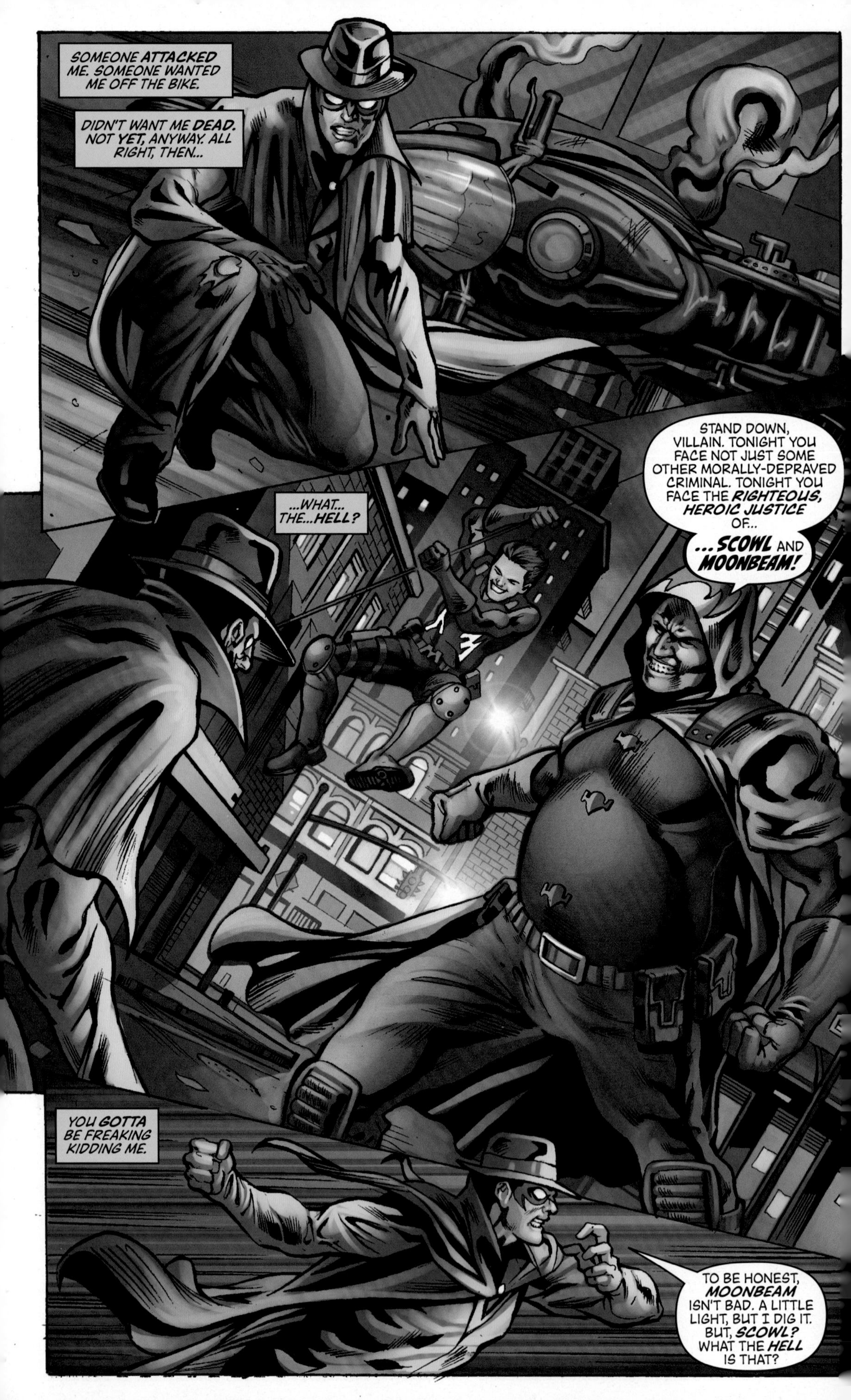
SOMEONE ATTACKED ME. SOMEONE WANTED ME OFF THE BIKE.
DIDN'T WANT ME DEAD. NOT YET, ANYWAY. ALL RIGHT, THEN...
...WHAT... THE...HELL?
STAND DOWN, VILLAIN. TONIGHT YOU FACE NOT JUST SOME OTHER MORALLY-DEPRAVED CRIMINAL. TONIGHT YOU FACE THE RIGHTEOUS, HEROIC JUSTICE OF... ...SCOWL AND MOONBEAM!
YOU GOTTA BE FREAKING KIDDING ME.
TO BE HONEST, MOONBEAM ISN'T BAD. A LITTLE LIGHT, BUT I DIG IT. BUT, SCOWL? WHAT THE HELL IS THAT?

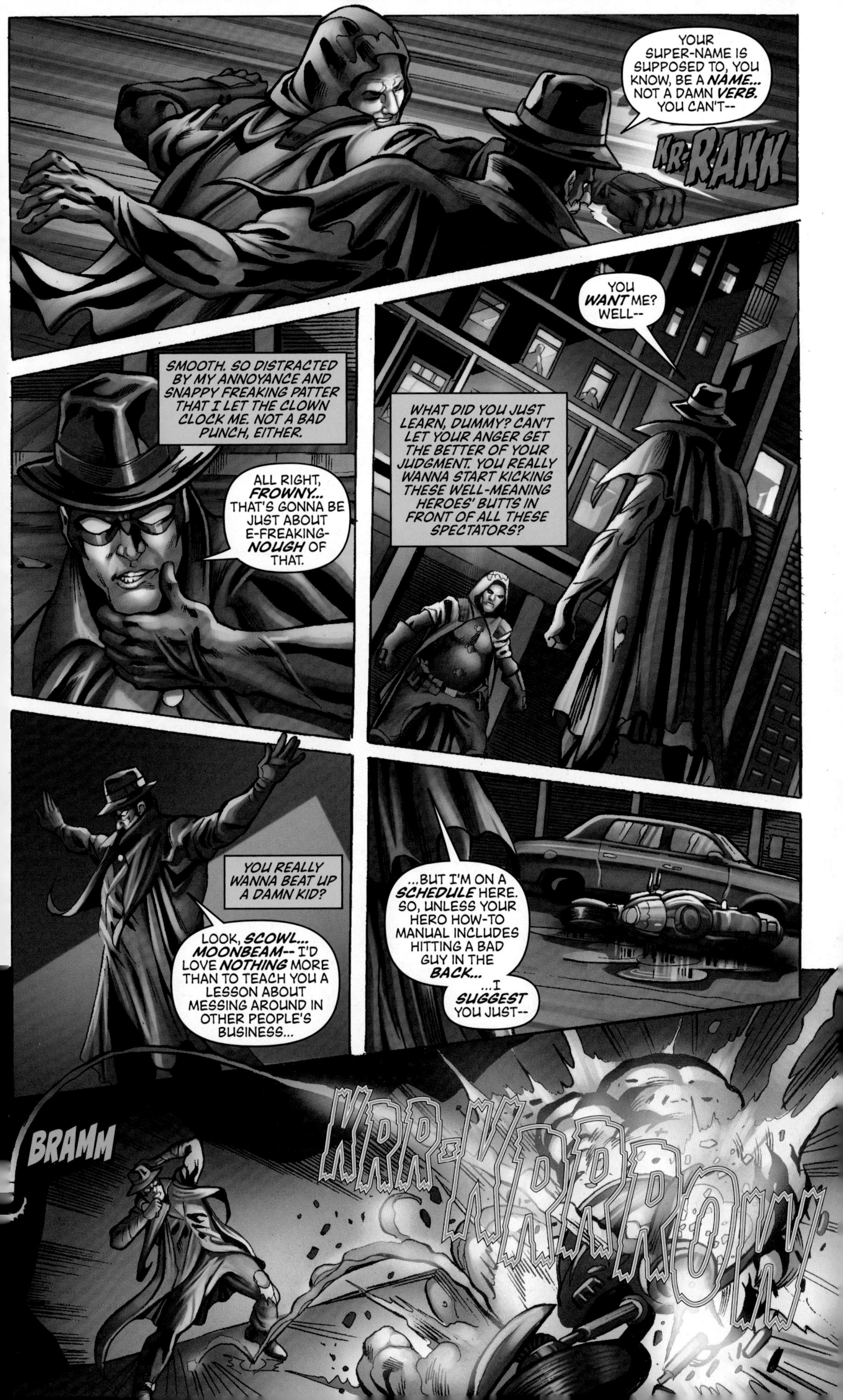

YOUR SUPER-NAME IS SUPPOSED TO, YOU KNOW, BE A NAME... NOT A DAMN VERB. YOU CAN'T--
KR-RAKK
SMOOTH. SO DISTRACTED BY MY ANNOYANCE AND SNAPPY FREAKING PATTER THAT I LET THE CLOWN CLOCK ME. NOT A BAD PUNCH, EITHER.
ALL RIGHT, FROWNY... THAT'S GONNA BE JUST ABOUT E-FREAKING-NOUGH OF THAT.
YOU WANT ME? WELL--
WHAT DID YOU JUST LEARN, DUMMY? CAN'T LET YOUR ANGER GET THE BETTER OF YOUR JUDGMENT. YOU REALLY WANNA START KICKING THESE WELL-MEANING HEROES' BUTTS IN FRONT OF ALL THESE SPECTATORS?
YOU REALLY WANNA BEAT UP A DAMN KID?
LOOK, SCOWL... MOONBEAM-- I'D LOVE NOTHING MORE THAN TO TEACH YOU A LESSON ABOUT MESSING AROUND IN OTHER PEOPLE'S BUSINESS...
...BUT I'M ON A SCHEDULE HERE. SO, UNLESS YOUR HERO HOW-TO MANUAL INCLUDES HITTING A BAD GUY IN THE BACK...
...I SUGGEST YOU JUST--
BRAMM
KRR-VRRROWW

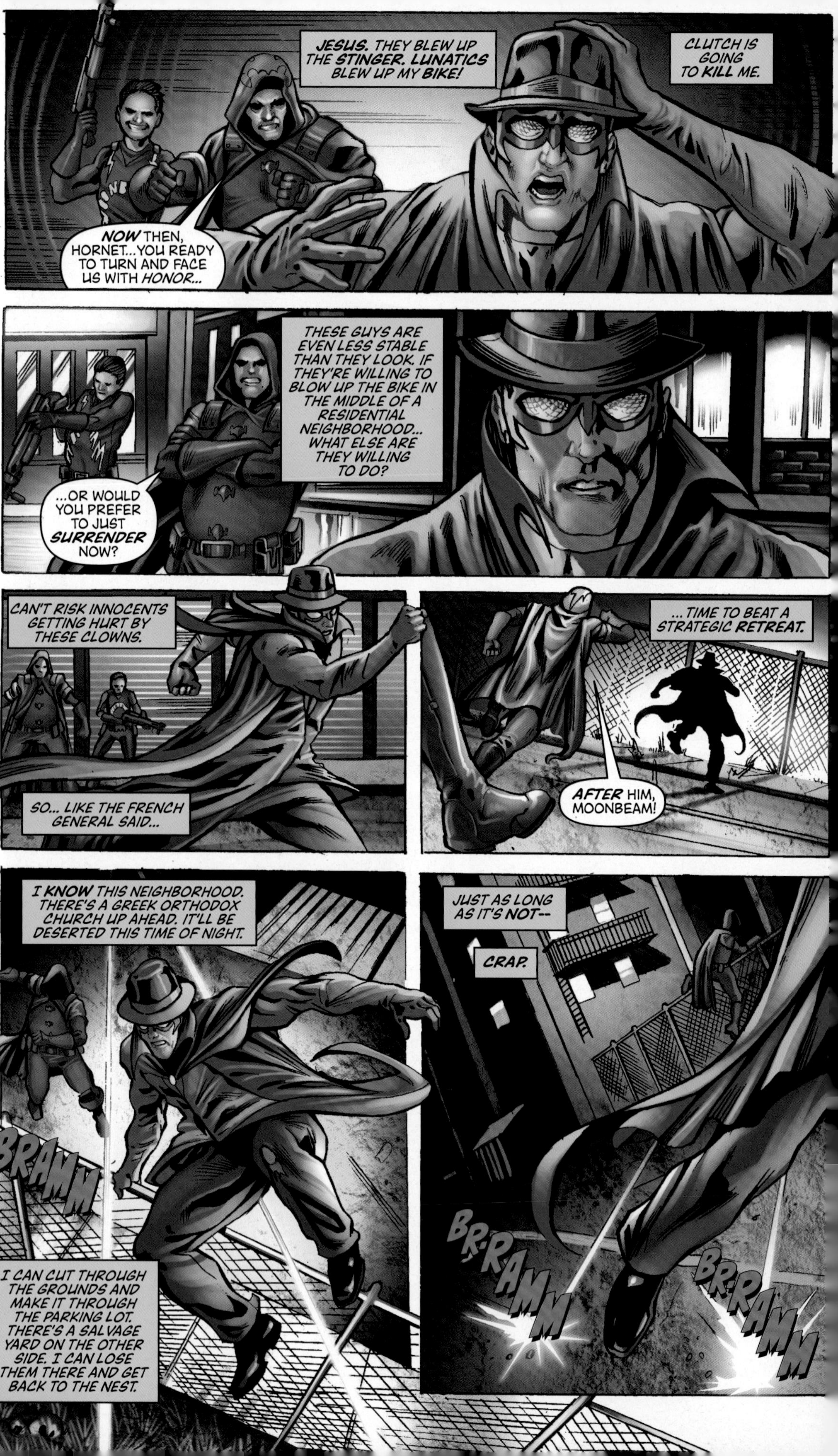

JESUS. THEY BLEW UP THE STINGER. LUNATICS BLEW UP MY BIKE!
CLUTCH IS GOING TO KILL ME.
NOW THEN, HORNET...YOU READY TO TURN AND FACE US WITH HONOR...
THESE GUYS ARE EVEN LESS STABLE THAN THEY LOOK. IF THEY'RE WILLING TO BLOW UP THE BIKE IN THE MIDDLE OF A RESIDENTIAL NEIGHBORHOOD... WHAT ELSE ARE THEY WILLING TO DO?
...OR WOULD YOU PREFER TO JUST SURRENDER NOW?
CAN'T RISK INNOCENTS GETTING HURT BY THESE CLOWNS.
SO... LIKE THE FRENCH GENERAL SAID...
...TIME TO BEAT A STRATEGIC RETREAT.
AFTER HIM, MOONBEAM!
I KNOW THIS NEIGHBORHOOD. THERE'S A GREEK ORTHODOX CHURCH UP AHEAD. IT'LL BE DESERTED THIS TIME OF NIGHT.
BRAMM
I CAN CUT THROUGH THE GROUNDS AND MAKE IT THROUGH THE PARKING LOT. THERE'S A SALVAGE YARD ON THE OTHER SIDE. I CAN LOSE THEM THERE AND GET BACK TO THE NEST.
JUST AS LONG AS IT'S NOT--
CRAP.
BR-RAMM
BR-RAMM

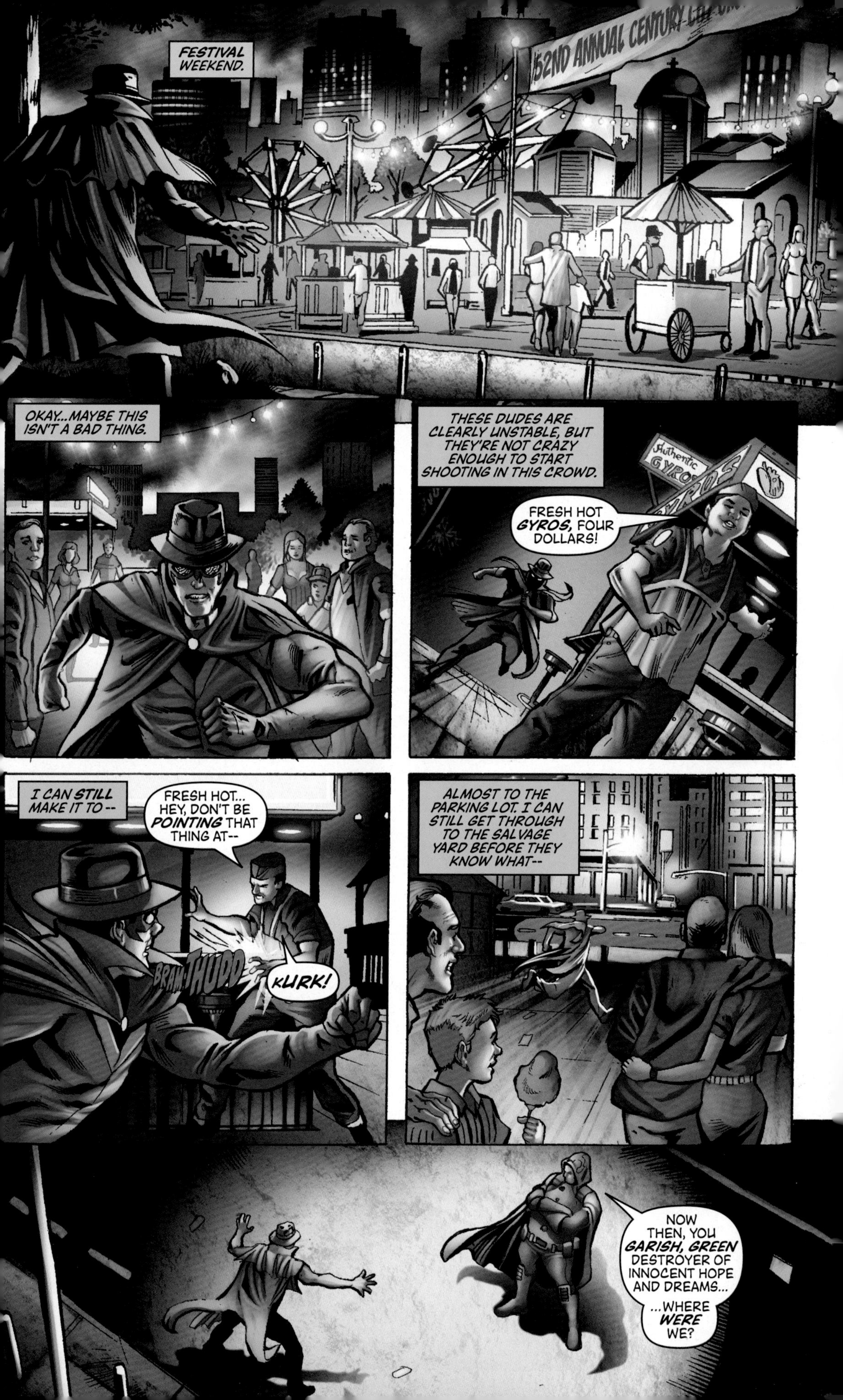
FESTIVAL WEEKEND.
52ND ANNUAL CENTURY
OKAY...MAYBE THIS ISN'T A BAD THING.
THESE DUDES ARE CLEARLY UNSTABLE, BUT THEY'RE NOT CRAZY ENOUGH TO START SHOOTING IN THIS CROWD.
Authentic GYROS
FRESH HOT GYROS, FOUR DOLLARS!
I CAN STILL MAKE IT TO --
FRESH HOT... HEY, DON'T BE POINTING THAT THING AT--
BRAM-THUDD
KURK!
ALMOST TO THE PARKING LOT. I CAN STILL GET THROUGH TO THE SALVAGE YARD BEFORE THEY KNOW WHAT--
NOW THEN, YOU GARISH, GREEN DESTROYER OF INNOCENT HOPE AND DREAMS...
...WHERE WERE WE?

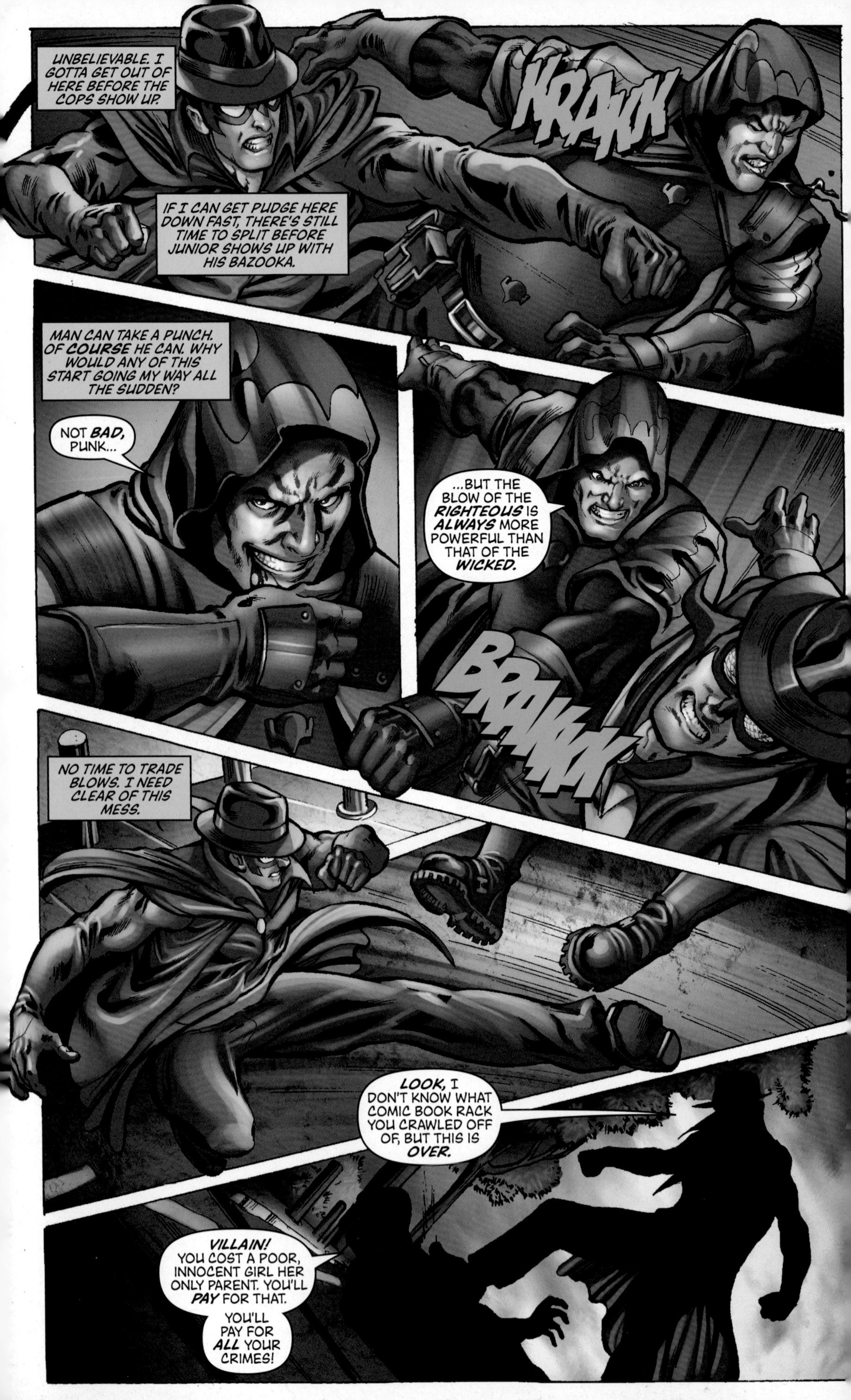
UNBELIEVABLE. I GOTTA GET OUT OF HERE BEFORE THE COPS SHOW UP.
KRAKK
IF I CAN GET PUDGE HERE DOWN FAST, THERE'S STILL TIME TO SPLIT BEFORE JUNIOR SHOWS UP WITH HIS BAZOOKA.
MAN CAN TAKE A PUNCH. OF COURSE HE CAN. WHY WOULD ANY OF THIS START GOING MY WAY ALL THE SUDDEN?
NOT BAD, PUNK...
...BUT THE BLOW OF THE RIGHTEOUS IS ALWAYS MORE POWERFUL THAN THAT OF THE WICKED.
BRAKKK
NO TIME TO TRADE BLOWS. I NEED CLEAR OF THIS MESS.
LOOK, I DON'T KNOW WHAT COMIC BOOK RACK YOU CRAWLED OFF OF, BUT THIS IS OVER.
VILLAIN! YOU COST A POOR, INNOCENT GIRL HER ONLY PARENT. YOU'LL PAY FOR THAT.
YOU'LL PAY FOR ALL YOUR CRIMES!

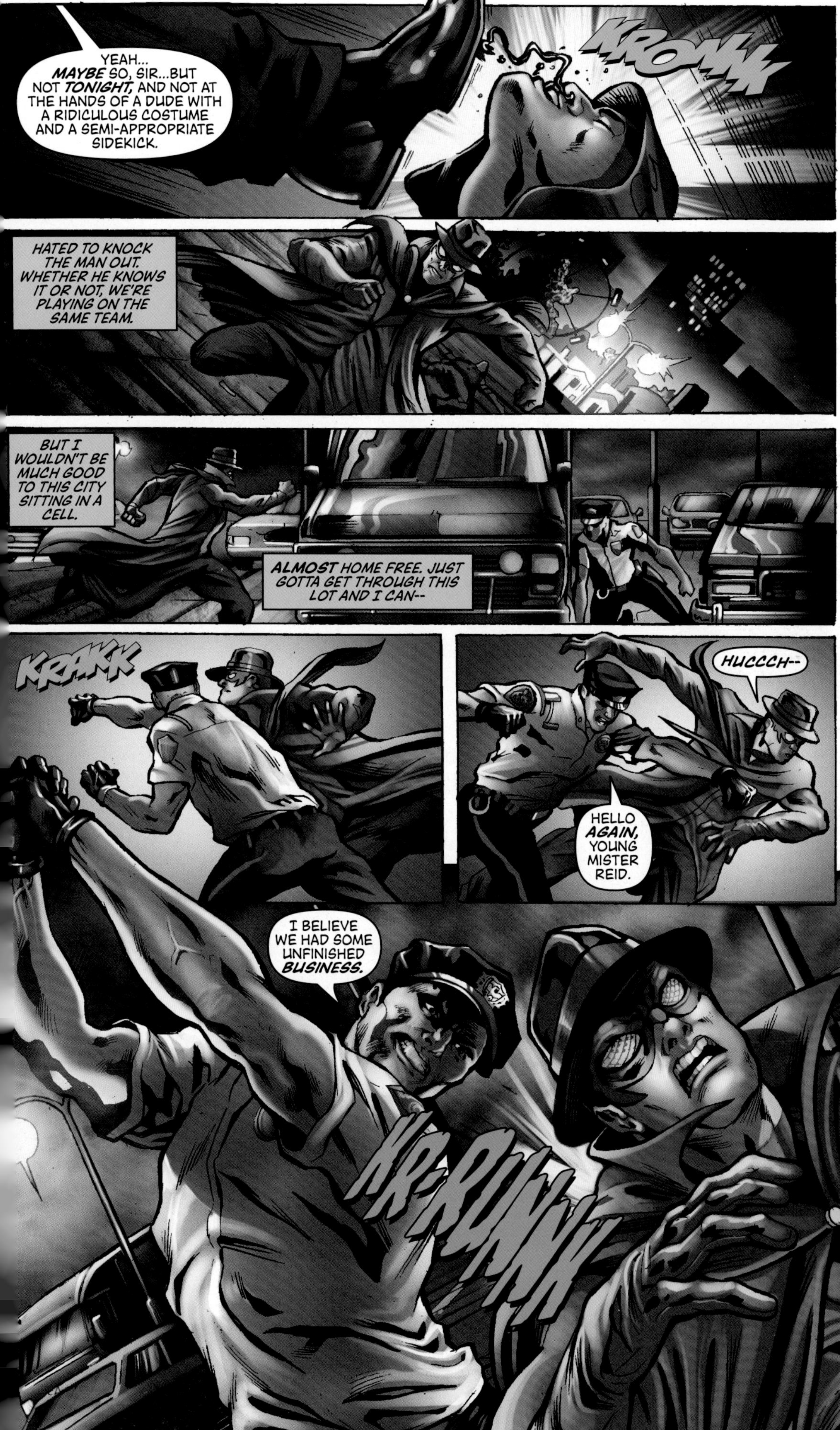
YEAH... MAYBE SO, SIR...BUT NOT TONIGHT, AND NOT AT THE HANDS OF A DUDE WITH A RIDICULOUS COSTUME AND A SEMI-APPROPRIATE SIDEKICK.
KRONK
HATED TO KNOCK THE MAN OUT. WHETHER HE KNOWS IT OR NOT, WE'RE PLAYING ON THE SAME TEAM.
BUT I WOULDN'T BE MUCH GOOD TO THIS CITY SITTING IN A CELL.
ALMOST HOME FREE. JUST GOTTA GET THROUGH THIS LOT AND I CAN--
KRAKK
HUCCCH--
HELLO AGAIN, YOUNG MISTER REID.
I BELIEVE WE HAD SOME UNFINISHED BUSINESS.
KR-RUNNK

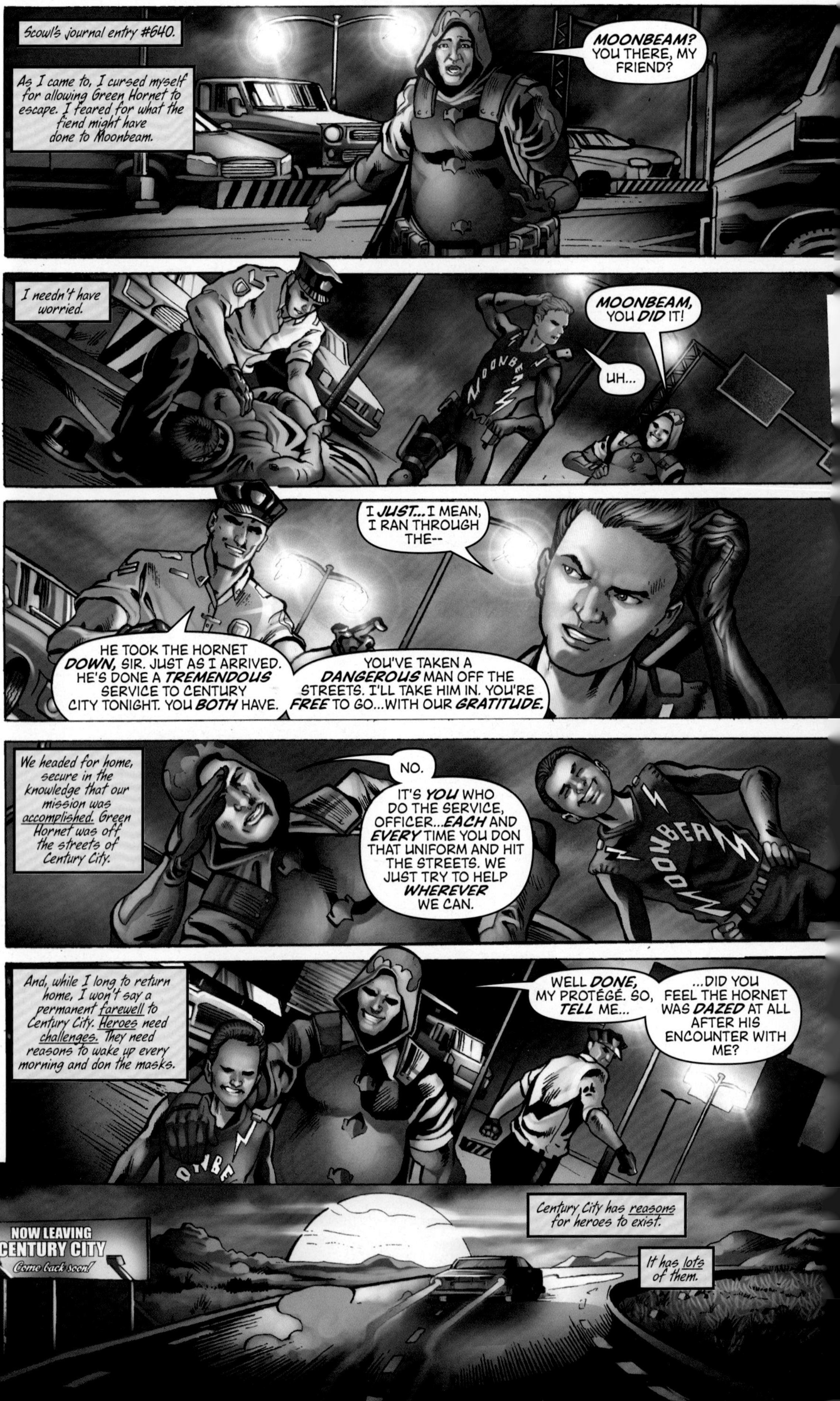
Scowl's journal entry #640.
As I came to, I cursed myself for allowing Green Hornet to escape. I feared for what the fiend might have done to Moonbeam.
MOONBEAM? YOU THERE, MY FRIEND?
I needn't have worried.
MOONBEAM, YOU DID IT!
UH...
I JUST... I MEAN, I RAN THROUGH THE--
HE TOOK THE HORNET DOWN, SIR. JUST AS I ARRIVED. HE'S DONE A TREMENDOUS SERVICE TO CENTURY CITY TONIGHT. YOU BOTH HAVE.
YOU'VE TAKEN A DANGEROUS MAN OFF THE STREETS. I'LL TAKE HIM IN. YOU'RE FREE TO GO...WITH OUR GRATITUDE.
We headed for home, secure in the knowledge that our mission was accomplished. Green Hornet was off the streets of Century City.
NO.
IT'S YOU WHO DO THE SERVICE, OFFICER...EACH AND EVERY TIME YOU DON THAT UNIFORM AND HIT THE STREETS. WE JUST TRY TO HELP WHEREVER WE CAN.
And, while I long to return home, I won't say a permanent farewell to Century City. Heroes need challenges. They need reasons to wake up every morning and don the masks.
WELL DONE, MY PROTÉGÉ. SO, TELL ME...
...DID YOU FEEL THE HORNET WAS DAZED AT ALL AFTER HIS ENCOUNTER WITH ME?
NOW LEAVING
CENTURY CITY
Come back soon!
Century City has reasons for heroes to exist.
It has lots of them.

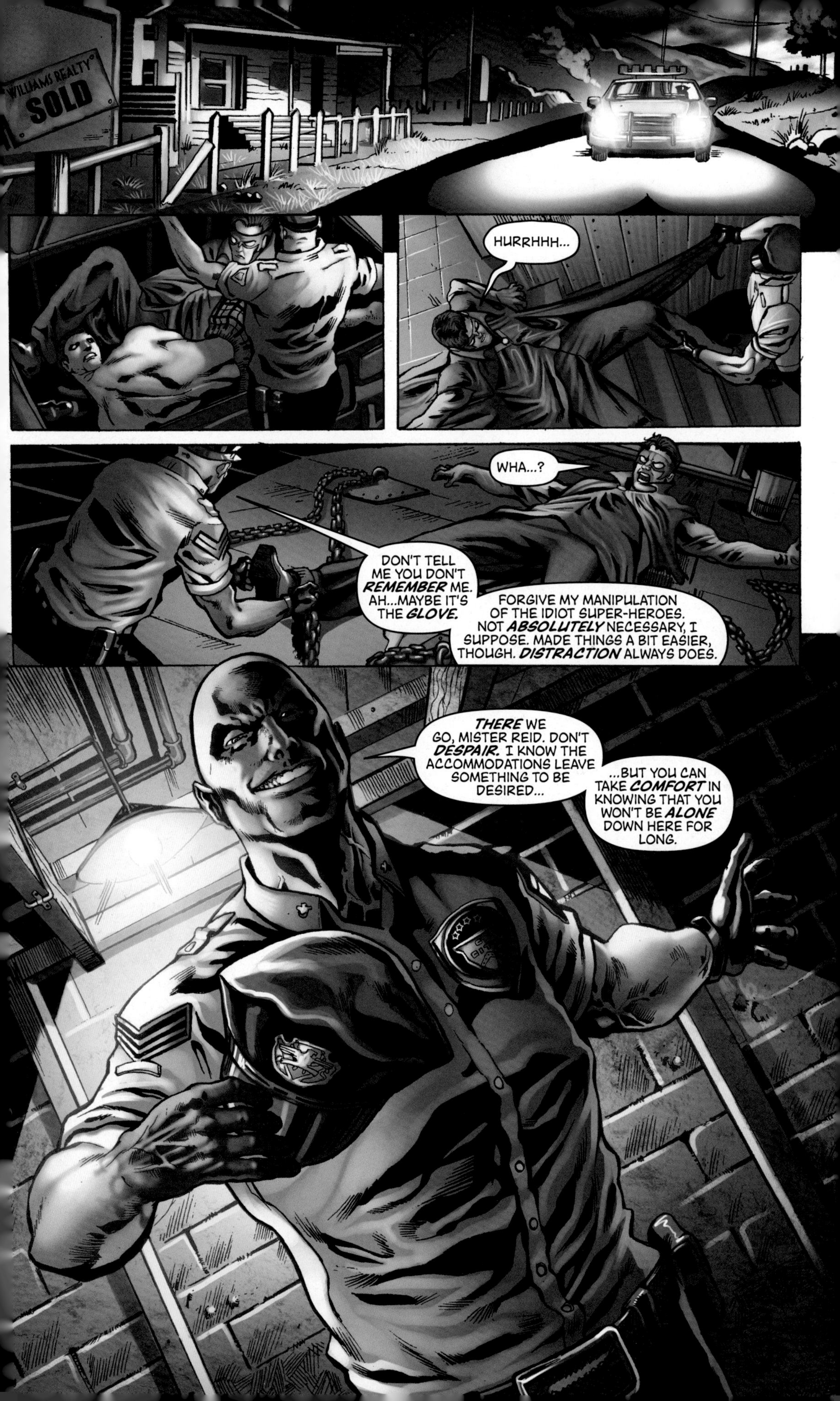
WILLIAMS REALTY
SOLD
HURRHHH...
WHA...?
DON'T TELL ME YOU DON'T REMEMBER ME. AH...MAYBE IT'S THE GLOVE.
FORGIVE MY MANIPULATION OF THE IDIOT SUPER-HEROES. NOT ABSOLUTELY NECESSARY, I SUPPOSE. MADE THINGS A BIT EASIER, THOUGH. DISTRACTION ALWAYS DOES.
THERE WE GO, MISTER REID. DON'T DESPAIR. I KNOW THE ACCOMMODATIONS LEAVE SOMETHING TO BE DESIRED...
...BUT YOU CAN TAKE COMFORT IN KNOWING THAT YOU WON'T BE ALONE DOWN HERE FOR LONG.

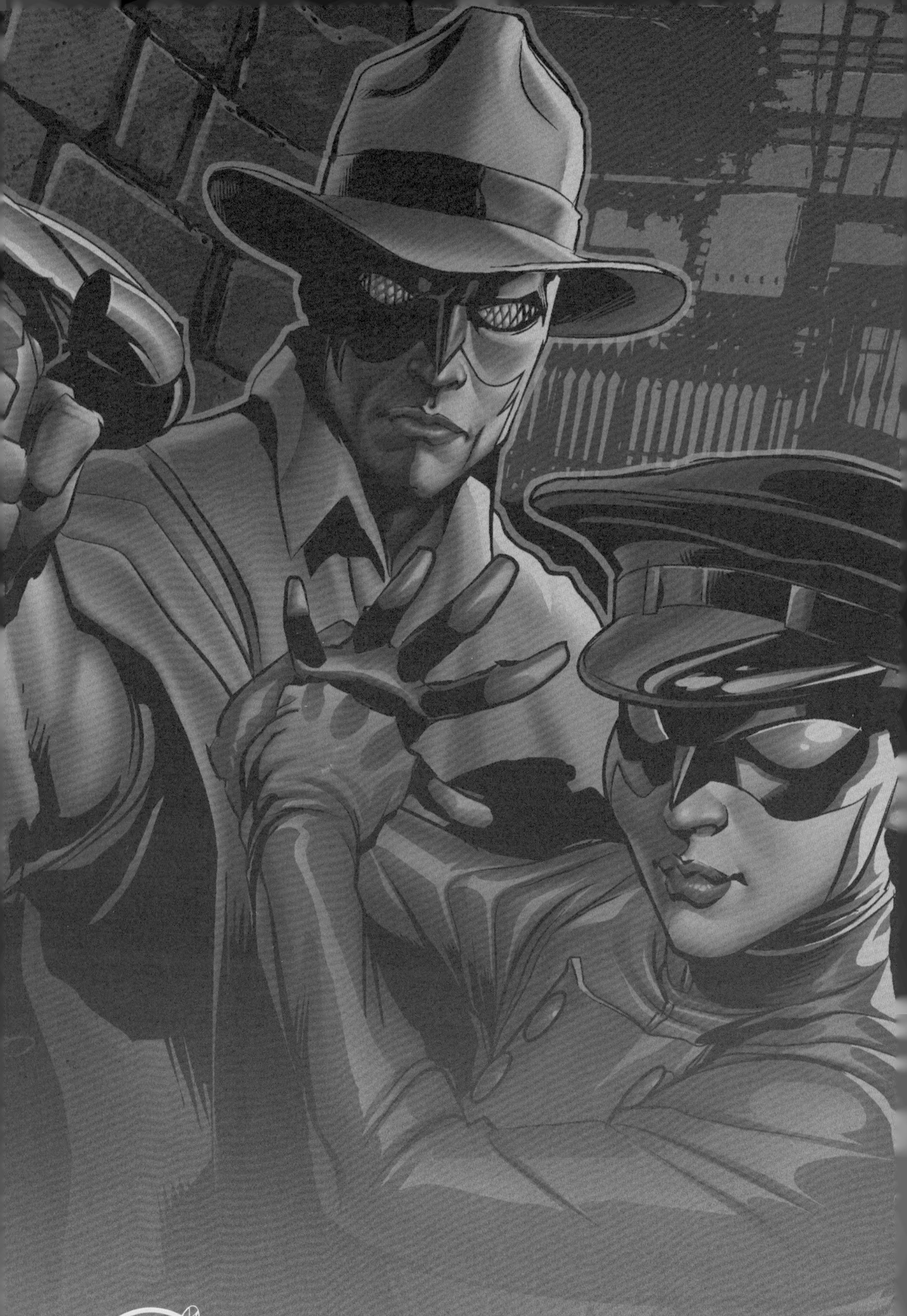

EPISODE SEVENTEEN: THE DEVIL YOU KNOW PART TWO

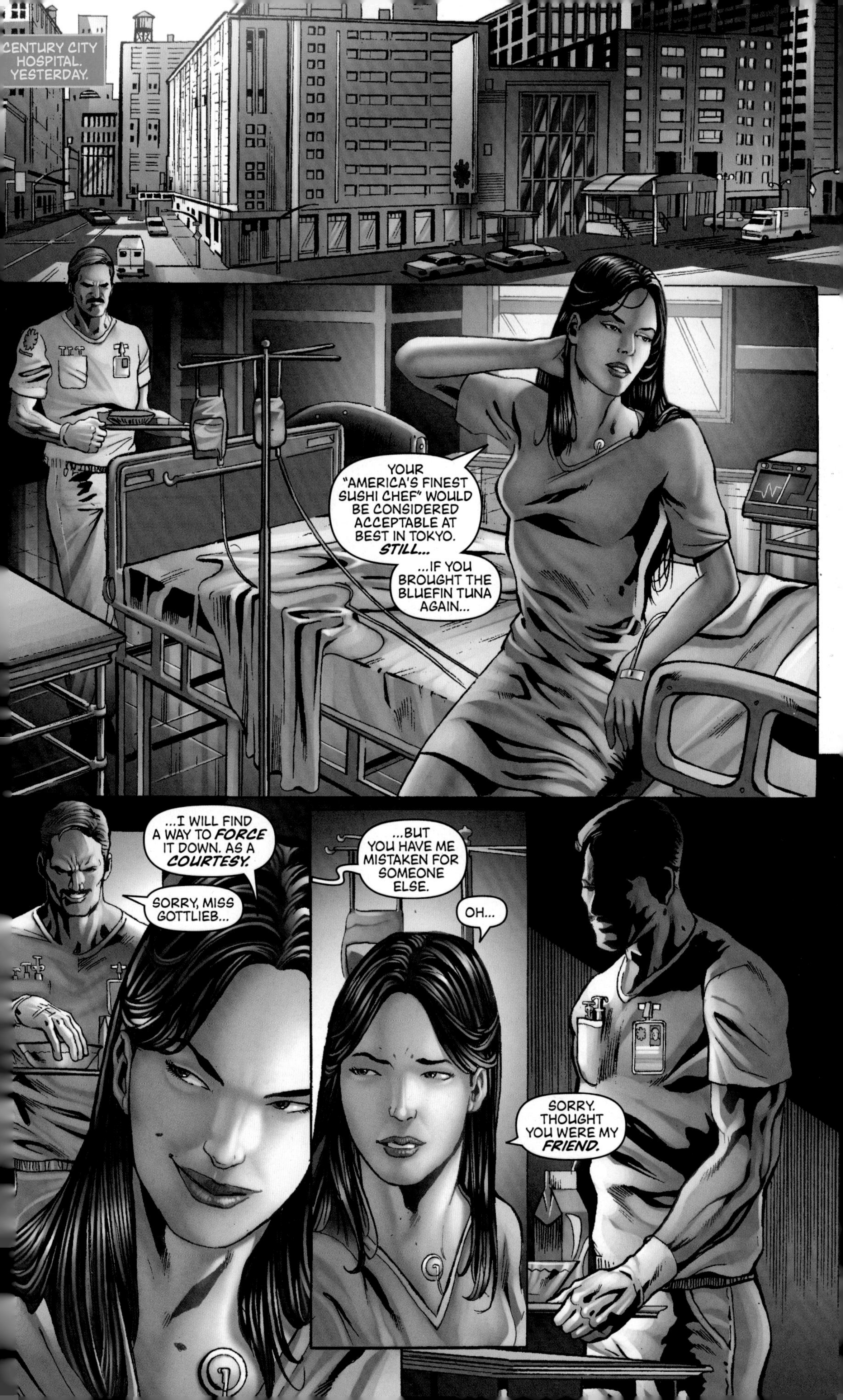
CENTURY CITY HOSPITAL. YESTERDAY.
YOUR "AMERICA'S FINEST SUSHI CHEF" WOULD BE CONSIDERED ACCEPTABLE AT BEST IN TOKYO. STILL...
...IF YOU BROUGHT THE BLUEFIN TUNA AGAIN...
...I WILL FIND A WAY TO FORCE IT DOWN. AS A COURTESY.
SORRY, MISS GOTTLIEB...
...BUT YOU HAVE ME MISTAKEN FOR SOMEONE ELSE.
OH...
SORRY. THOUGHT YOU WERE MY FRIEND.

NOT COMING TODAY, I GUESS. LEAVES ME WITH THIS... *DELIGHTFUL* NOURISHMENT.

YOU MUST BE NEW. I'VE BEEN HERE A WEEK AND HAVEN'T SEEN YOU BEFORE.

FILLING IN, MISS GOTTLIEB. JUST HERE FOR A FEW SHIFTS.

I BRING THE TRAYS...

CHECK THE DRUGS...

...SEE THAT ALL THE PATIENTS ARE CHECKED IN... UNDER THEIR *PROPER* NAMES.

WHA...?

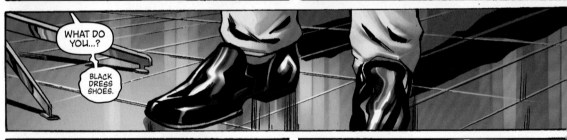

WHAT DO YOU...?

BLACK DRESS SHOES.

WHO THE *HELL* ARE YOU?

WHA... HUHHNN...

CLEVER GIRL. ABOUT *HALF* CLEVER ENOUGH.

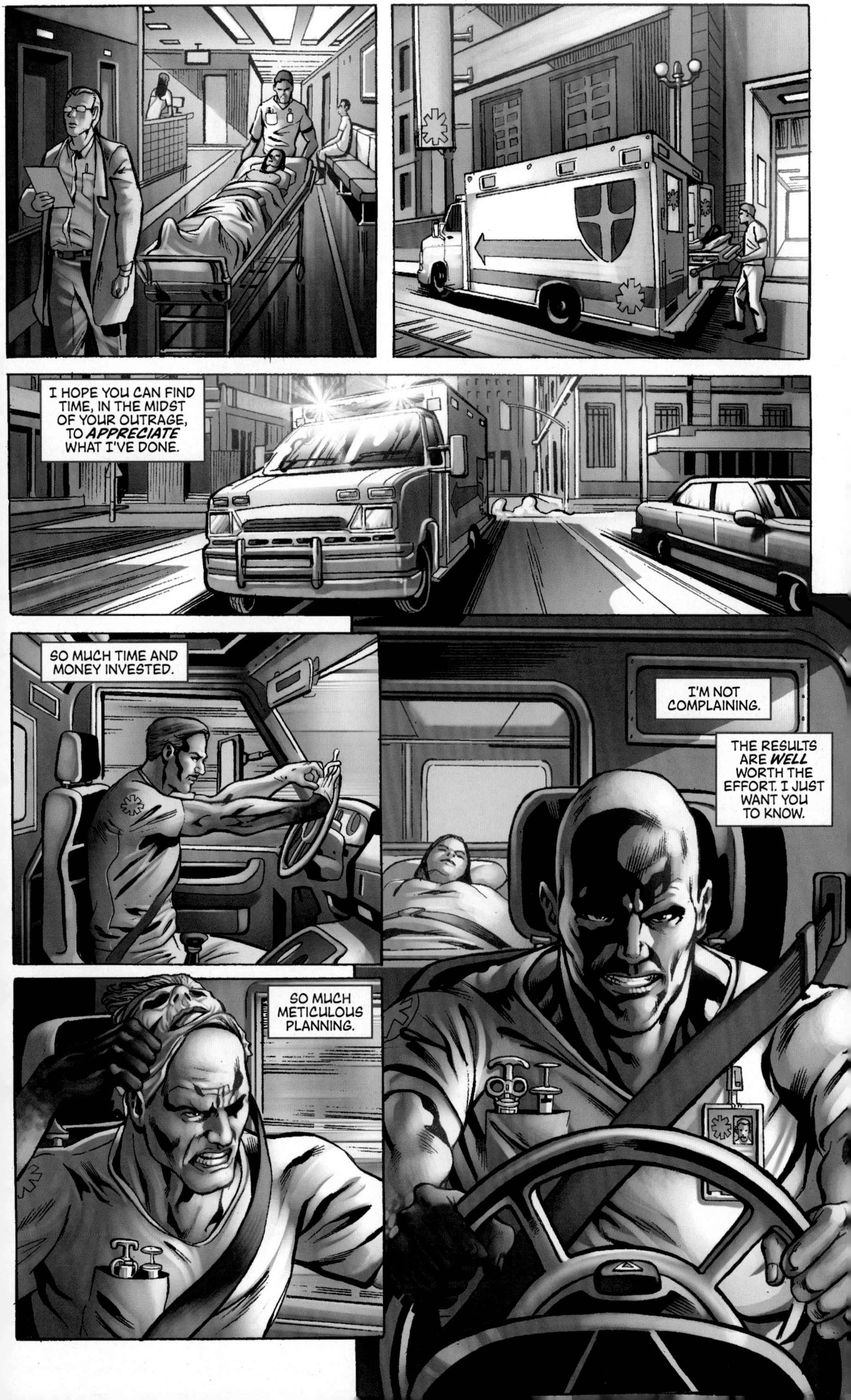
I HOPE YOU CAN FIND TIME, IN THE MIDST OF YOUR OUTRAGE, TO *APPRECIATE* WHAT I'VE DONE.
SO MUCH TIME AND MONEY INVESTED.
I'M NOT COMPLAINING.
THE RESULTS ARE *WELL* WORTH THE EFFORT. I JUST WANT YOU TO KNOW.
SO MUCH METICULOUS PLANNING.

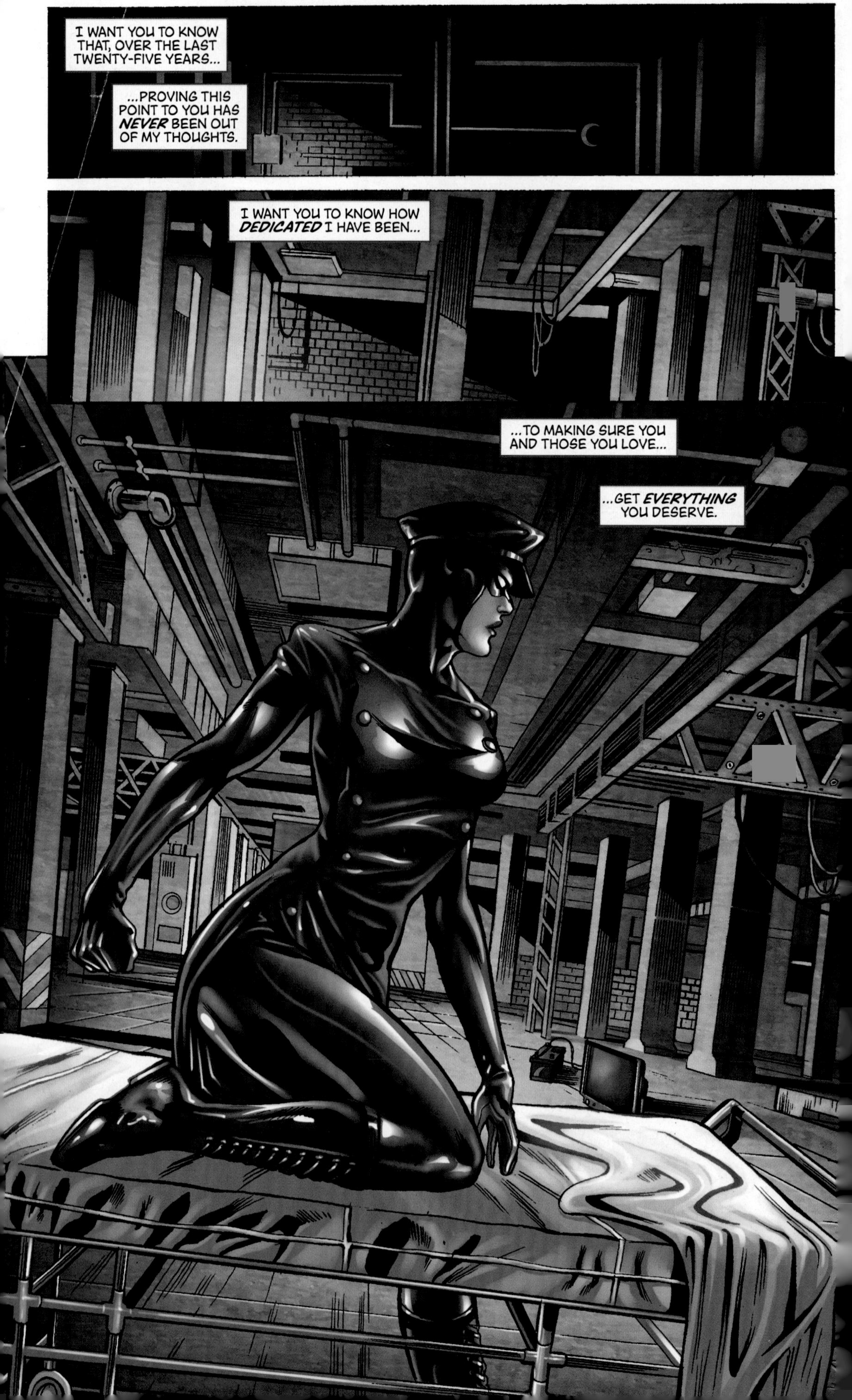
I WANT YOU TO KNOW THAT, OVER THE LAST TWENTY-FIVE YEARS...
...PROVING THIS POINT TO YOU HAS *NEVER* BEEN OUT OF MY THOUGHTS.
I WANT YOU TO KNOW HOW *DEDICATED* I HAVE BEEN...
...TO MAKING SURE YOU AND THOSE YOU LOVE...
...GET *EVERYTHING* YOU DESERVE.

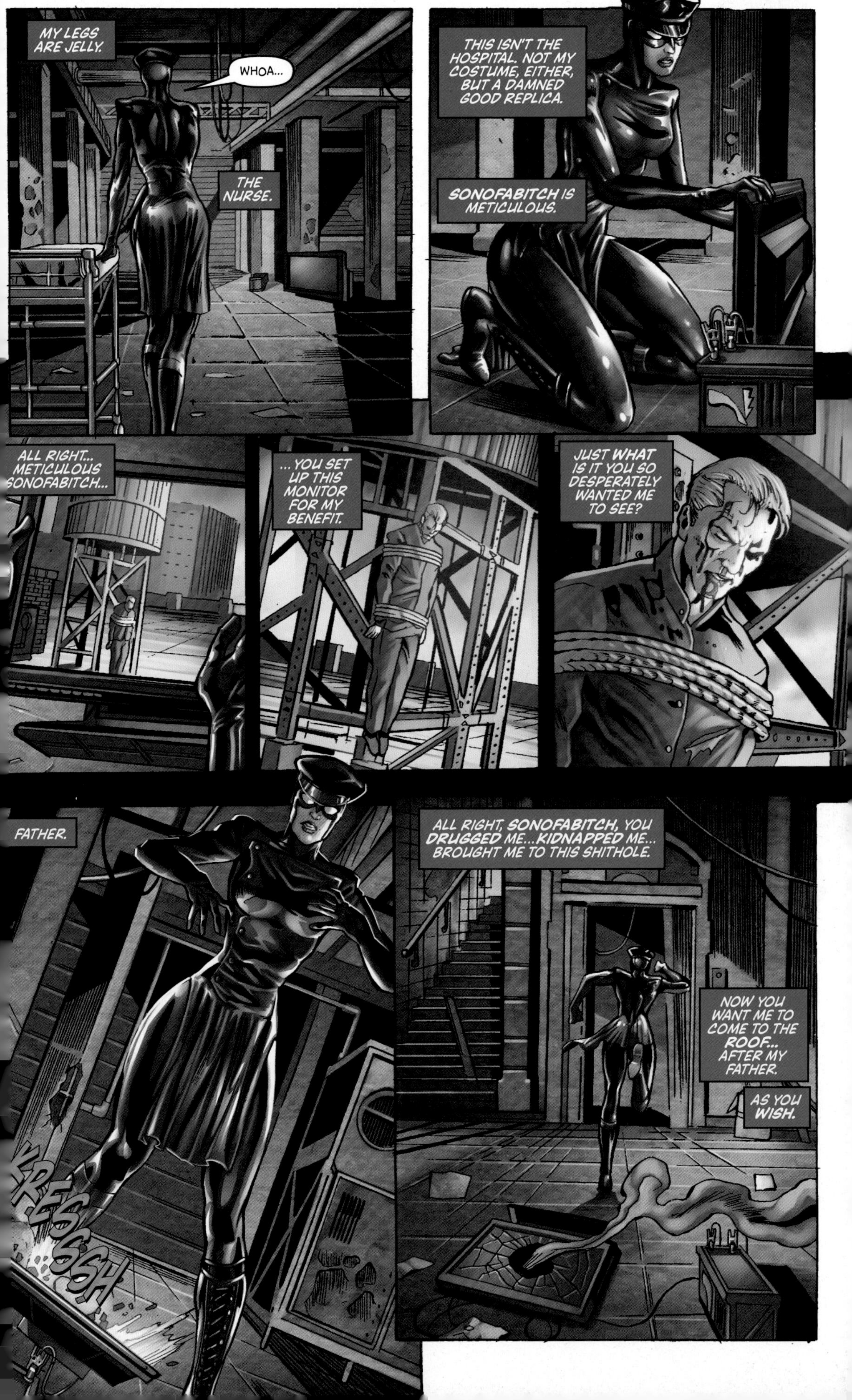

MY LEGS ARE JELLY.
WHOA...
THE NURSE.
THIS ISN'T THE HOSPITAL. NOT MY COSTUME, EITHER, BUT A DAMNED GOOD REPLICA.
SONOFABITCH IS METICULOUS.
ALL RIGHT... METICULOUS SONOFABITCH...
...YOU SET UP THIS MONITOR FOR MY BENEFIT.
JUST WHAT IS IT YOU SO DESPERATELY WANTED ME TO SEE?
FATHER.
KRESSSH
ALL RIGHT, SONOFABITCH, YOU DRUGGED ME...KIDNAPPED ME... BROUGHT ME TO THIS SHITHOLE.
NOW YOU WANT ME TO COME TO THE ROOF... AFTER MY FATHER.
AS YOU WISH.

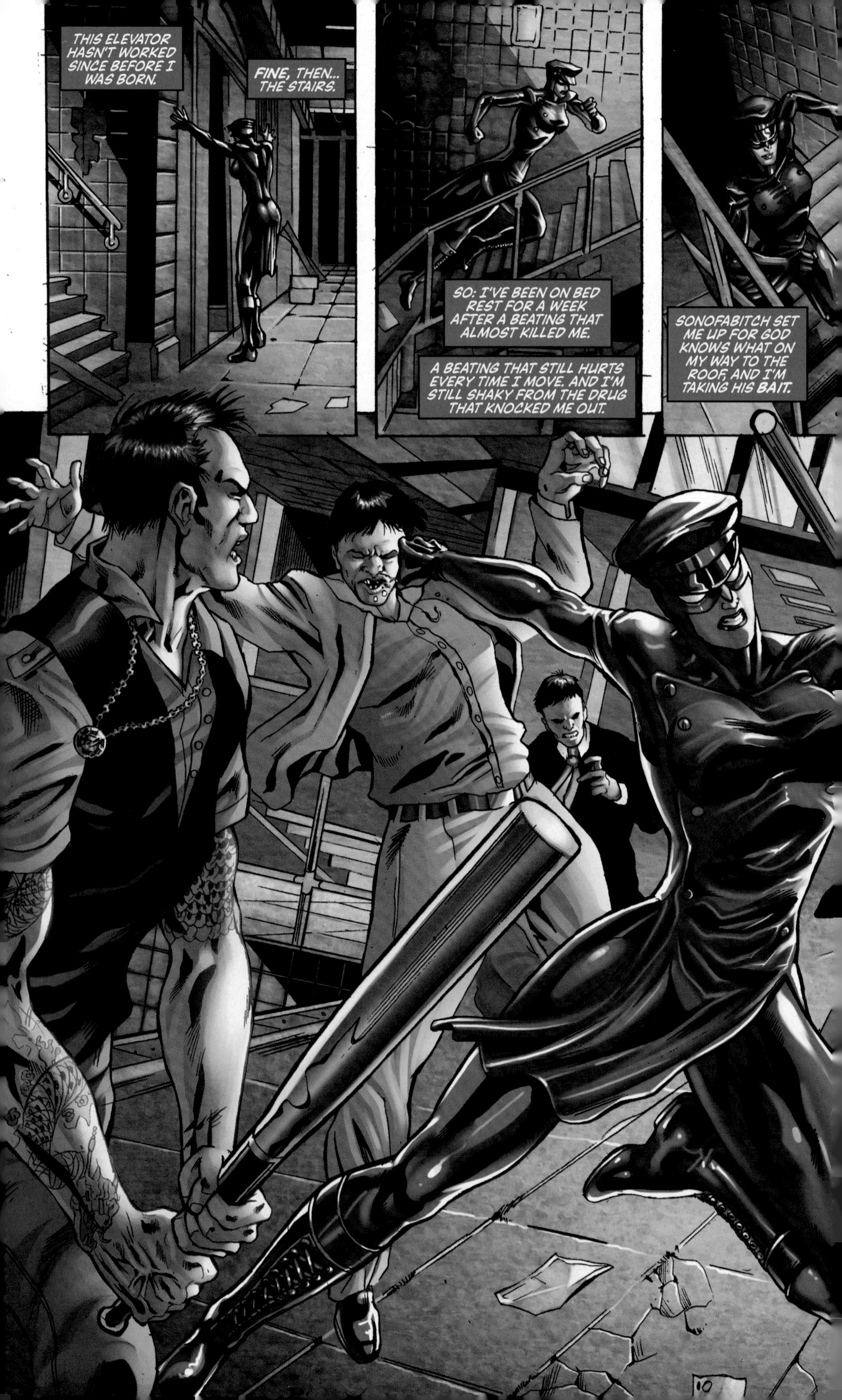

THIS ELEVATOR HASN'T WORKED SINCE BEFORE I WAS BORN.
FINE, THEN... THE STAIRS.
SO: I'VE BEEN ON BED REST FOR A WEEK AFTER A BEATING THAT ALMOST KILLED ME.
A BEATING THAT STILL HURTS EVERY TIME I MOVE. AND I'M STILL SHAKY FROM THE DRUG THAT KNOCKED ME OUT.
SONOFABITCH SET ME UP FOR GOD KNOWS WHAT ON MY WAY TO THE ROOF, AND I'M TAKING HIS BAIT.

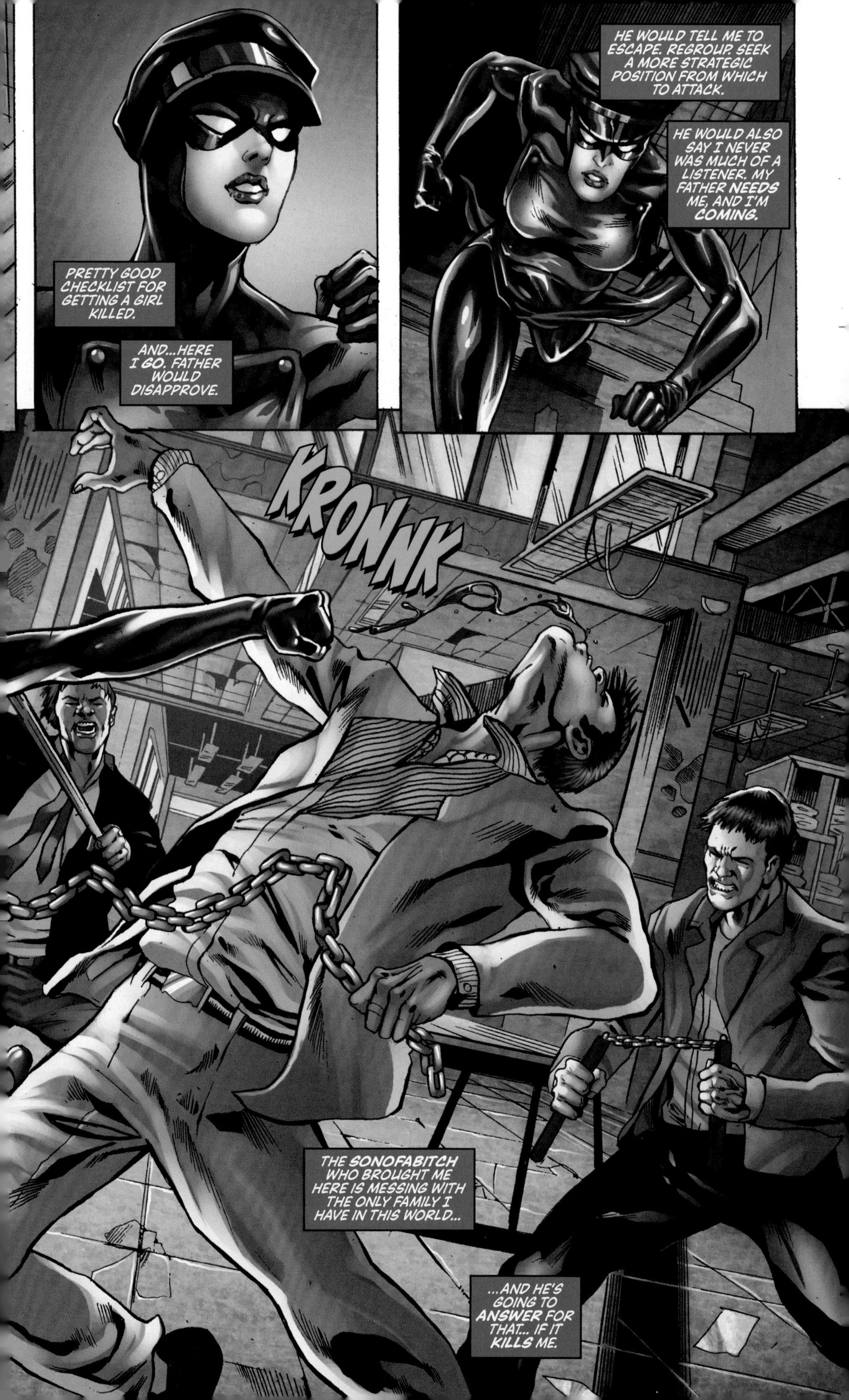
PRETTY GOOD CHECKLIST FOR GETTING A GIRL KILLED.
AND...HERE I GO. FATHER WOULD DISAPPROVE.
HE WOULD TELL ME TO ESCAPE. REGROUP. SEEK A MORE STRATEGIC POSITION FROM WHICH TO ATTACK.
HE WOULD ALSO SAY I NEVER WAS MUCH OF A LISTENER. MY FATHER NEEDS ME, AND I'M COMING.
KRONNK
THE SONOFABITCH WHO BROUGHT ME HERE IS MESSING WITH THE ONLY FAMILY I HAVE IN THIS WORLD...
...AND HE'S GOING TO ANSWER FOR THAT... IF IT KILLS ME.

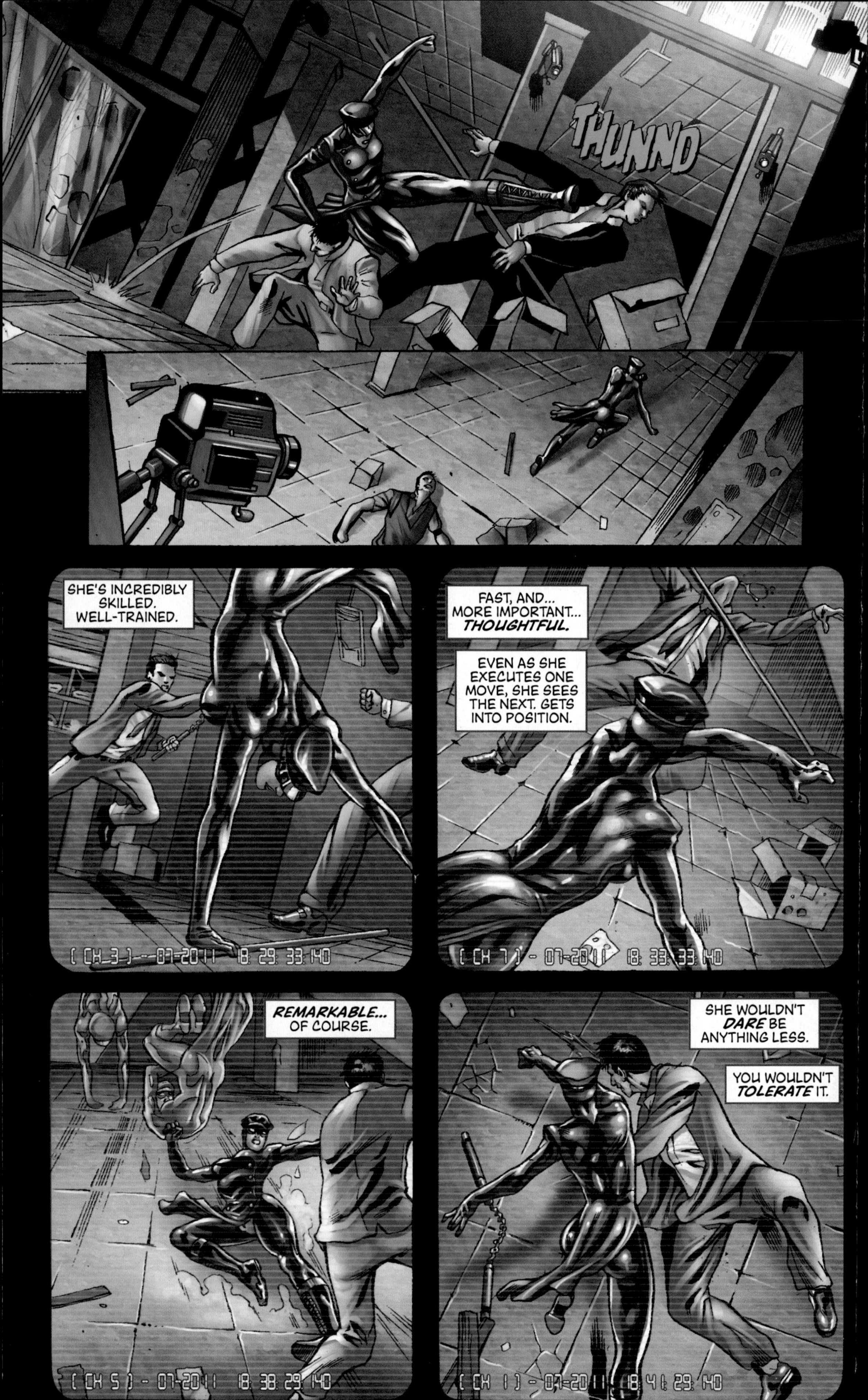
THUNND
SHE'S INCREDIBLY SKILLED. WELL-TRAINED.
[CH 3] - 07-2011 18: 29: 33: 140
FAST, AND... MORE IMPORTANT... *THOUGHTFUL.*
EVEN AS SHE EXECUTES ONE MOVE, SHE SEES THE NEXT. GETS INTO POSITION.
[CH 7] - 07-2011 18: 33: 33: 140
REMARKABLE... OF COURSE.
[CH 5] - 07-2011 18: 38: 29: 140
SHE WOULDN'T *DARE* BE ANYTHING LESS.
YOU WOULDN'T *TOLERATE* IT.
[CH 1] - 07-2011 18: 41: 29: 140

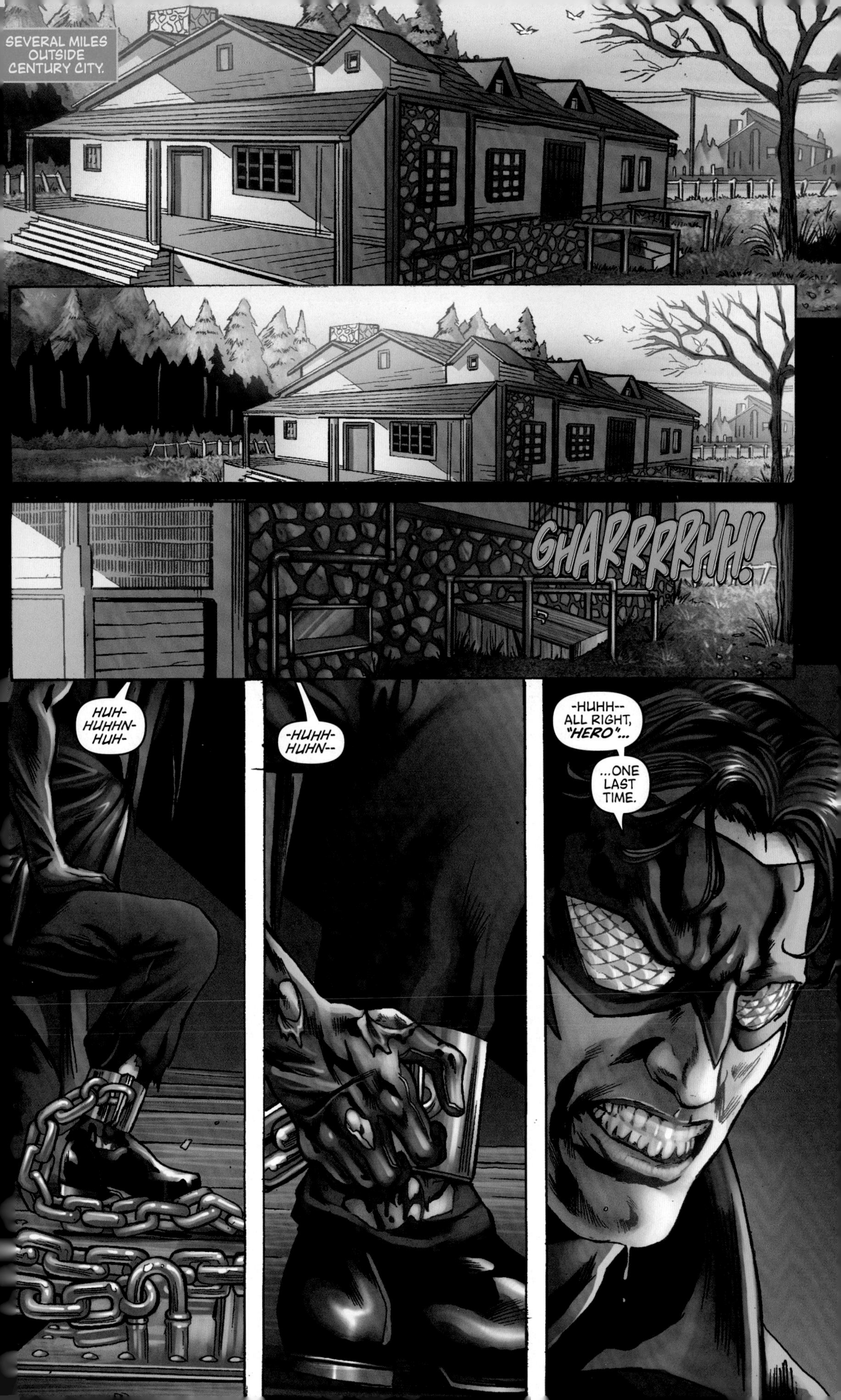
SEVERAL MILES OUTSIDE CENTURY CITY.
GHARRRRHH!
HUH-HUHHN-HUH-
-HUHH-HUHN--
-HUHH-- ALL RIGHT, "HERO"...
...ONE LAST TIME.

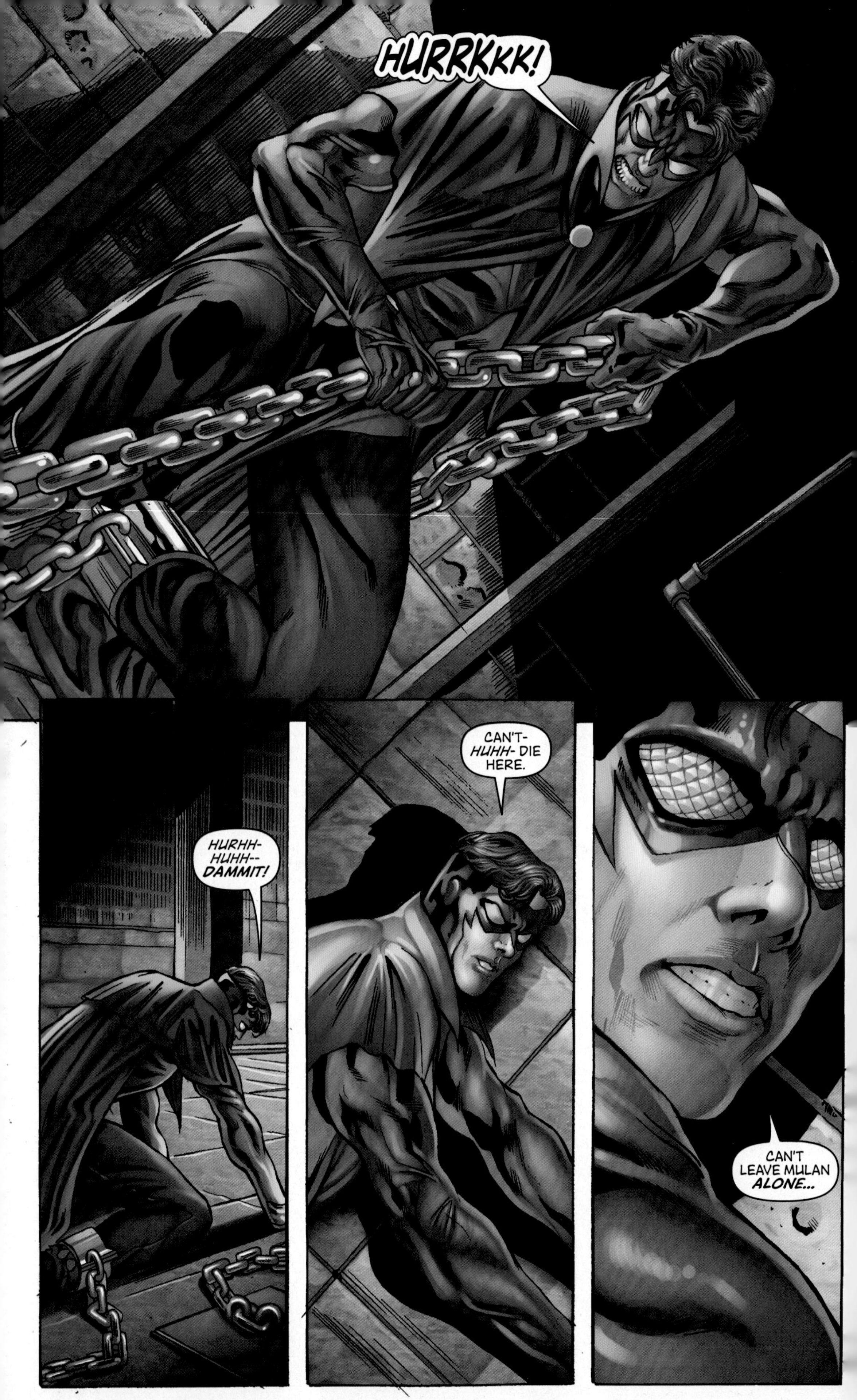
HURRKKK!
HURHH-
HUHH--
DAMMIT!
CAN'T-
HUHH- DIE
HERE.
CAN'T
LEAVE MULAN
ALONE...

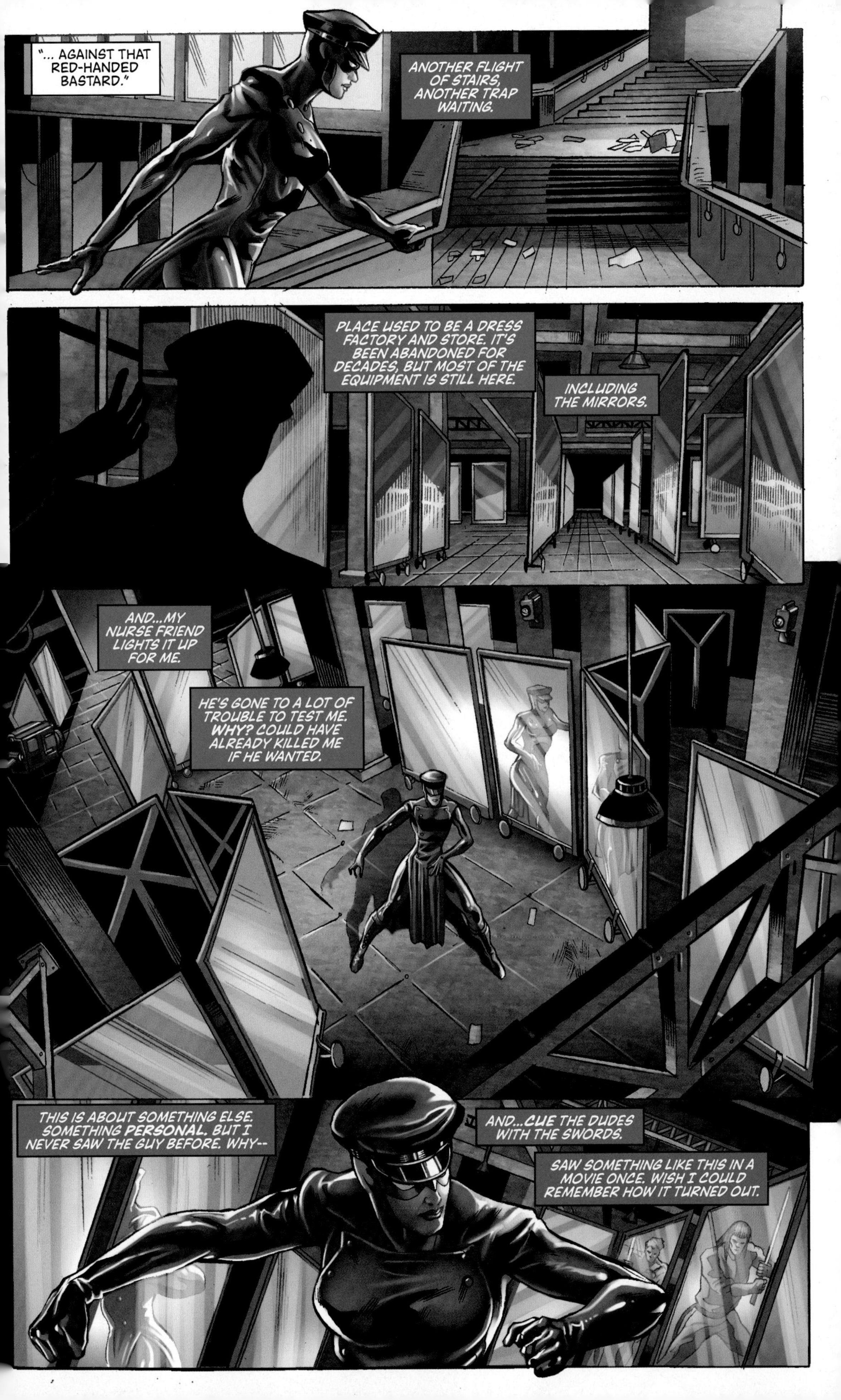
"... AGAINST THAT RED-HANDED BASTARD."
ANOTHER FLIGHT OF STAIRS, ANOTHER TRAP WAITING.
PLACE USED TO BE A DRESS FACTORY AND STORE. IT'S BEEN ABANDONED FOR DECADES, BUT MOST OF THE EQUIPMENT IS STILL HERE.
INCLUDING THE MIRRORS.
AND...MY NURSE FRIEND LIGHTS IT UP FOR ME.
HE'S GONE TO A LOT OF TROUBLE TO TEST ME. WHY? COULD HAVE ALREADY KILLED ME IF HE WANTED.
THIS IS ABOUT SOMETHING ELSE. SOMETHING PERSONAL. BUT I NEVER SAW THE GUY BEFORE. WHY--
AND...CUE THE DUDES WITH THE SWORDS.
SAW SOMETHING LIKE THIS IN A MOVIE ONCE. WISH I COULD REMEMBER HOW IT TURNED OUT.

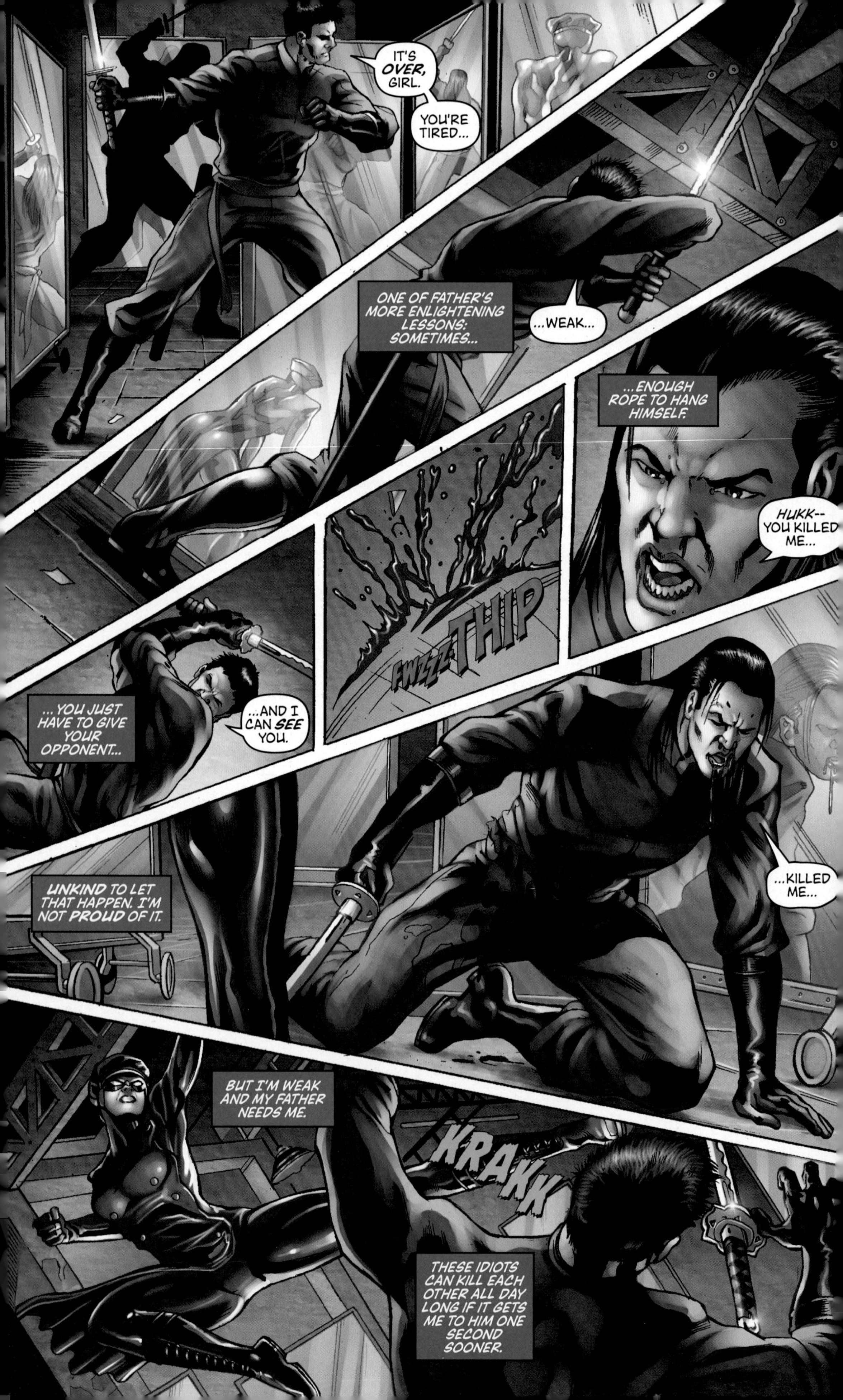

IT'S OVER, GIRL.
YOU'RE TIRED...
ONE OF FATHER'S MORE ENLIGHTENING LESSONS: SOMETIMES...
...WEAK...
...ENOUGH ROPE TO HANG HIMSELF.
HUKK-- YOU KILLED ME...
...YOU JUST HAVE TO GIVE YOUR OPPONENT...
...AND I CAN SEE YOU.
FWSSZ THIP
UNKIND TO LET THAT HAPPEN. I'M NOT PROUD OF IT.
...KILLED ME...
BUT I'M WEAK AND MY FATHER NEEDS ME.
KRAKK
THESE IDIOTS CAN KILL EACH OTHER ALL DAY LONG IF IT GETS ME TO HIM ONE SECOND SOONER.

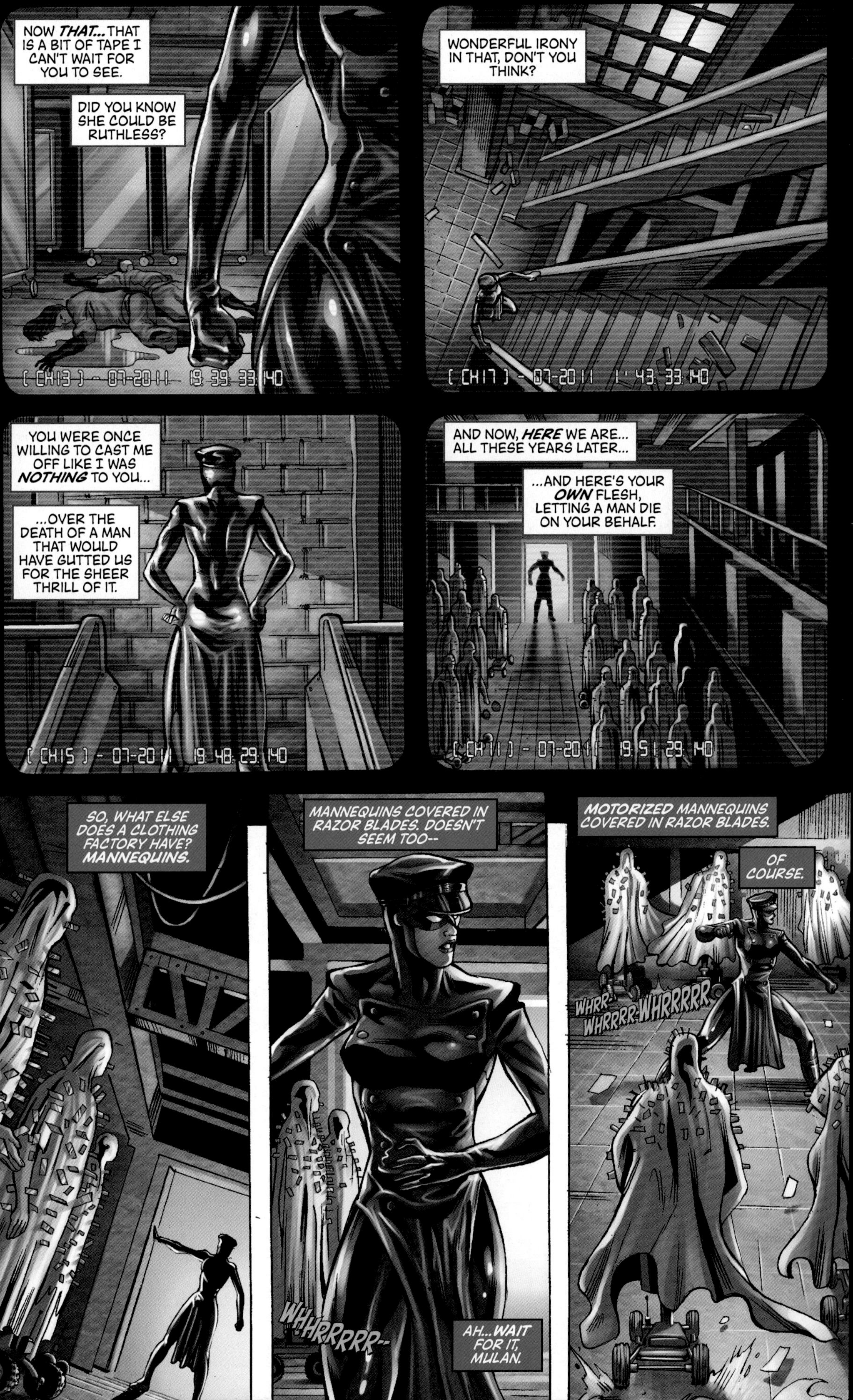

NOW THAT... THAT IS A BIT OF TAPE I CAN'T WAIT FOR YOU TO SEE.
DID YOU KNOW SHE COULD BE RUTHLESS?
[CH13] - 07-2011 19:39:33:140
WONDERFUL IRONY IN THAT, DON'T YOU THINK?
[CH17] - 07-2011 1:43:33:140
YOU WERE ONCE WILLING TO CAST ME OFF LIKE I WAS NOTHING TO YOU...
...OVER THE DEATH OF A MAN THAT WOULD HAVE GUTTED US FOR THE SHEER THRILL OF IT.
[CH15] - 07-2011 19:48:29:140
AND NOW, HERE WE ARE... ALL THESE YEARS LATER...
...AND HERE'S YOUR OWN FLESH, LETTING A MAN DIE ON YOUR BEHALF.
[CH11] - 07-2011 19:51:29:140
SO, WHAT ELSE DOES A CLOTHING FACTORY HAVE? MANNEQUINS.
MANNEQUINS COVERED IN RAZOR BLADES. DOESN'T SEEM TOO--
WHHRRRRR--
AH... WAIT FOR IT, MULAN.
MOTORIZED MANNEQUINS COVERED IN RAZOR BLADES.
OF COURSE.
WHRR-WHRRRR-WHRRRRR

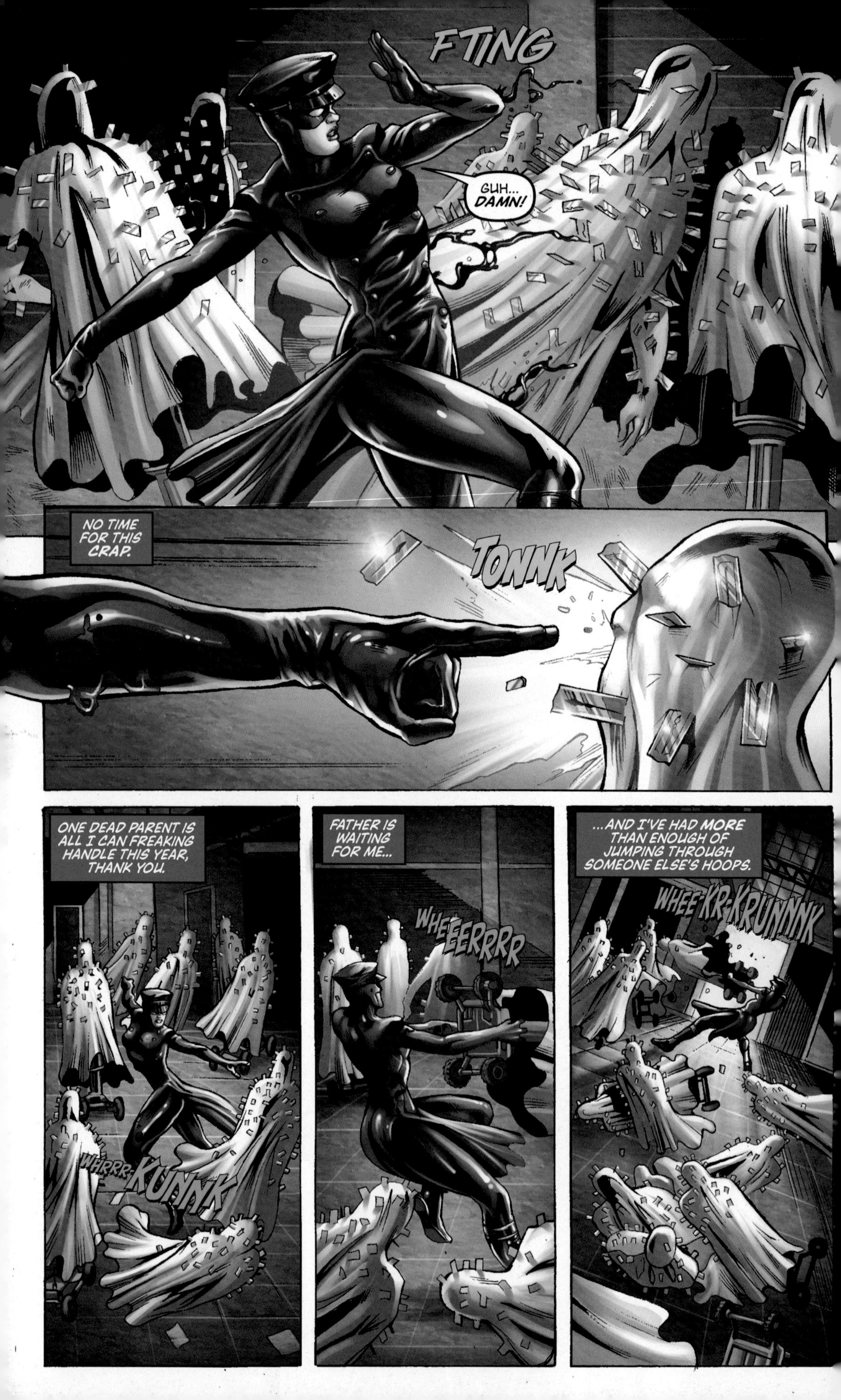
FTING
GUH... DAMN!
NO TIME FOR THIS CRAP.
TONNK
ONE DEAD PARENT IS ALL I CAN FREAKING HANDLE THIS YEAR, THANK YOU.
WHRRR-KUNNK
FATHER IS WAITING FOR ME...
WHEEERRRR
...AND I'VE HAD MORE THAN ENOUGH OF JUMPING THROUGH SOMEONE ELSE'S HOOPS.
WHEE-KR-KRUNNNK

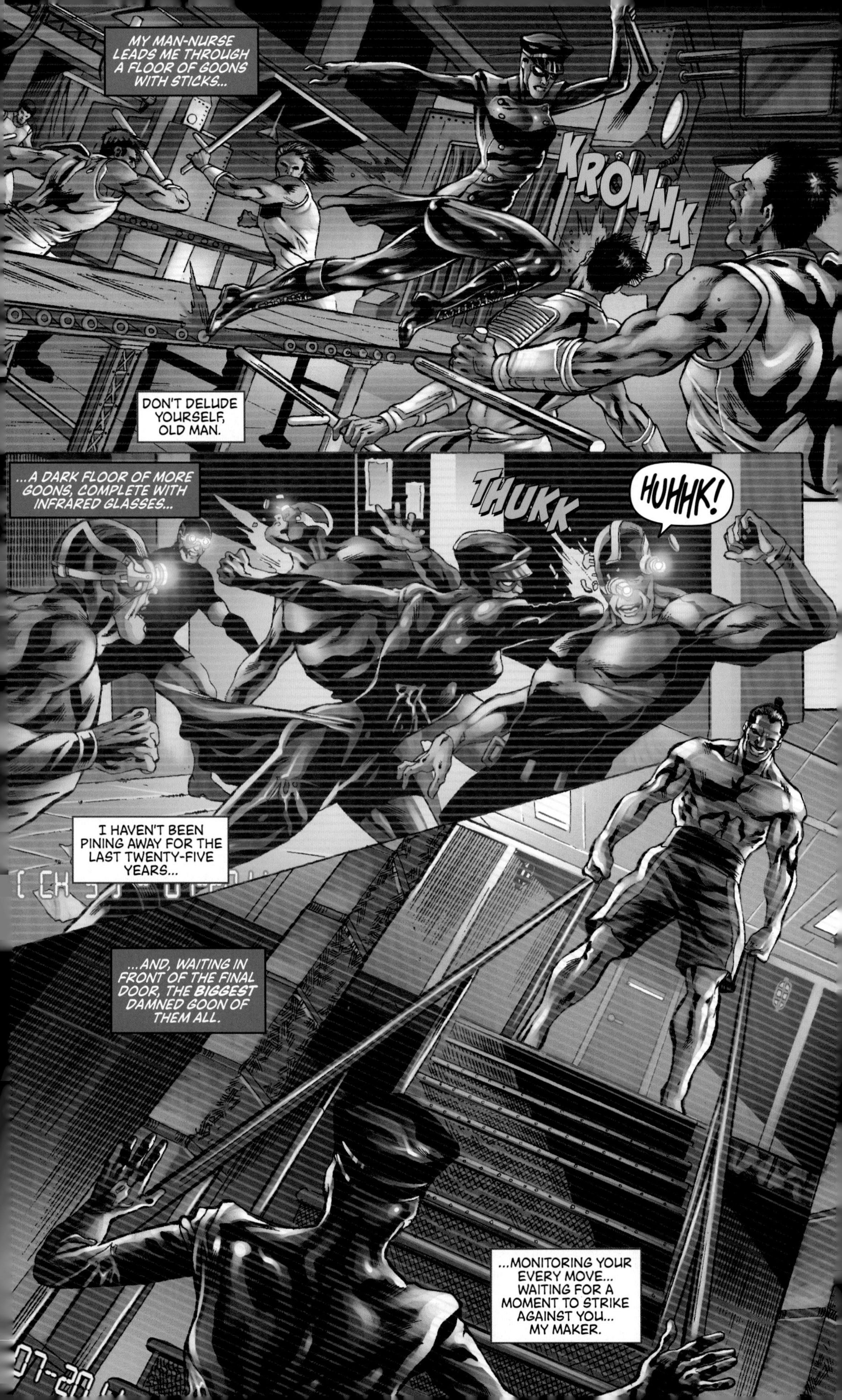

MY MAN-NURSE LEADS ME THROUGH A FLOOR OF GOONS WITH STICKS...
KRONNK
DON'T DELUDE YOURSELF, OLD MAN.
...A DARK FLOOR OF MORE GOONS, COMPLETE WITH INFRARED GLASSES...
THUKK
HUHHK!
I HAVEN'T BEEN PINING AWAY FOR THE LAST TWENTY-FIVE YEARS...
...AND, WAITING IN FRONT OF THE FINAL DOOR, THE BIGGEST DAMNED GOON OF THEM ALL.
...MONITORING YOUR EVERY MOVE... WAITING FOR A MOMENT TO STRIKE AGAINST YOU... MY MAKER.

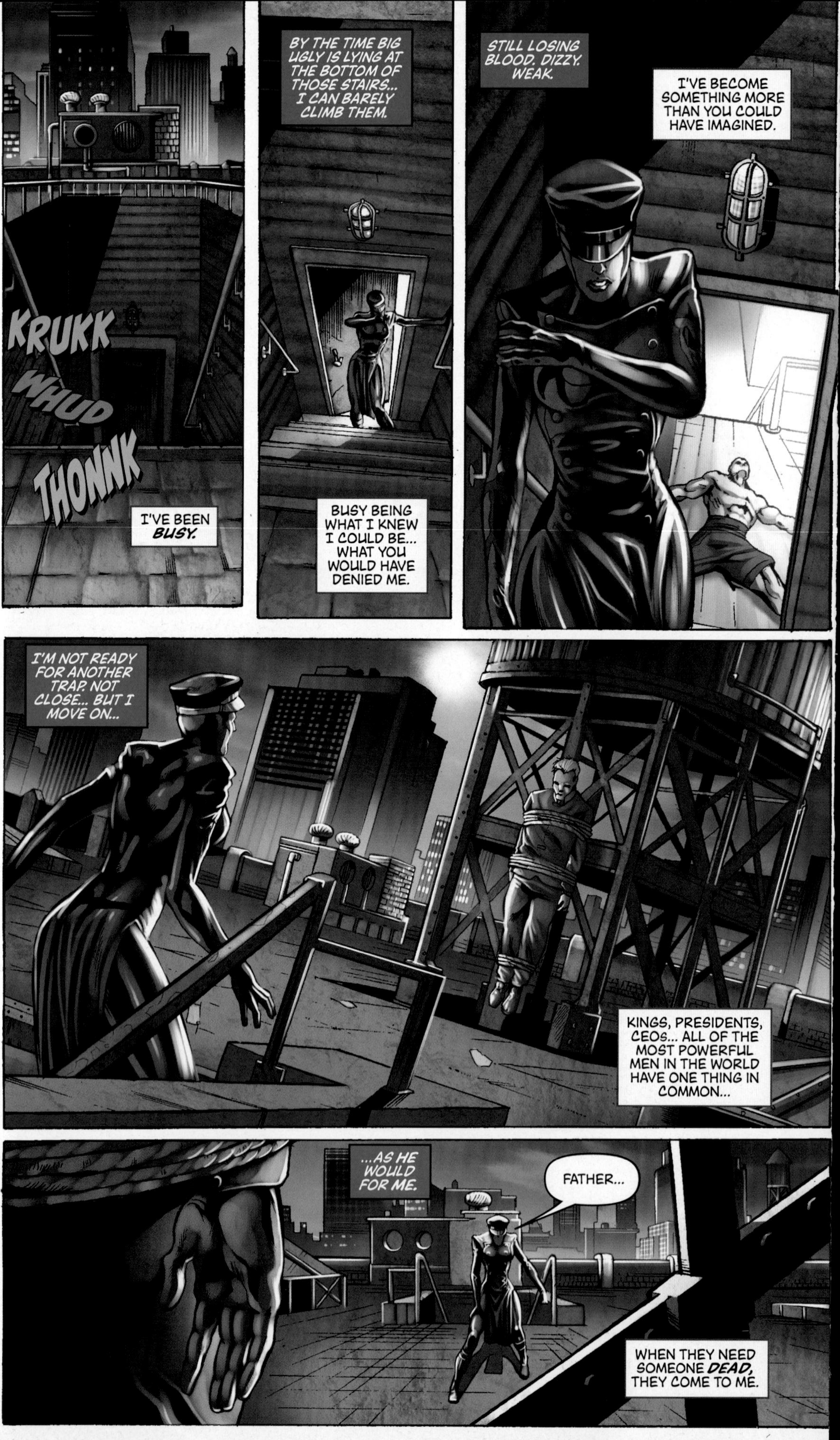
KRUKK
WHUD
THONNK
I'VE BEEN BUSY.
BY THE TIME BIG UGLY IS LYING AT THE BOTTOM OF THOSE STAIRS... I CAN BARELY CLIMB THEM.
BUSY BEING WHAT I KNEW I COULD BE... WHAT YOU WOULD HAVE DENIED ME.
STILL LOSING BLOOD. DIZZY. WEAK.
I'VE BECOME SOMETHING MORE THAN YOU COULD HAVE IMAGINED.
I'M NOT READY FOR ANOTHER TRAP. NOT CLOSE... BUT I MOVE ON...
KINGS, PRESIDENTS, CEOS... ALL OF THE MOST POWERFUL MEN IN THE WORLD HAVE ONE THING IN COMMON...
WHEN THEY NEED SOMEONE DEAD, THEY COME TO ME.
...AS HE WOULD FOR ME.
FATHER...

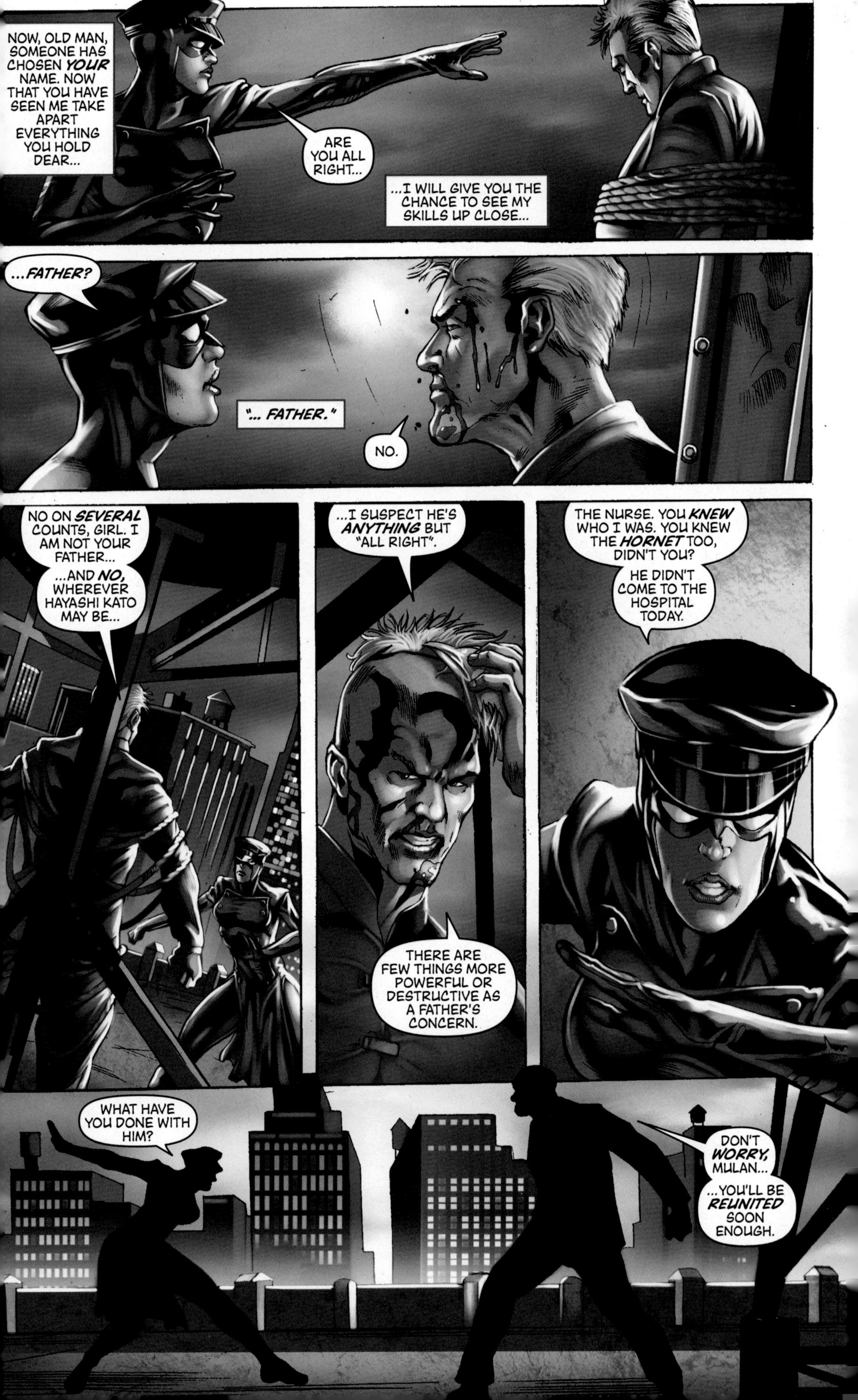
NOW, OLD MAN, SOMEONE HAS CHOSEN YOUR NAME. NOW THAT YOU HAVE SEEN ME TAKE APART EVERYTHING YOU HOLD DEAR...
ARE YOU ALL RIGHT...
...I WILL GIVE YOU THE CHANCE TO SEE MY SKILLS UP CLOSE...
...FATHER?
"... FATHER."
NO.
NO ON SEVERAL COUNTS, GIRL. I AM NOT YOUR FATHER...
...AND NO, WHEREVER HAYASHI KATO MAY BE...
...I SUSPECT HE'S ANYTHING BUT "ALL RIGHT".
THERE ARE FEW THINGS MORE POWERFUL OR DESTRUCTIVE AS A FATHER'S CONCERN.
THE NURSE. YOU KNEW WHO I WAS. YOU KNEW THE HORNET TOO, DIDN'T YOU?
HE DIDN'T COME TO THE HOSPITAL TODAY.
WHAT HAVE YOU DONE WITH HIM?
DON'T WORRY, MULAN...
...YOU'LL BE REUNITED SOON ENOUGH.

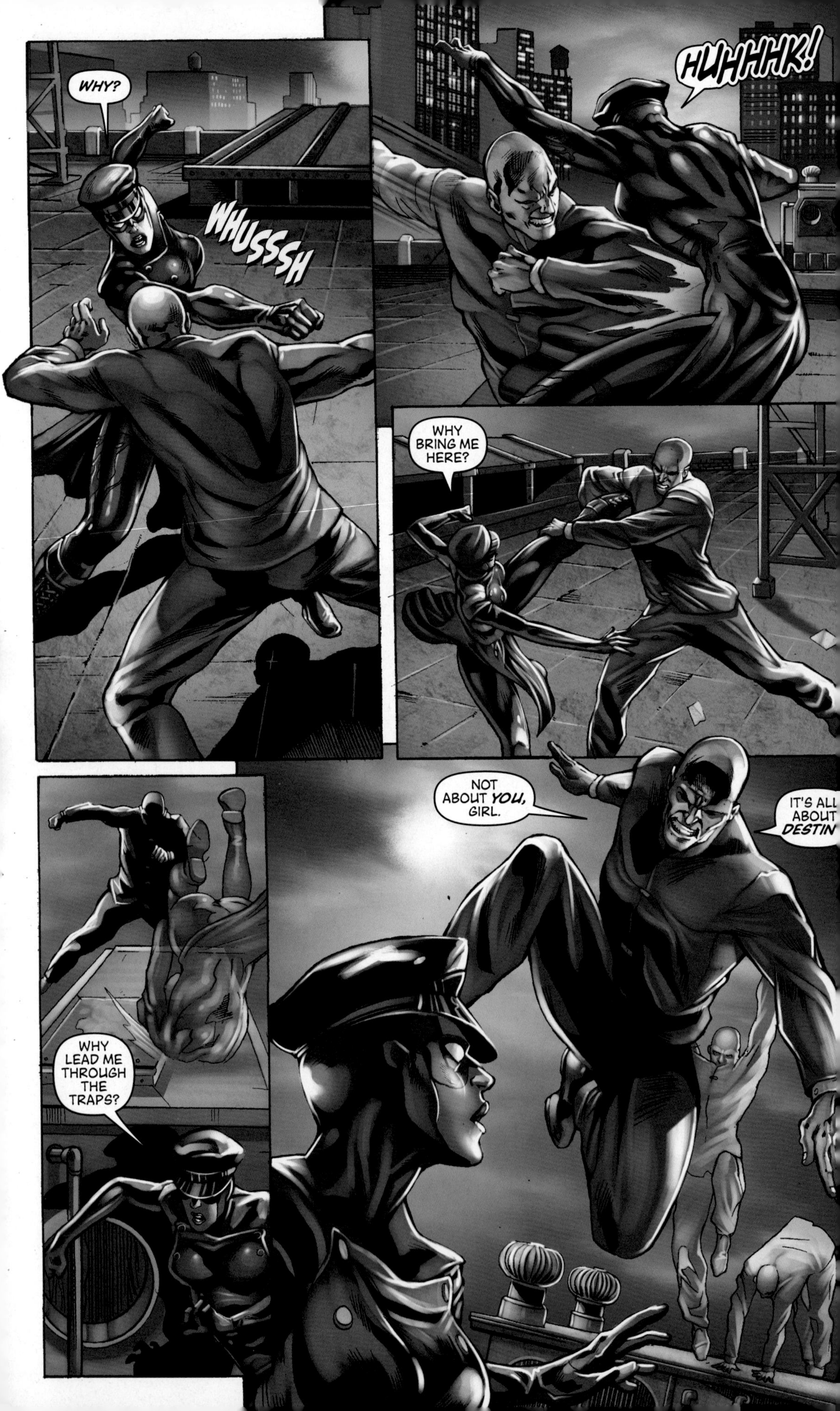
WHY?
WHUSSSH
HUHHHK!
WHY BRING ME HERE?
WHY LEAD ME THROUGH THE TRAPS?
NOT ABOUT YOU, GIRL.
IT'S ALL ABOUT DESTIN

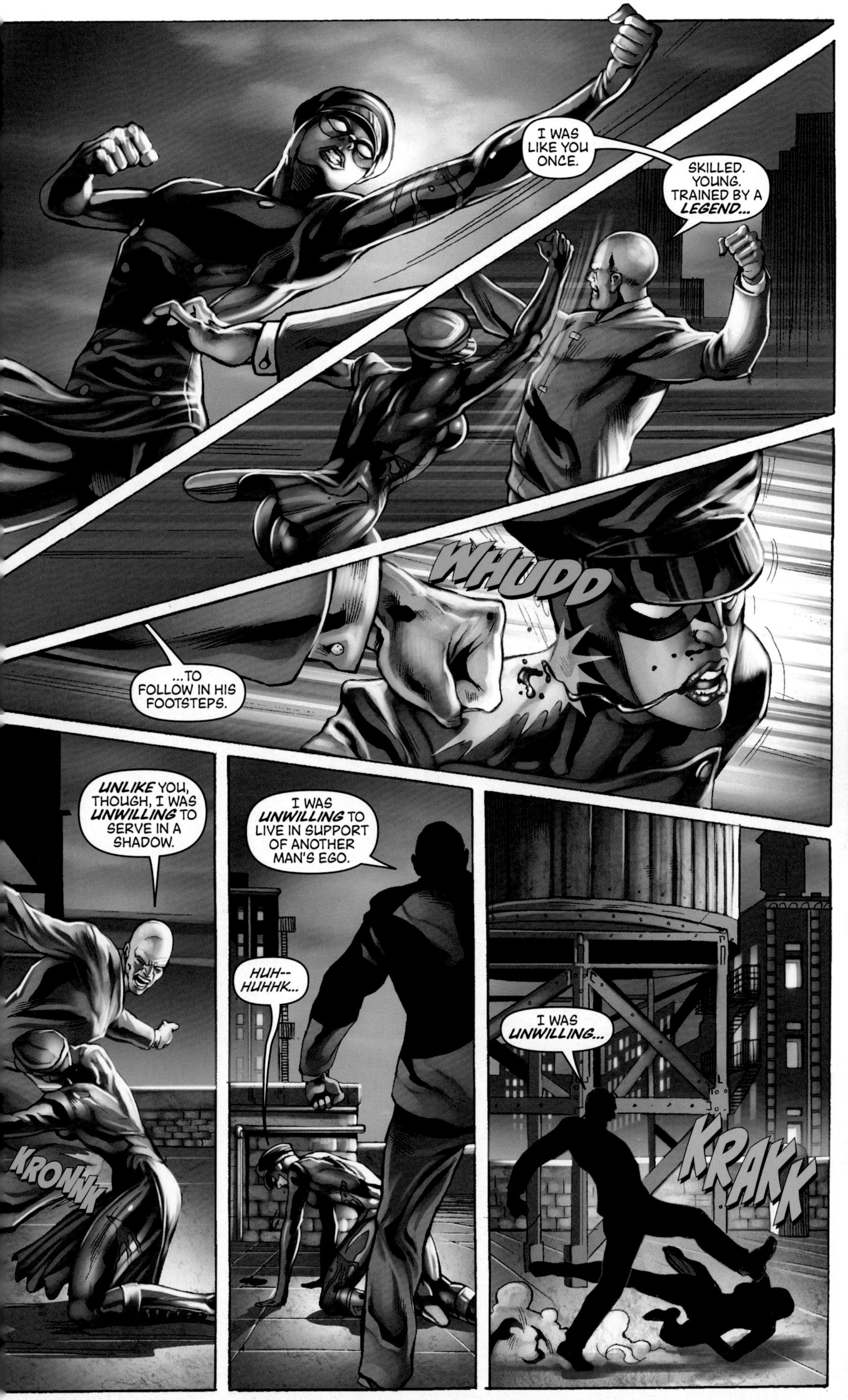
I WAS LIKE YOU ONCE.
SKILLED. YOUNG. TRAINED BY A LEGEND...
WHUDD
...TO FOLLOW IN HIS FOOTSTEPS.
UNLIKE YOU, THOUGH, I WAS UNWILLING TO SERVE IN A SHADOW.
KRONNK
I WAS UNWILLING TO LIVE IN SUPPORT OF ANOTHER MAN'S EGO.
HUH-- HUHHK...
I WAS UNWILLING...
KRAKK

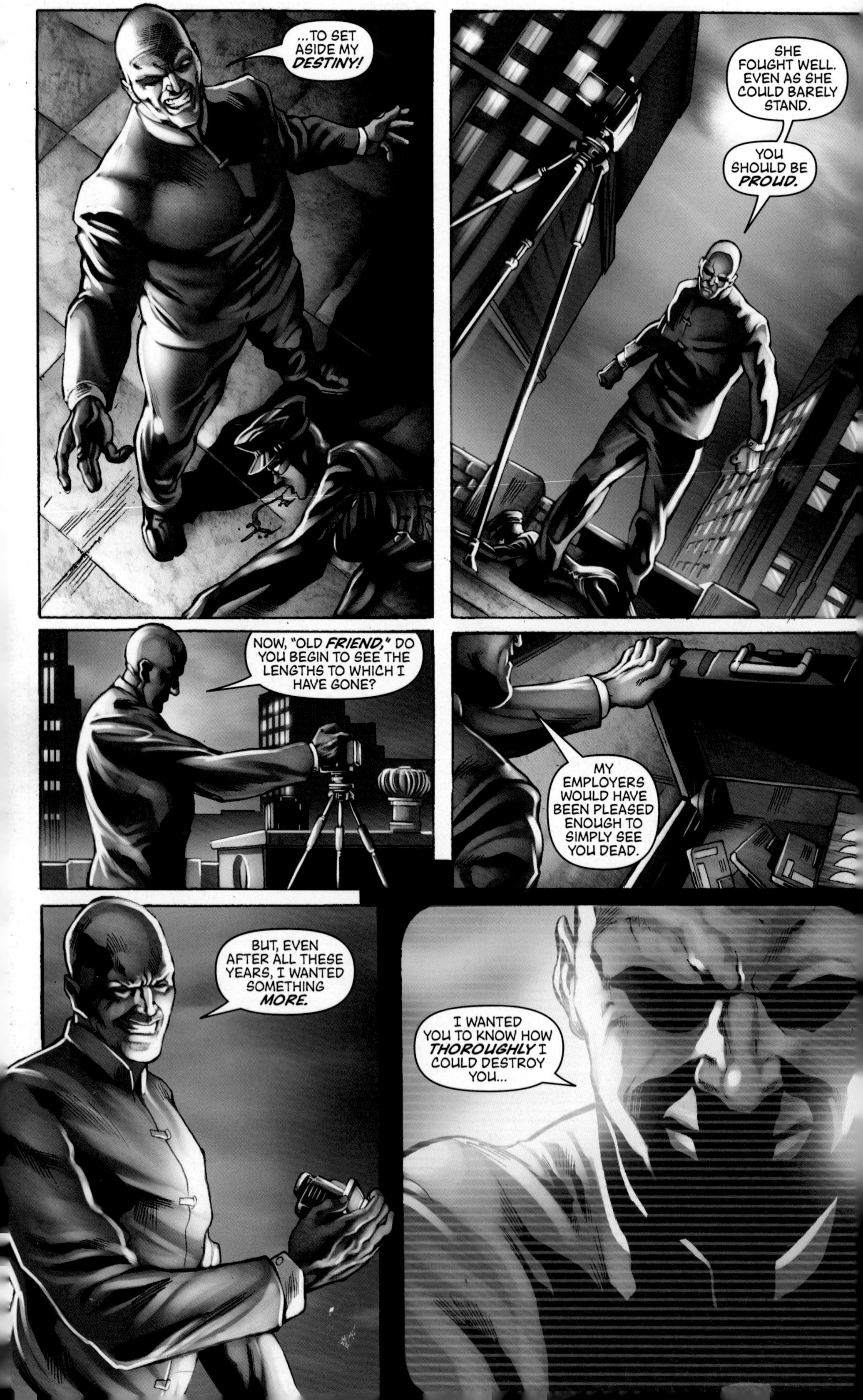
...TO SET ASIDE MY *DESTINY!*
SHE FOUGHT WELL. EVEN AS SHE COULD BARELY STAND.
YOU SHOULD BE *PROUD.*
NOW, "OLD *FRIEND,*" DO YOU BEGIN TO SEE THE LENGTHS TO WHICH I HAVE GONE?
MY EMPLOYERS WOULD HAVE BEEN PLEASED ENOUGH TO SIMPLY SEE YOU DEAD.
BUT, EVEN AFTER ALL THESE YEARS, I WANTED SOMETHING *MORE.*
I WANTED YOU TO KNOW HOW *THOROUGHLY* I COULD DESTROY YOU...

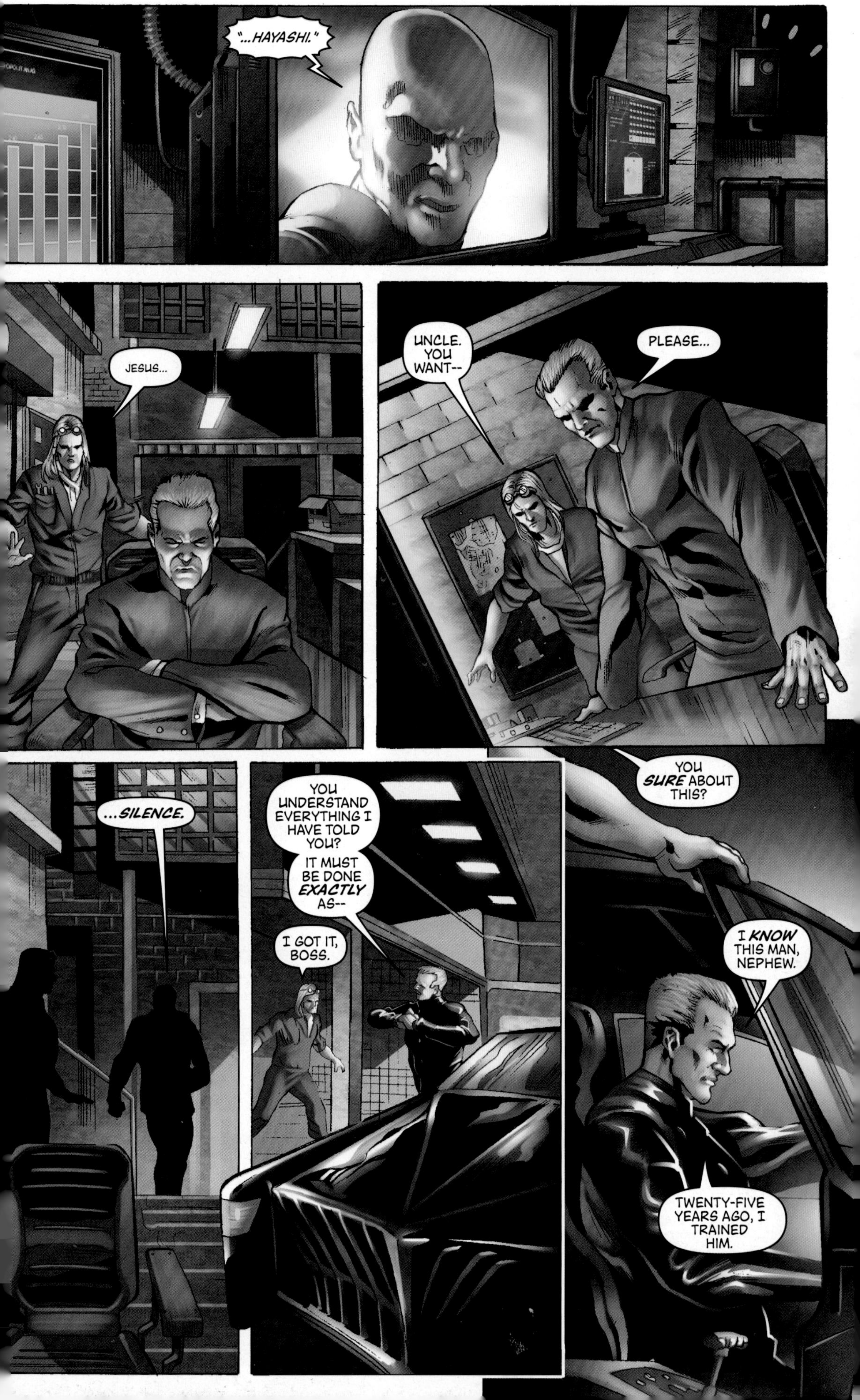
"...HAYASHI."
JESUS...
UNCLE. YOU WANT--
PLEASE...
...SILENCE.
YOU UNDERSTAND EVERYTHING I HAVE TOLD YOU?
IT MUST BE DONE EXACTLY AS--
I GOT IT, BOSS.
YOU SURE ABOUT THIS?
I KNOW THIS MAN, NEPHEW.
TWENTY-FIVE YEARS AGO, I TRAINED HIM.

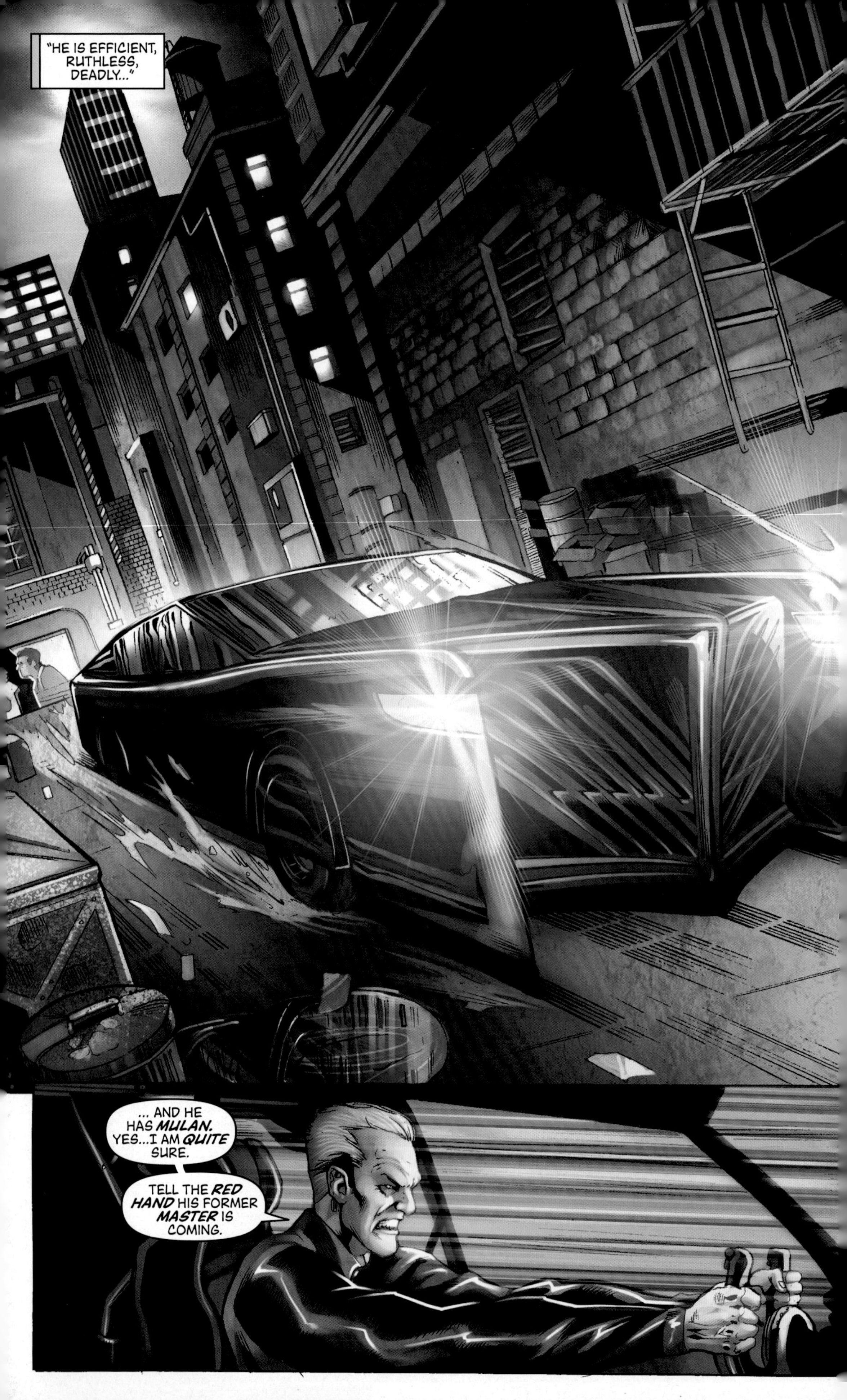
"HE IS EFFICIENT, RUTHLESS, DEADLY..."
... AND HE HAS MULAN. YES...I AM QUITE SURE.
TELL THE RED HAND HIS FORMER MASTER IS COMING.

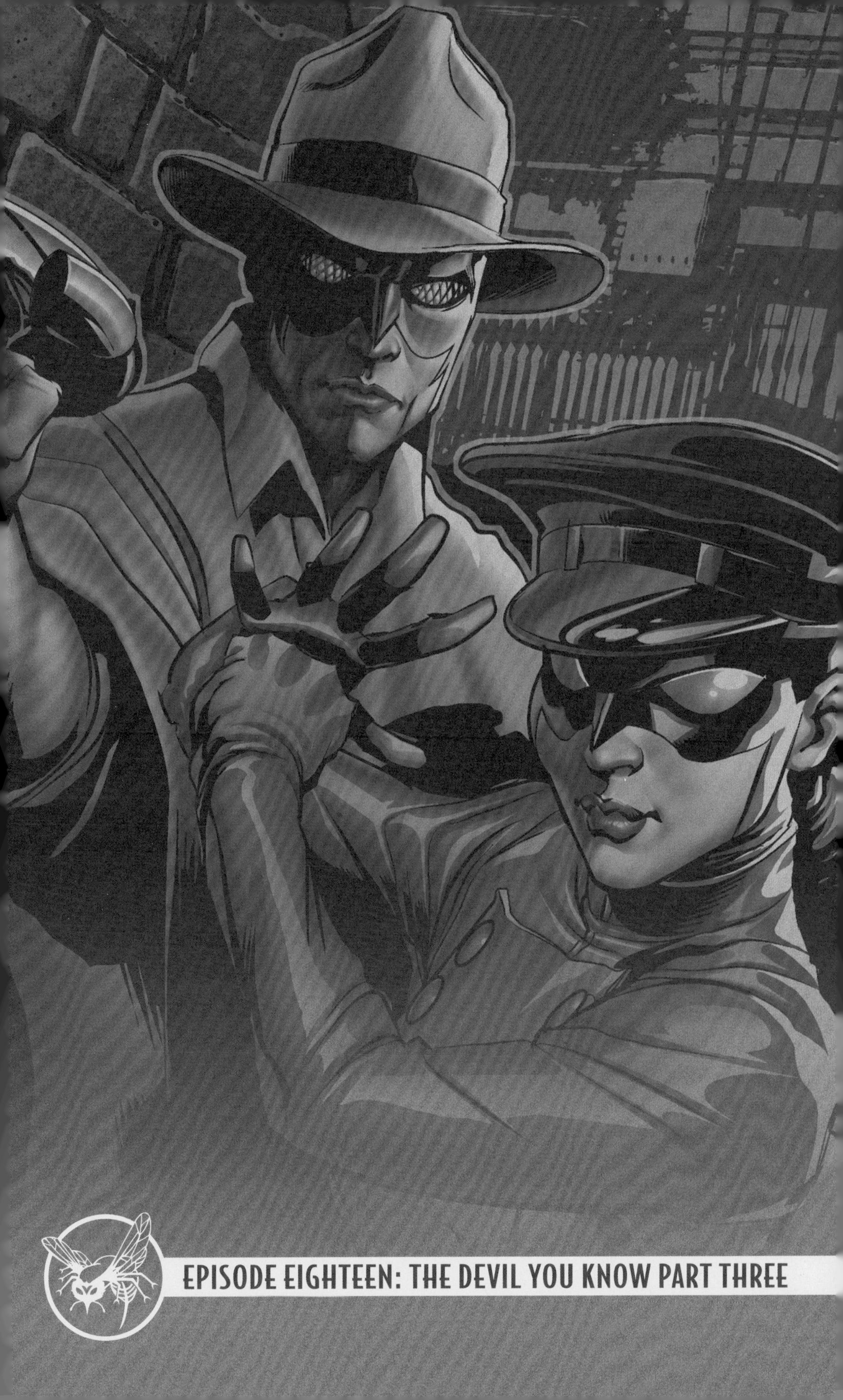

EPISODE EIGHTEEN: THE DEVIL YOU KNOW PART THREE

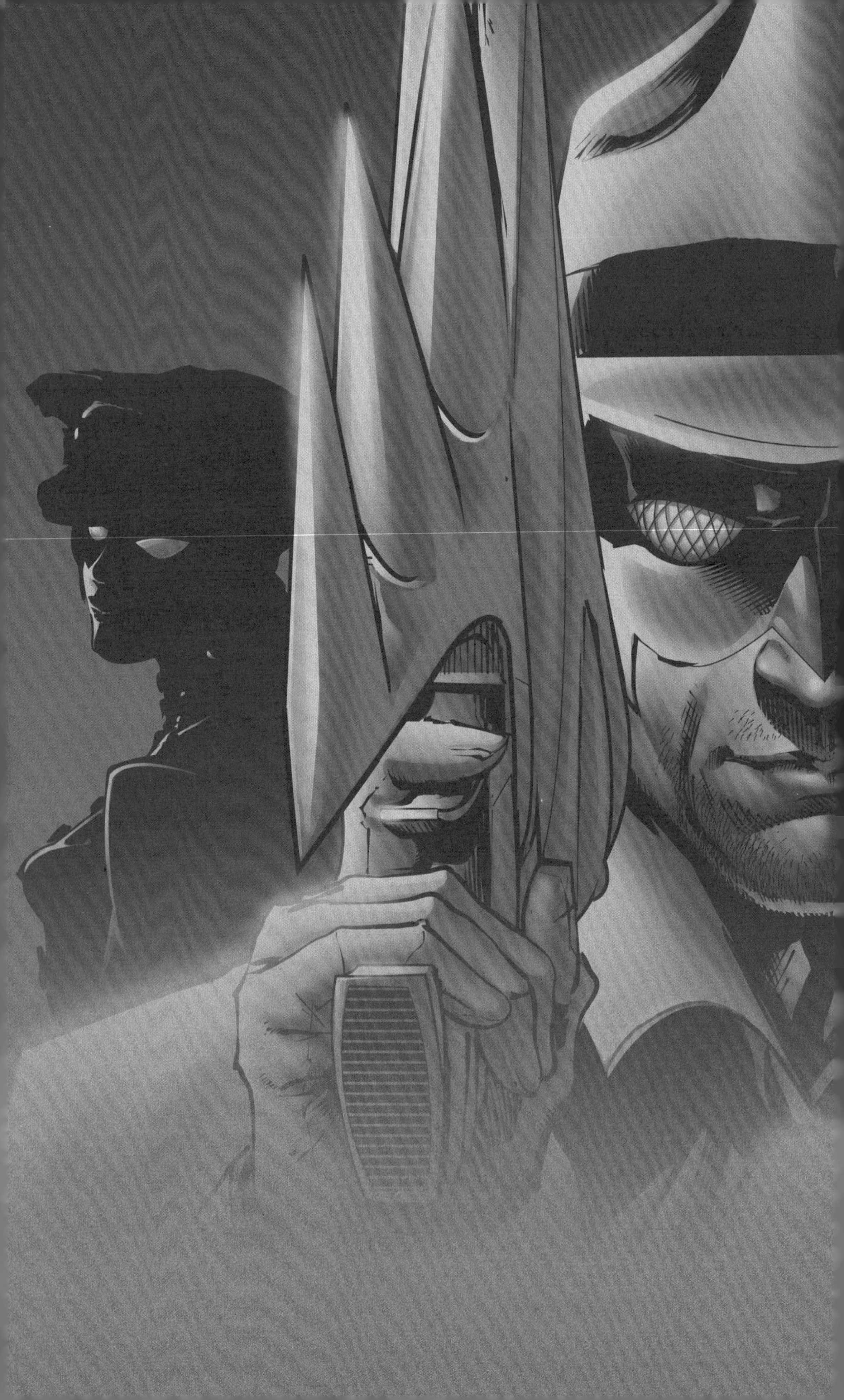

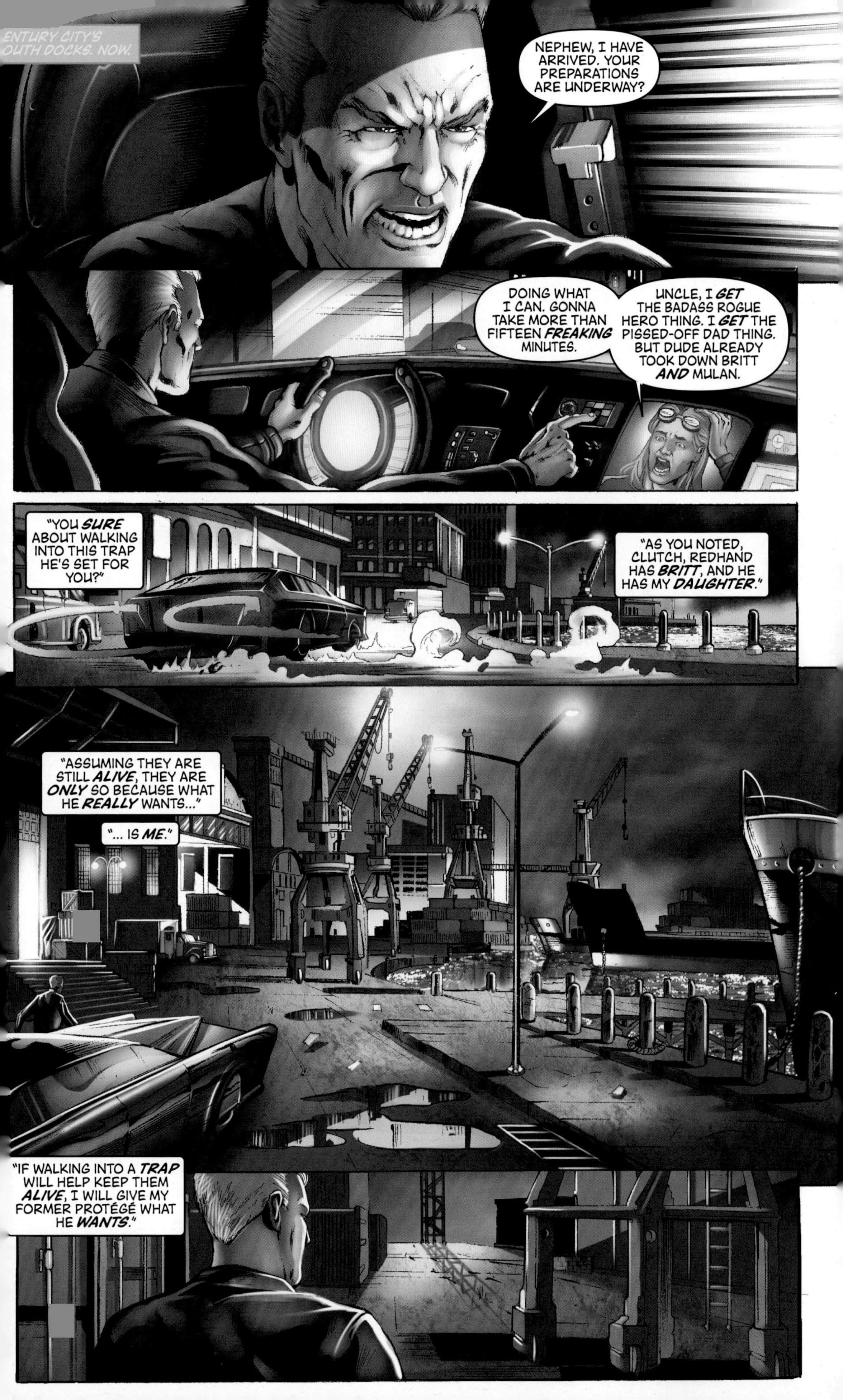
ENTURY CITY'S
OUTH DOCKS. NOW.
NEPHEW, I HAVE ARRIVED. YOUR PREPARATIONS ARE UNDERWAY?
DOING WHAT I CAN. GONNA TAKE MORE THAN FIFTEEN FREAKING MINUTES.
UNCLE, I GET THE BADASS ROGUE HERO THING. I GET THE PISSED-OFF DAD THING. BUT DUDE ALREADY TOOK DOWN BRITT AND MULAN.
"YOU SURE ABOUT WALKING INTO THIS TRAP HE'S SET FOR YOU?"
"AS YOU NOTED, CLUTCH, REDHAND HAS BRITT, AND HE HAS MY DAUGHTER."
"ASSUMING THEY ARE STILL ALIVE, THEY ARE ONLY SO BECAUSE WHAT HE REALLY WANTS..."
"... IS ME."
"IF WALKING INTO A TRAP WILL HELP KEEP THEM ALIVE, I WILL GIVE MY FORMER PROTÉGÉ WHAT HE WANTS."

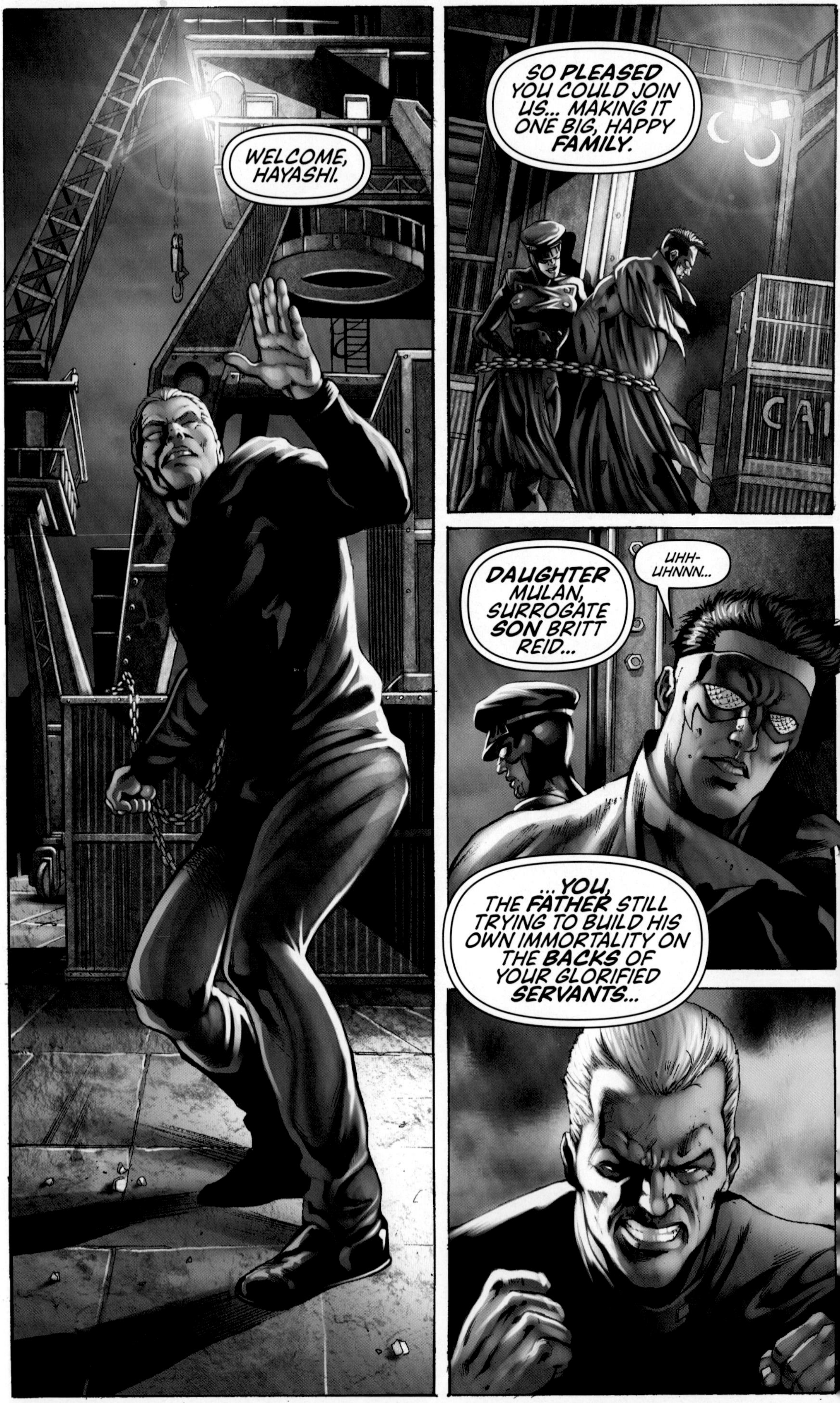

WELCOME, HAYASHI.
SO PLEASED YOU COULD JOIN US... MAKING IT ONE BIG, HAPPY FAMILY.
DAUGHTER MULAN, SURROGATE SON BRITT REID...
UHH-UHNNN...
...YOU, THE FATHER STILL TRYING TO BUILD HIS OWN IMMORTALITY ON THE BACKS OF YOUR GLORIFIED SERVANTS...

... AND YOUR FIRST *DISCIPLE*, BACK TO *CLAIM* WHAT YOU *TOOK* FROM ME.

EITHER YOUR *MEMORY* OR YOUR *LOGIC* IS TRAGICALLY *FLAWED*, REDHAND.

I OFFERED YOU A *CHANCE* TO BUILD ON A *NOBLE* LEGACY. A *CHANCE* TO MAKE IT YOUR *OWN*.

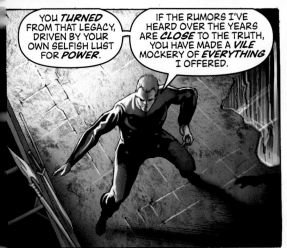

YOU *TURNED* FROM THAT LEGACY, DRIVEN BY YOUR OWN SELFISH LUST FOR *POWER*.

IF THE RUMORS I'VE HEARD OVER THE YEARS ARE *CLOSE* TO THE TRUTH, YOU HAVE MADE A *VILE* MOCKERY OF *EVERYTHING* I OFFERED.

YOU *WANTED* ME HERE, VILLAIN. AND *SO* HERE I AM.

I WILL SEE THIS ENDED. *TONIGHT*.

AS WILL *I*, OLD FOOL.

NOW... *PREPARE* YOURSELF...

I THINK YOU WILL FIND I AM *NOT* THE AMATEUR YOU KNEW IN JAPAN...

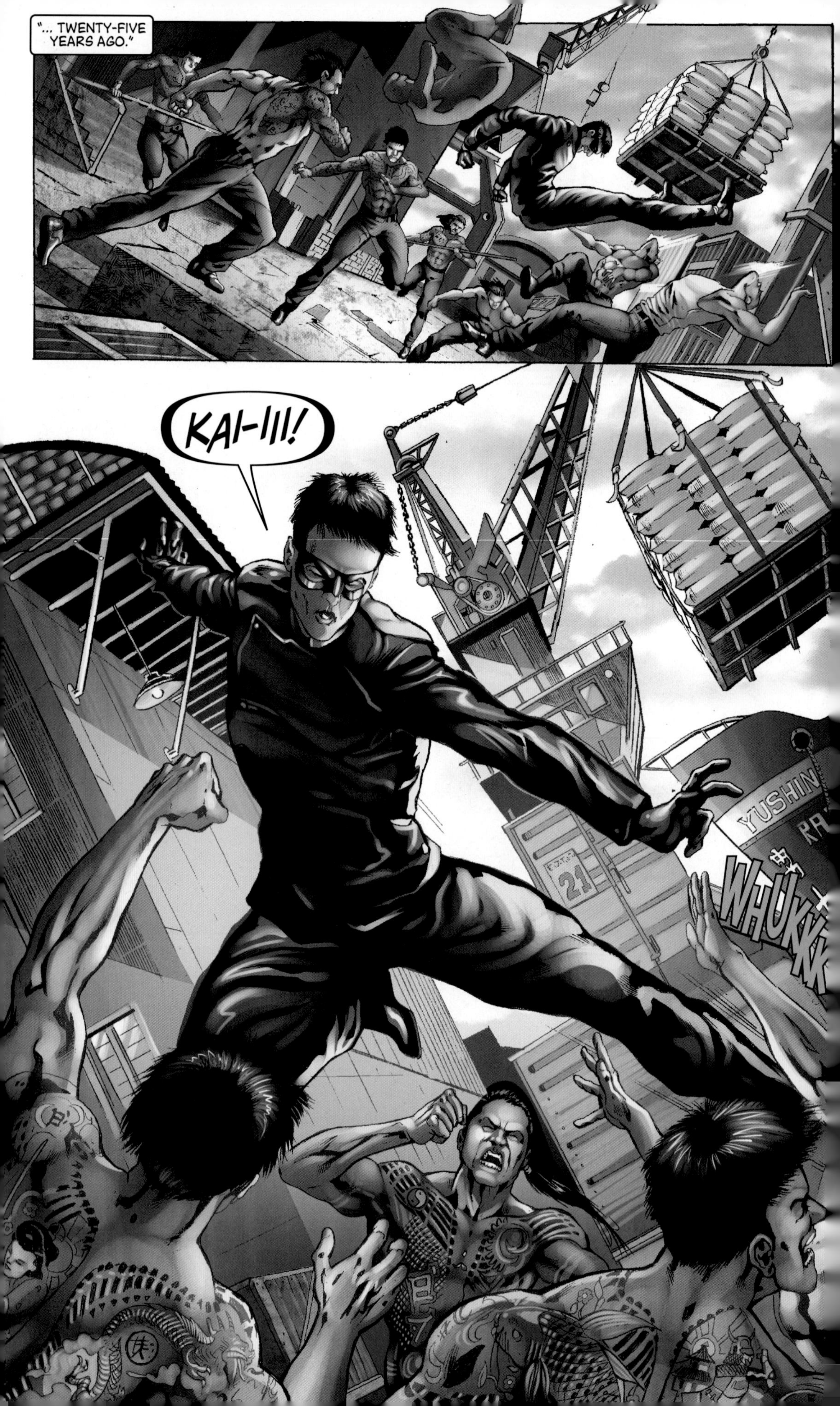
"... TWENTY-FIVE YEARS AGO."
KAI-III!
WHUKKK
YUSHIN

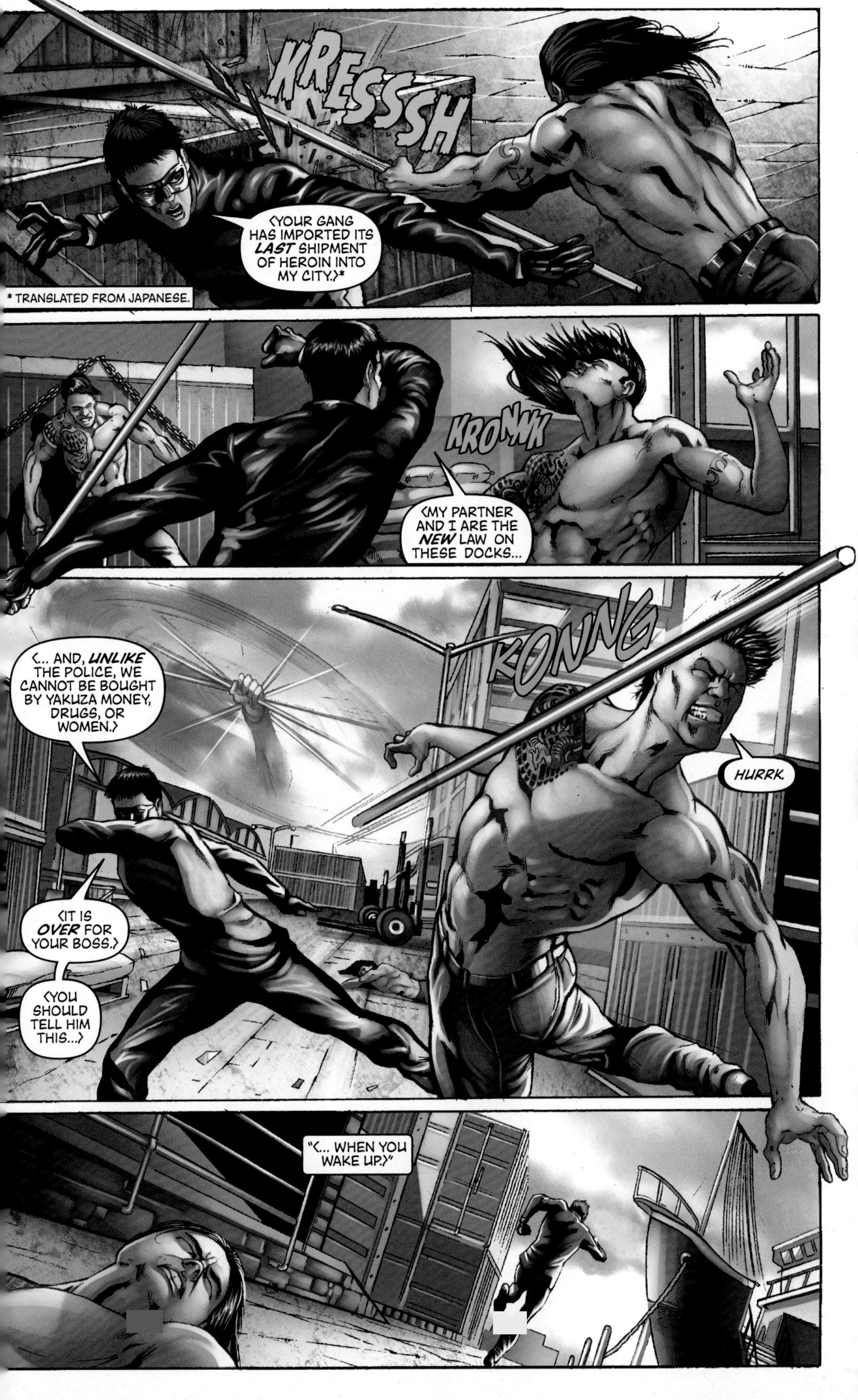
KRESSSH
<YOUR GANG HAS IMPORTED ITS LAST SHIPMENT OF HEROIN INTO MY CITY.>*
* TRANSLATED FROM JAPANESE.
KRONK
<MY PARTNER AND I ARE THE NEW LAW ON THESE DOCKS...
<... AND, UNLIKE THE POLICE, WE CANNOT BE BOUGHT BY YAKUZA MONEY, DRUGS, OR WOMEN.>
KONNG
HURRK.
<IT IS OVER FOR YOUR BOSS.>
<YOU SHOULD TELL HIM THIS...>
"<... WHEN YOU WAKE UP.>"

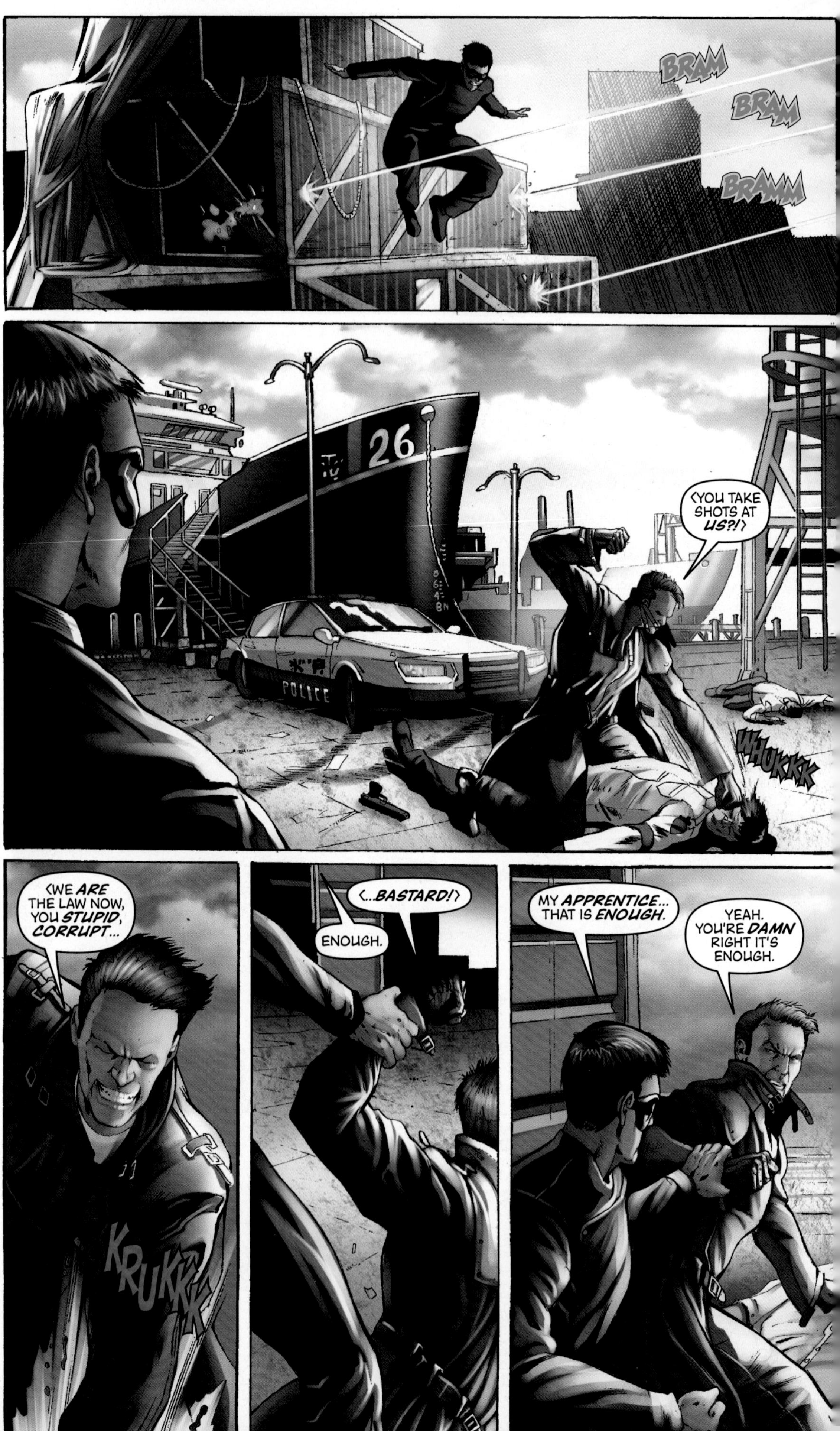
BRAM
BRAM
BRAMM
‹YOU TAKE SHOTS AT US?!›
WHUKKK
‹WE ARE THE LAW NOW, YOU STUPID, CORRUPT...
KRUKKK
‹...BASTARD!›
ENOUGH.
MY APPRENTICE... THAT IS ENOUGH.
YEAH. YOU'RE DAMN RIGHT IT'S ENOUGH.

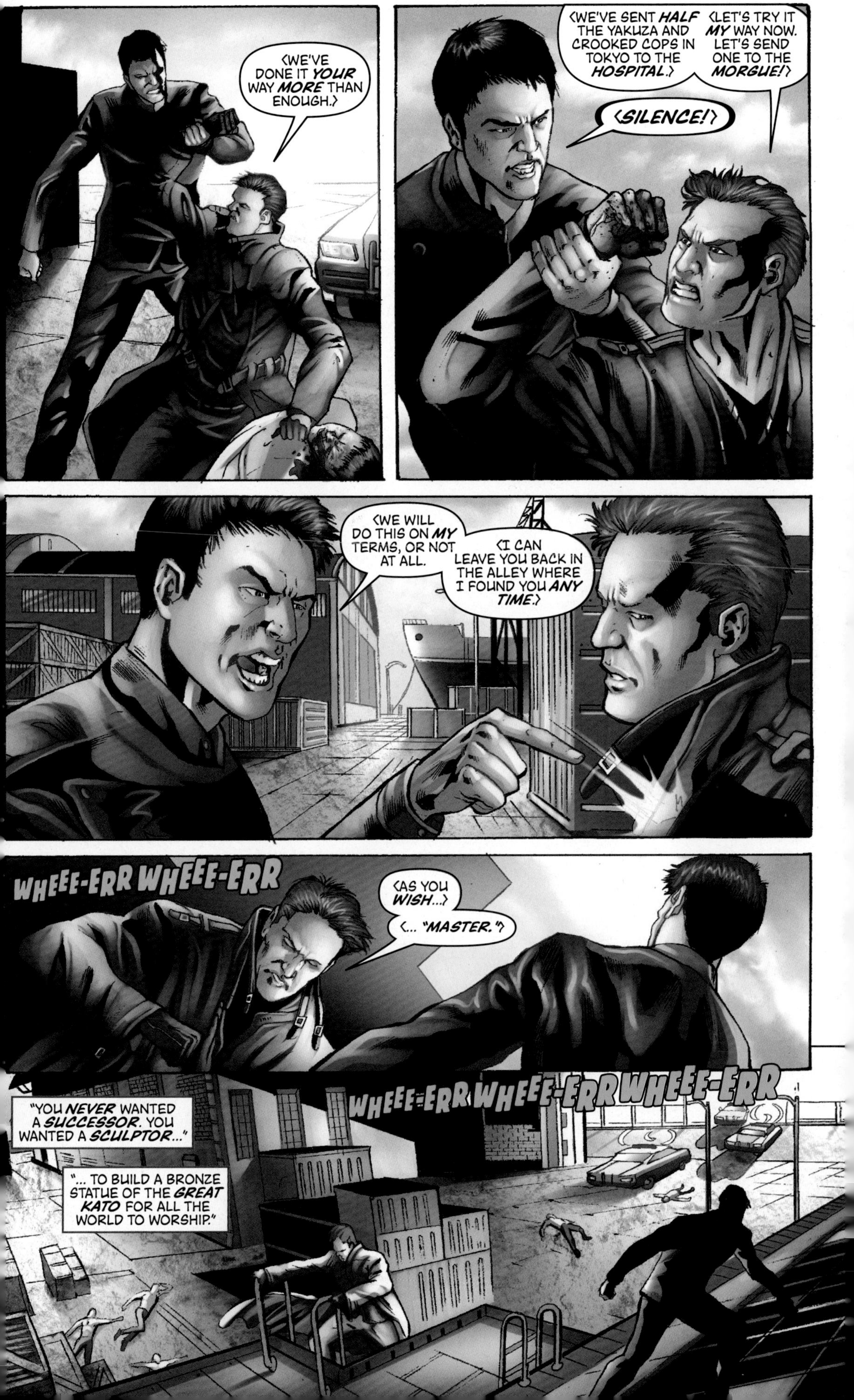

‹WE'VE DONE IT YOUR WAY MORE THAN ENOUGH.›
‹WE'VE SENT HALF THE YAKUZA AND CROOKED COPS IN TOKYO TO THE HOSPITAL.›
‹LET'S TRY IT MY WAY NOW. LET'S SEND ONE TO THE MORGUE!›
‹SILENCE!›
‹WE WILL DO THIS ON MY TERMS, OR NOT AT ALL.
‹I CAN LEAVE YOU BACK IN THE ALLEY WHERE I FOUND YOU ANY TIME.›
WHEEE-ERR WHEEE-ERR
‹AS YOU WISH...›
‹... "MASTER."›
"YOU NEVER WANTED A SUCCESSOR. YOU WANTED A SCULPTOR..."
WHEEE-ERR WHEEE-ERR WHEEE-ERR
"... TO BUILD A BRONZE STATUE OF THE GREAT KATO FOR ALL THE WORLD TO WORSHIP."

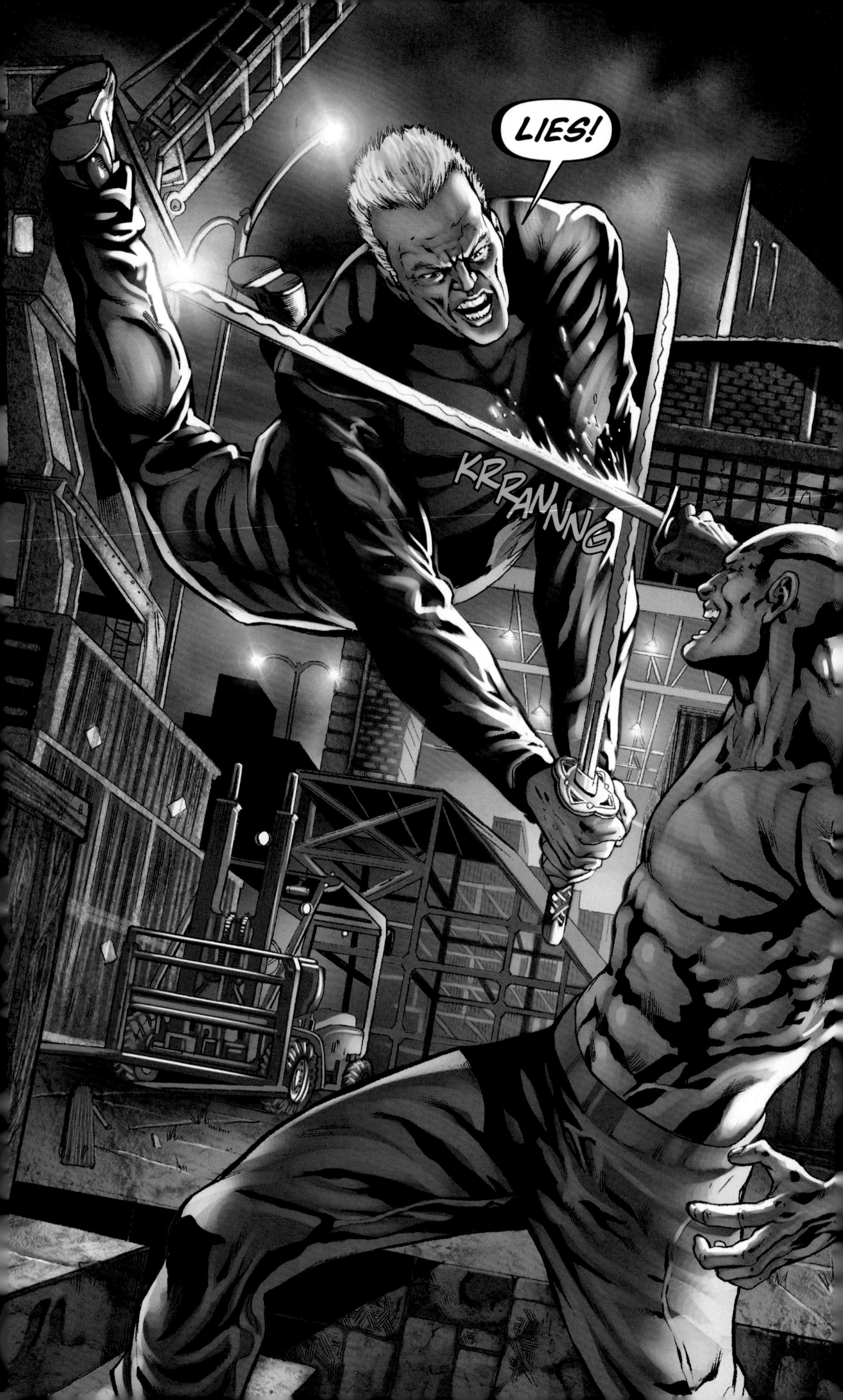
LIES!
KRRANNNG

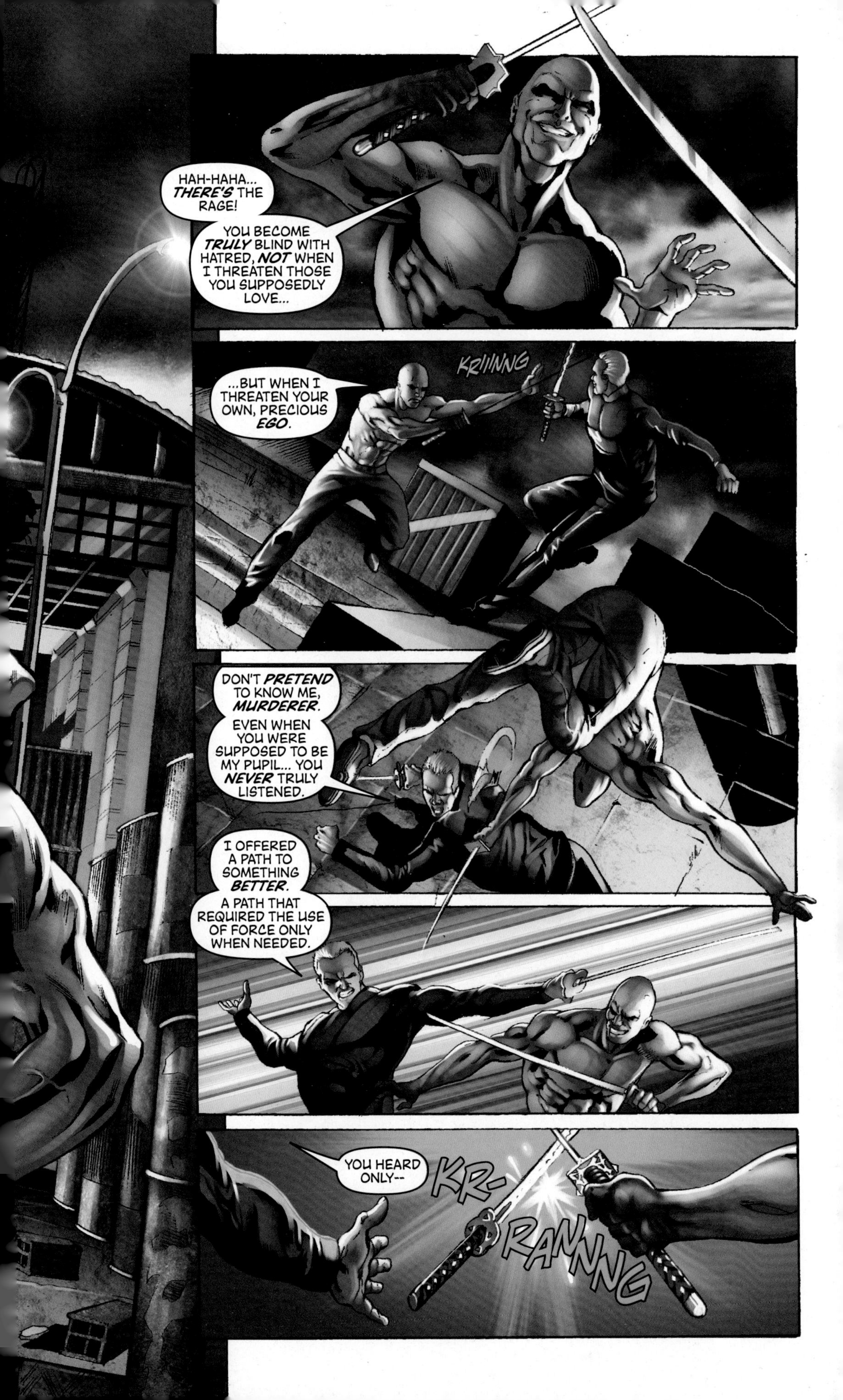
HAH-HAHA... THERE'S THE RAGE!
YOU BECOME TRULY BLIND WITH HATRED, NOT WHEN I THREATEN THOSE YOU SUPPOSEDLY LOVE...
...BUT WHEN I THREATEN YOUR OWN, PRECIOUS EGO.
KRIIINNG
DON'T PRETEND TO KNOW ME, MURDERER.
EVEN WHEN YOU WERE SUPPOSED TO BE MY PUPIL... YOU NEVER TRULY LISTENED.
I OFFERED A PATH TO SOMETHING BETTER.
A PATH THAT REQUIRED THE USE OF FORCE ONLY WHEN NEEDED.
YOU HEARD ONLY--
KR-RANNNG

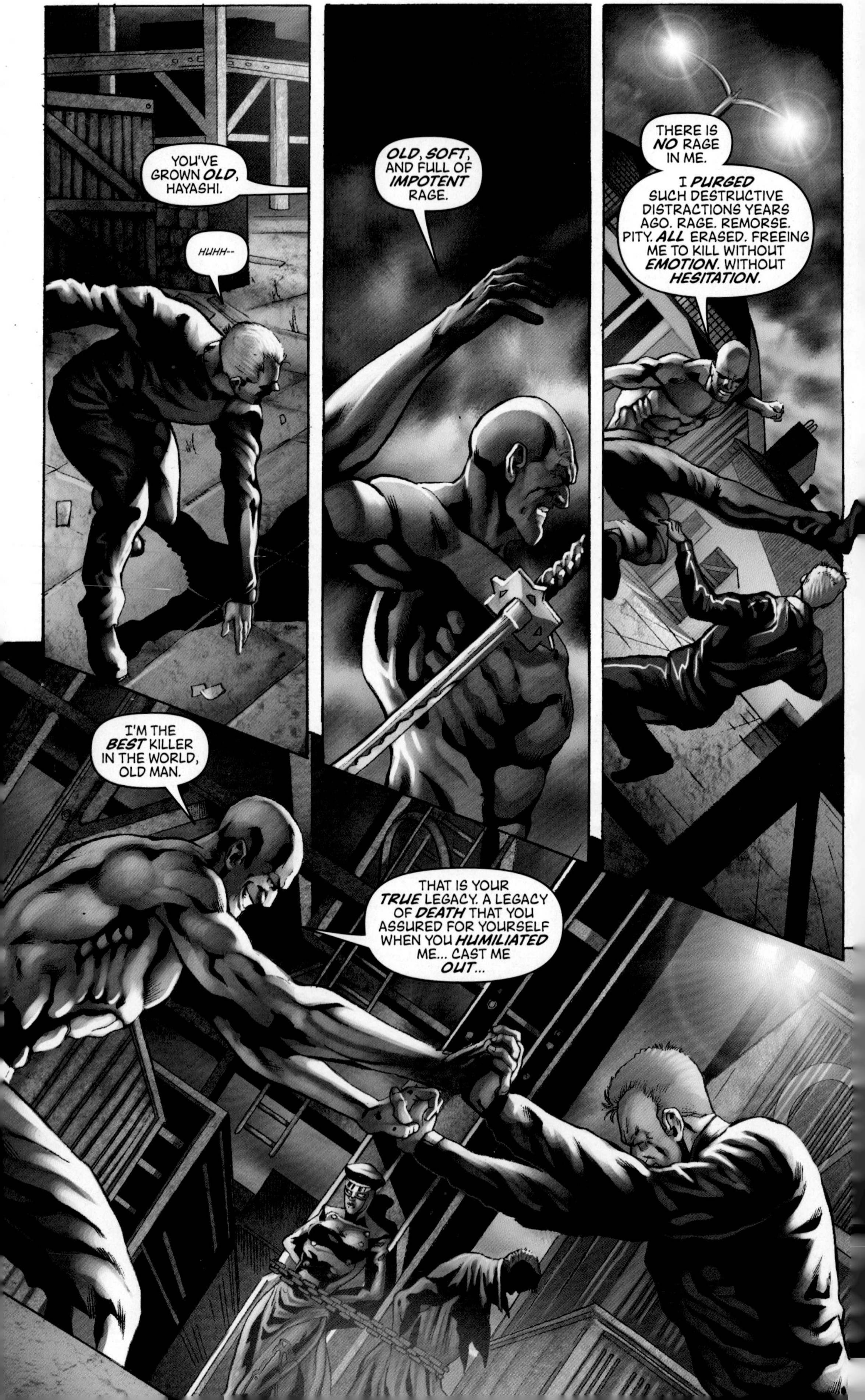

YOU'VE GROWN OLD, HAYASHI.
HUHH--
OLD, SOFT, AND FULL OF IMPOTENT RAGE.
THERE IS NO RAGE IN ME.
I PURGED SUCH DESTRUCTIVE DISTRACTIONS YEARS AGO. RAGE. REMORSE. PITY. ALL ERASED. FREEING ME TO KILL WITHOUT EMOTION. WITHOUT HESITATION.
I'M THE BEST KILLER IN THE WORLD, OLD MAN.
THAT IS YOUR TRUE LEGACY. A LEGACY OF DEATH THAT YOU ASSURED FOR YOURSELF WHEN YOU HUMILIATED ME... CAST ME OUT...

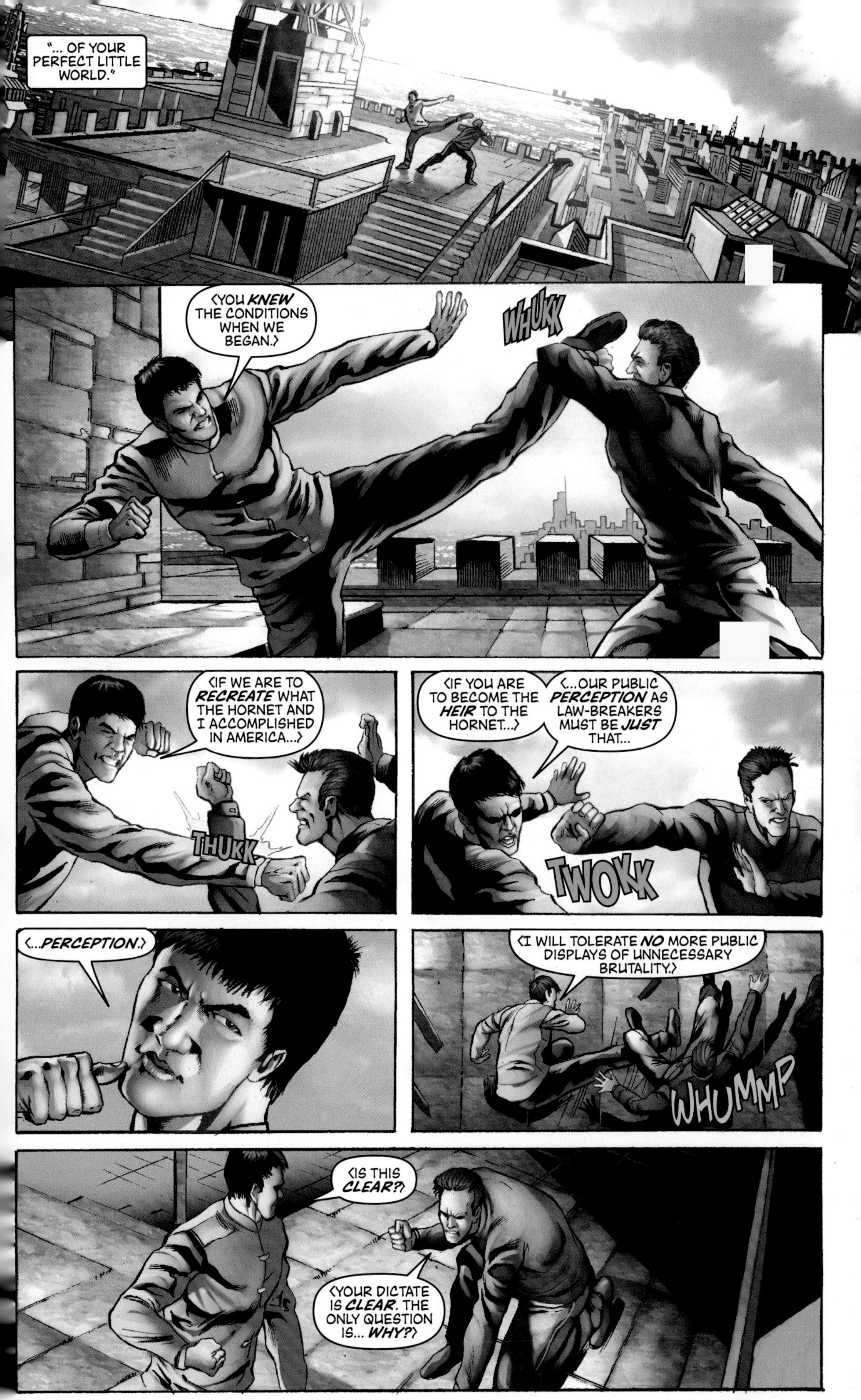
"... OF YOUR PERFECT LITTLE WORLD."
‹YOU KNEW THE CONDITIONS WHEN WE BEGAN.›
WHUKK
‹IF WE ARE TO RECREATE WHAT THE HORNET AND I ACCOMPLISHED IN AMERICA...›
THUKK
‹IF YOU ARE TO BECOME THE HEIR TO THE HORNET...›
‹...OUR PUBLIC PERCEPTION AS LAW-BREAKERS MUST BE JUST THAT...
TWOKK
‹...PERCEPTION.›
‹I WILL TOLERATE NO MORE PUBLIC DISPLAYS OF UNNECESSARY BRUTALITY.›
WHUMMP
‹IS THIS CLEAR?›
‹YOUR DICTATE IS CLEAR. THE ONLY QUESTION IS... WHY?›

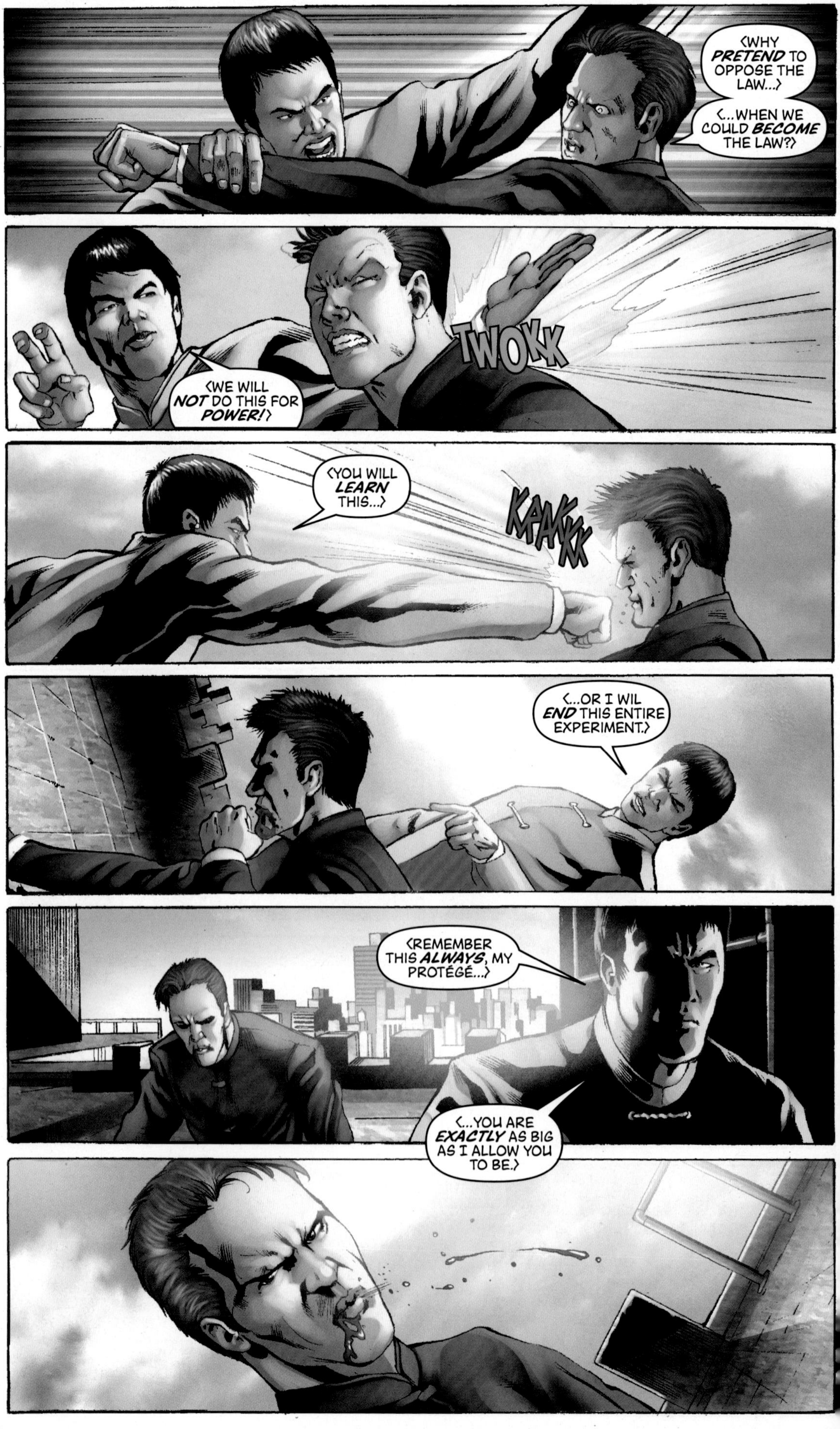
‹WHY PRETEND TO OPPOSE THE LAW...›
‹...WHEN WE COULD BECOME THE LAW?›
TWOKK
‹WE WILL NOT DO THIS FOR POWER!›
‹YOU WILL LEARN THIS...›
KRAKKK
‹...OR I WIL END THIS ENTIRE EXPERIMENT.›
‹REMEMBER THIS ALWAYS, MY PROTÉGÉ...›
‹...YOU ARE EXACTLY AS BIG AS I ALLOW YOU TO BE.›

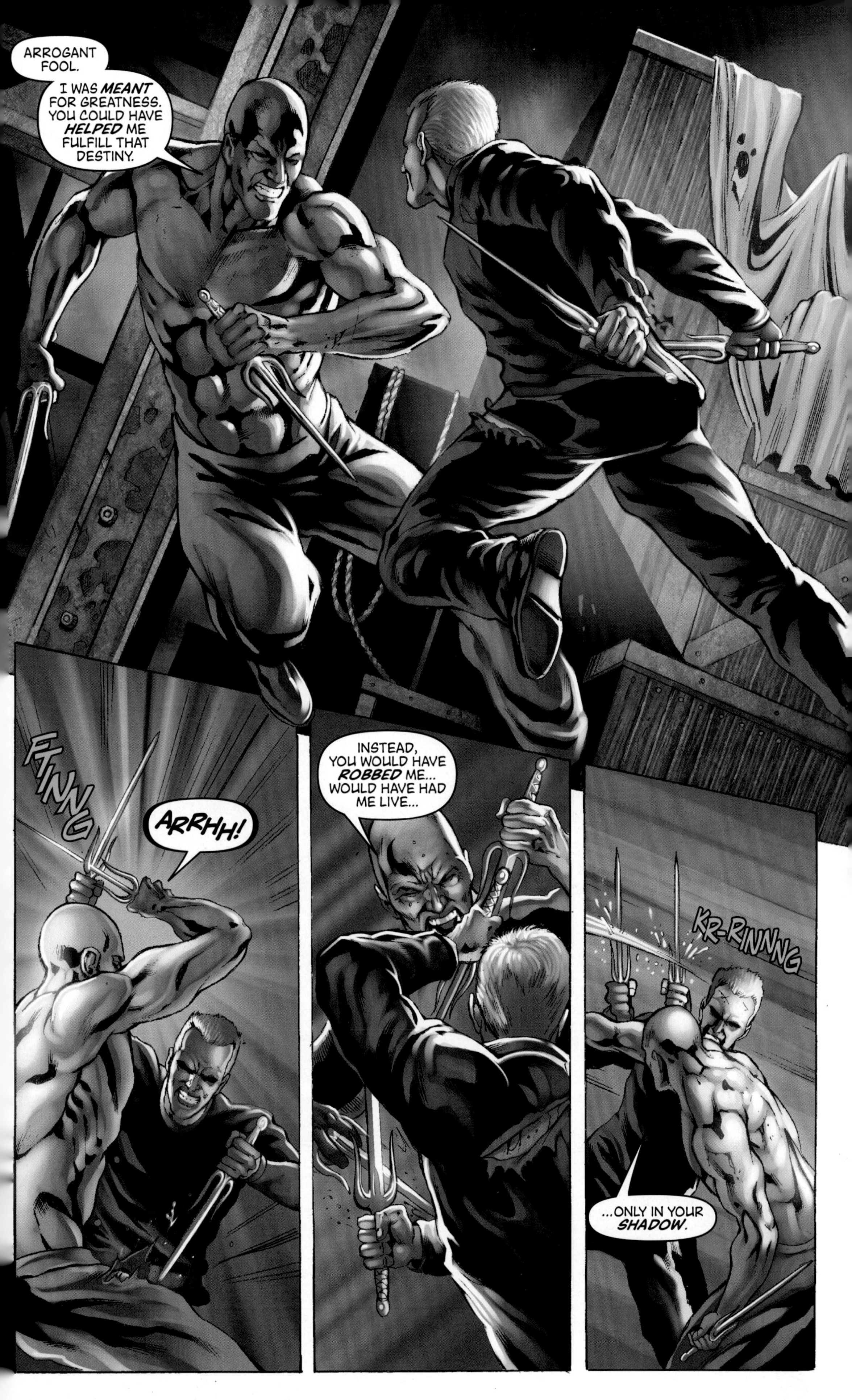

ARROGANT FOOL.
I WAS MEANT FOR GREATNESS. YOU COULD HAVE HELPED ME FULFILL THAT DESTINY.
FTINNG
ARRHH!
INSTEAD, YOU WOULD HAVE ROBBED ME... WOULD HAVE HAD ME LIVE...
KR-RINNNG
...ONLY IN YOUR SHADOW.

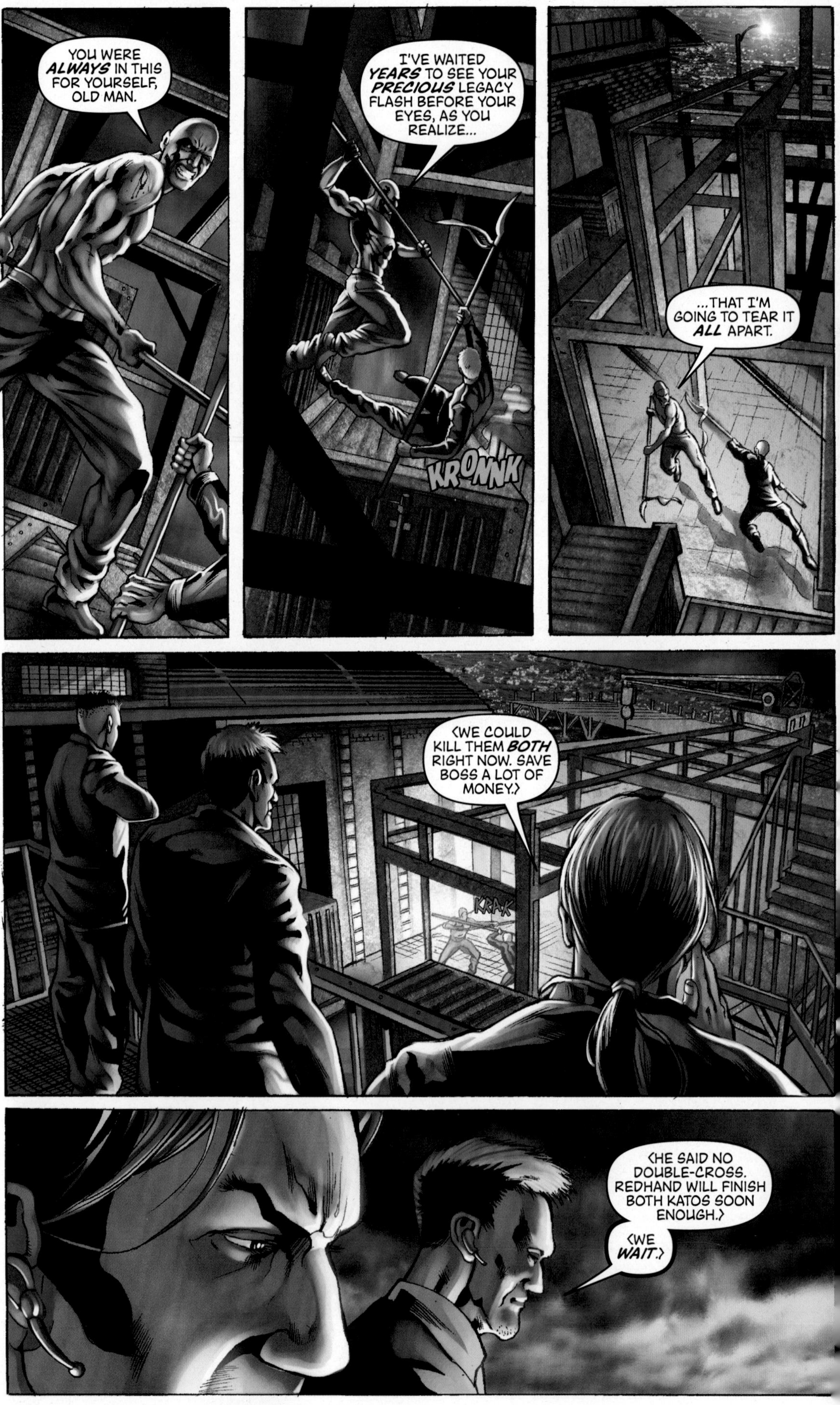
YOU WERE ALWAYS IN THIS FOR YOURSELF, OLD MAN.
I'VE WAITED YEARS TO SEE YOUR PRECIOUS LEGACY FLASH BEFORE YOUR EYES, AS YOU REALIZE...
KRONNK
...THAT I'M GOING TO TEAR IT ALL APART.
<WE COULD KILL THEM BOTH RIGHT NOW. SAVE BOSS A LOT OF MONEY.>
KRAK
<HE SAID NO DOUBLE-CROSS. REDHAND WILL FINISH BOTH KATOS SOON ENOUGH.>
<WE WAIT.>

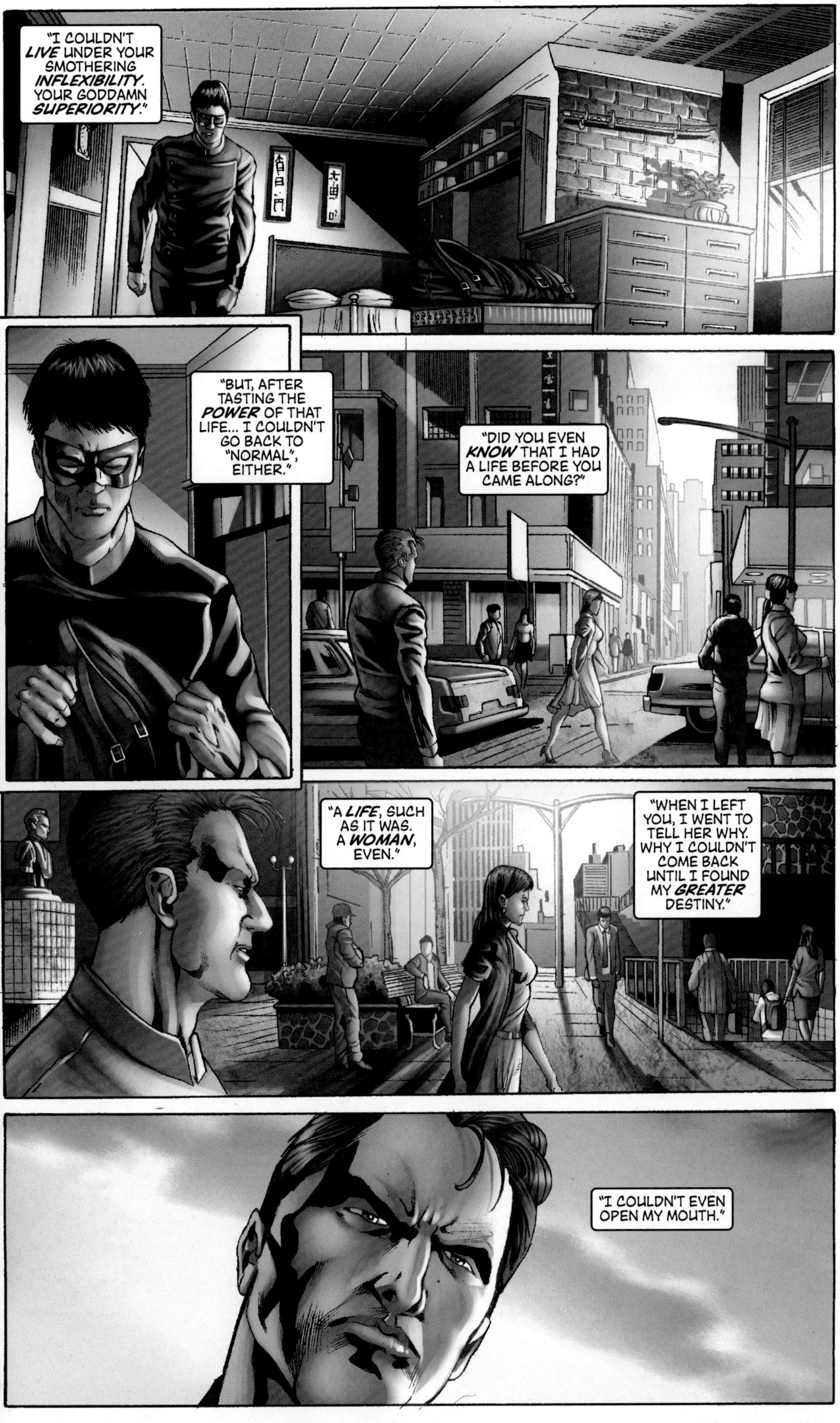
"I COULDN'T LIVE UNDER YOUR SMOTHERING INFLEXIBILITY. YOUR GODDAMN SUPERIORITY."
"BUT, AFTER TASTING THE POWER OF THAT LIFE... I COULDN'T GO BACK TO "NORMAL", EITHER."
"DID YOU EVEN KNOW THAT I HAD A LIFE BEFORE YOU CAME ALONG?"
"A LIFE, SUCH AS IT WAS. A WOMAN, EVEN."
"WHEN I LEFT YOU, I WENT TO TELL HER WHY. WHY I COULDN'T COME BACK UNTIL I FOUND MY GREATER DESTINY."
"I COULDN'T EVEN OPEN MY MOUTH."

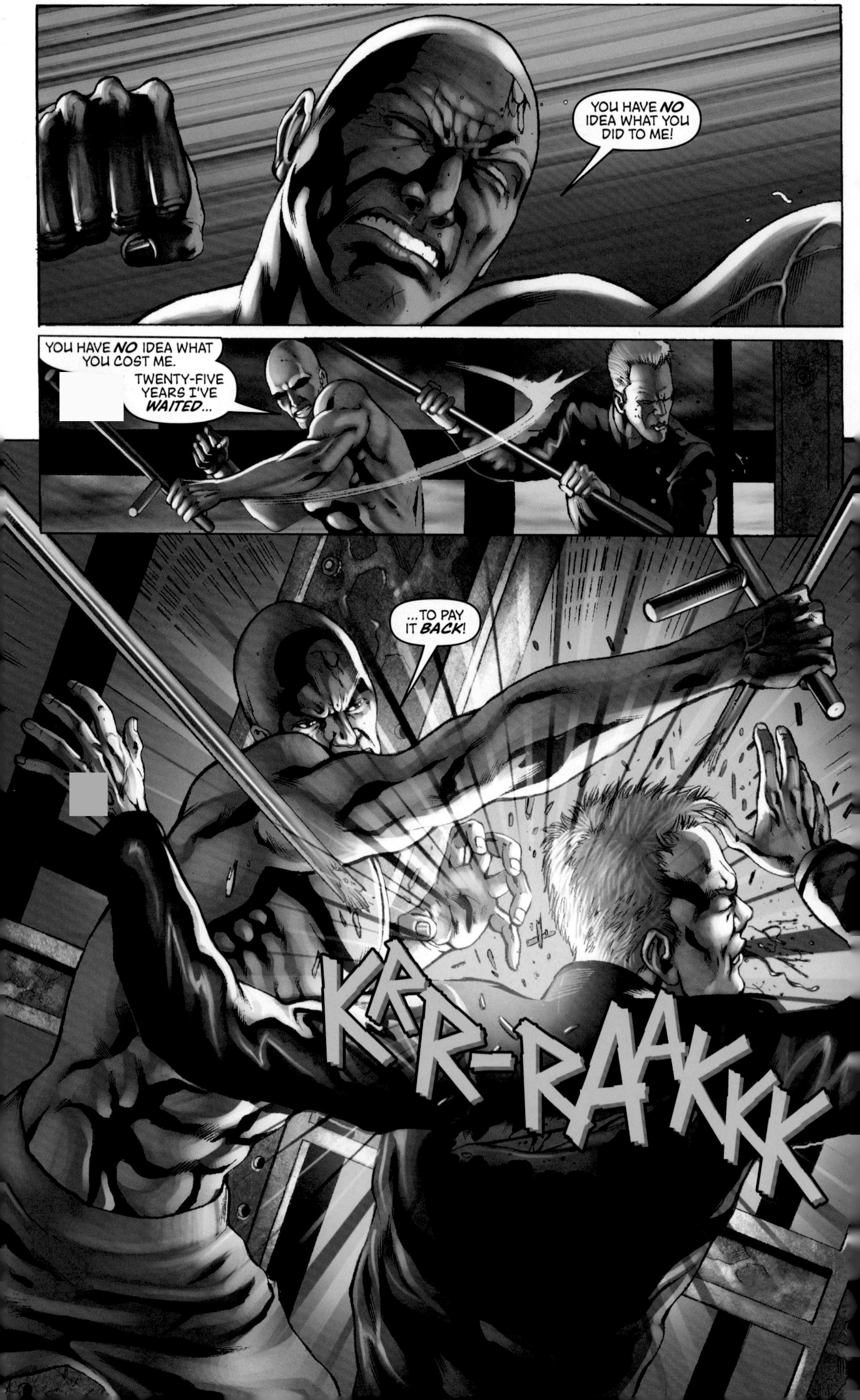
YOU HAVE NO IDEA WHAT YOU DID TO ME!
YOU HAVE NO IDEA WHAT YOU COST ME.
TWENTY-FIVE YEARS I'VE WAITED...
...TO PAY IT BACK!
KRR-RAAKKK

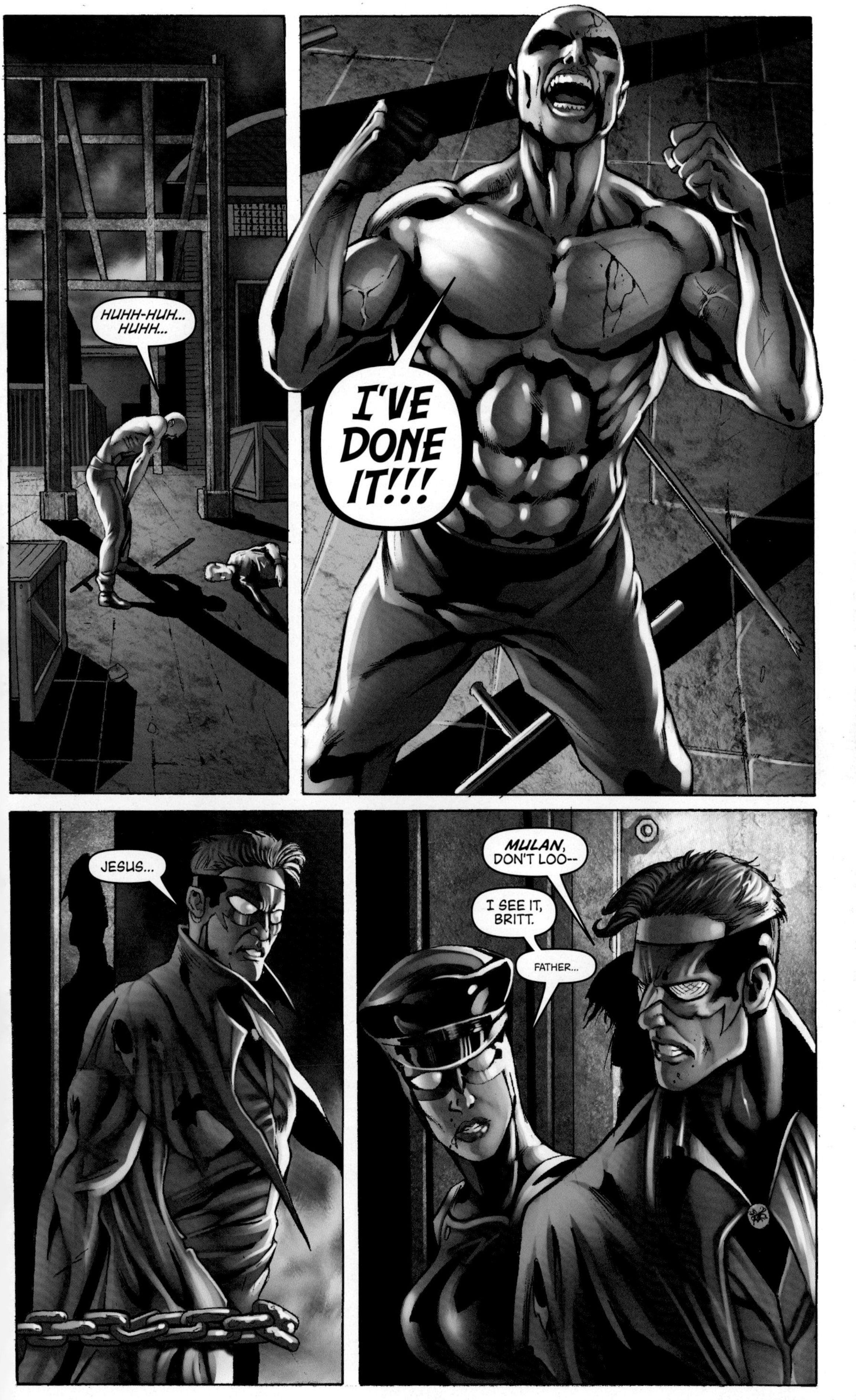
HUHH-HUH...
HUHH...
I'VE DONE IT!!!
JESUS...
MULAN, DON'T LOO--
I SEE IT, BRITT.
FATHER...

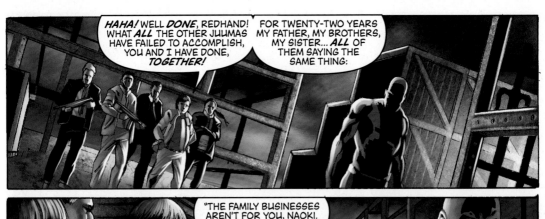

HAHA! WELL *DONE*, REDHAND! WHAT *ALL* THE OTHER JUUMAS HAVE FAILED TO ACCOMPLISH, YOU AND I HAVE DONE, *TOGETHER!*

FOR TWENTY-TWO YEARS MY FATHER, MY BROTHERS, MY SISTER... *ALL* OF THEM SAYING THE SAME THING:

"THE FAMILY BUSINESSES AREN'T FOR YOU, NAOKI. YOU'RE TOO *STUPID.* TOO *WEAK.*"

AND NOW, THE KATOS ARE DEAD, AND *I* AM THE ONE WHO DID IT. *KILL* THEM, REDHAND. AS OUR CONTRACT--

BRAMM BRAMM BRAMMM

NO, NAOKI...

BRAMM

...I DON'T THINK SO.

I'M AFRAID I'VE COME *TOO* FAR...

BRRAAM

...TO SIMPLY *KILL* THEM.

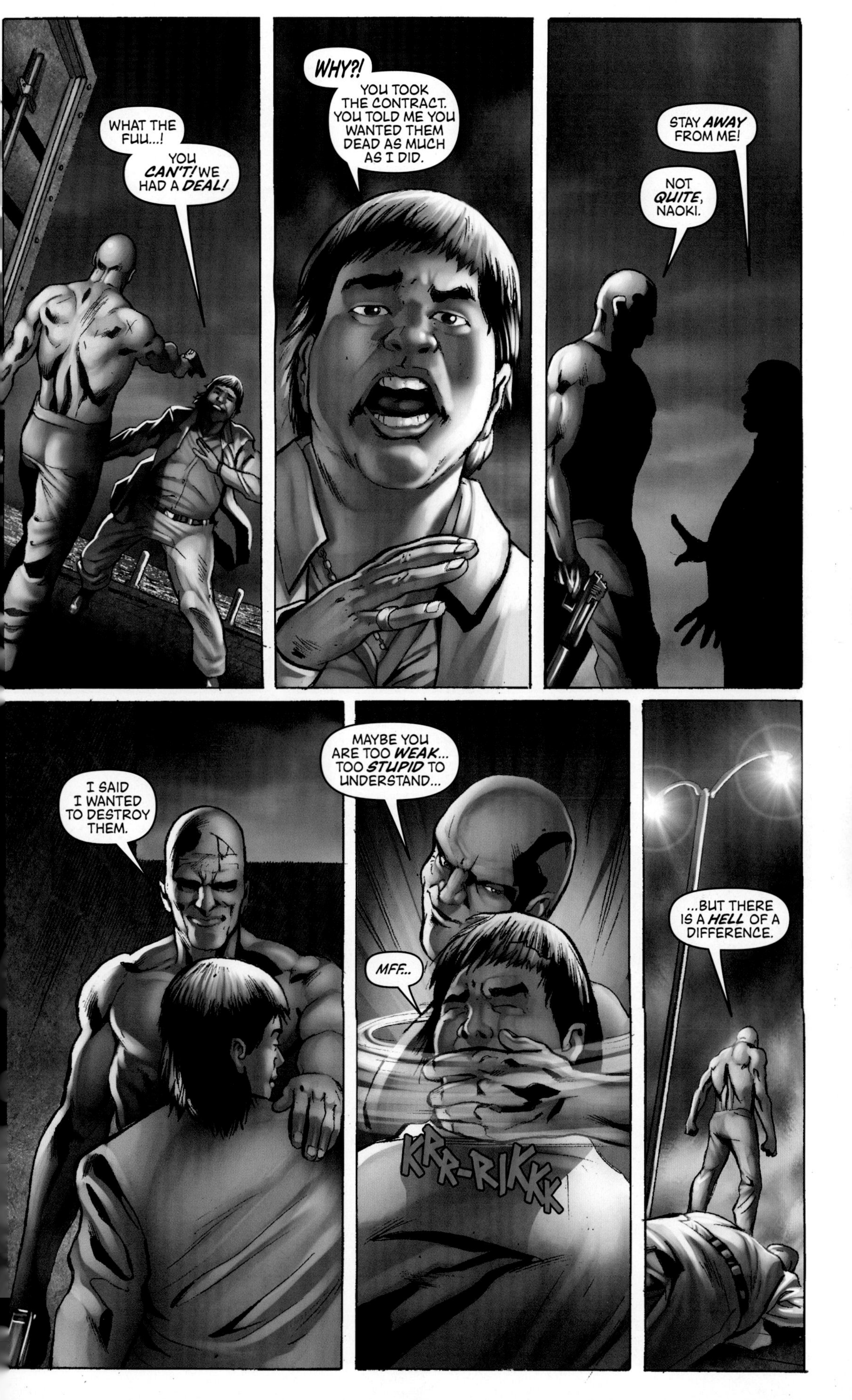
WHAT THE FUU...!
YOU CAN'T! WE HAD A DEAL!
WHY?!
YOU TOOK THE CONTRACT. YOU TOLD ME YOU WANTED THEM DEAD AS MUCH AS I DID.
STAY AWAY FROM ME!
NOT QUITE, NAOKI.
I SAID I WANTED TO DESTROY THEM.
MAYBE YOU ARE TOO WEAK... TOO STUPID TO UNDERSTAND...
MFF...
KRR-RIKKK
...BUT THERE IS A HELL OF A DIFFERENCE.

NOW THEN...

I BELIEVE I HAVE SOME UNFINISHED *BUSINESS* WITH YOU...

..."*SISTER.*"

I WANT TO KNOW *EVERYTHING.* TELL ME, GIRL...

...WHERE DO YOU PARK THAT *LOVELY* BLACK CAR OF YOURS?

WHERE IS THE *HORNET'S NEST?*

HORNET'S NEST? SOUNDS *RIDICULOUS.* EVEN *IF* I KNEW WHAT THE *HELL* YOU WERE TALKING ABOUT, THE ANSWER WOULD BE THE SAME...

...GO TO *HELL,* FREAK.

PROBABLY, YES. BUT YOU'LL BE THERE *LONG* BEFORE ME.

MULAN!

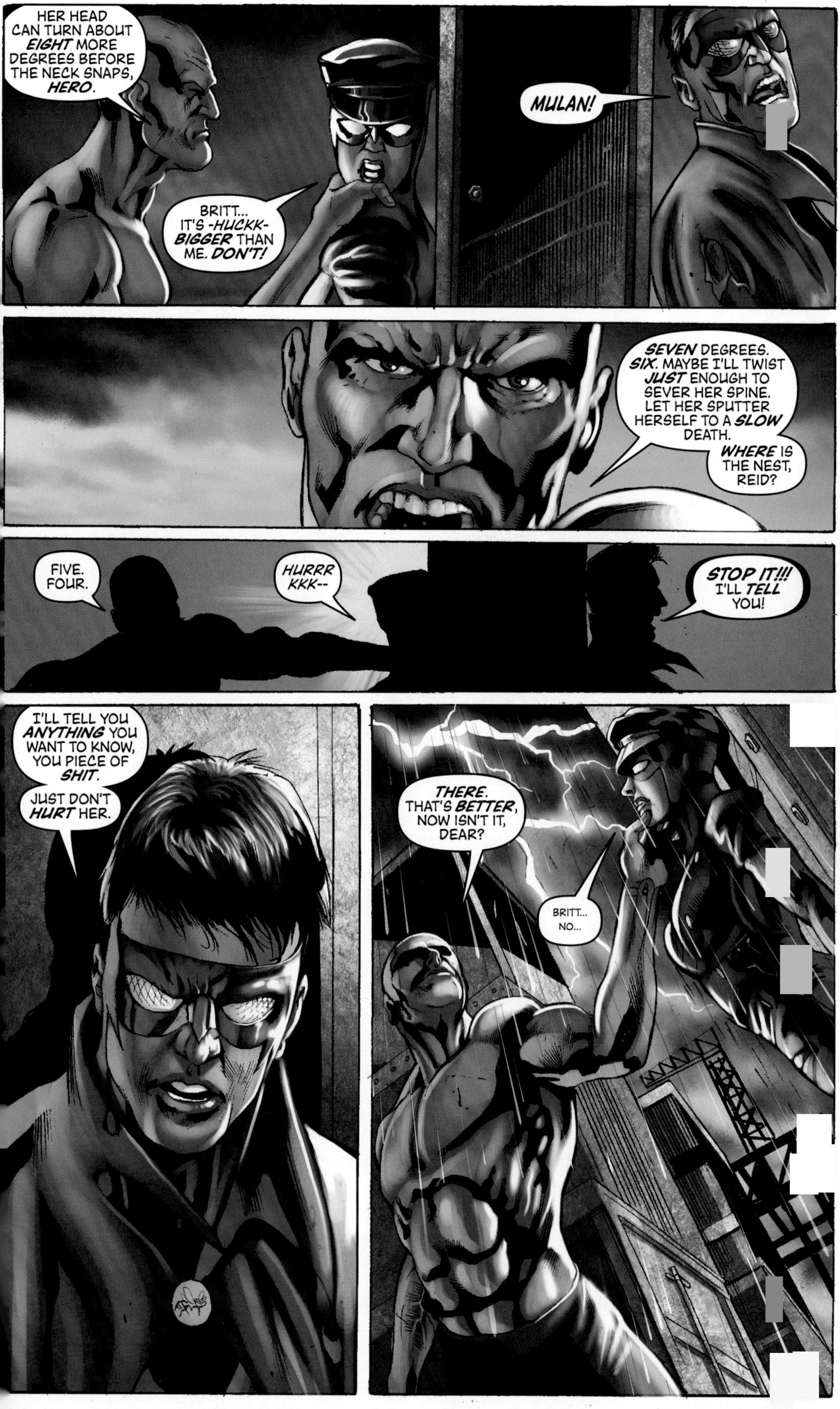
HER HEAD CAN TURN ABOUT EIGHT MORE DEGREES BEFORE THE NECK SNAPS, HERO.
BRITT... IT'S -HUCKK- BIGGER THAN ME. DON'T!
MULAN!
SEVEN DEGREES. SIX. MAYBE I'LL TWIST JUST ENOUGH TO SEVER HER SPINE. LET HER SPUTTER HERSELF TO A SLOW DEATH.
WHERE IS THE NEST, REID?
FIVE. FOUR.
HURRR KKK--
STOP IT!!! I'LL TELL YOU!
I'LL TELL YOU ANYTHING YOU WANT TO KNOW, YOU PIECE OF SHIT.
JUST DON'T HURT HER.
THERE. THAT'S BETTER, NOW ISN'T IT, DEAR?
BRITT... NO...

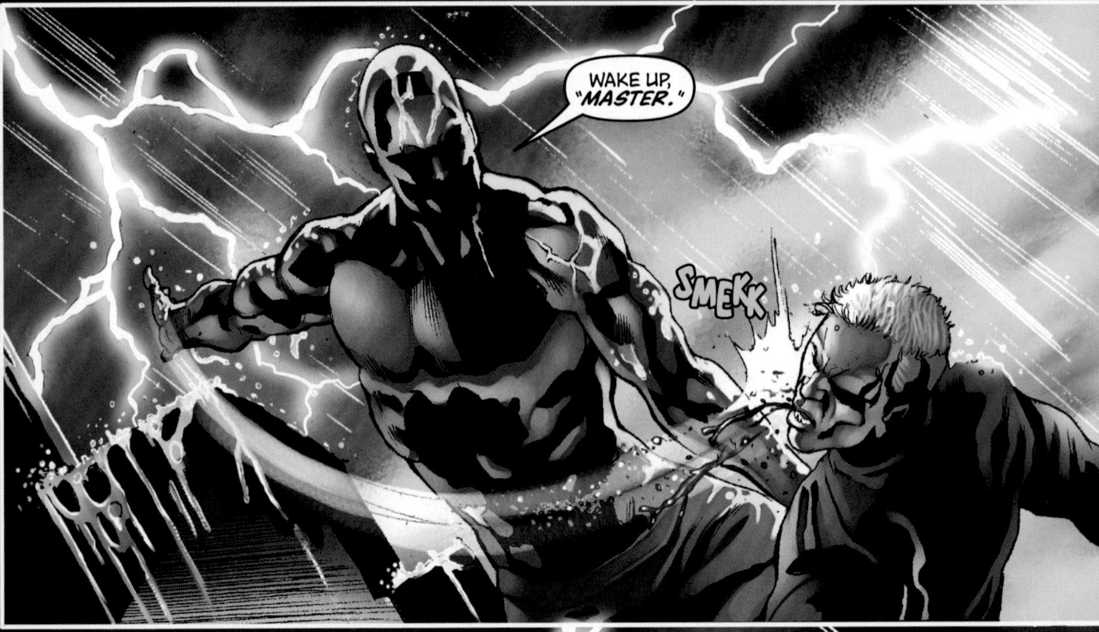
WAKE UP, "MASTER."
SMEKK

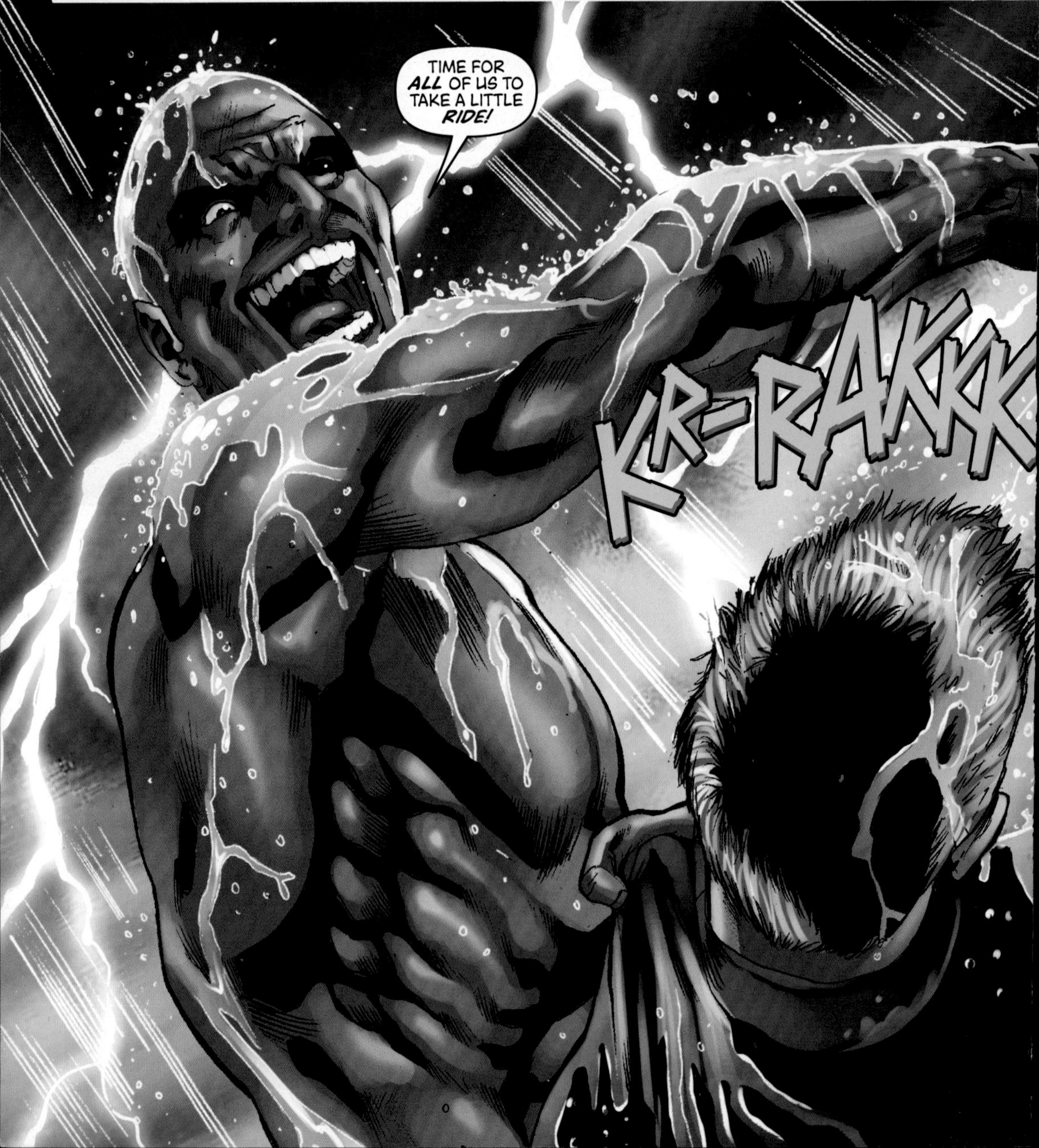
TIME FOR ALL OF US TO TAKE A LITTLE RIDE!
KR-RAKKK

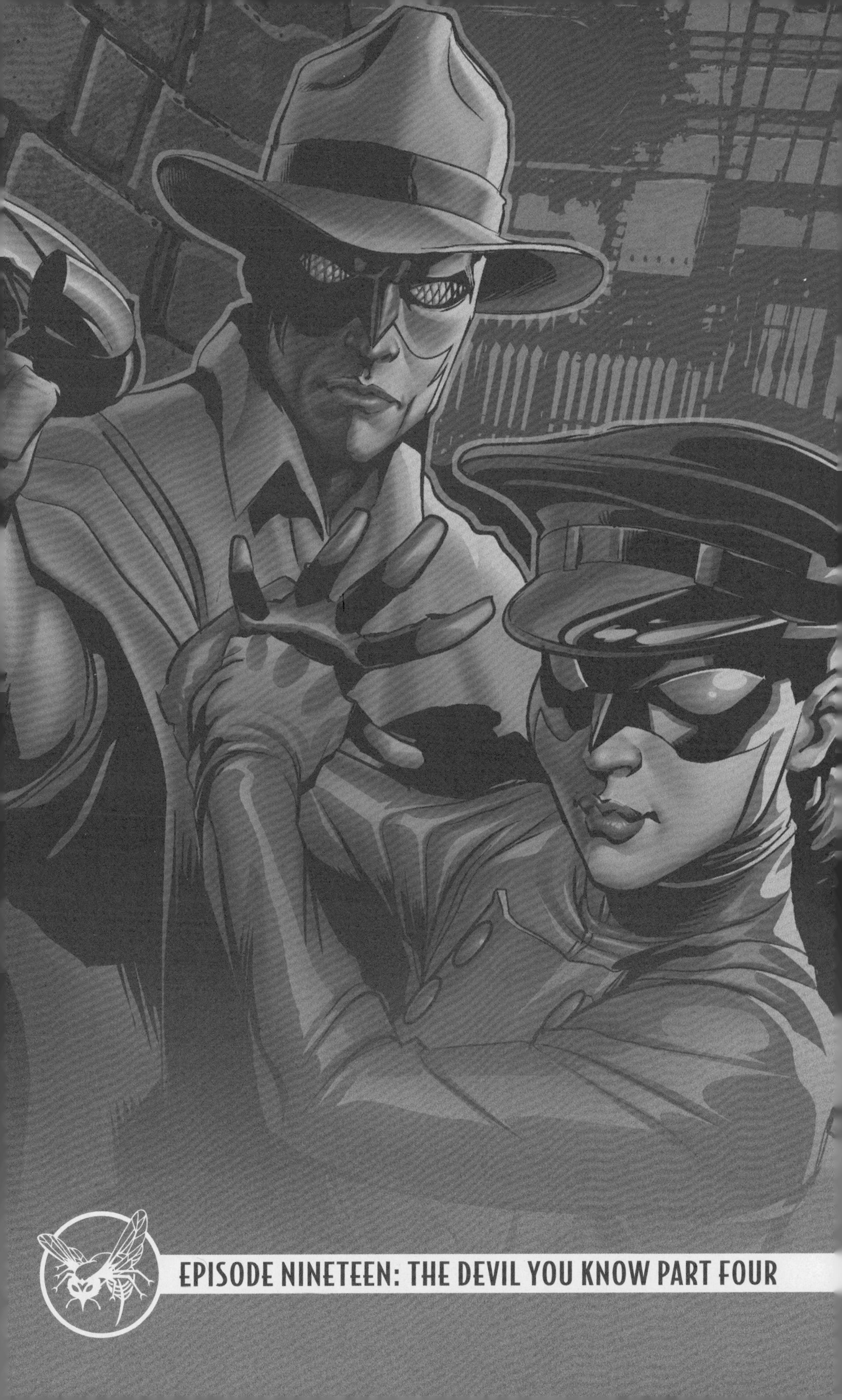

EPISODE NINETEEN: THE DEVIL YOU KNOW PART FOUR

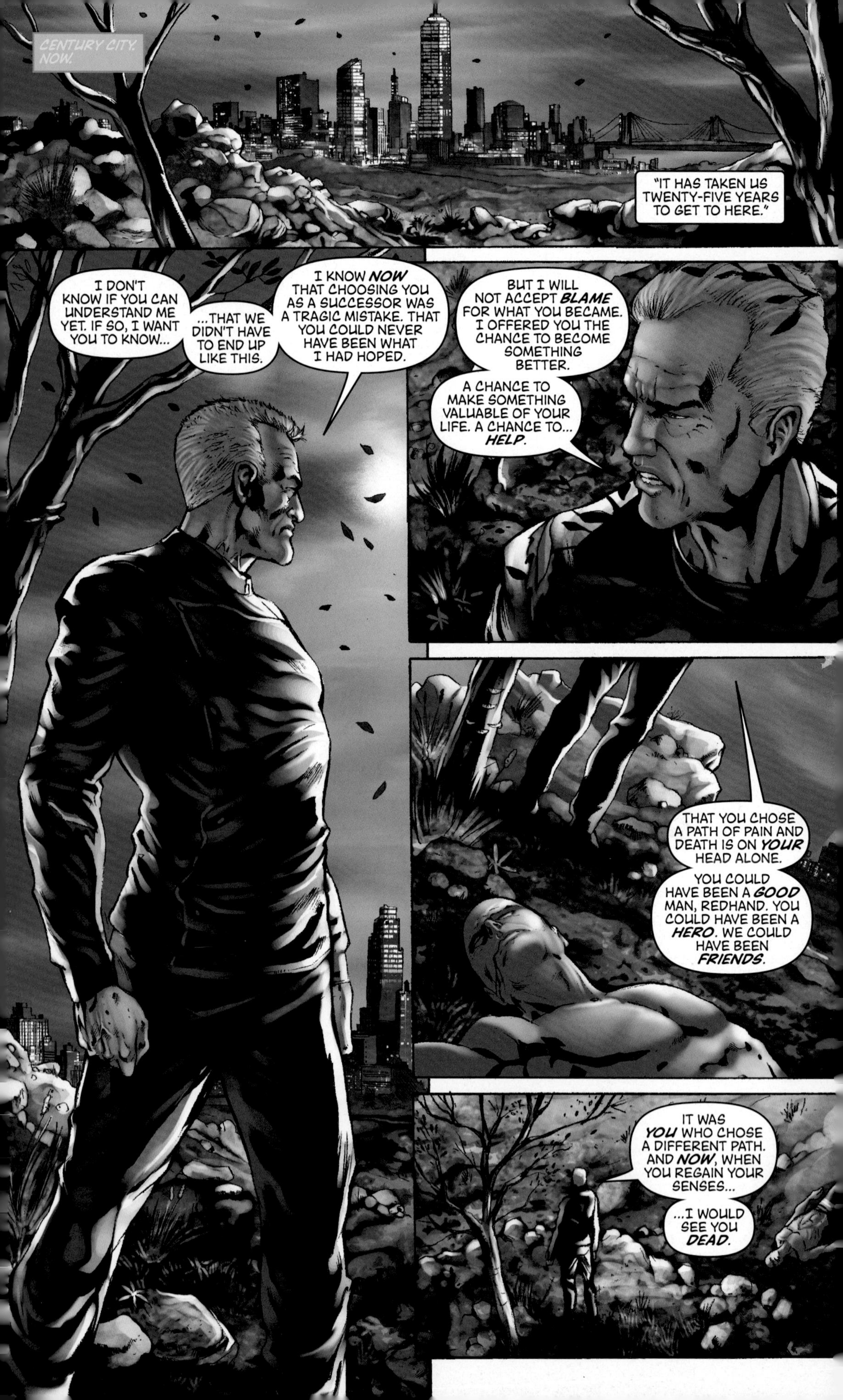
CENTURY CITY. NOW.
"IT HAS TAKEN US TWENTY-FIVE YEARS TO GET TO HERE."
I DON'T KNOW IF YOU CAN UNDERSTAND ME YET. IF SO, I WANT YOU TO KNOW...
...THAT WE DIDN'T HAVE TO END UP LIKE THIS.
I KNOW NOW THAT CHOOSING YOU AS A SUCCESSOR WAS A TRAGIC MISTAKE. THAT YOU COULD NEVER HAVE BEEN WHAT I HAD HOPED.
BUT I WILL NOT ACCEPT BLAME FOR WHAT YOU BECAME. I OFFERED YOU THE CHANCE TO BECOME SOMETHING BETTER.
A CHANCE TO MAKE SOMETHING VALUABLE OF YOUR LIFE. A CHANCE TO... HELP.
THAT YOU CHOSE A PATH OF PAIN AND DEATH IS ON YOUR HEAD ALONE.
YOU COULD HAVE BEEN A GOOD MAN, REDHAND. YOU COULD HAVE BEEN A HERO. WE COULD HAVE BEEN FRIENDS.
IT WAS YOU WHO CHOSE A DIFFERENT PATH. AND NOW, WHEN YOU REGAIN YOUR SENSES...
...I WOULD SEE YOU DEAD.

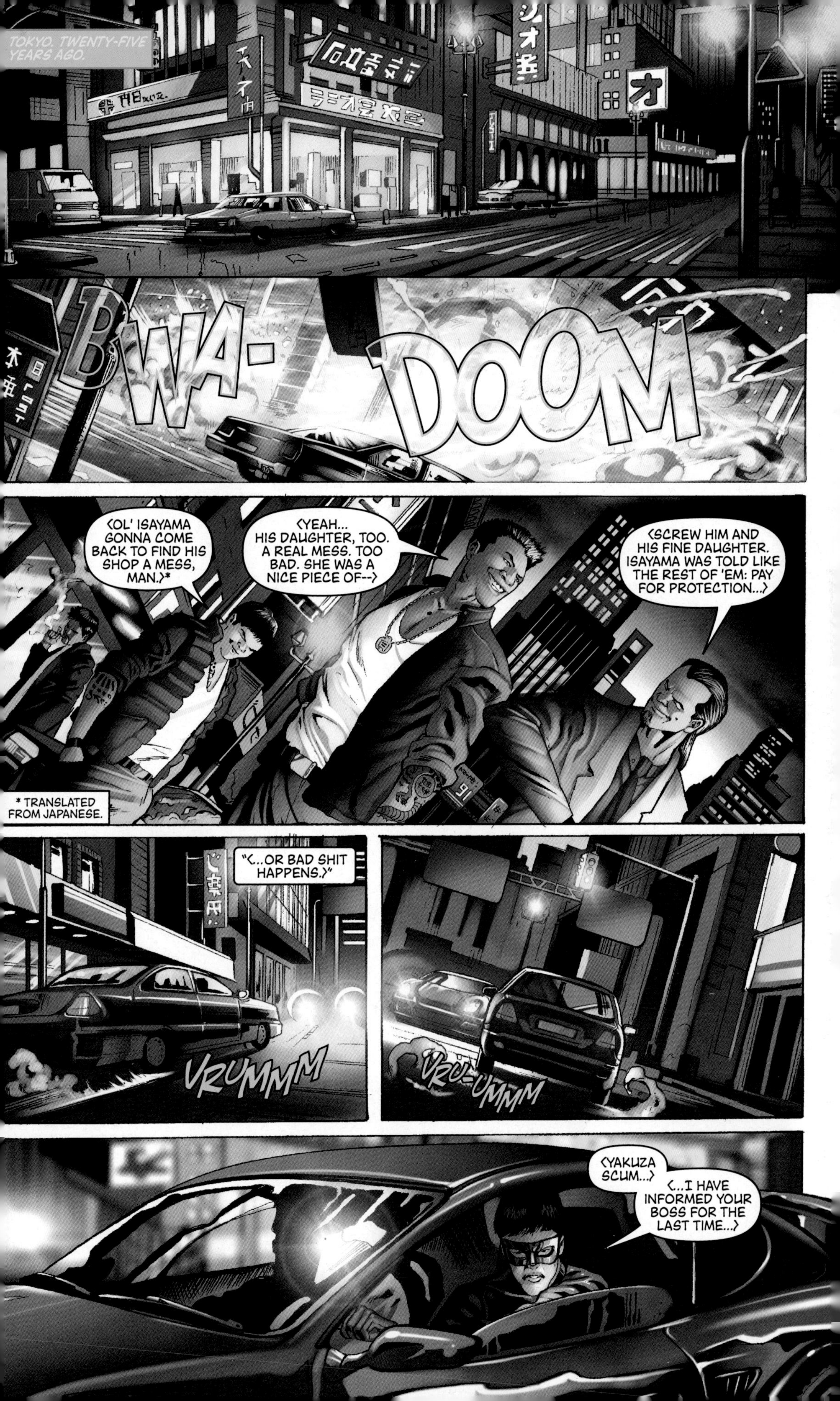
TOKYO. TWENTY-FIVE YEARS AGO.
BWA-DOOM
‹OL' ISAYAMA GONNA COME BACK TO FIND HIS SHOP A MESS, MAN.›*
‹YEAH... HIS DAUGHTER, TOO. A REAL MESS. TOO BAD. SHE WAS A NICE PIECE OF--›
‹SCREW HIM AND HIS FINE DAUGHTER. ISAYAMA WAS TOLD LIKE THE REST OF 'EM: PAY FOR PROTECTION...›
* TRANSLATED FROM JAPANESE.
"‹...OR BAD SHIT HAPPENS.›"
VRUMMM
VRU-UMMM
‹YAKUZA SCUM...›
‹...I HAVE INFORMED YOUR BOSS FOR THE LAST TIME...›

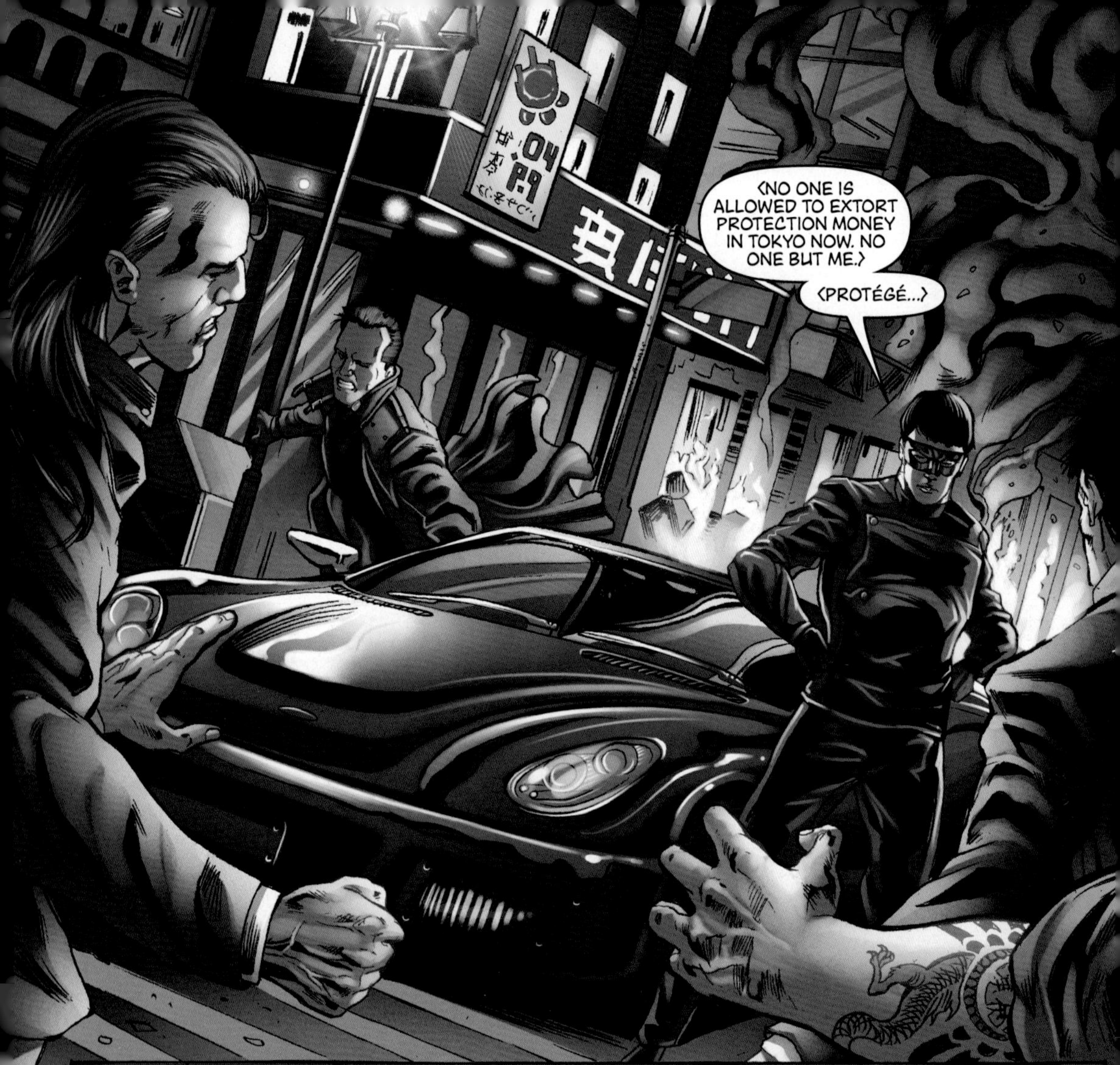
‹NO ONE IS ALLOWED TO EXTORT PROTECTION MONEY IN TOKYO NOW. NO ONE BUT ME.›
‹PROTÉGÉ...›

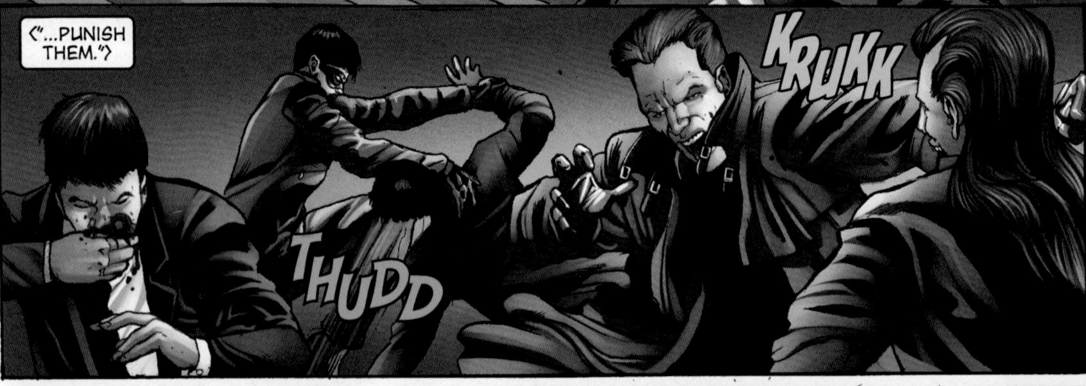
‹"...PUNISH THEM."›
KRUKK
THUDD

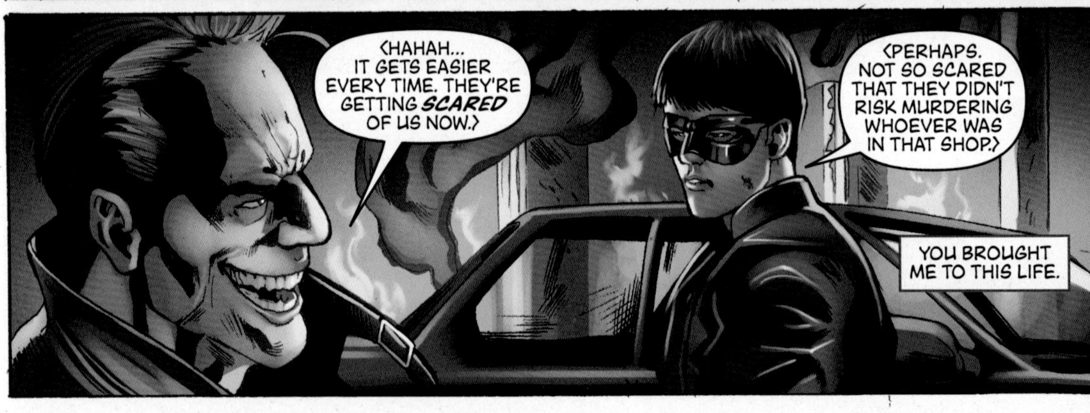
‹HAHAH... IT GETS EASIER EVERY TIME. THEY'RE GETTING *SCARED* OF US NOW.›
‹PERHAPS. NOT SO SCARED THAT THEY DIDN'T RISK MURDERING WHOEVER WAS IN THAT SHOP.›
YOU BROUGHT ME TO THIS LIFE.

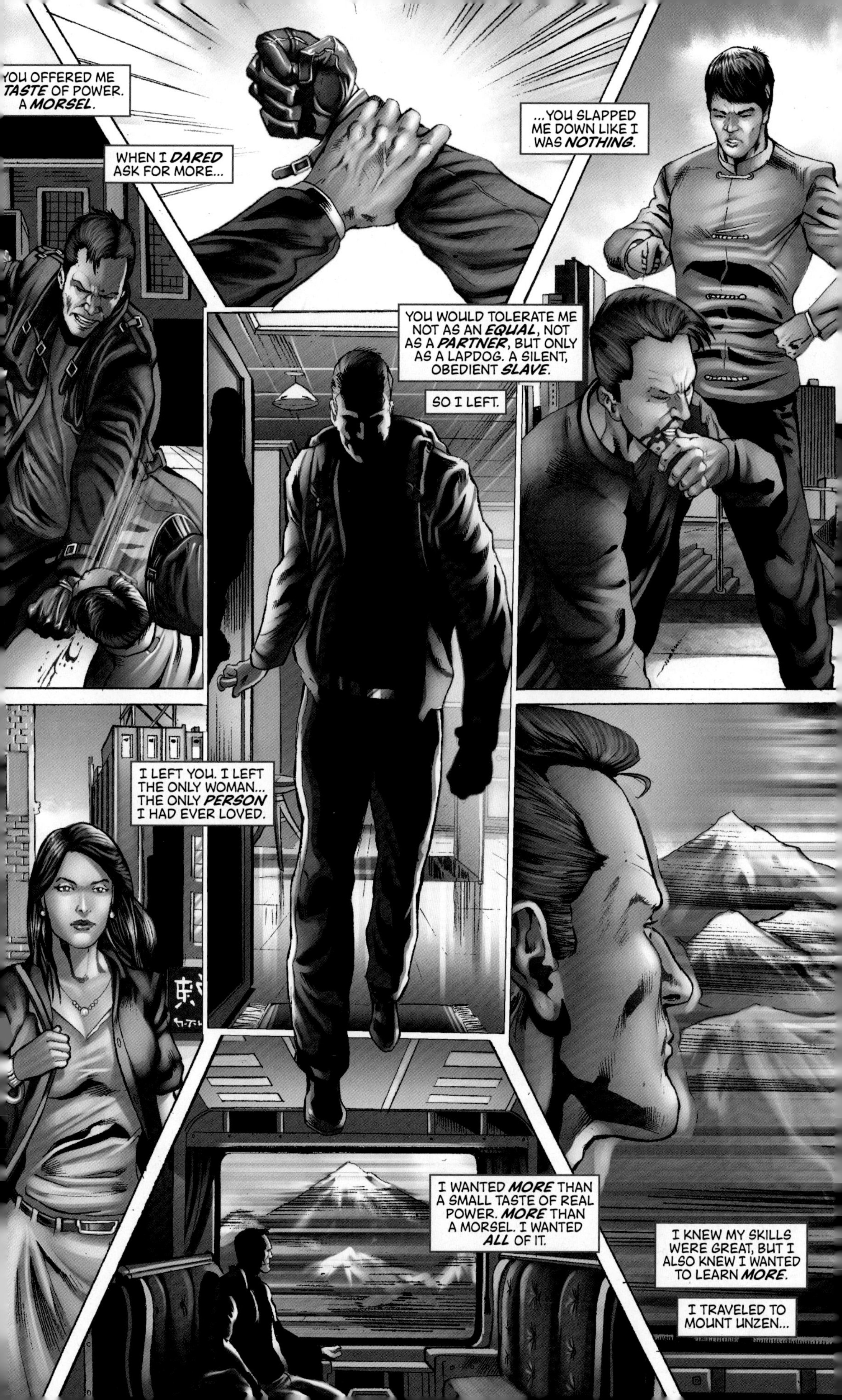
YOU OFFERED ME TASTE OF POWER. A MORSEL.
WHEN I DARED ASK FOR MORE...
...YOU SLAPPED ME DOWN LIKE I WAS NOTHING.
YOU WOULD TOLERATE ME NOT AS AN EQUAL, NOT AS A PARTNER, BUT ONLY AS A LAPDOG. A SILENT, OBEDIENT SLAVE.
SO I LEFT.
I LEFT YOU. I LEFT THE ONLY WOMAN... THE ONLY PERSON I HAD EVER LOVED.
I WANTED MORE THAN A SMALL TASTE OF REAL POWER. MORE THAN A MORSEL. I WANTED ALL OF IT.
I KNEW MY SKILLS WERE GREAT, BUT I ALSO KNEW I WANTED TO LEARN MORE.
I TRAVELED TO MOUNT UNZEN...

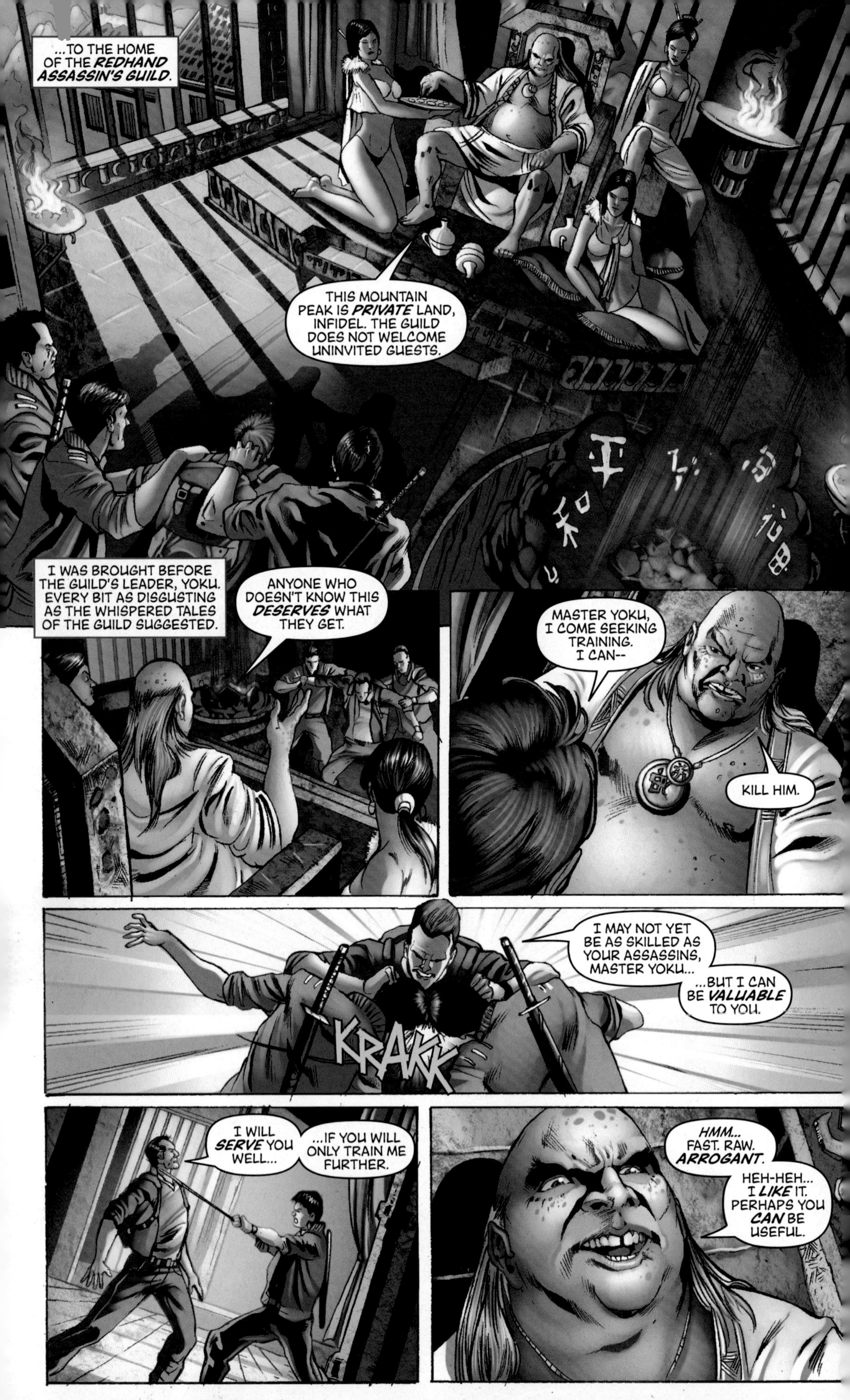
...TO THE HOME OF THE REDHAND ASSASSIN'S GUILD.
THIS MOUNTAIN PEAK IS PRIVATE LAND, INFIDEL. THE GUILD DOES NOT WELCOME UNINVITED GUESTS.
I WAS BROUGHT BEFORE THE GUILD'S LEADER, YOKU. EVERY BIT AS DISGUSTING AS THE WHISPERED TALES OF THE GUILD SUGGESTED.
ANYONE WHO DOESN'T KNOW THIS DESERVES WHAT THEY GET.
MASTER YOKU, I COME SEEKING TRAINING. I CAN--
KILL HIM.
I MAY NOT YET BE AS SKILLED AS YOUR ASSASSINS, MASTER YOKU...
...BUT I CAN BE VALUABLE TO YOU.
KRAKK
I WILL SERVE YOU WELL...
...IF YOU WILL ONLY TRAIN ME FURTHER.
HMM... FAST. RAW. ARROGANT.
HEH-HEH... I LIKE IT. PERHAPS YOU CAN BE USEFUL.

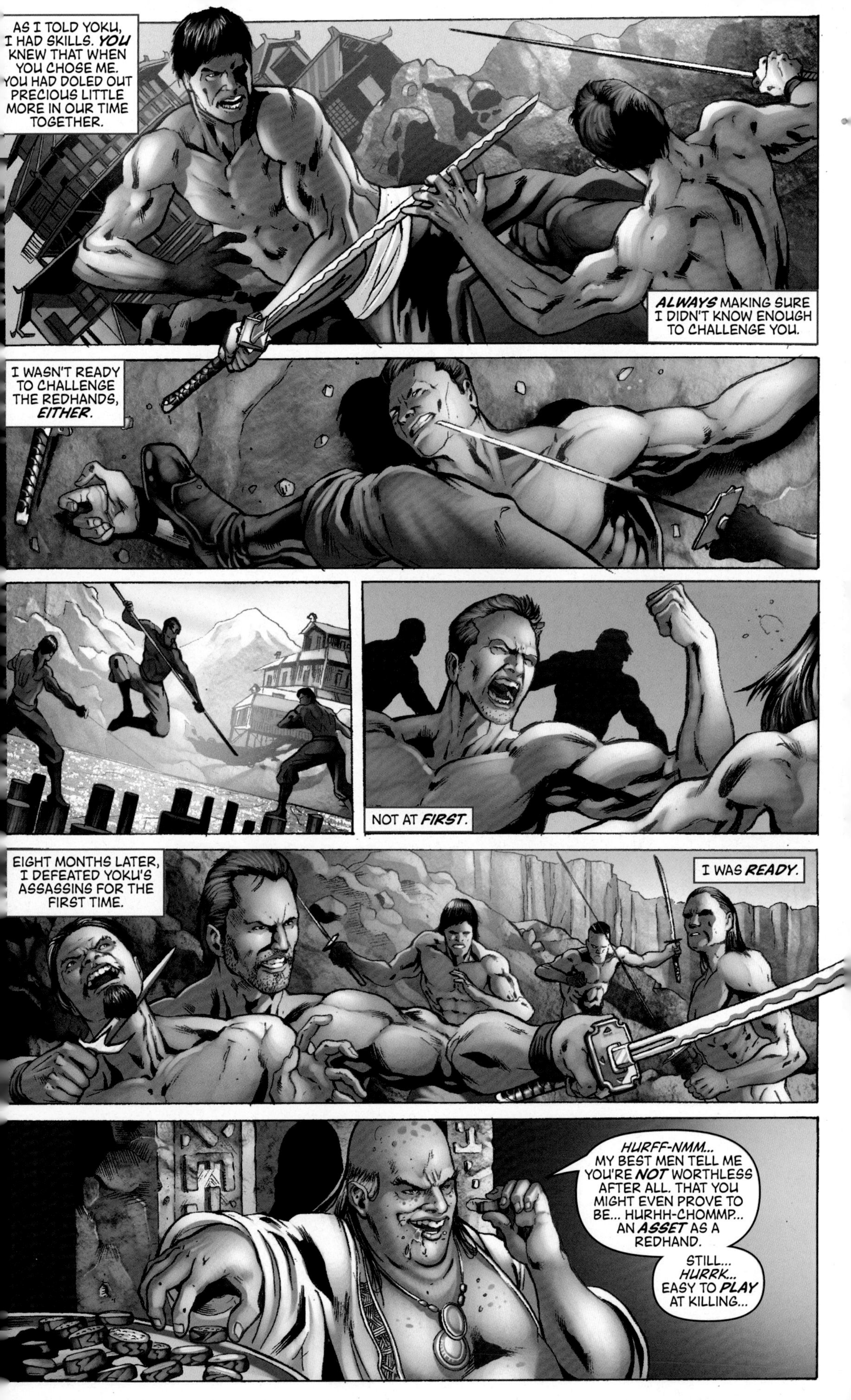
AS I TOLD YOKU, I HAD SKILLS. YOU KNEW THAT WHEN YOU CHOSE ME. YOU HAD DOLED OUT PRECIOUS LITTLE MORE IN OUR TIME TOGETHER.
ALWAYS MAKING SURE I DIDN'T KNOW ENOUGH TO CHALLENGE YOU.
I WASN'T READY TO CHALLENGE THE REDHANDS, EITHER.
NOT AT FIRST.
EIGHT MONTHS LATER, I DEFEATED YOKU'S ASSASSINS FOR THE FIRST TIME.
I WAS READY.
HURFF-NMM... MY BEST MEN TELL ME YOU'RE NOT WORTHLESS AFTER ALL. THAT YOU MIGHT EVEN PROVE TO BE... HURHH-CHOMMP... AN ASSET AS A REDHAND.
STILL... HURRK... EASY TO PLAY AT KILLING...

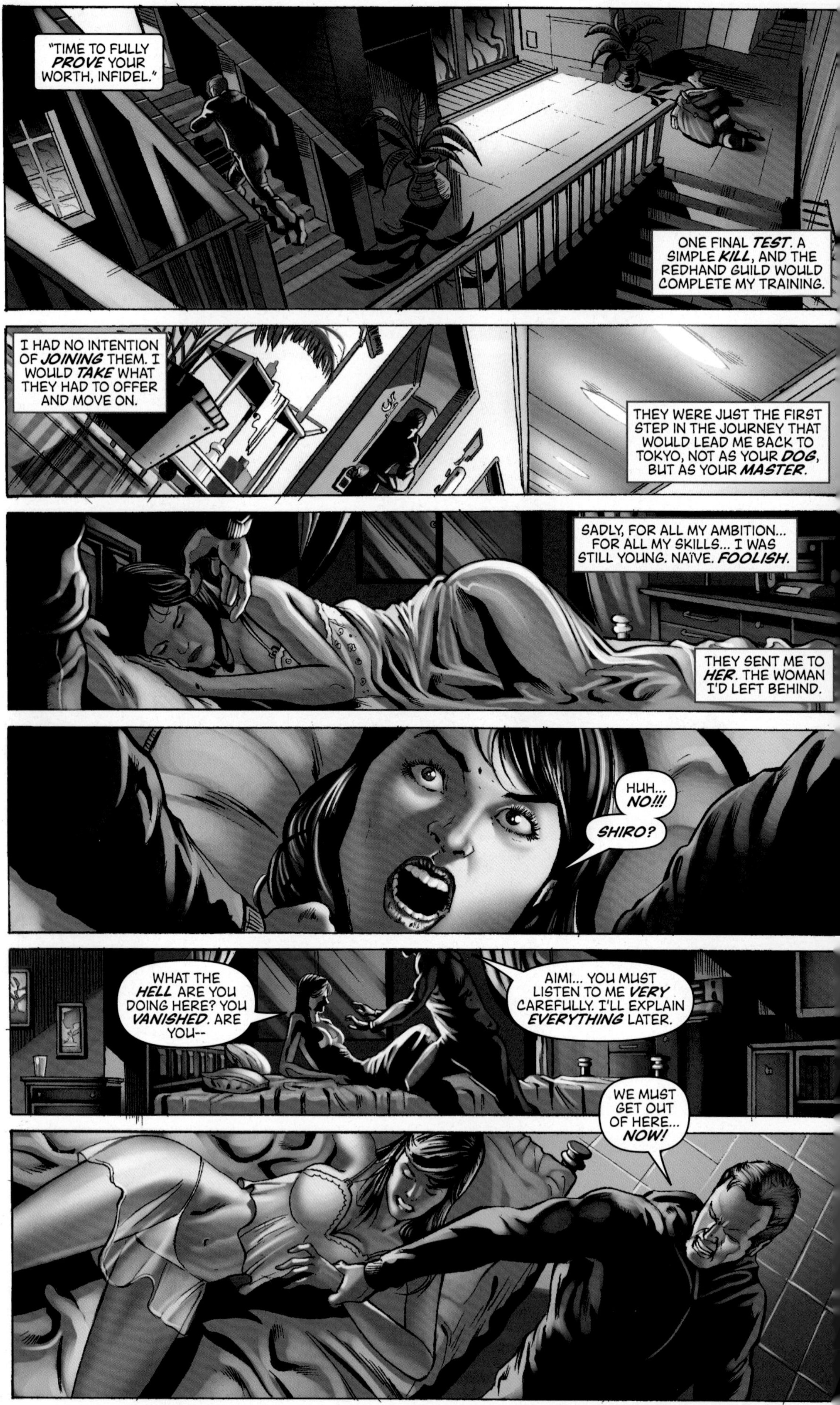
"TIME TO FULLY PROVE YOUR WORTH, INFIDEL."
ONE FINAL TEST. A SIMPLE KILL, AND THE REDHAND GUILD WOULD COMPLETE MY TRAINING.
I HAD NO INTENTION OF JOINING THEM. I WOULD TAKE WHAT THEY HAD TO OFFER AND MOVE ON.
THEY WERE JUST THE FIRST STEP IN THE JOURNEY THAT WOULD LEAD ME BACK TO TOKYO, NOT AS YOUR DOG, BUT AS YOUR MASTER.
SADLY, FOR ALL MY AMBITION... FOR ALL MY SKILLS... I WAS STILL YOUNG. NAÏVE. FOOLISH.
THEY SENT ME TO HER. THE WOMAN I'D LEFT BEHIND.
HUH... NO!!!
SHIRO?
WHAT THE HELL ARE YOU DOING HERE? YOU VANISHED. ARE YOU--
AIMI... YOU MUST LISTEN TO ME VERY CAREFULLY. I'LL EXPLAIN EVERYTHING LATER.
WE MUST GET OUT OF HERE... NOW!

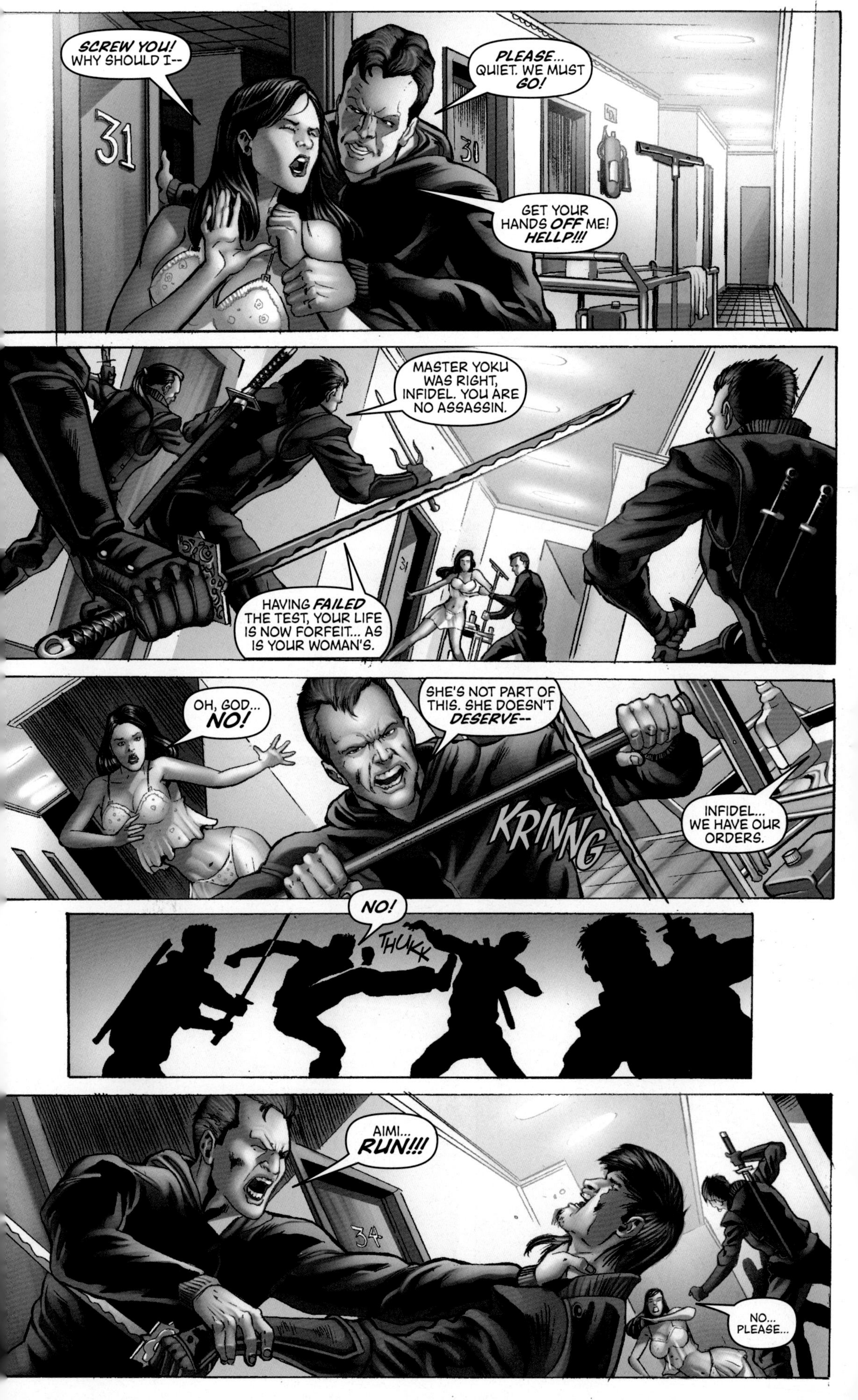
SCREW YOU! WHY SHOULD I--
PLEASE... QUIET. WE MUST GO!
GET YOUR HANDS OFF ME! HELLP!!!
MASTER YOKU WAS RIGHT, INFIDEL. YOU ARE NO ASSASSIN.
HAVING FAILED THE TEST, YOUR LIFE IS NOW FORFEIT... AS IS YOUR WOMAN'S.
OH, GOD... NO!
SHE'S NOT PART OF THIS. SHE DOESN'T DESERVE--
KRINNG
INFIDEL... WE HAVE OUR ORDERS.
NO!
THUKK
AIMI... RUN!!!
NO... PLEASE...

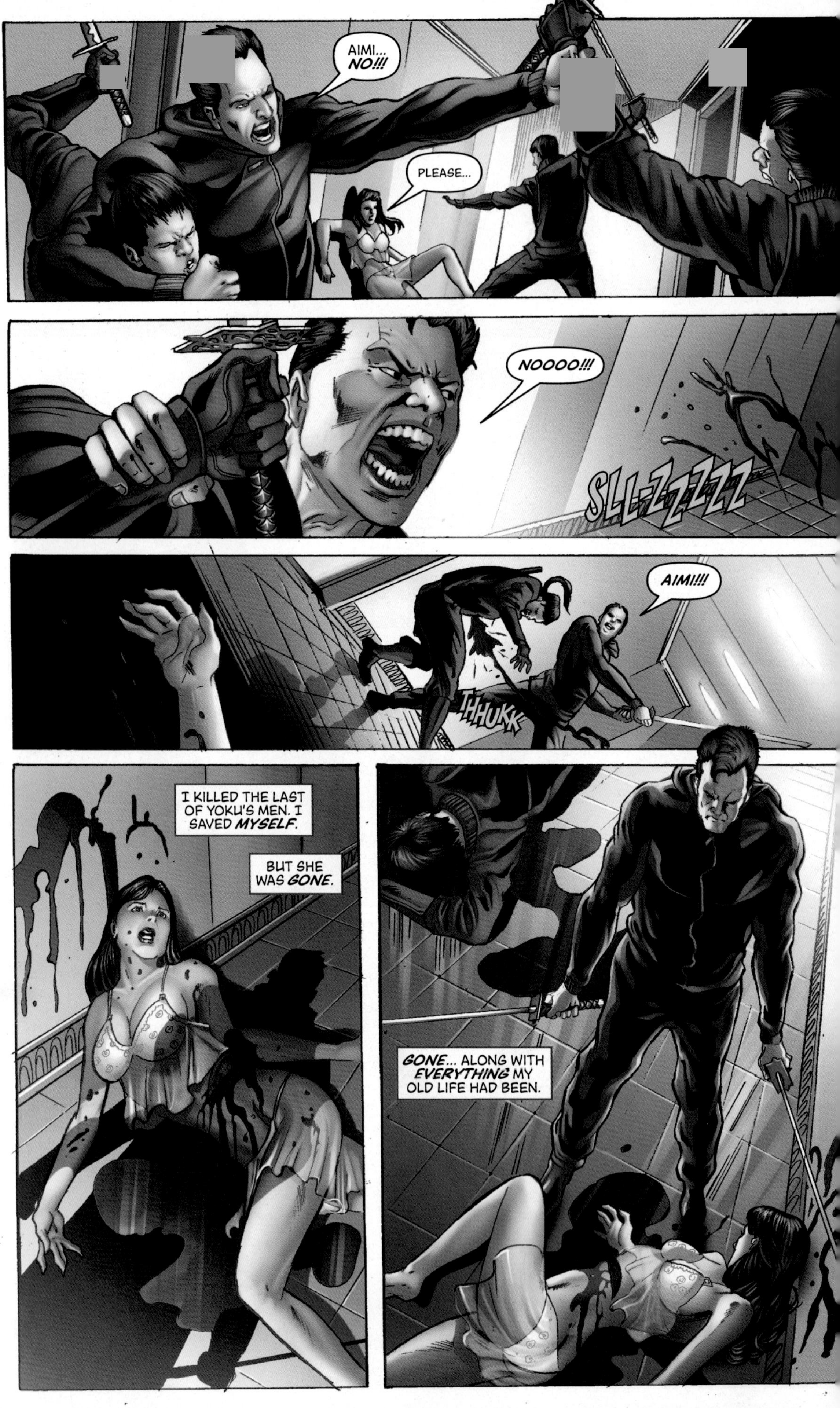
AIMI... NO!!!
PLEASE...
NOOOO!!!
SLL-ZZZZZ
AIMI!!!
THHUKK
I KILLED THE LAST OF YOKU'S MEN. I SAVED MYSELF.
BUT SHE WAS GONE.
GONE... ALONG WITH EVERYTHING MY OLD LIFE HAD BEEN.

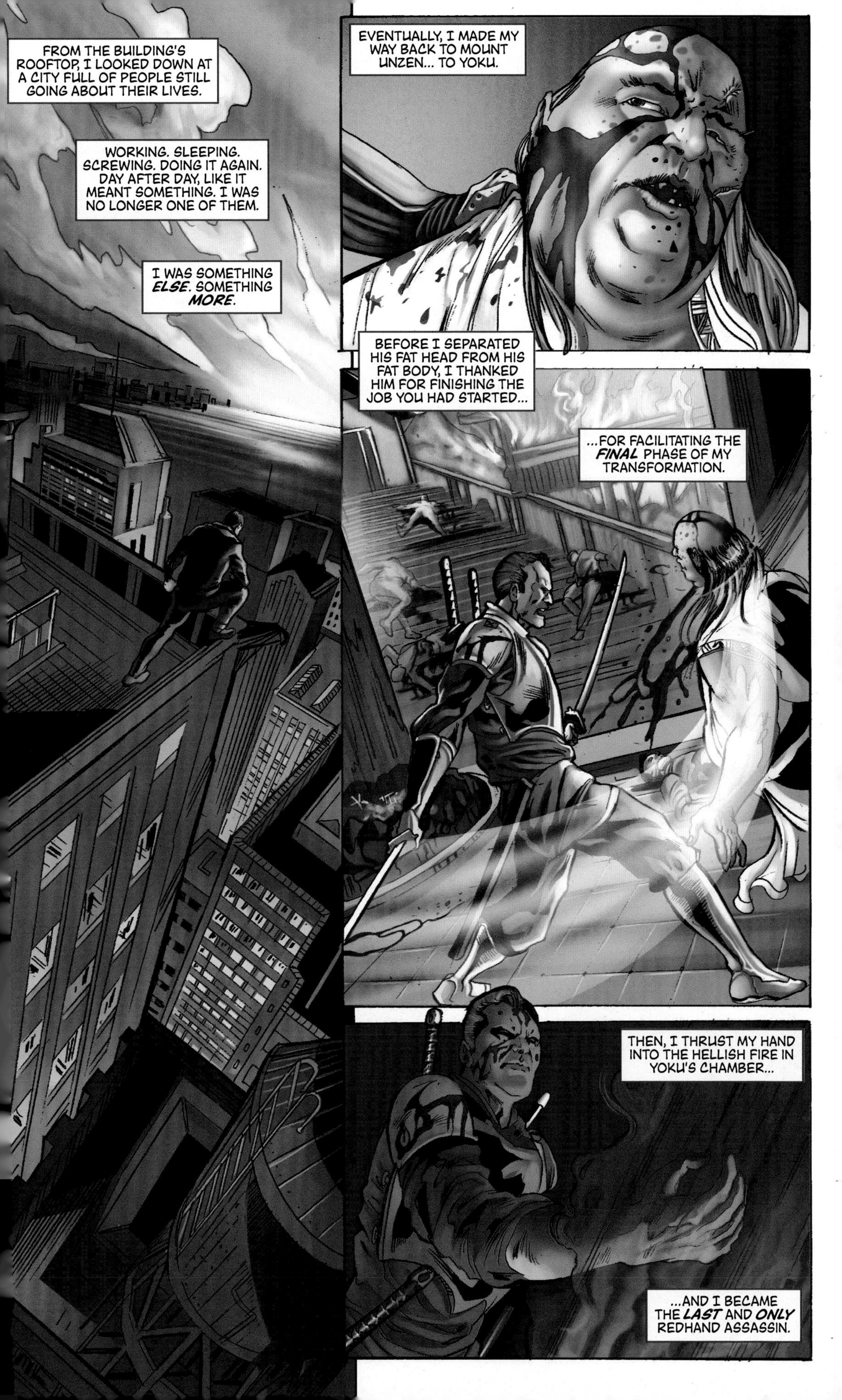
FROM THE BUILDING'S ROOFTOP, I LOOKED DOWN AT A CITY FULL OF PEOPLE STILL GOING ABOUT THEIR LIVES.
WORKING. SLEEPING. SCREWING. DOING IT AGAIN. DAY AFTER DAY, LIKE IT MEANT SOMETHING. I WAS NO LONGER ONE OF THEM.
I WAS SOMETHING *ELSE*. SOMETHING *MORE*.
EVENTUALLY, I MADE MY WAY BACK TO MOUNT UNZEN... TO YOKU.
BEFORE I SEPARATED HIS FAT HEAD FROM HIS FAT BODY, I THANKED HIM FOR FINISHING THE JOB YOU HAD STARTED...
...FOR FACILITATING THE *FINAL* PHASE OF MY TRANSFORMATION.
THEN, I THRUST MY HAND INTO THE HELLISH FIRE IN YOKU'S CHAMBER...
...AND I BECAME THE *LAST* AND *ONLY* REDHAND ASSASSIN.

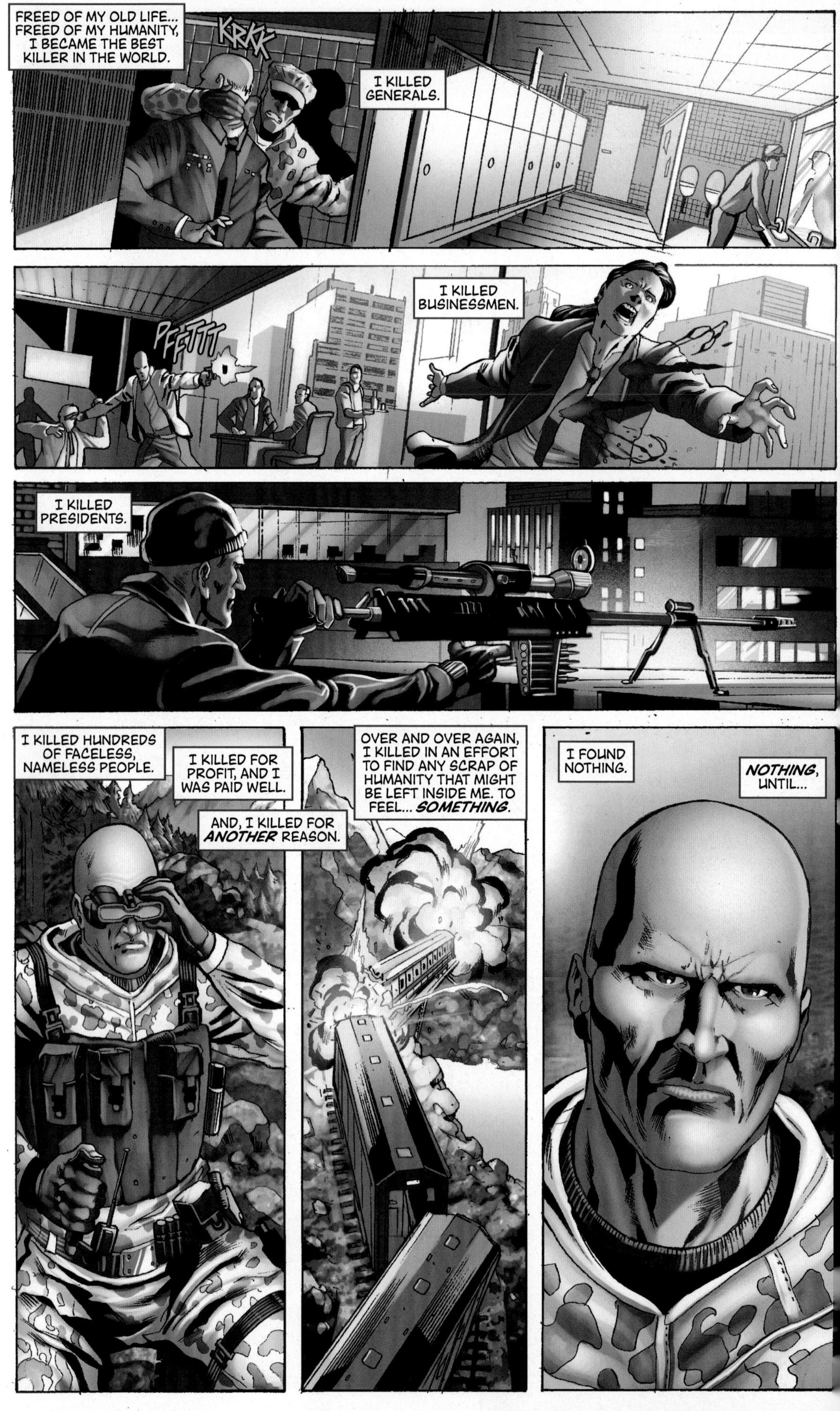

FREED OF MY OLD LIFE... FREED OF MY HUMANITY, I BECAME THE BEST KILLER IN THE WORLD.
KRKK
I KILLED GENERALS.
I KILLED BUSINESSMEN.
PFFTTT
I KILLED PRESIDENTS.
I KILLED HUNDREDS OF FACELESS, NAMELESS PEOPLE.
I KILLED FOR PROFIT, AND I WAS PAID WELL.
AND, I KILLED FOR ANOTHER REASON.
OVER AND OVER AGAIN, I KILLED IN AN EFFORT TO FIND ANY SCRAP OF HUMANITY THAT MIGHT BE LEFT INSIDE ME. TO FEEL... SOMETHING.
I FOUND NOTHING.
NOTHING, UNTIL...

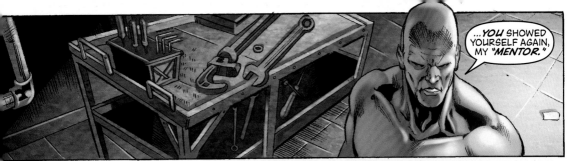

...*YOU* SHOWED YOURSELF AGAIN, MY *"MENTOR."*

WHEN I SAW YOU PARADING YOUR OLD, SELF-SERVING ASS AROUND AGAIN, COMPLETE WITH ALL-NEW PUPPETS YOU'D CREATED IN YOUR OWN IMAGE...

...I FELT SOMETHING.

LET ME *ASSURE* YOU, HAYASHI... ...WE'RE BOTH GOING TO FEEL A *GREAT* DEAL IN THE NEXT FEW DAYS.

THIS IS ABOUT *YOU* AND *ME* ALONE. LET THEM GO. YOU HAVE *NOTHING* TO GAIN BY--

KRAKK

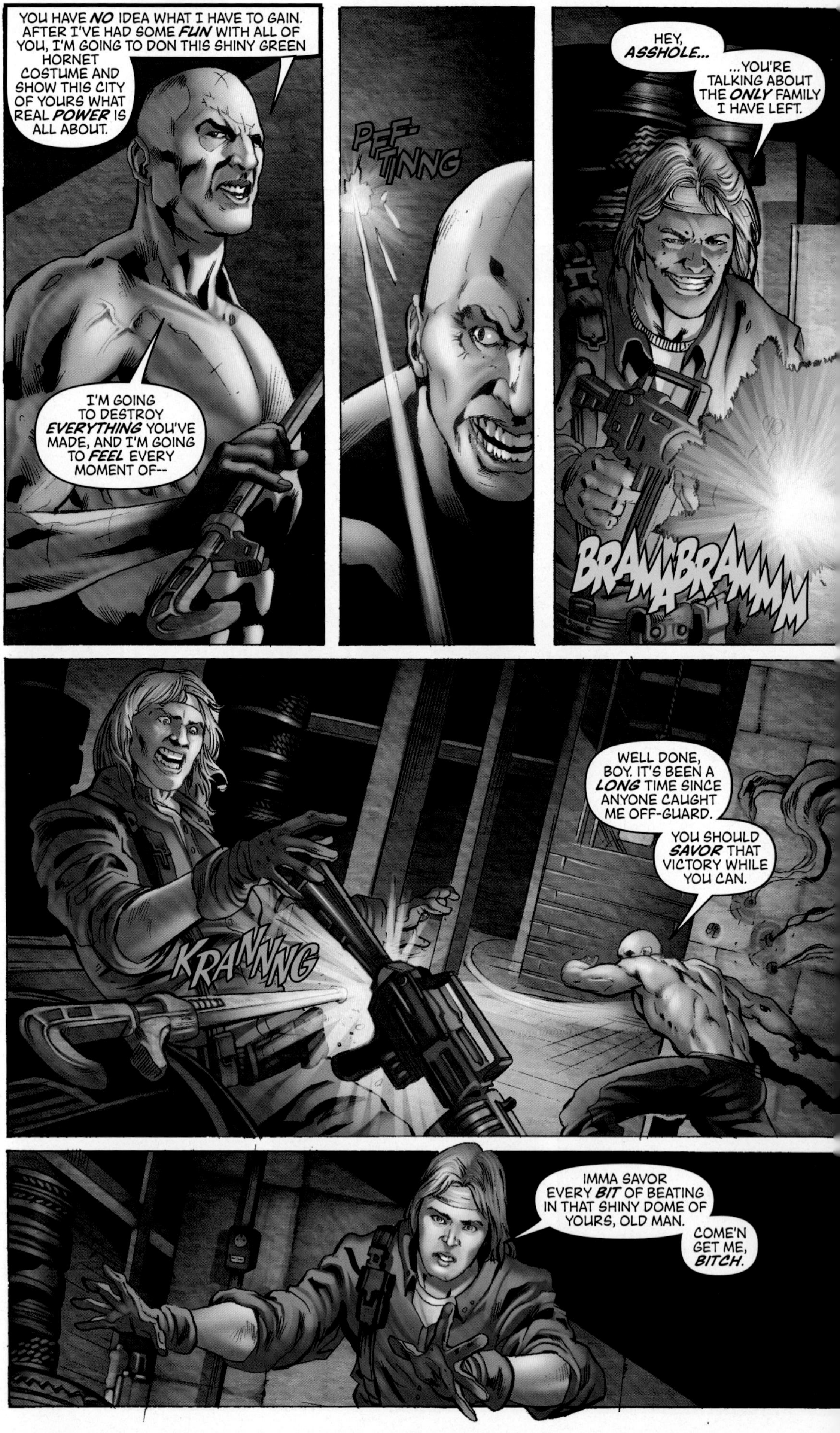

YOU HAVE NO IDEA WHAT I HAVE TO GAIN. AFTER I'VE HAD SOME FUN WITH ALL OF YOU, I'M GOING TO DON THIS SHINY GREEN HORNET COSTUME AND SHOW THIS CITY OF YOURS WHAT REAL POWER IS ALL ABOUT.
I'M GOING TO DESTROY EVERYTHING YOU'VE MADE, AND I'M GOING TO FEEL EVERY MOMENT OF--
PFF-TINNG
HEY, ASSHOLE...
...YOU'RE TALKING ABOUT THE ONLY FAMILY I HAVE LEFT.
BRAMABRAMMMM
KRANNNG
WELL DONE, BOY. IT'S BEEN A LONG TIME SINCE ANYONE CAUGHT ME OFF-GUARD.
YOU SHOULD SAVOR THAT VICTORY WHILE YOU CAN.
IMMA SAVOR EVERY BIT OF BEATING IN THAT SHINY DOME OF YOURS, OLD MAN.
COME'N GET ME, BITCH.

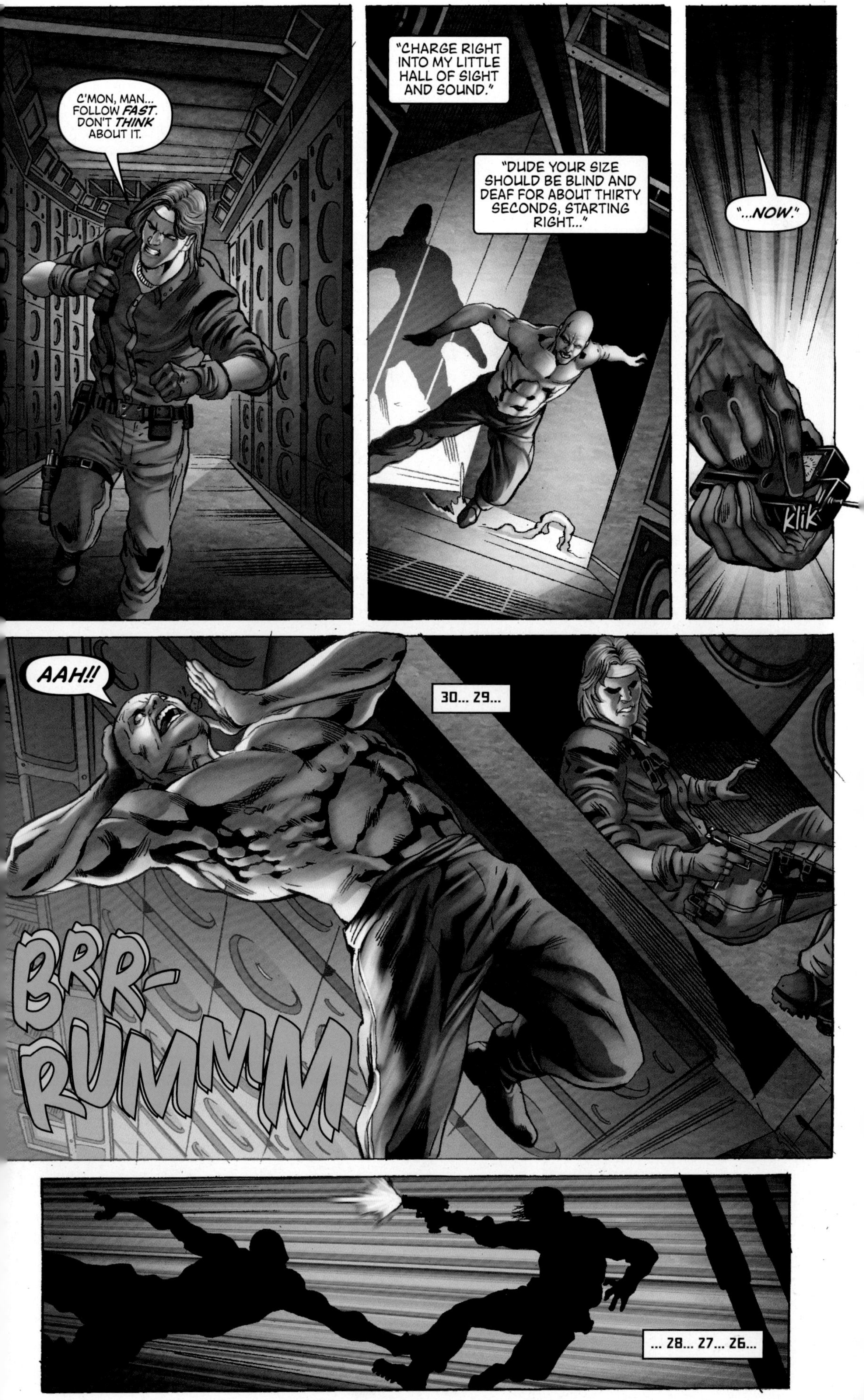
C'MON, MAN... FOLLOW *FAST*. DON'T *THINK* ABOUT IT.
"CHARGE RIGHT INTO MY LITTLE HALL OF SIGHT AND SOUND."
"DUDE YOUR SIZE SHOULD BE BLIND AND DEAF FOR ABOUT THIRTY SECONDS, STARTING RIGHT..."
"...*NOW*."
klik
AAH!!
30... 29...
BRR-RUMMM
... 28... 27... 26...

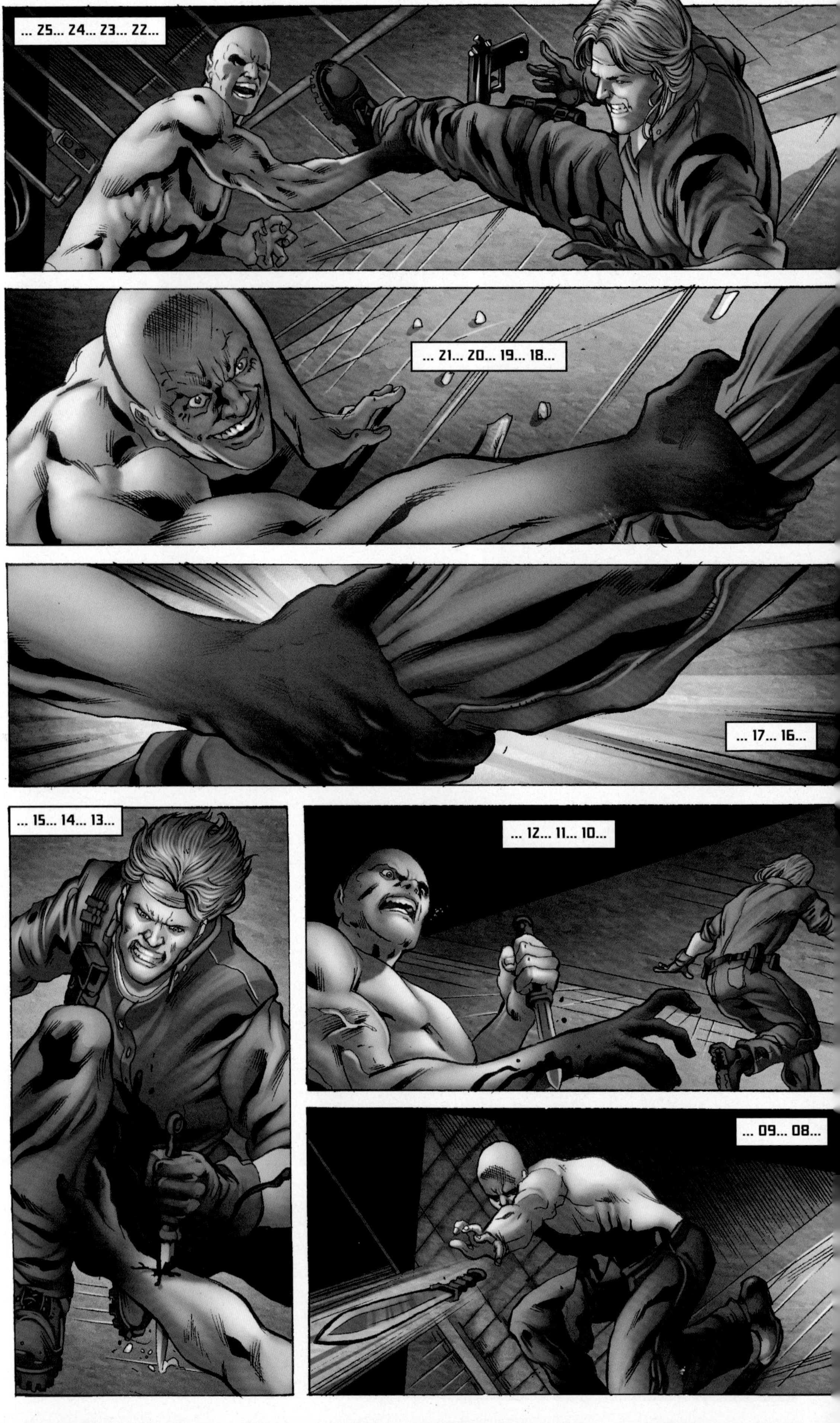
... 25... 24... 23... 22...
... 21... 20... 19... 18...
... 17... 16...
... 15... 14... 13...
... 12... 11... 10...
... 09... 08...

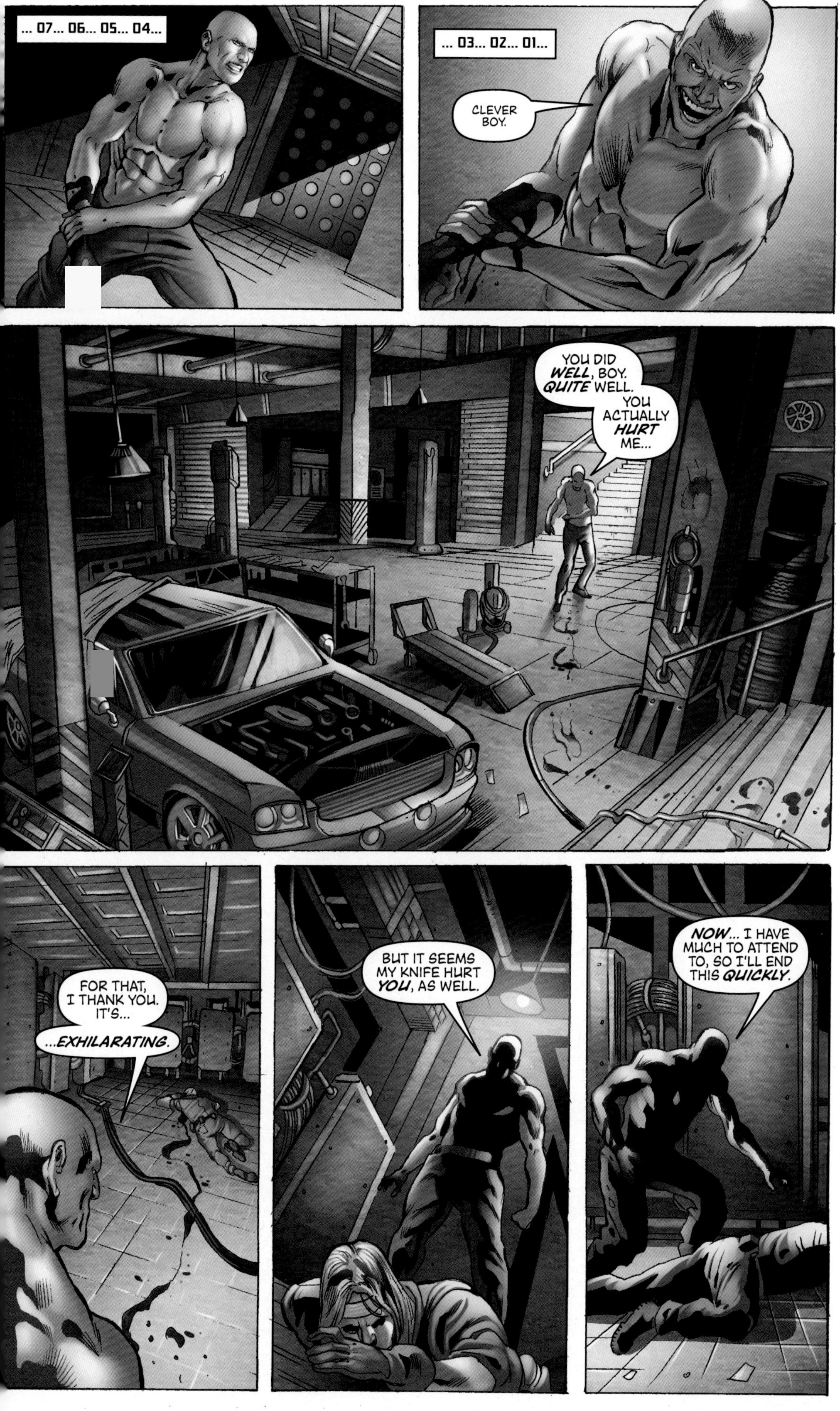

... 07... 06... 05... 04...
... 03... 02... 01...
CLEVER BOY.
YOU DID WELL, BOY. QUITE WELL.
YOU ACTUALLY HURT ME...
FOR THAT, I THANK YOU. IT'S...
...EXHILARATING.
BUT IT SEEMS MY KNIFE HURT YOU, AS WELL.
NOW... I HAVE MUCH TO ATTEND TO, SO I'LL END THIS QUICKLY.

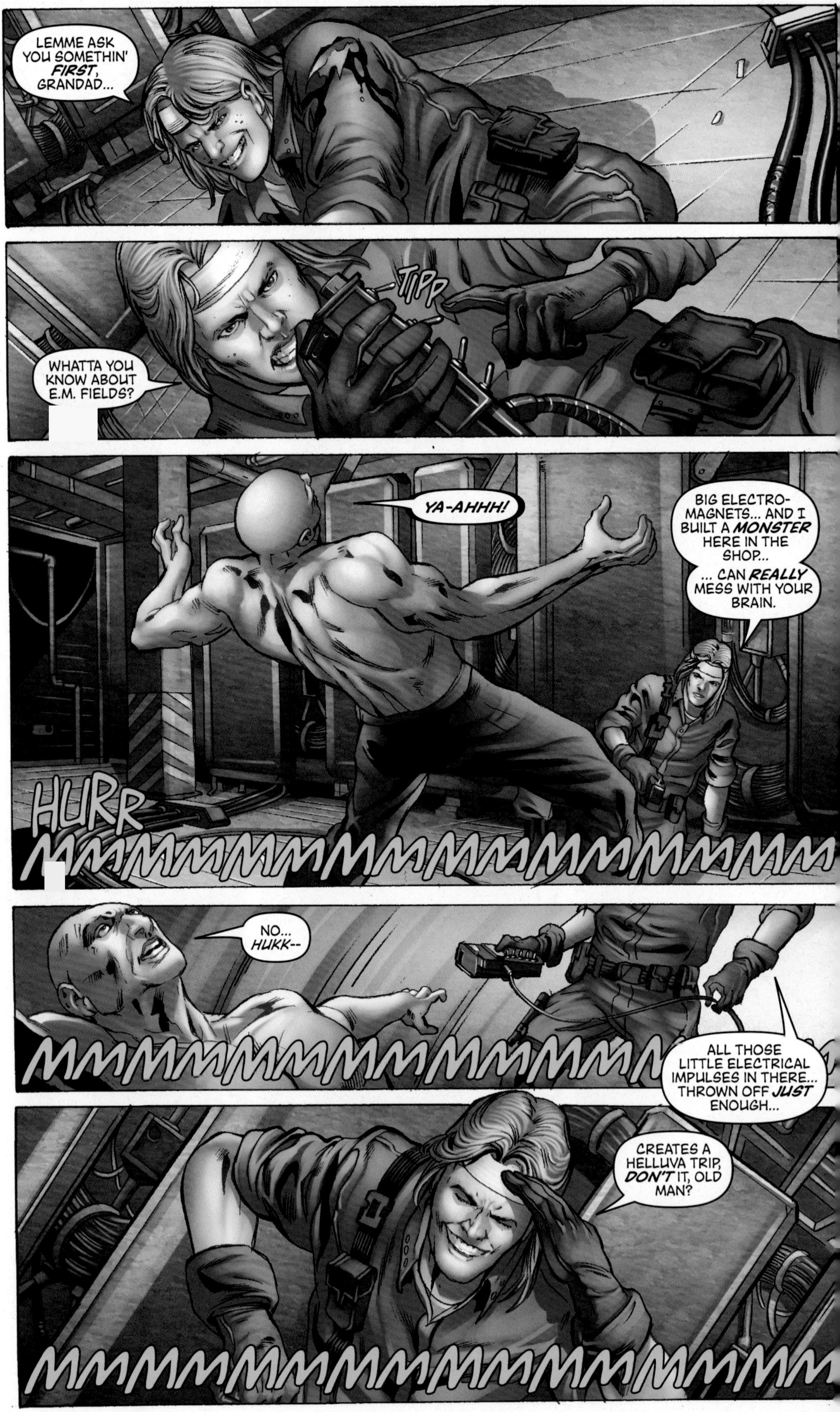
LEMME ASK YOU SOMETHIN' FIRST, GRANDAD...
TIPP
WHATTA YOU KNOW ABOUT E.M. FIELDS?
YA-AHHH!
BIG ELECTRO-MAGNETS... AND I BUILT A MONSTER HERE IN THE SHOP...
... CAN REALLY MESS WITH YOUR BRAIN.
HURR
MMMMMMMMMMMMMMMMMMMM
NO... HUKK--
MMMMMMMMMMMMMMMMMM
ALL THOSE LITTLE ELECTRICAL IMPULSES IN THERE... THROWN OFF JUST ENOUGH...
CREATES A HELLUVA TRIP, DON'T IT, OLD MAN?
MMMMMMMMMMMMMMMMMMMMMM

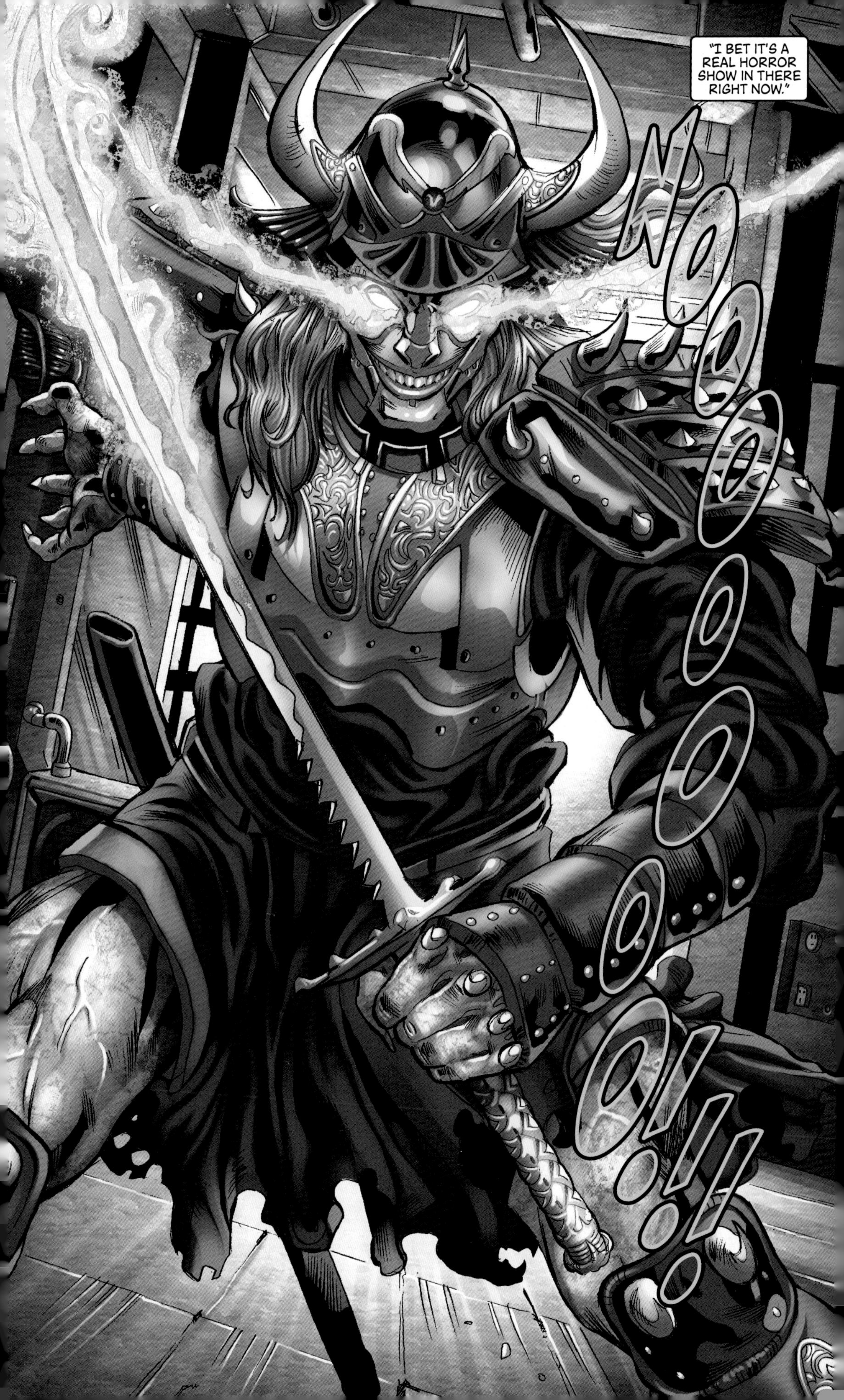
"I BET IT'S A REAL HORROR SHOW IN THERE RIGHT NOW."
NOOOOOOO!!!

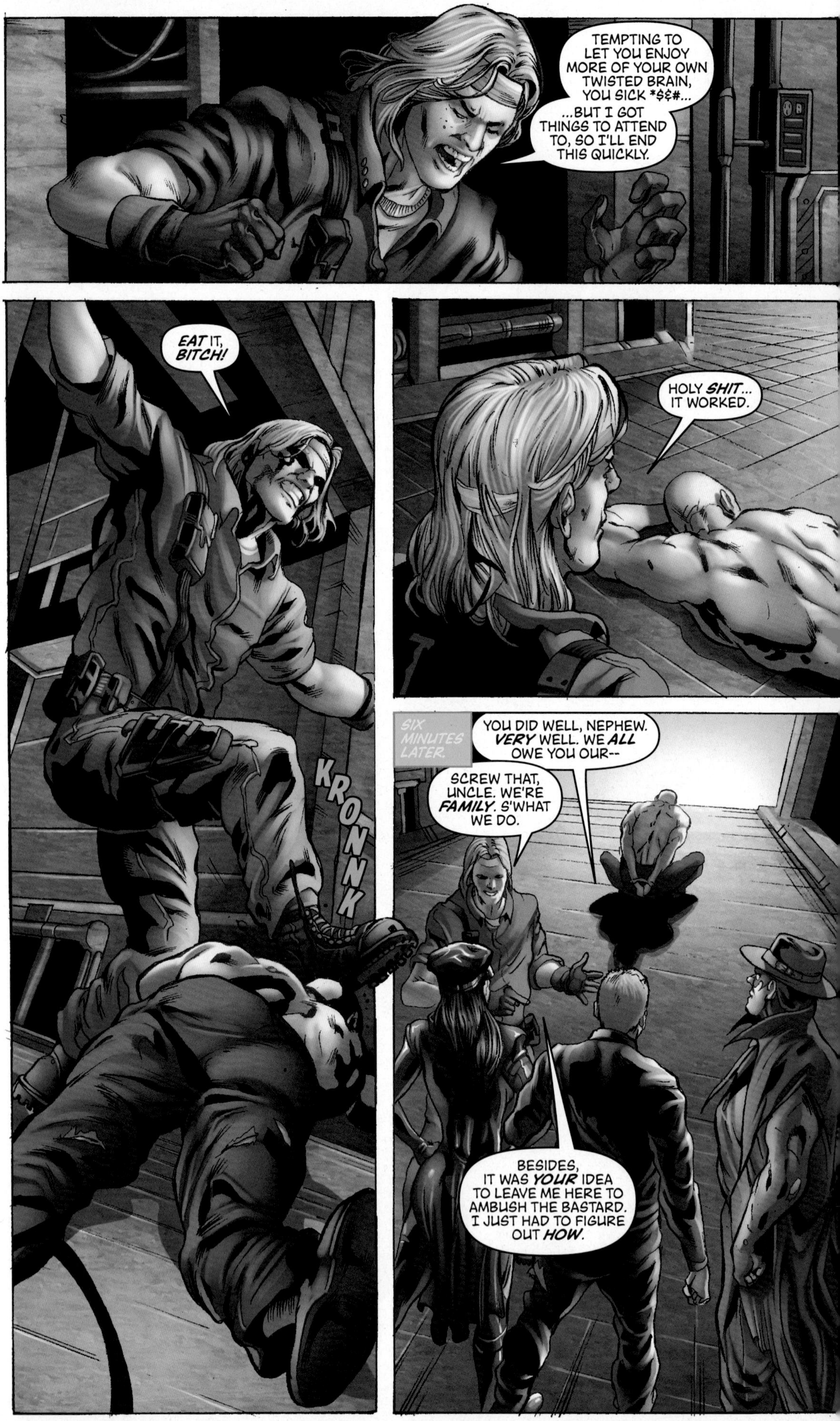
TEMPTING TO LET YOU ENJOY MORE OF YOUR OWN TWISTED BRAIN, YOU SICK *$&#...
...BUT I GOT THINGS TO ATTEND TO, SO I'LL END THIS QUICKLY.
EAT IT, BITCH!
KRONNNK
HOLY SHIT... IT WORKED.
SIX MINUTES LATER.
YOU DID WELL, NEPHEW. VERY WELL. WE ALL OWE YOU OUR--
SCREW THAT, UNCLE. WE'RE FAMILY. S'WHAT WE DO.
BESIDES, IT WAS YOUR IDEA TO LEAVE ME HERE TO AMBUSH THE BASTARD. I JUST HAD TO FIGURE OUT HOW.

ONE QUESTION: IF THE ELECTROMAGNETIC FIELD WAS STRONG ENOUGH TO COMPLETELY SCRAMBLE REDHAND'S BRAIN...

...WHY WEREN'T *YOU* AFFECTED?

YEAH, WELL... PRETTY *EXTENSIVE* EXPERIENCE WITH POWERFUL HALLUCINOGENS, BRAH.

NEPHEW, YOU HAVE MY *WORD* THAT I WILL NOT DISPARAGE YOUR CHOICE OF RECREATIONAL ACTIVITIES...

...FOR A FULL WEEK.

I'M ALL ABOUT THE HAPPY-HAPPY FAMILY LOVE HOUR...

...BUT WHAT ARE WE GOING TO DO WITH THIS SONOFABITCH?

I WILL LOAD HIM INTO THE BLACK BEAUTY.

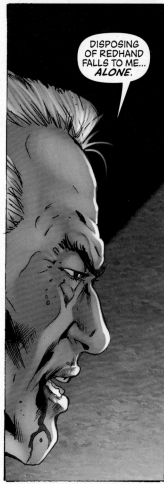

DISPOSING OF REDHAND FALLS TO ME... *ALONE.*

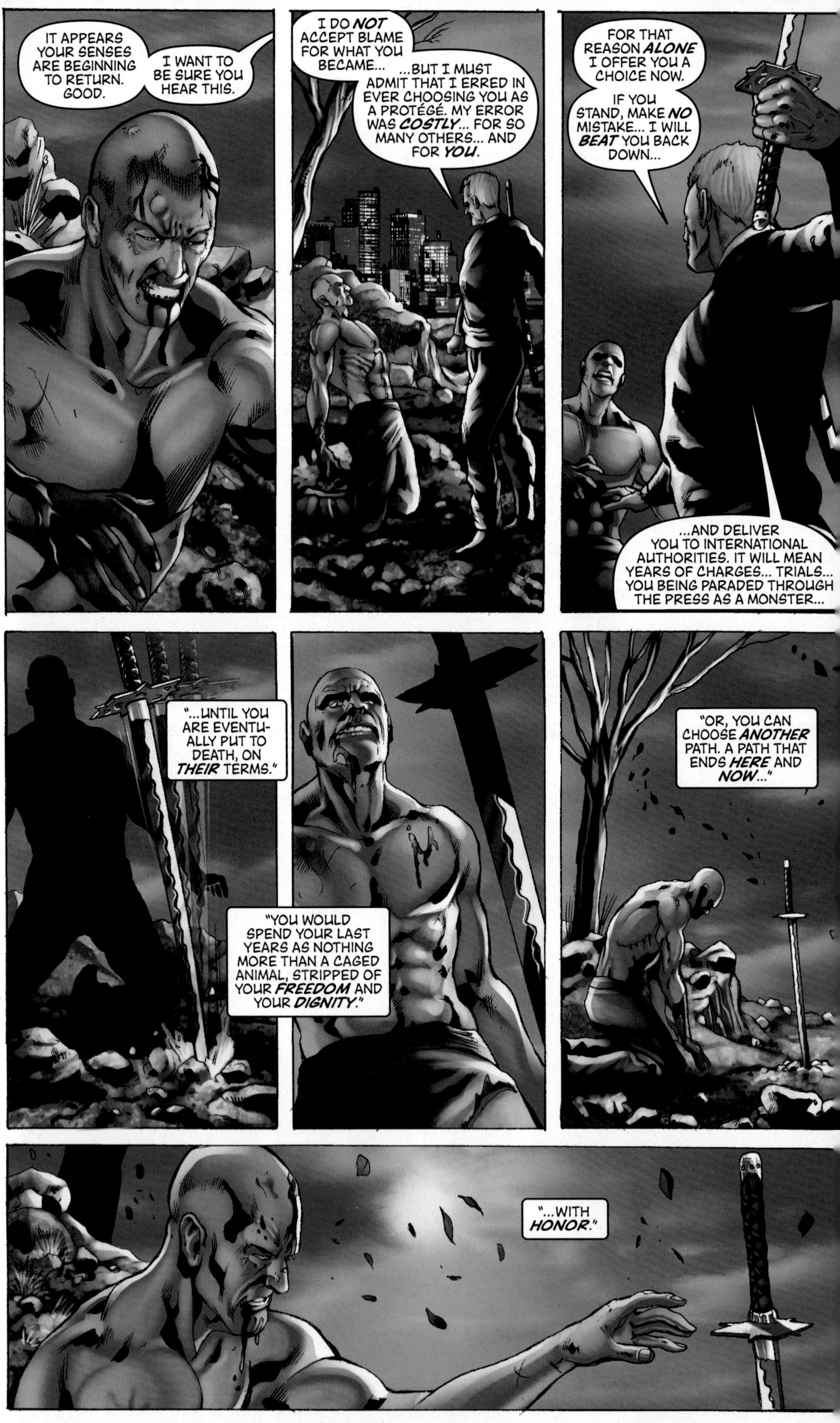
IT APPEARS YOUR SENSES ARE BEGINNING TO RETURN. GOOD.
I WANT TO BE SURE YOU HEAR THIS.
I DO NOT ACCEPT BLAME FOR WHAT YOU BECAME...
...BUT I MUST ADMIT THAT I ERRED IN EVER CHOOSING YOU AS A PROTÉGÉ. MY ERROR WAS COSTLY... FOR SO MANY OTHERS... AND FOR YOU.
FOR THAT REASON ALONE I OFFER YOU A CHOICE NOW.
IF YOU STAND, MAKE NO MISTAKE... I WILL BEAT YOU BACK DOWN...
...AND DELIVER YOU TO INTERNATIONAL AUTHORITIES. IT WILL MEAN YEARS OF CHARGES... TRIALS... YOU BEING PARADED THROUGH THE PRESS AS A MONSTER...
"...UNTIL YOU ARE EVENTU-ALLY PUT TO DEATH, ON THEIR TERMS."
"YOU WOULD SPEND YOUR LAST YEARS AS NOTHING MORE THAN A CAGED ANIMAL, STRIPPED OF YOUR FREEDOM AND YOUR DIGNITY."
"OR, YOU CAN CHOOSE ANOTHER PATH. A PATH THAT ENDS HERE AND NOW..."
"...WITH HONOR."

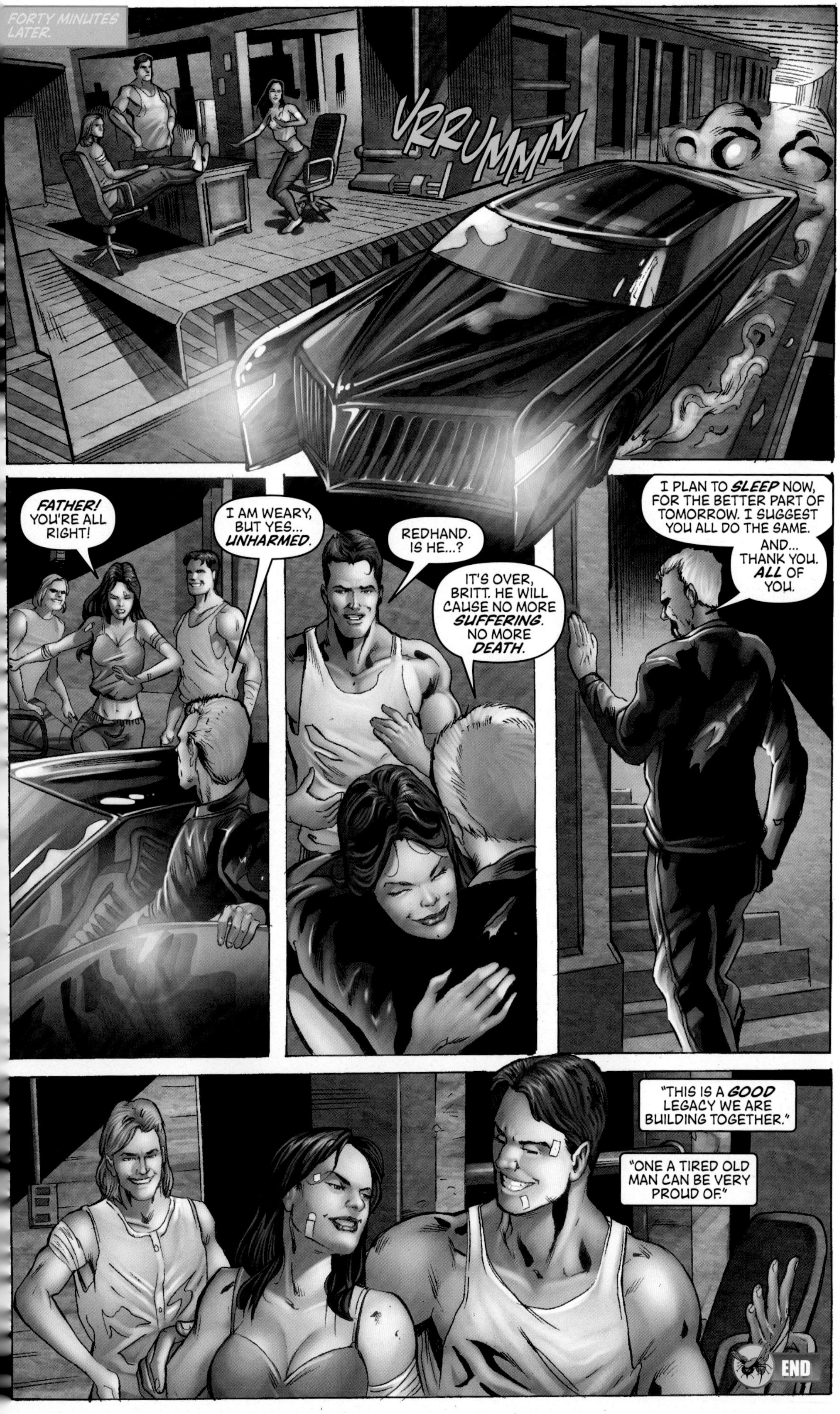

FORTY MINUTES LATER.
VRRUMMMM
FATHER! YOU'RE ALL RIGHT!
I AM WEARY, BUT YES... UNHARMED.
REDHAND. IS HE...?
IT'S OVER, BRITT. HE WILL CAUSE NO MORE SUFFERING. NO MORE DEATH.
I PLAN TO SLEEP NOW, FOR THE BETTER PART OF TOMORROW. I SUGGEST YOU ALL DO THE SAME.
AND... THANK YOU. ALL OF YOU.
"THIS IS A GOOD LEGACY WE ARE BUILDING TOGETHER."
"ONE A TIRED OLD MAN CAN BE VERY PROUD OF."
END

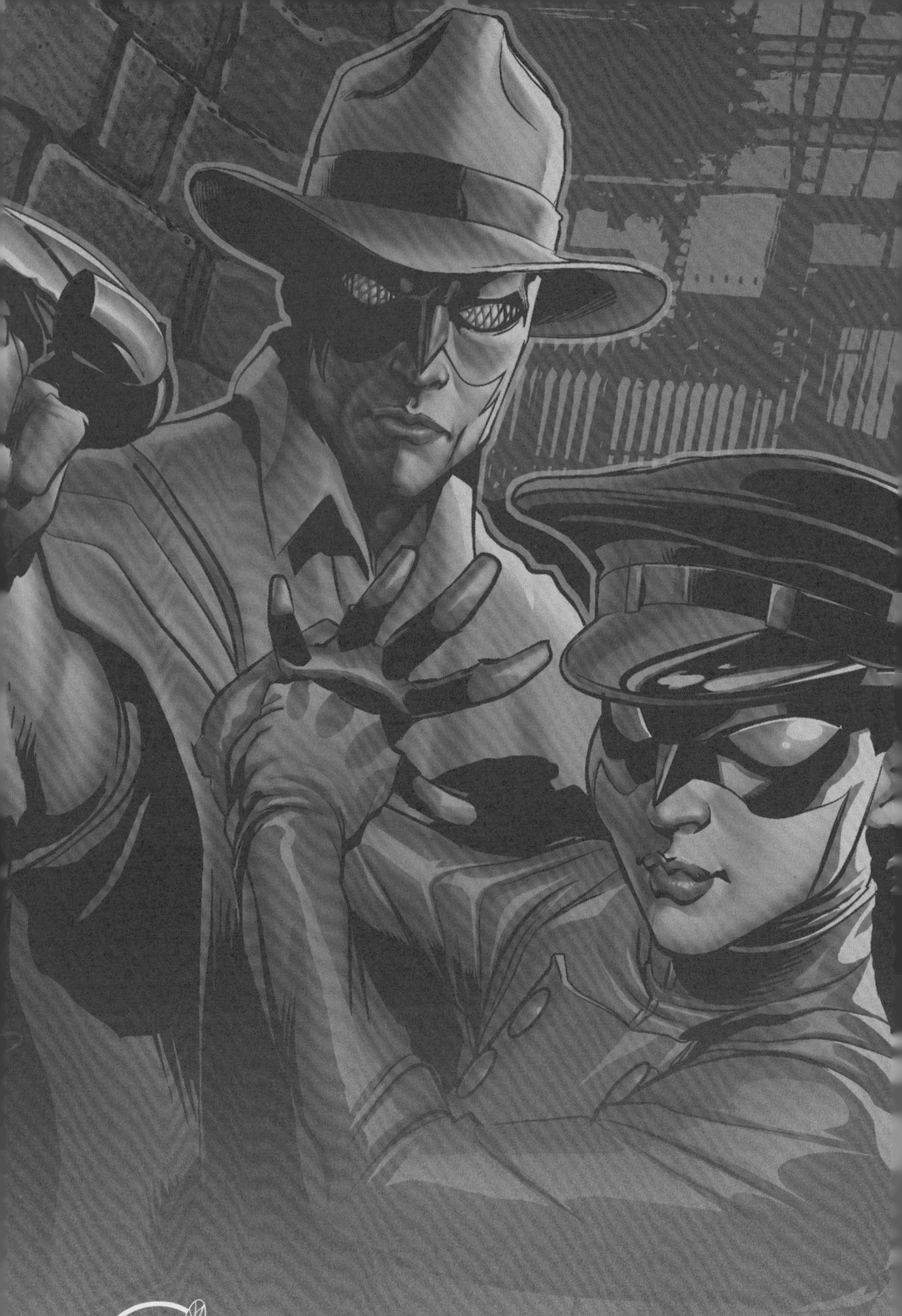

EPISODE TWENTY: LIKE MY FATHER BEFORE ME

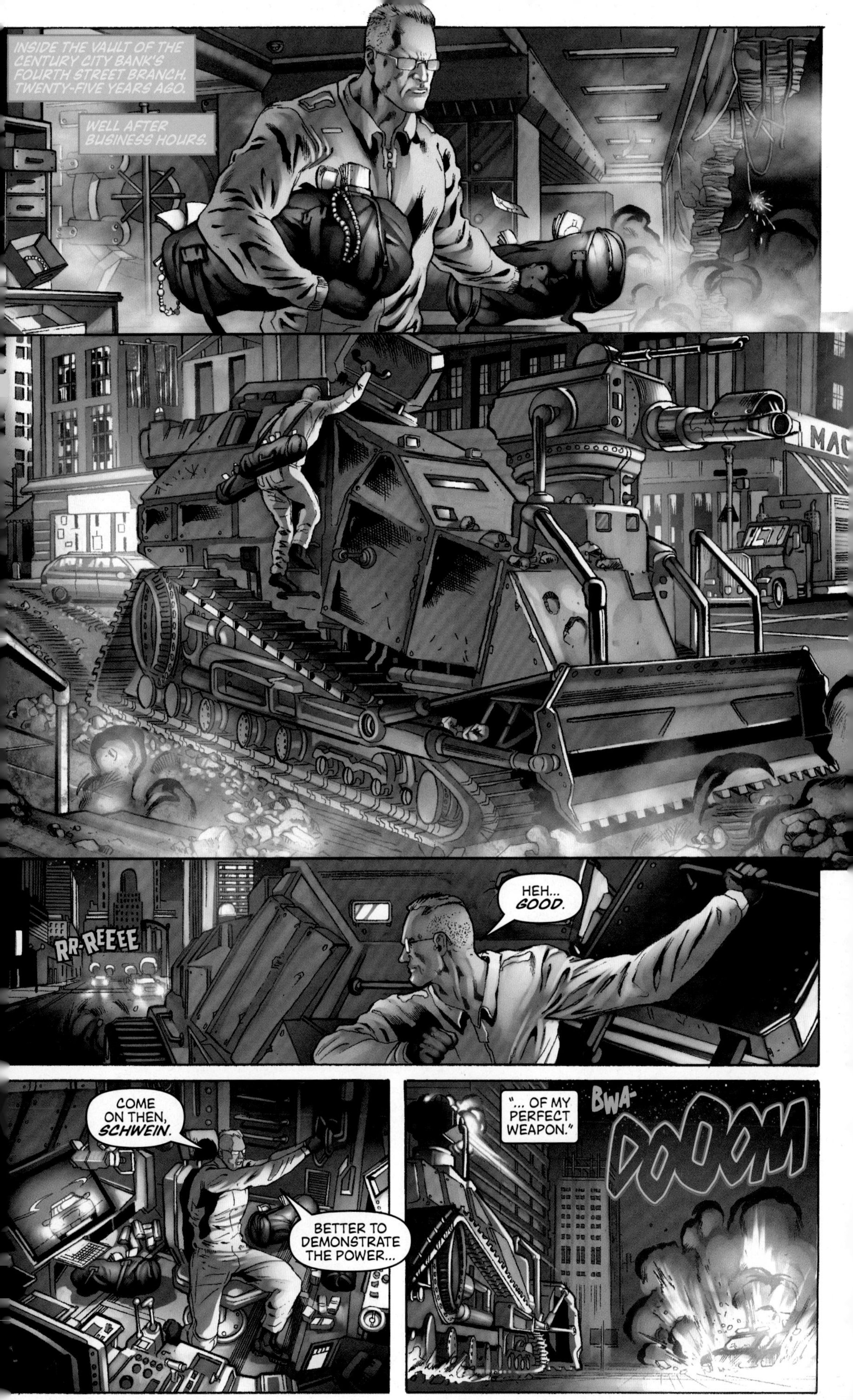

INSIDE THE VAULT OF THE CENTURY CITY BANK'S FOURTH STREET BRANCH. TWENTY-FIVE YEARS AGO.
WELL AFTER BUSINESS HOURS.
RR-REEEE
HEH... GOOD.
COME ON THEN, SCHWEIN.
BETTER TO DEMONSTRATE THE POWER...
"... OF MY PERFECT WEAPON."
BWA-DOOOM

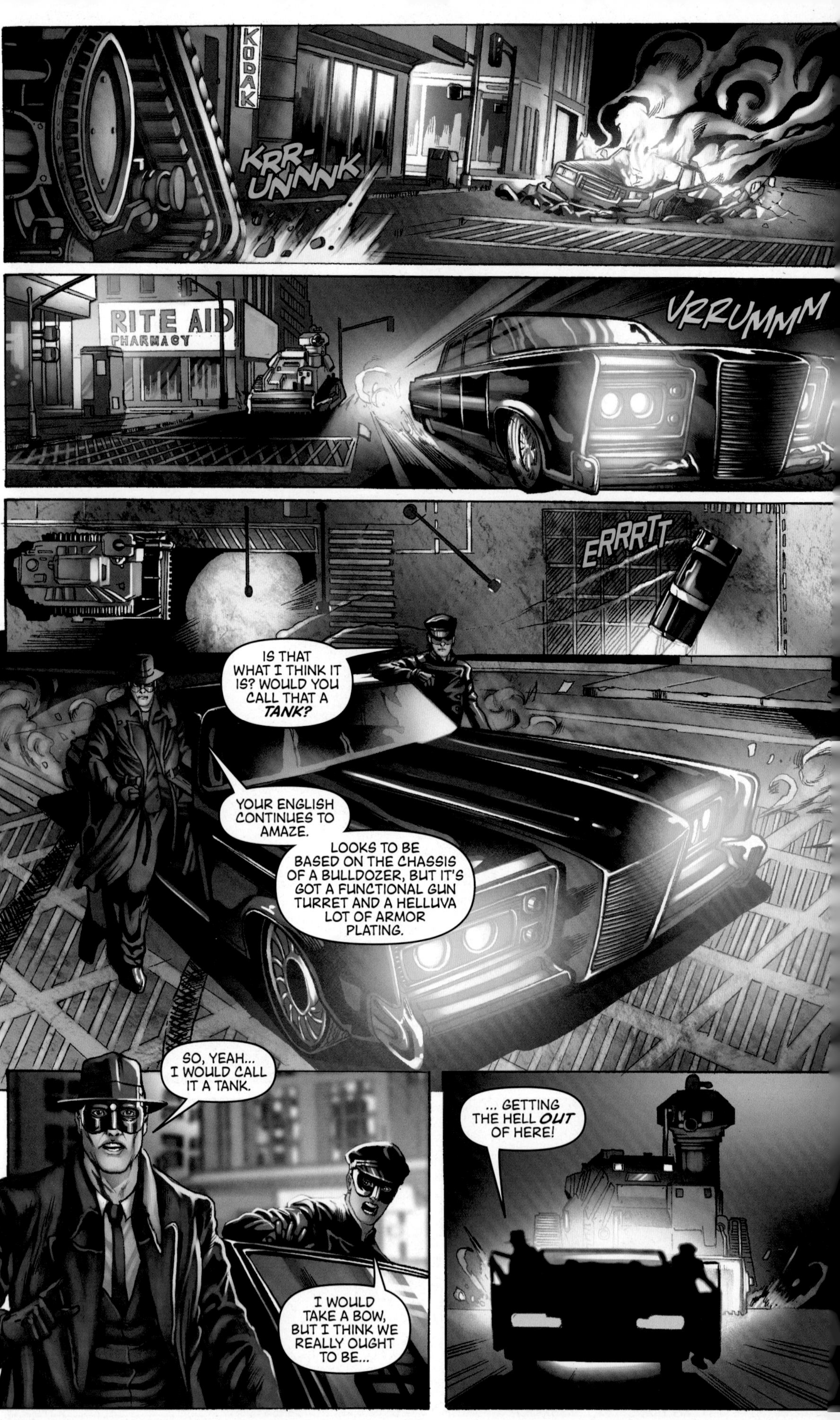
KODAK
KRR-UNNNK
RITE AID PHARMACY
VRRUMMM
ERRRTT
IS THAT WHAT I THINK IT IS? WOULD YOU CALL THAT A *TANK?*
YOUR ENGLISH CONTINUES TO AMAZE.
LOOKS TO BE BASED ON THE CHASSIS OF A BULLDOZER, BUT IT'S GOT A FUNCTIONAL GUN TURRET AND A HELLUVA LOT OF ARMOR PLATING.
SO, YEAH... I WOULD CALL IT A TANK.
I WOULD TAKE A BOW, BUT I THINK WE REALLY OUGHT TO BE...
... GETTING THE HELL *OUT* OF HERE!

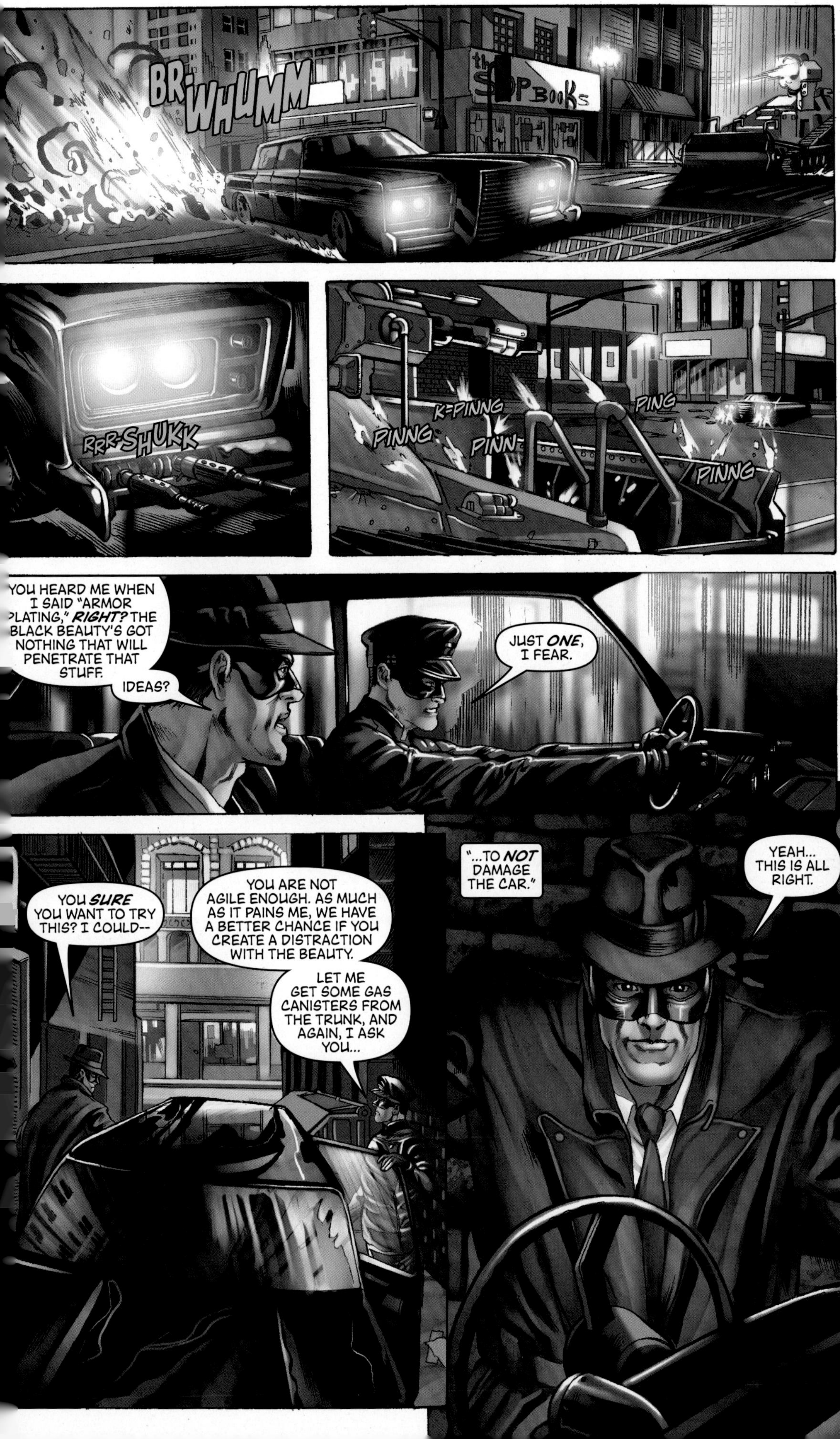
BR-WHUMM
THE SOP BOOKS
RRR-SHUKK
PING
K-PINNG
PINN
PING
PINNG
YOU HEARD ME WHEN I SAID "ARMOR PLATING," RIGHT? THE BLACK BEAUTY'S GOT NOTHING THAT WILL PENETRATE THAT STUFF.
IDEAS?
JUST ONE, I FEAR.
YOU SURE YOU WANT TO TRY THIS? I COULD--
YOU ARE NOT AGILE ENOUGH. AS MUCH AS IT PAINS ME, WE HAVE A BETTER CHANCE IF YOU CREATE A DISTRACTION WITH THE BEAUTY.
LET ME GET SOME GAS CANISTERS FROM THE TRUNK, AND AGAIN, I ASK YOU...
"...TO NOT DAMAGE THE CAR."
YEAH... THIS IS ALL RIGHT.

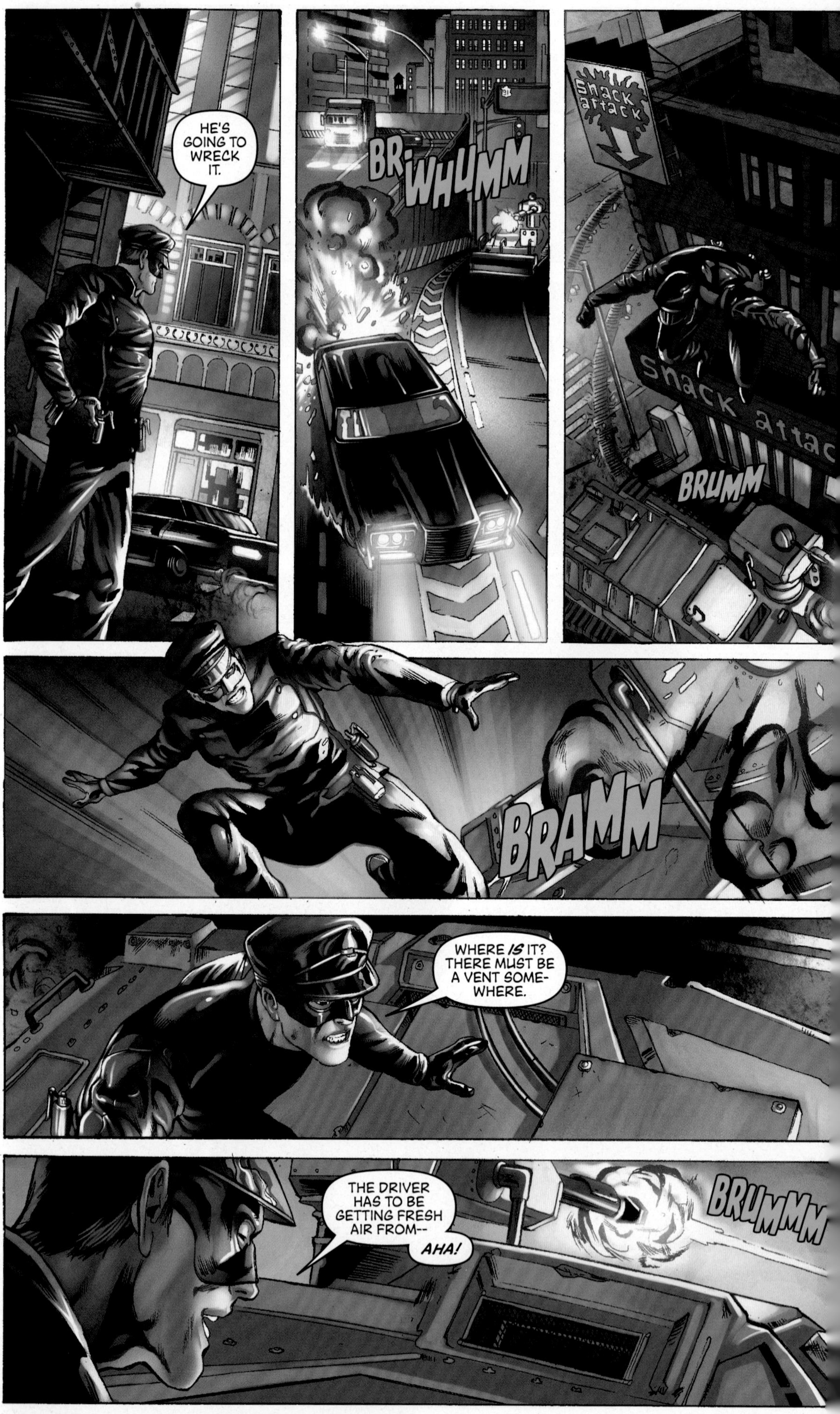
HE'S GOING TO WRECK IT.
BR-WHUMM
snack attack
snack attac
BRUMM
BRAMM
WHERE *IS* IT? THERE MUST BE A VENT SOMEWHERE.
THE DRIVER HAS TO BE GETTING FRESH AIR FROM--
AHA!
BRUMMM

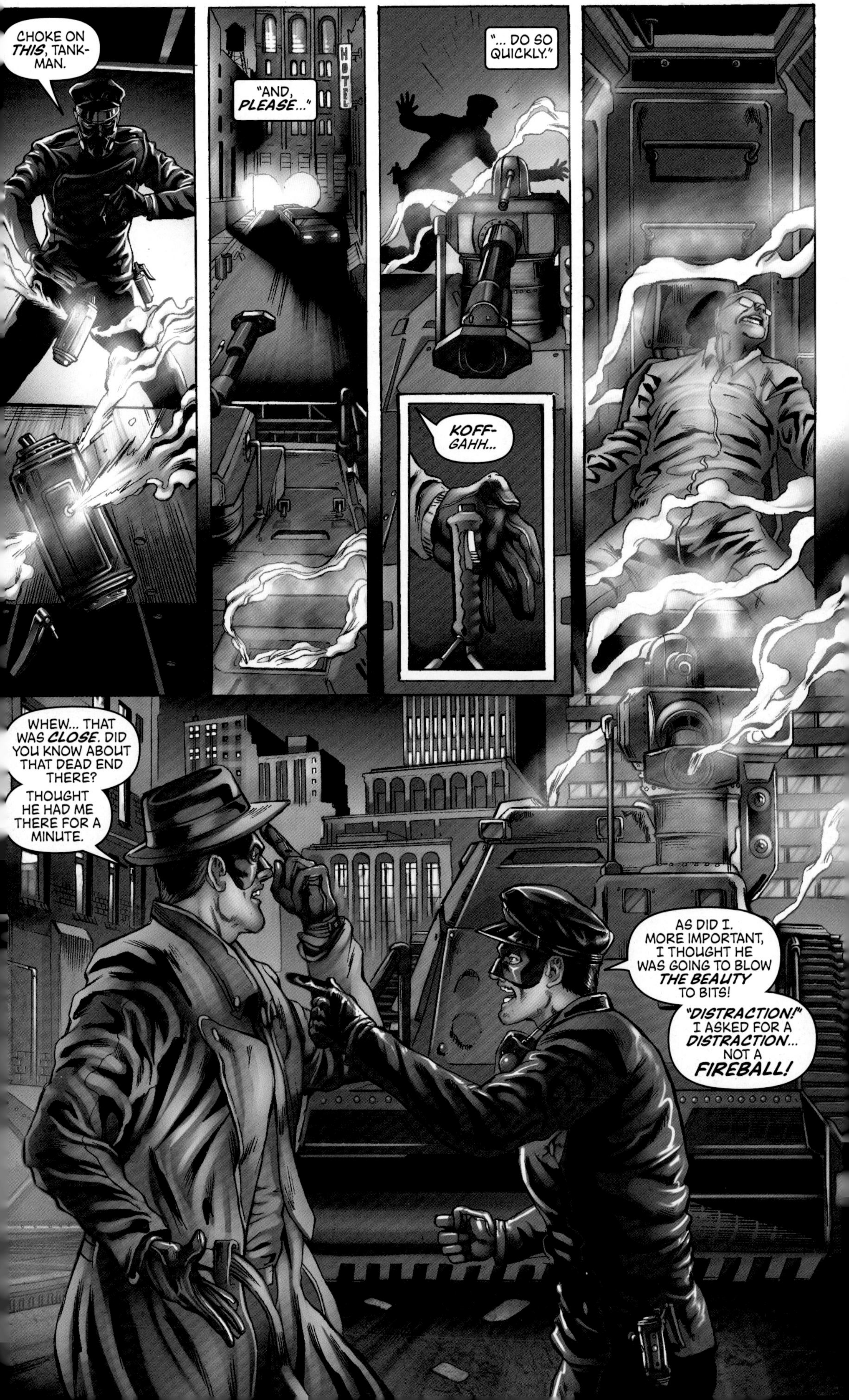

CHOKE ON *THIS*, TANK-MAN.
"AND, *PLEASE*..."
"... DO SO QUICKLY."
KOFF-GAHH...
WHEW... THAT WAS *CLOSE*. DID YOU KNOW ABOUT THAT DEAD END THERE?
THOUGHT HE HAD ME THERE FOR A MINUTE.
AS DID I. MORE IMPORTANT, I THOUGHT HE WAS GOING TO BLOW *THE BEAUTY* TO BITS!
"DISTRACTION!" I ASKED FOR A *DISTRACTION*... NOT A *FIREBALL!*

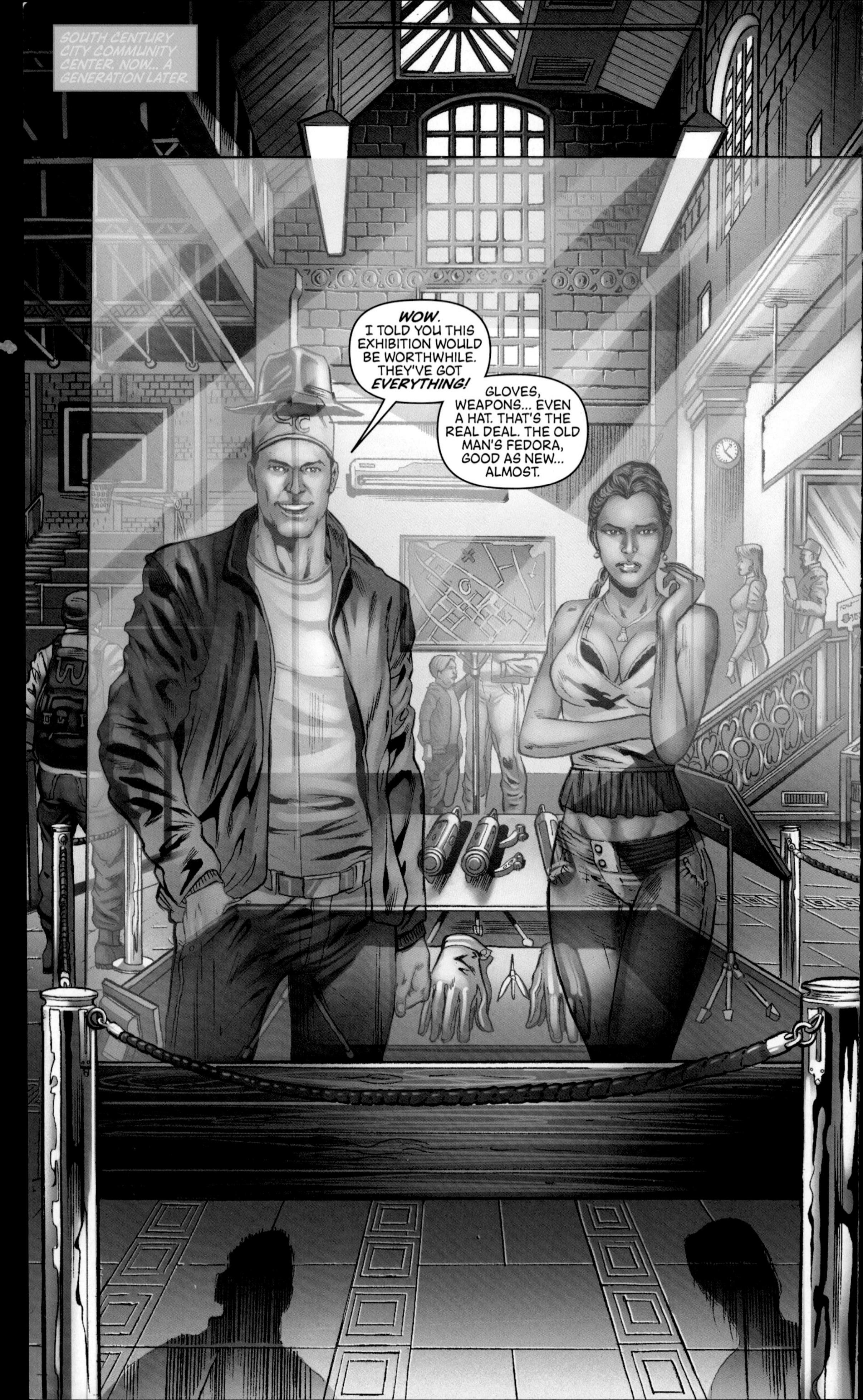
SOUTH CENTURY CITY COMMUNITY CENTER. NOW... A GENERATION LATER.
WOW. I TOLD YOU THIS EXHIBITION WOULD BE WORTHWHILE. THEY'VE GOT EVERYTHING!
GLOVES, WEAPONS... EVEN A HAT. THAT'S THE REAL DEAL. THE OLD MAN'S FEDORA, GOOD AS NEW... ALMOST.

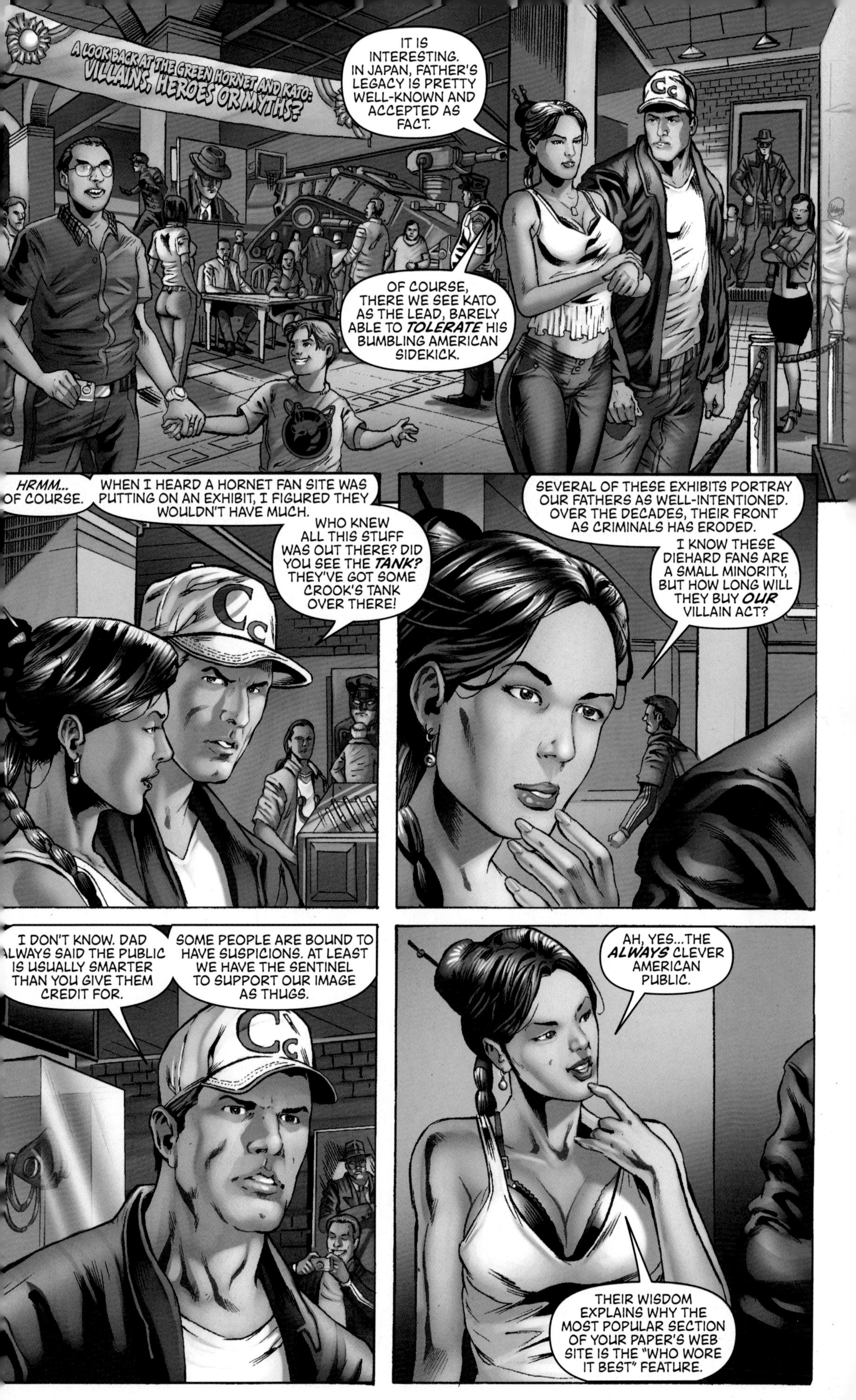
A LOOK BACK AT THE GREEN HORNET AND KATO:
VILLAINS, HEROES OR MYTHS?
IT IS INTERESTING. IN JAPAN, FATHER'S LEGACY IS PRETTY WELL-KNOWN AND ACCEPTED AS FACT.
OF COURSE, THERE WE SEE KATO AS THE LEAD, BARELY ABLE TO TOLERATE HIS BUMBLING AMERICAN SIDEKICK.
HRMM... OF COURSE.
WHEN I HEARD A HORNET FAN SITE WAS PUTTING ON AN EXHIBIT, I FIGURED THEY WOULDN'T HAVE MUCH.
WHO KNEW ALL THIS STUFF WAS OUT THERE? DID YOU SEE THE TANK? THEY'VE GOT SOME CROOK'S TANK OVER THERE!
SEVERAL OF THESE EXHIBITS PORTRAY OUR FATHERS AS WELL-INTENTIONED. OVER THE DECADES, THEIR FRONT AS CRIMINALS HAS ERODED.
I KNOW THESE DIEHARD FANS ARE A SMALL MINORITY, BUT HOW LONG WILL THEY BUY OUR VILLAIN ACT?
I DON'T KNOW. DAD ALWAYS SAID THE PUBLIC IS USUALLY SMARTER THAN YOU GIVE THEM CREDIT FOR.
SOME PEOPLE ARE BOUND TO HAVE SUSPICIONS. AT LEAST WE HAVE THE SENTINEL TO SUPPORT OUR IMAGE AS THUGS.
AH, YES...THE ALWAYS CLEVER AMERICAN PUBLIC.
THEIR WISDOM EXPLAINS WHY THE MOST POPULAR SECTION OF YOUR PAPER'S WEB SITE IS THE "WHO WORE IT BEST" FEATURE.

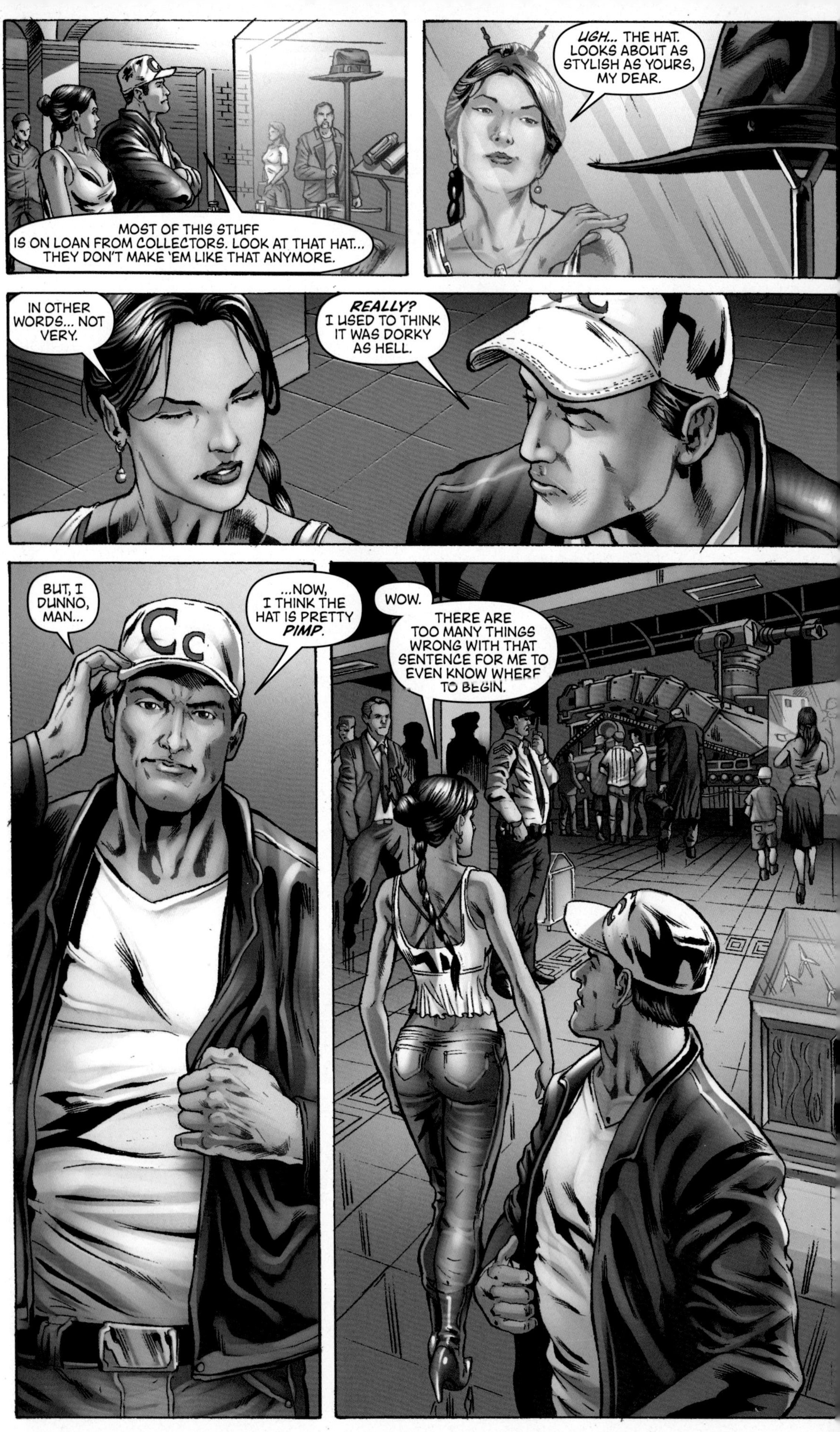
MOST OF THIS STUFF IS ON LOAN FROM COLLECTORS. LOOK AT THAT HAT... THEY DON'T MAKE 'EM LIKE THAT ANYMORE.
UGH... THE HAT. LOOKS ABOUT AS STYLISH AS YOURS, MY DEAR.
IN OTHER WORDS... NOT VERY.
REALLY? I USED TO THINK IT WAS DORKY AS HELL.
BUT, I DUNNO, MAN...
...NOW, I THINK THE HAT IS PRETTY PIMP.
WOW.
THERE ARE TOO MANY THINGS WRONG WITH THAT SENTENCE FOR ME TO EVEN KNOW WHERE TO BEGIN.

THE HAT IS CUTTING EDGE! LIDS ARE COMING BACK. YOU SEE GQ LAST MONTH?

NO, BUT BY ALL MEANS, KEEP *YELLING* ABOUT IT. *VERY* INCOGNITO.

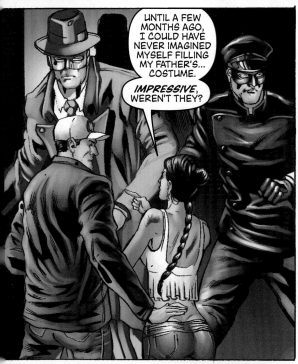

UNTIL A FEW MONTHS AGO, I COULD HAVE NEVER IMAGINED MYSELF FILLING MY FATHER'S... COSTUME.

IMPRESSIVE, WEREN'T THEY?

YEAH.

YOU THINK THEY WOULD HAVE HAD THEIR ASSES HANDED TO THEM BY REDHAND?

WELL, I *DID* LAST SEVERAL MINUTES AGAINST HIM, AFTER A WEEK'S HOSPITAL STAY AND FIGHTING MY WAY THROUGH A WHOLE BUILDING OF NINJAS.

HOW LONG DID *YOU* MANAGE TO HOLD OUT AGAINST REDHAND, AGAIN?

SNEAKY BASTARD CAUGHT ME *OFF-GUARD!*

LESSON *LEARNED*. TRUST ME, THAT IS *NOT* GOING TO HAPPEN--

...A-MUHHH...

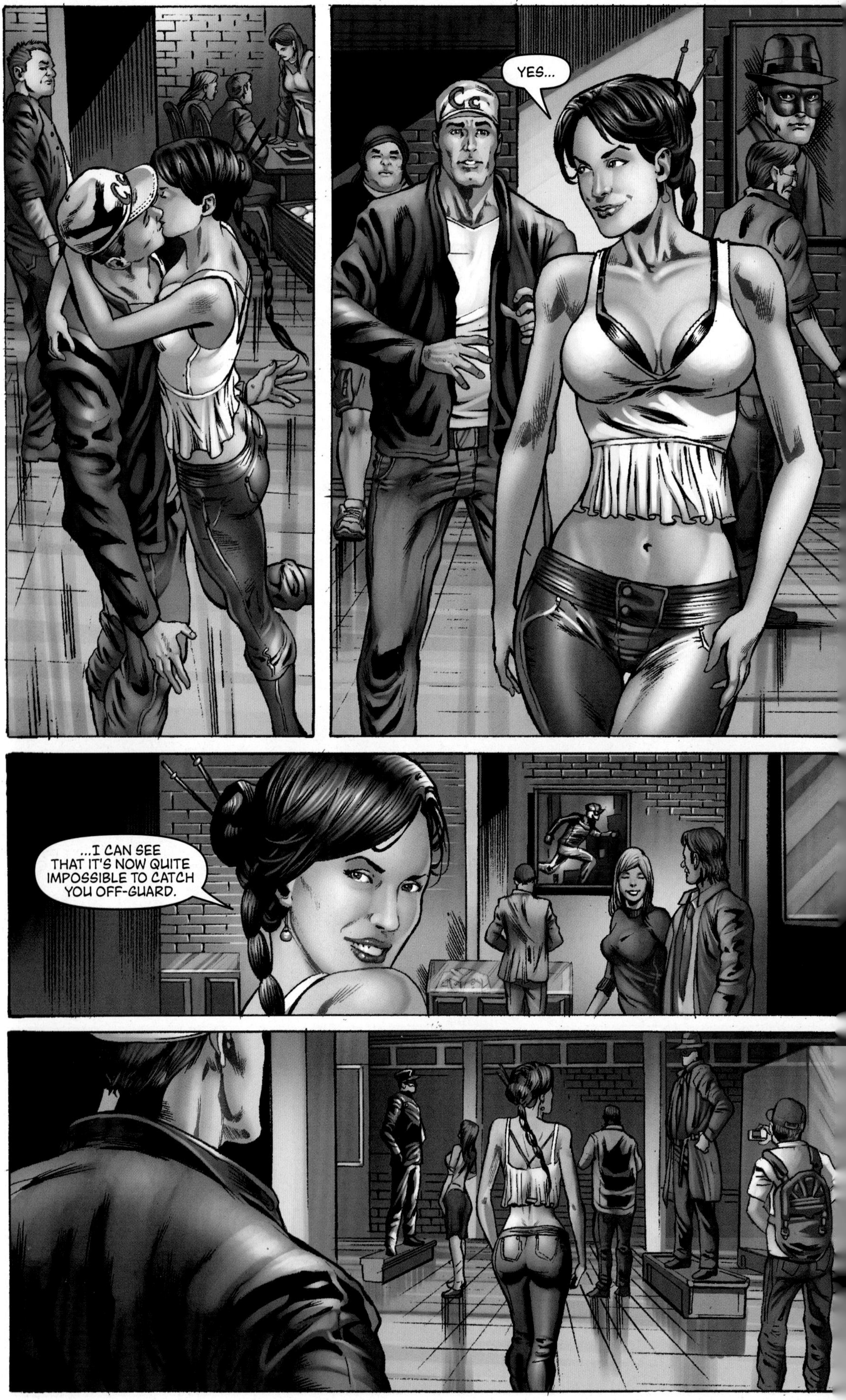
YES...
...I CAN SEE THAT IT'S NOW QUITE IMPOSSIBLE TO CATCH YOU OFF-GUARD.

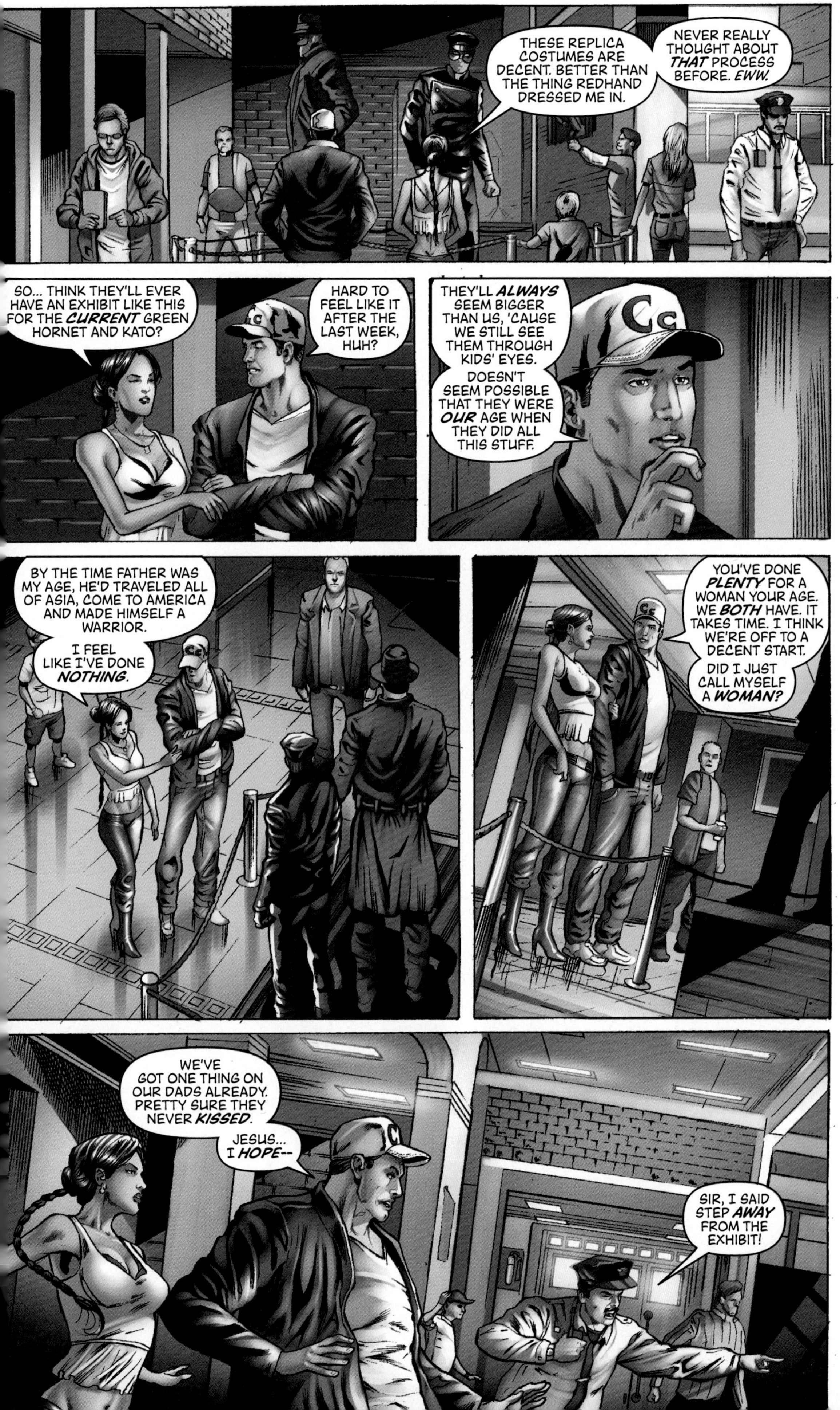
THESE REPLICA COSTUMES ARE DECENT. BETTER THAN THE THING REDHAND DRESSED ME IN.
NEVER REALLY THOUGHT ABOUT *THAT* PROCESS BEFORE. *EWW.*
SO... THINK THEY'LL EVER HAVE AN EXHIBIT LIKE THIS FOR THE *CURRENT* GREEN HORNET AND KATO?
HARD TO FEEL LIKE IT AFTER THE LAST WEEK, HUH?
THEY'LL *ALWAYS* SEEM BIGGER THAN US, 'CAUSE WE STILL SEE THEM THROUGH KIDS' EYES.
DOESN'T SEEM POSSIBLE THAT THEY WERE *OUR* AGE WHEN THEY DID ALL THIS STUFF.
BY THE TIME FATHER WAS MY AGE, HE'D TRAVELED ALL OF ASIA, COME TO AMERICA AND MADE HIMSELF A WARRIOR.
I FEEL LIKE I'VE DONE *NOTHING*.
YOU'VE DONE *PLENTY* FOR A WOMAN YOUR AGE. WE *BOTH* HAVE. IT TAKES TIME. I THINK WE'RE OFF TO A DECENT START.
DID I JUST CALL MYSELF A *WOMAN?*
WE'VE GOT ONE THING ON OUR DADS ALREADY. PRETTY SURE THEY NEVER *KISSED*.
JESUS... I *HOPE*--
SIR, I SAID STEP *AWAY* FROM THE EXHIBIT!

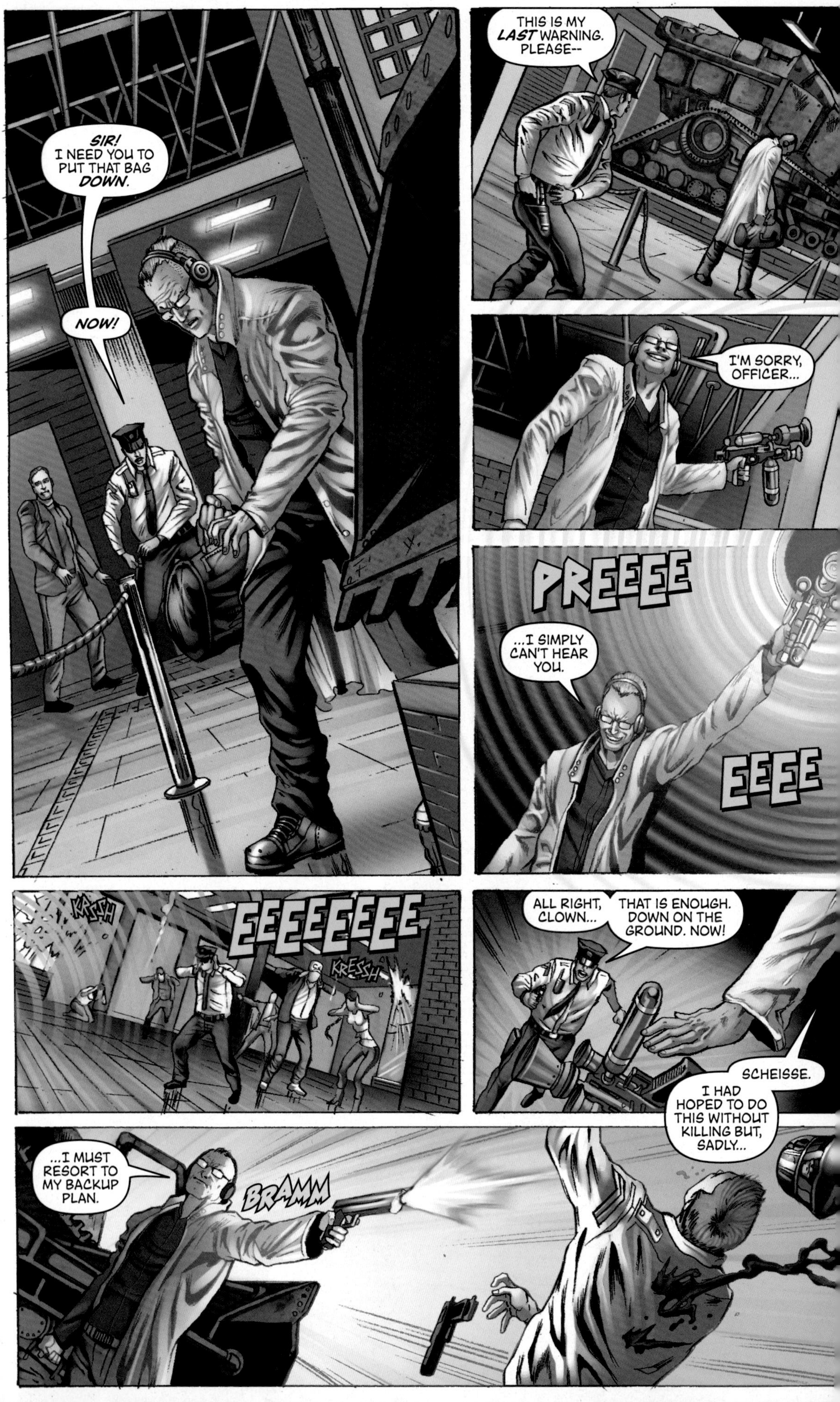
SIR! I NEED YOU TO PUT THAT BAG DOWN.
NOW!
THIS IS MY LAST WARNING. PLEASE--
I'M SORRY, OFFICER...
PREEEE
...I SIMPLY CAN'T HEAR YOU.
EEEE
KRASH
EEEEEEEE
KRESSH
ALL RIGHT, CLOWN...
THAT IS ENOUGH. DOWN ON THE GROUND. NOW!
SCHEISSE.
I HAD HOPED TO DO THIS WITHOUT KILLING BUT, SADLY...
...I MUST RESORT TO MY BACKUP PLAN.
BRAMM

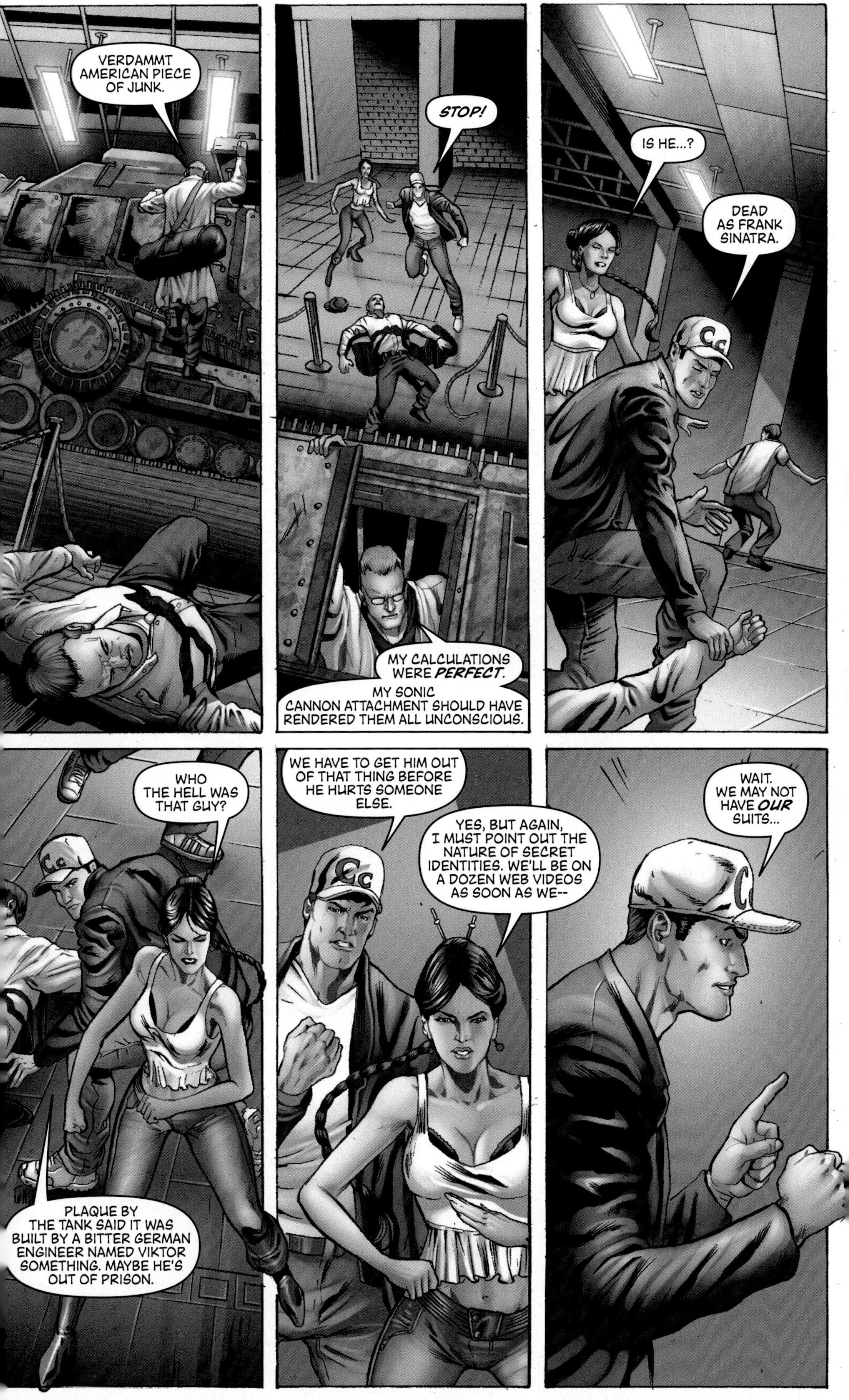
VERDAMMT AMERICAN PIECE OF JUNK.
STOP!
MY CALCULATIONS WERE *PERFECT*.
MY SONIC CANNON ATTACHMENT SHOULD HAVE RENDERED THEM ALL UNCONSCIOUS.
IS HE...?
DEAD AS FRANK SINATRA.
WHO THE HELL WAS THAT GUY?
PLAQUE BY THE TANK SAID IT WAS BUILT BY A BITTER GERMAN ENGINEER NAMED VIKTOR SOMETHING. MAYBE HE'S OUT OF PRISON.
WE HAVE TO GET HIM OUT OF THAT THING BEFORE HE HURTS SOMEONE ELSE.
YES, BUT AGAIN, I MUST POINT OUT THE NATURE OF SECRET IDENTITIES. WE'LL BE ON A DOZEN WEB VIDEOS AS SOON AS WE--
WAIT. WE MAY NOT HAVE *OUR* SUITS...

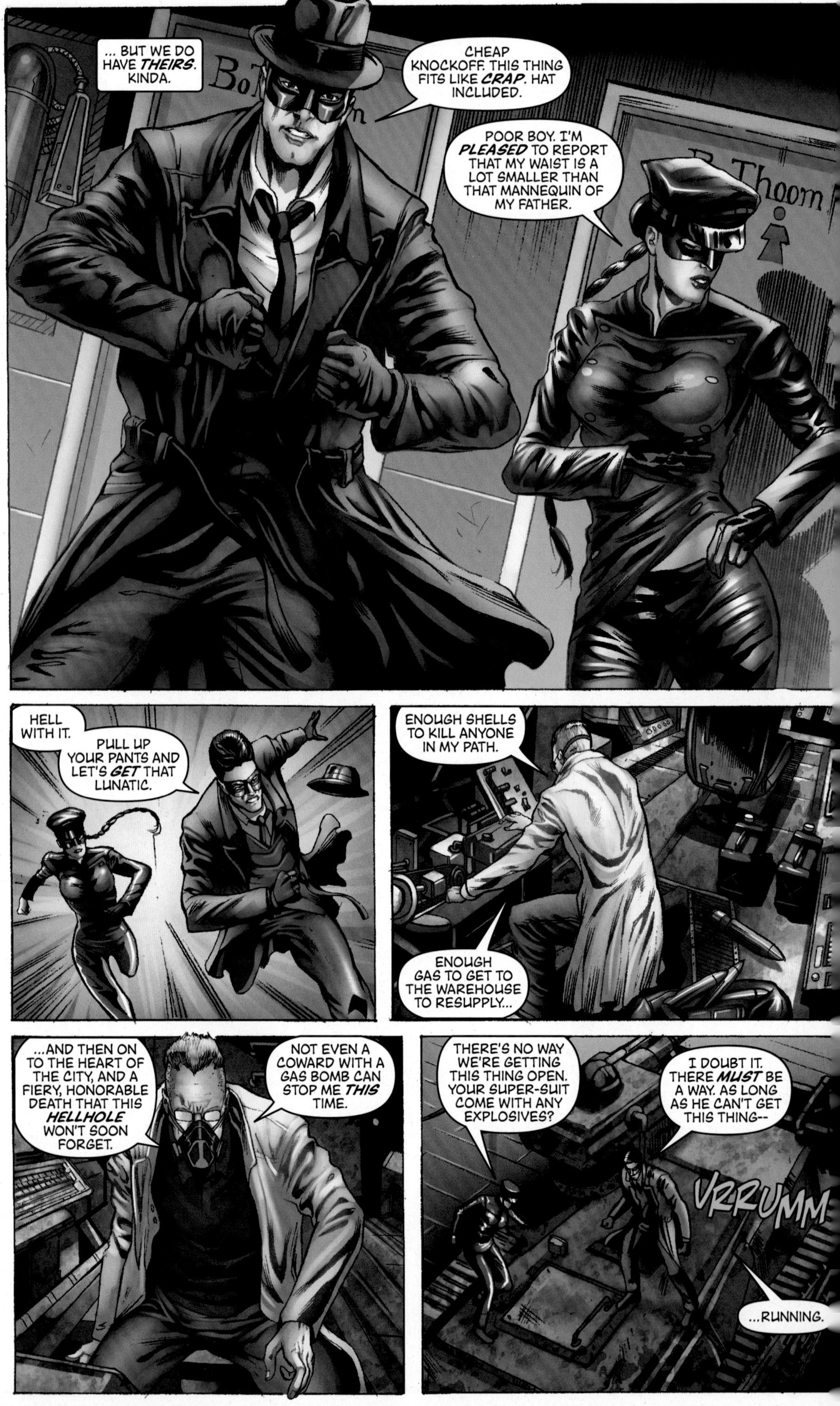

... BUT WE DO HAVE *THEIRS*. KINDA.
CHEAP KNOCKOFF. THIS THING FITS LIKE *CRAP*. HAT INCLUDED.
POOR BOY. I'M *PLEASED* TO REPORT THAT MY WAIST IS A LOT SMALLER THAN THAT MANNEQUIN OF MY FATHER.
HELL WITH IT.
PULL UP YOUR PANTS AND LET'S *GET* THAT LUNATIC.
ENOUGH SHELLS TO KILL ANYONE IN MY PATH.
ENOUGH GAS TO GET TO THE WAREHOUSE TO RESUPPLY...
...AND THEN ON TO THE HEART OF THE CITY, AND A FIERY, HONORABLE DEATH THAT THIS *HELLHOLE* WON'T SOON FORGET.
NOT EVEN A COWARD WITH A GAS BOMB CAN STOP ME *THIS* TIME.
THERE'S NO WAY WE'RE GETTING THIS THING OPEN. YOUR SUPER-SUIT COME WITH ANY EXPLOSIVES?
I DOUBT IT. THERE *MUST* BE A WAY. AS LONG AS HE CAN'T GET THIS THING--
VRRUMM
...RUNNING.

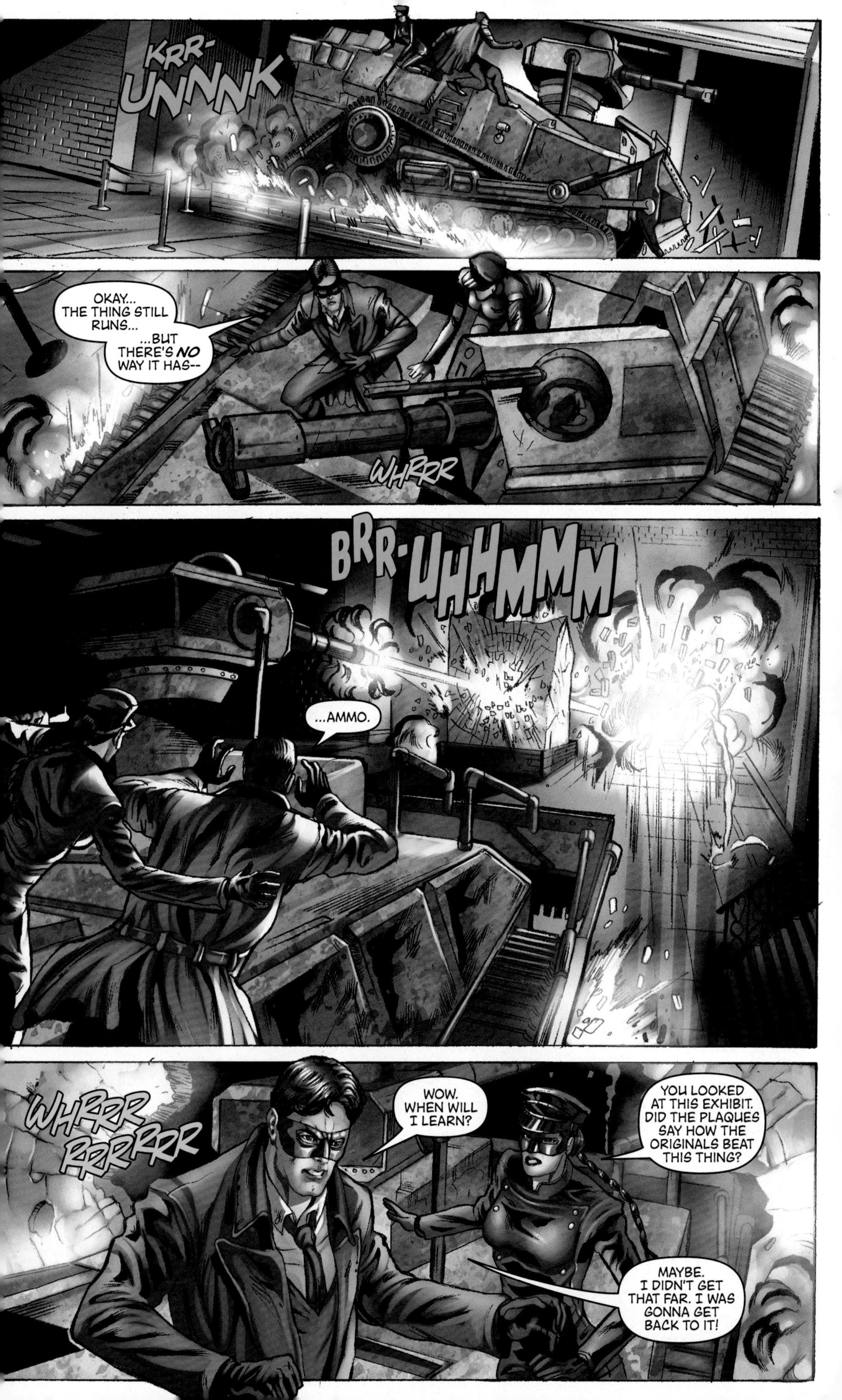
KRR-UNNNK
OKAY... THE THING STILL RUNS... ...BUT THERE'S NO WAY IT HAS--
WHRRR
BRR-UHHMMMM
...AMMO.
WHRRR RRRRRR
WOW. WHEN WILL I LEARN?
YOU LOOKED AT THIS EXHIBIT. DID THE PLAQUES SAY HOW THE ORIGINALS BEAT THIS THING?
MAYBE. I DIDN'T GET THAT FAR. I WAS GONNA GET BACK TO IT!

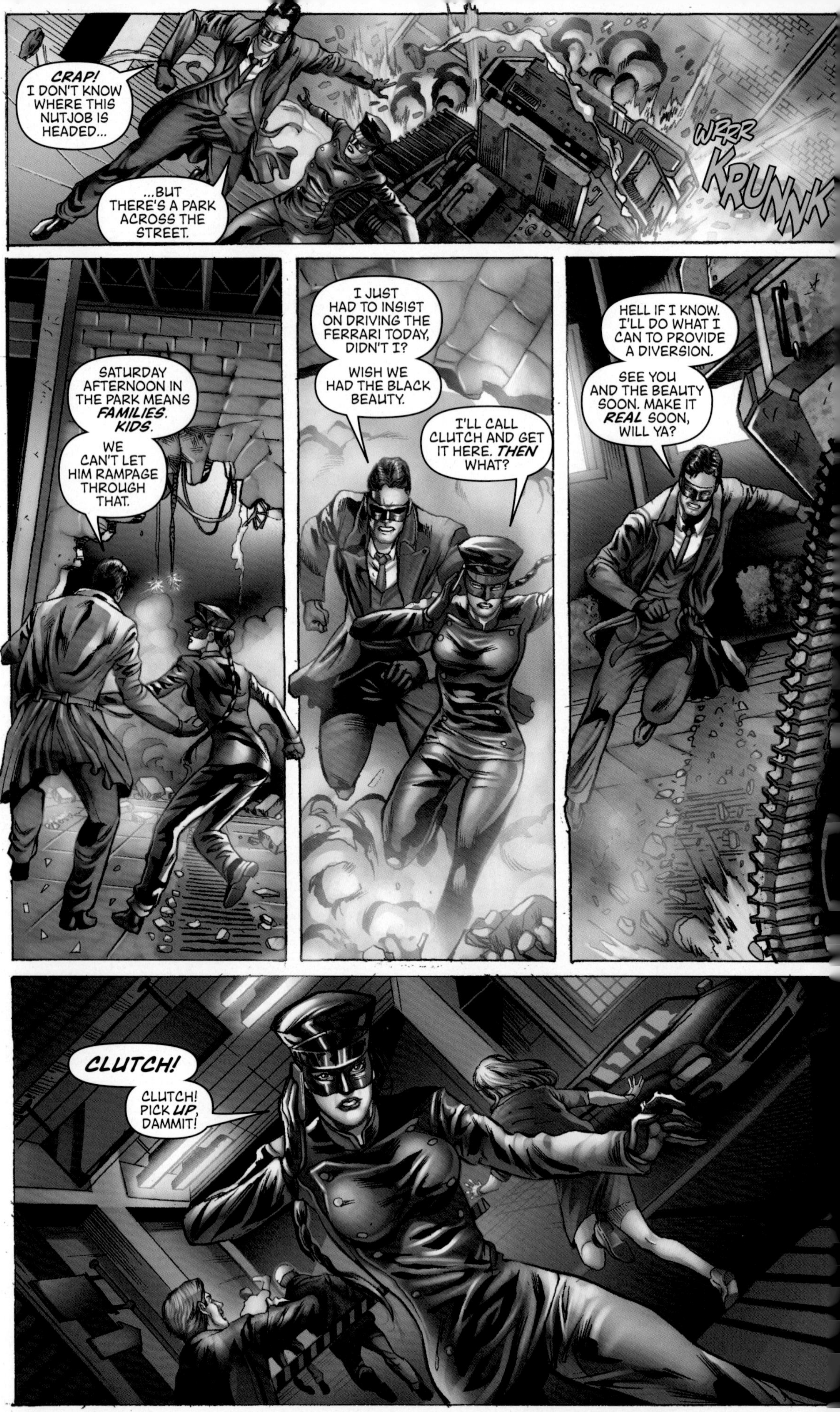

CRAP! I DON'T KNOW WHERE THIS NUTJOB IS HEADED...
...BUT THERE'S A PARK ACROSS THE STREET.
WRRR
KRUNNK
SATURDAY AFTERNOON IN THE PARK MEANS FAMILIES. KIDS.
WE CAN'T LET HIM RAMPAGE THROUGH THAT.
I JUST HAD TO INSIST ON DRIVING THE FERRARI TODAY, DIDN'T I?
WISH WE HAD THE BLACK BEAUTY.
I'LL CALL CLUTCH AND GET IT HERE. THEN WHAT?
HELL IF I KNOW. I'LL DO WHAT I CAN TO PROVIDE A DIVERSION.
SEE YOU AND THE BEAUTY SOON. MAKE IT REAL SOON, WILL YA?
CLUTCH!
CLUTCH! PICK UP, DAMMIT!

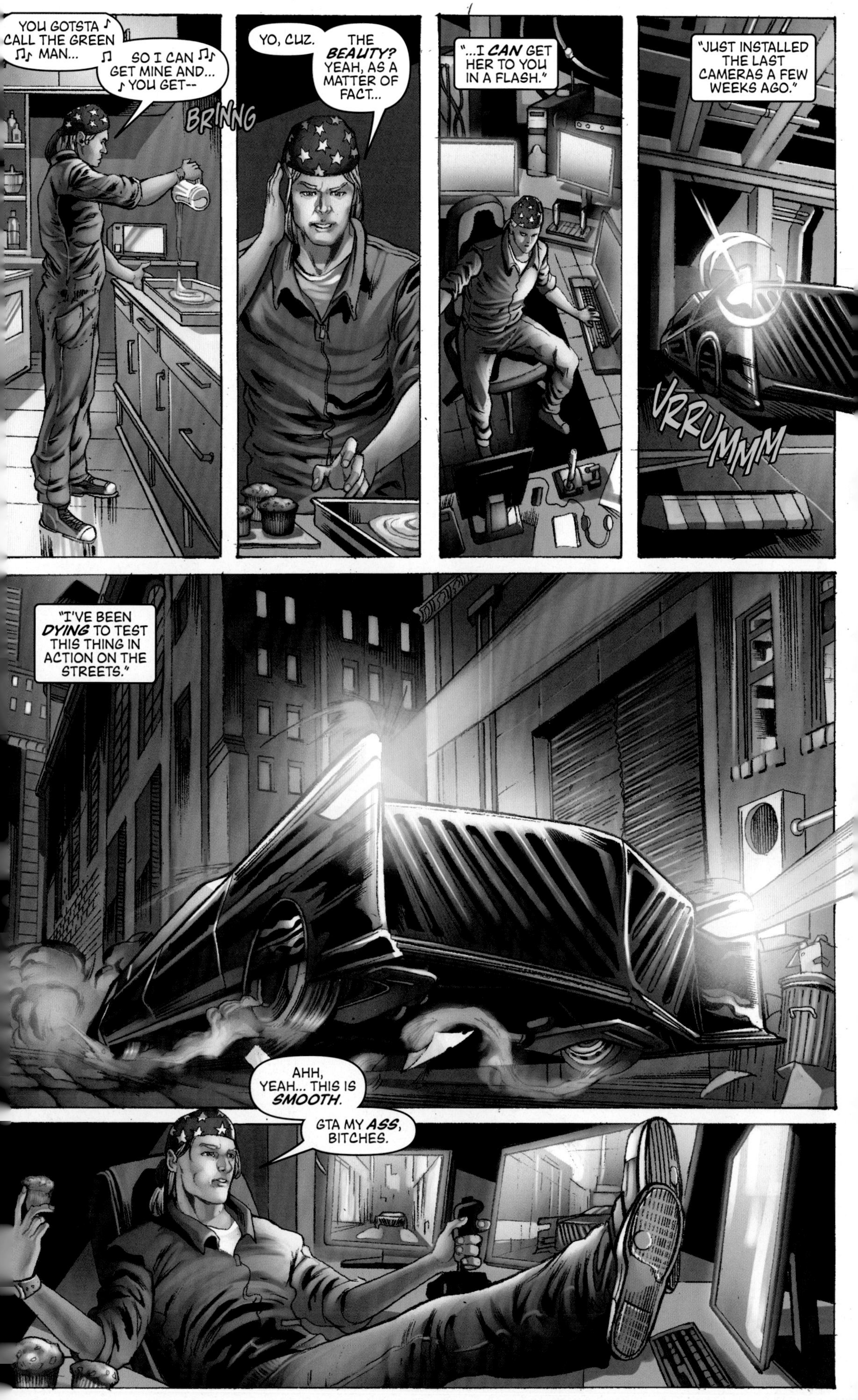

YOU GOTSTA ♪ CALL THE GREEN ♫ MAN... ♫
SO I CAN ♫ GET MINE AND... ♪ YOU GET--
BRINNG
YO, CUZ.
THE BEAUTY? YEAH, AS A MATTER OF FACT...
"...I CAN GET HER TO YOU IN A FLASH."
"JUST INSTALLED THE LAST CAMERAS A FEW WEEKS AGO."
VRRUMMM
"I'VE BEEN DYING TO TEST THIS THING IN ACTION ON THE STREETS."
AHH, YEAH... THIS IS SMOOTH.
GTA MY ASS, BITCHES.

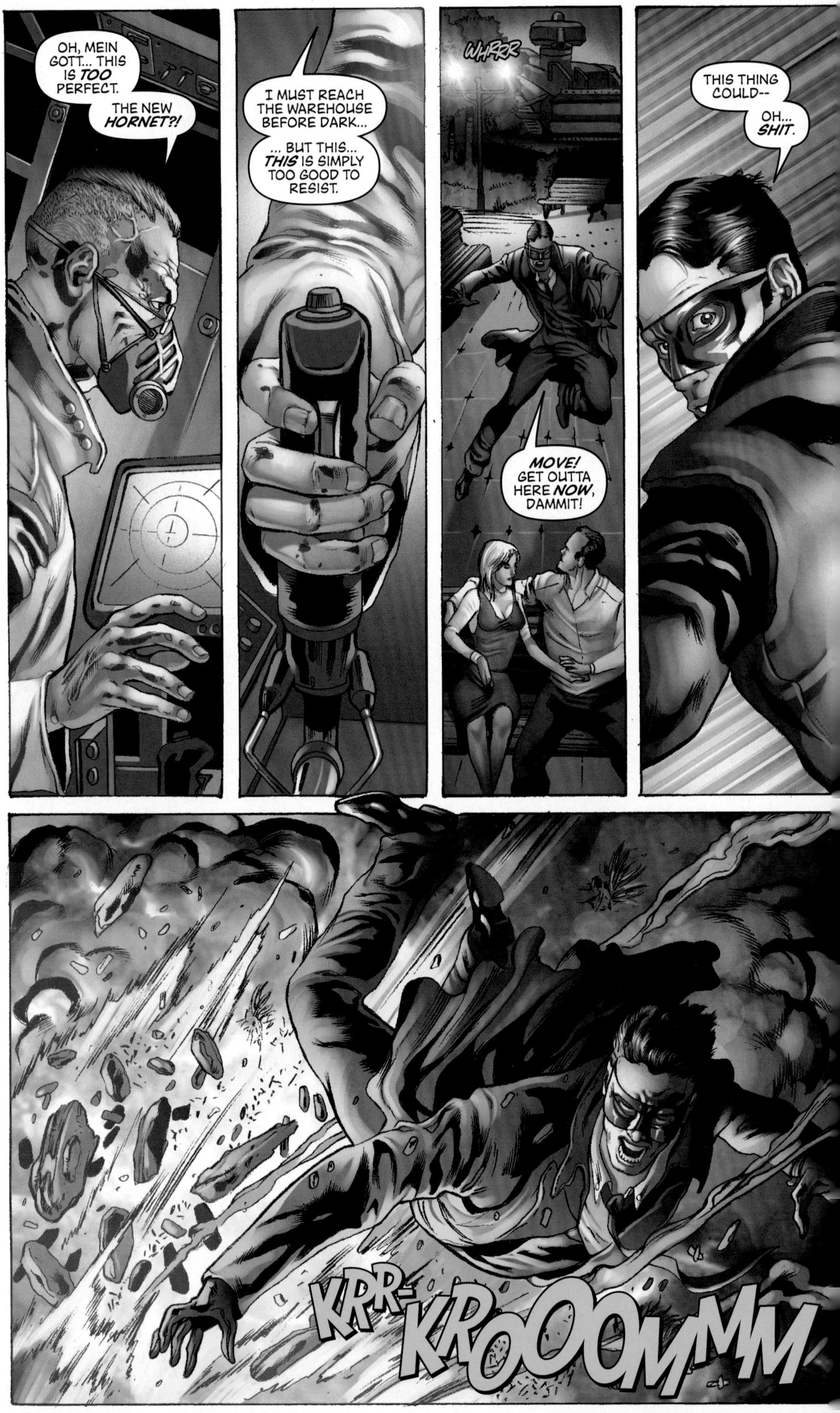
OH, MEIN GOTT... THIS IS TOO PERFECT.
THE NEW HORNET?!
I MUST REACH THE WAREHOUSE BEFORE DARK...
... BUT THIS... THIS IS SIMPLY TOO GOOD TO RESIST.
WHRRR
MOVE! GET OUTTA HERE NOW, DAMMIT!
THIS THING COULD--
OH... SHIT.
KRR-KROOOMMM

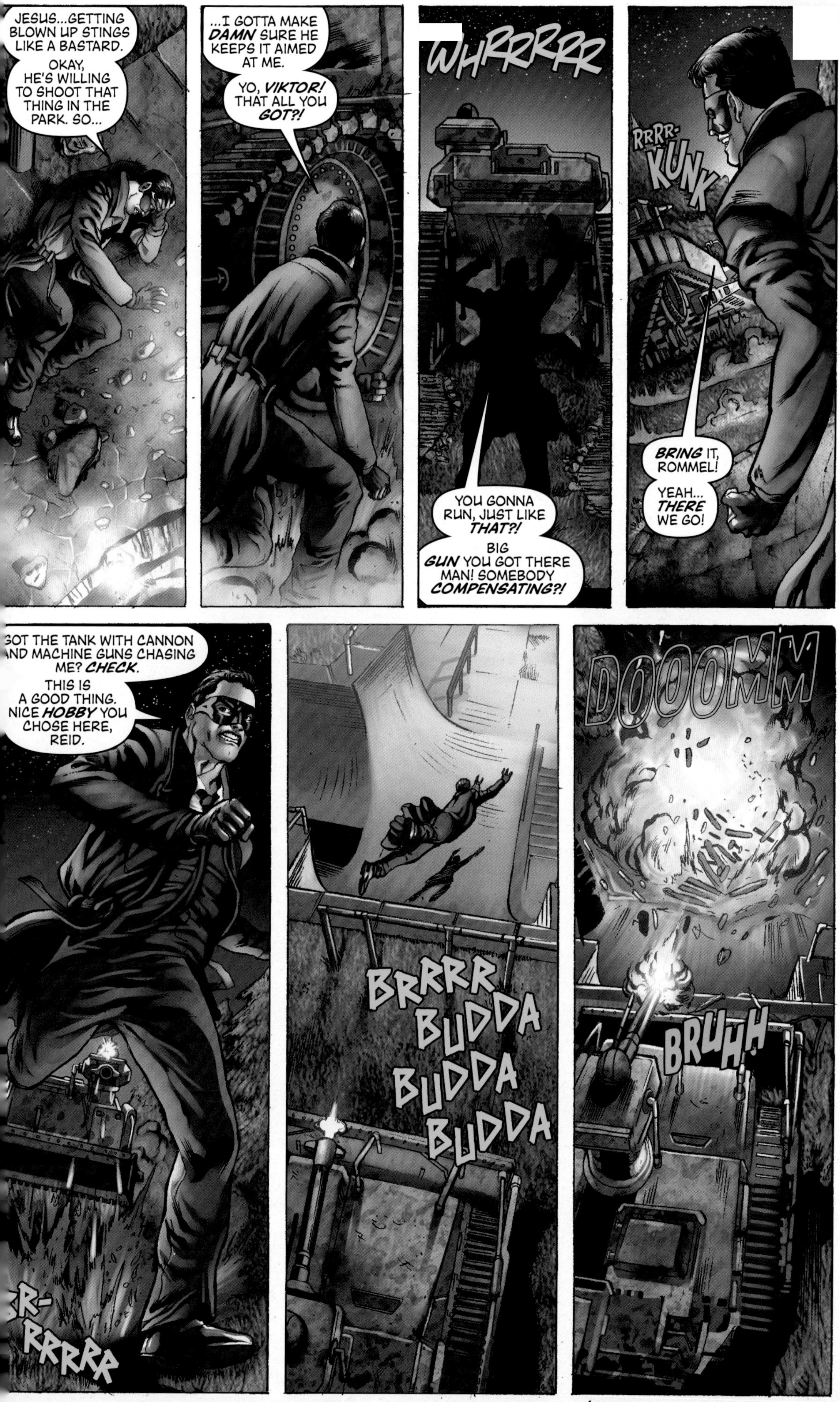

JESUS...GETTING BLOWN UP STINGS LIKE A BASTARD.
OKAY, HE'S WILLING TO SHOOT THAT THING IN THE PARK. SO...
...I GOTTA MAKE DAMN SURE HE KEEPS IT AIMED AT ME.
YO, VIKTOR! THAT ALL YOU GOT?!
WHRRRRR
YOU GONNA RUN, JUST LIKE THAT?!
BIG GUN YOU GOT THERE MAN! SOMEBODY COMPENSATING?!
RRRR-KUNK
BRING IT, ROMMEL!
YEAH... THERE WE GO!
GOT THE TANK WITH CANNON AND MACHINE GUNS CHASING ME? CHECK.
THIS IS A GOOD THING. NICE HOBBY YOU CHOSE HERE, REID.
R-RRRRR
BRRRR BUDDA BUDDA BUDDA
DOOOMM
BRUHH

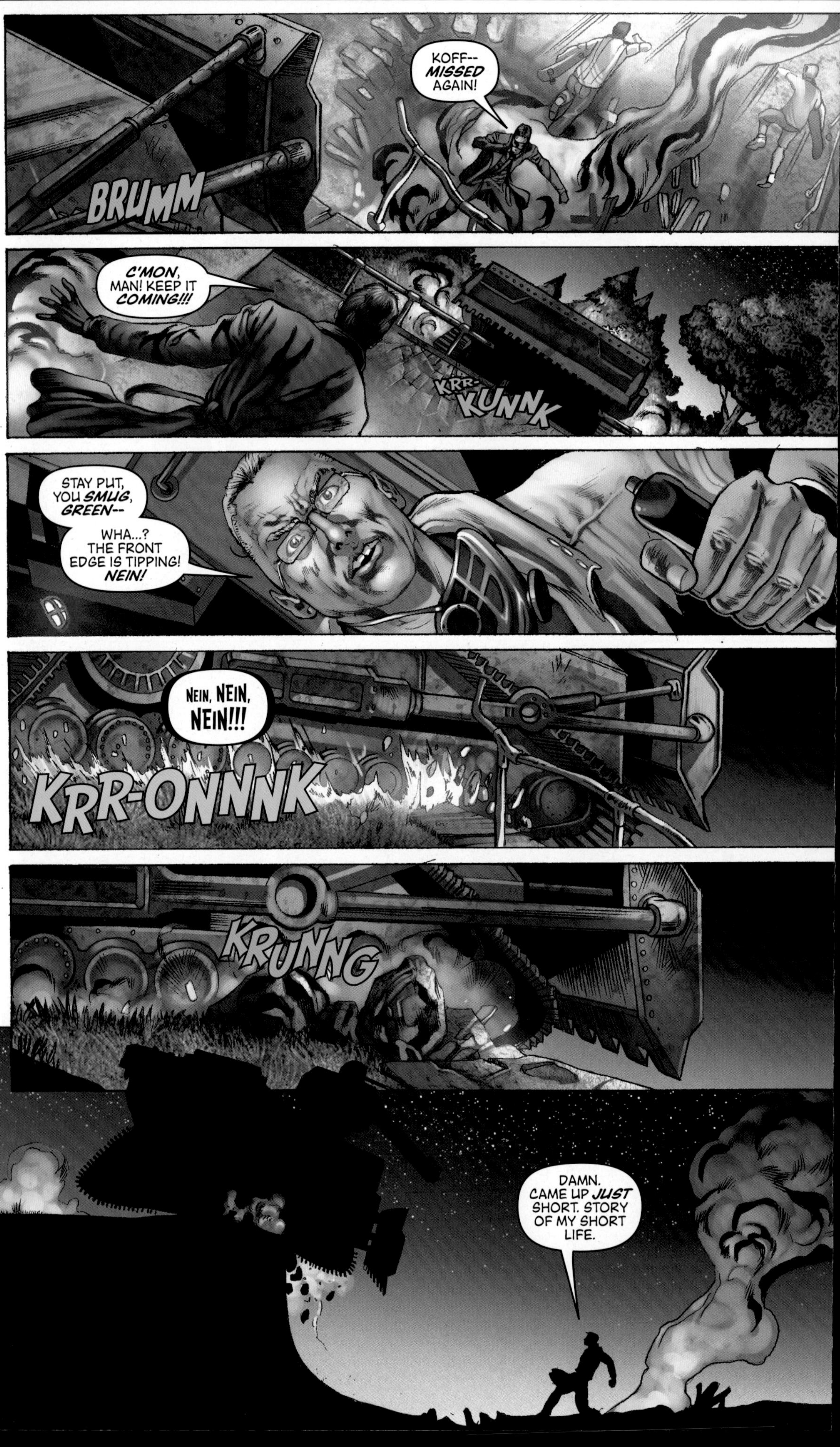
KOFF-- MISSED AGAIN!
BRUMM
C'MON, MAN! KEEP IT COMING!!!
KRR-KUNNK
STAY PUT, YOU SMUG, GREEN--
WHA...? THE FRONT EDGE IS TIPPING! NEIN!
NEIN, NEIN, NEIN!!!
KRR-ONNNK
KRUNNG
DAMN. CAME UP JUST SHORT. STORY OF MY SHORT LIFE.

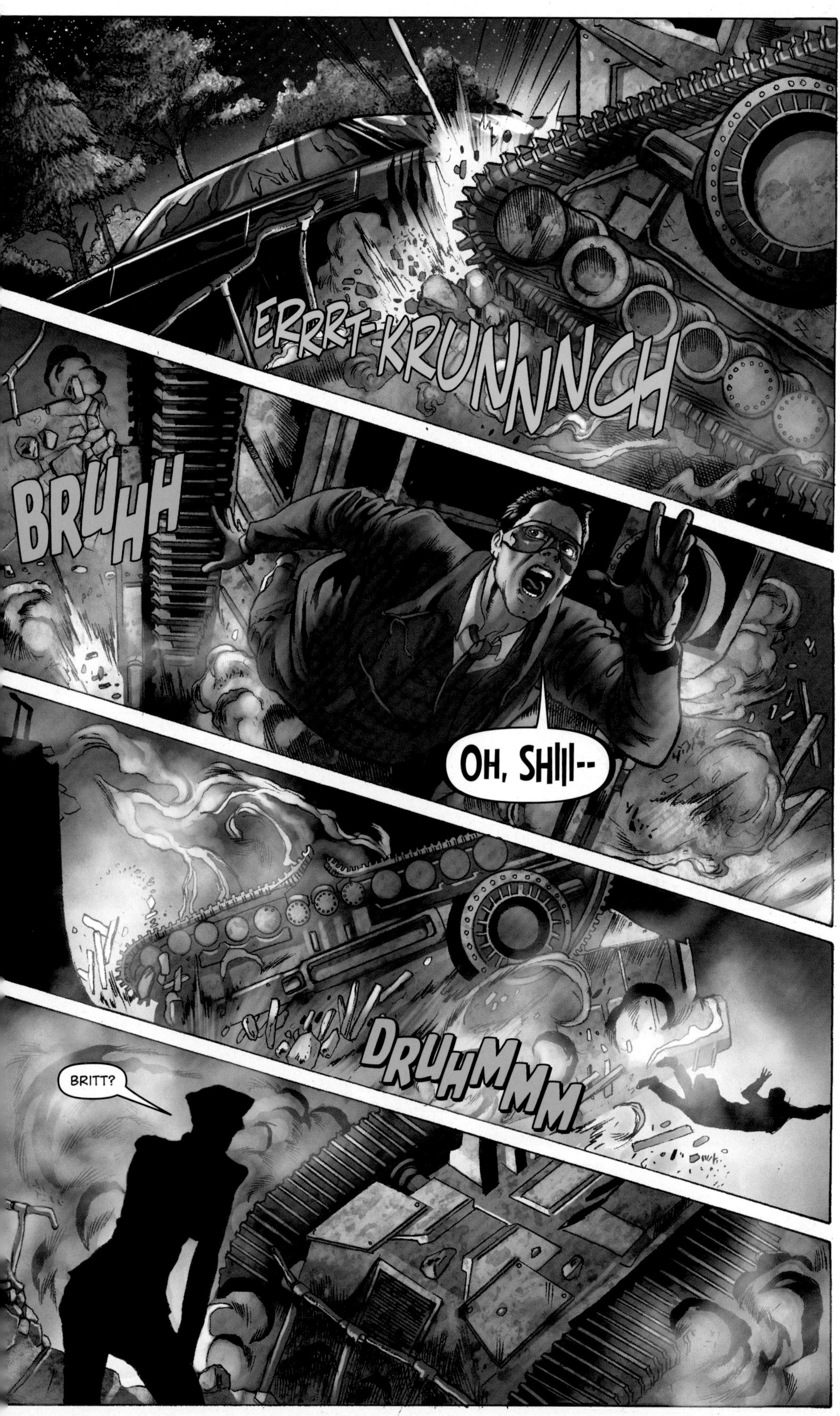
ERRRT-KRUNNNCH
BRUHH
OH, SHIII--
DRUHMMMM
BRITT?

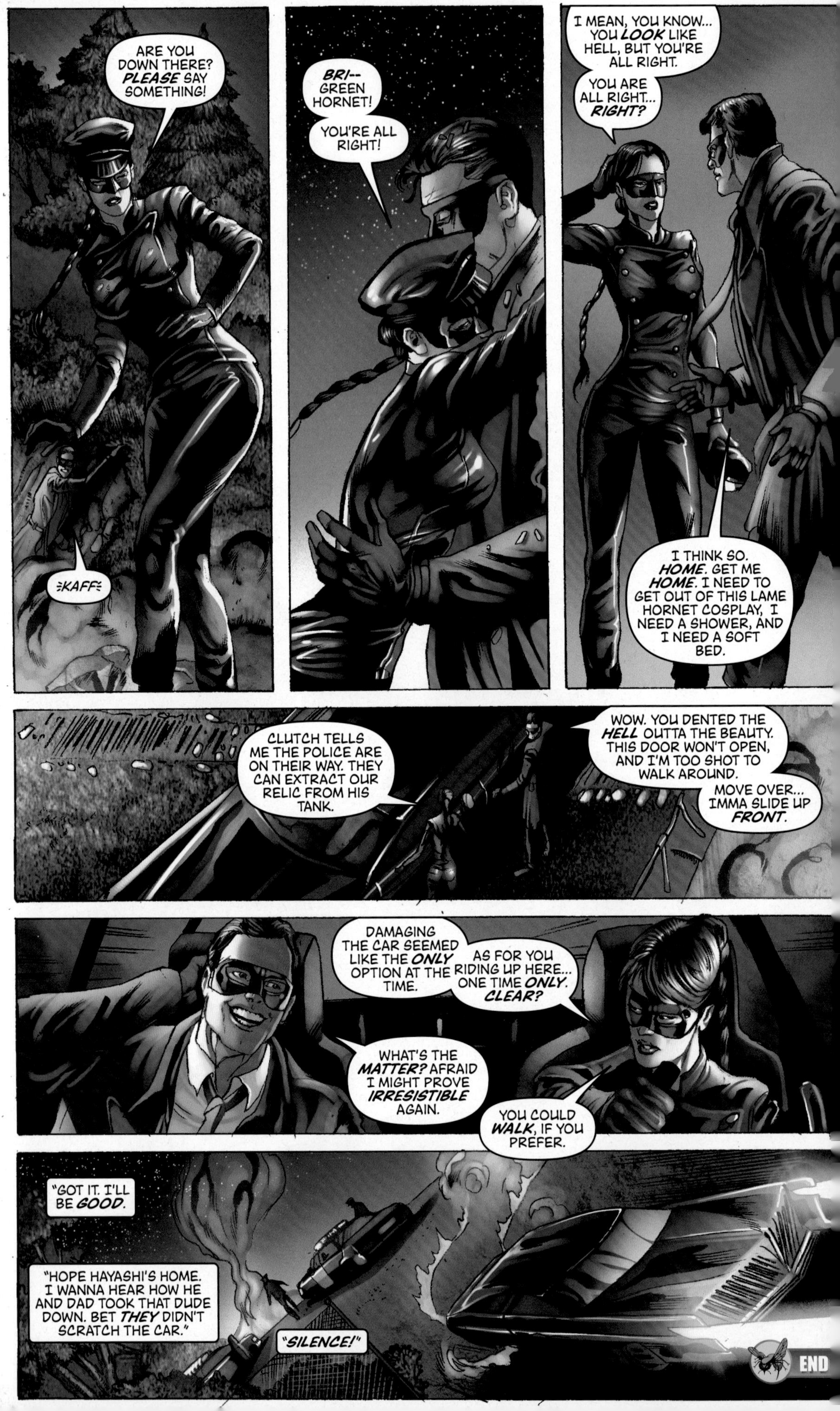
ARE YOU DOWN THERE? PLEASE SAY SOMETHING!
KAFF
BRI-- GREEN HORNET!
YOU'RE ALL RIGHT!
I MEAN, YOU KNOW... YOU LOOK LIKE HELL, BUT YOU'RE ALL RIGHT.
YOU ARE ALL RIGHT... RIGHT?
I THINK SO. HOME. GET ME HOME. I NEED TO GET OUT OF THIS LAME HORNET COSPLAY, I NEED A SHOWER, AND I NEED A SOFT BED.
CLUTCH TELLS ME THE POLICE ARE ON THEIR WAY. THEY CAN EXTRACT OUR RELIC FROM HIS TANK.
WOW. YOU DENTED THE HELL OUTTA THE BEAUTY. THIS DOOR WON'T OPEN, AND I'M TOO SHOT TO WALK AROUND.
MOVE OVER... IMMA SLIDE UP FRONT.
DAMAGING THE CAR SEEMED LIKE THE ONLY OPTION AT THE TIME.
AS FOR YOU RIDING UP HERE... ONE TIME ONLY. CLEAR?
WHAT'S THE MATTER? AFRAID I MIGHT PROVE IRRESISTIBLE AGAIN.
YOU COULD WALK, IF YOU PREFER.
"GOT IT. I'LL BE GOOD.
"HOPE HAYASHI'S HOME. I WANNA HEAR HOW HE AND DAD TOOK THAT DUDE DOWN. BET THEY DIDN'T SCRATCH THE CAR."
"SILENCE!"
END

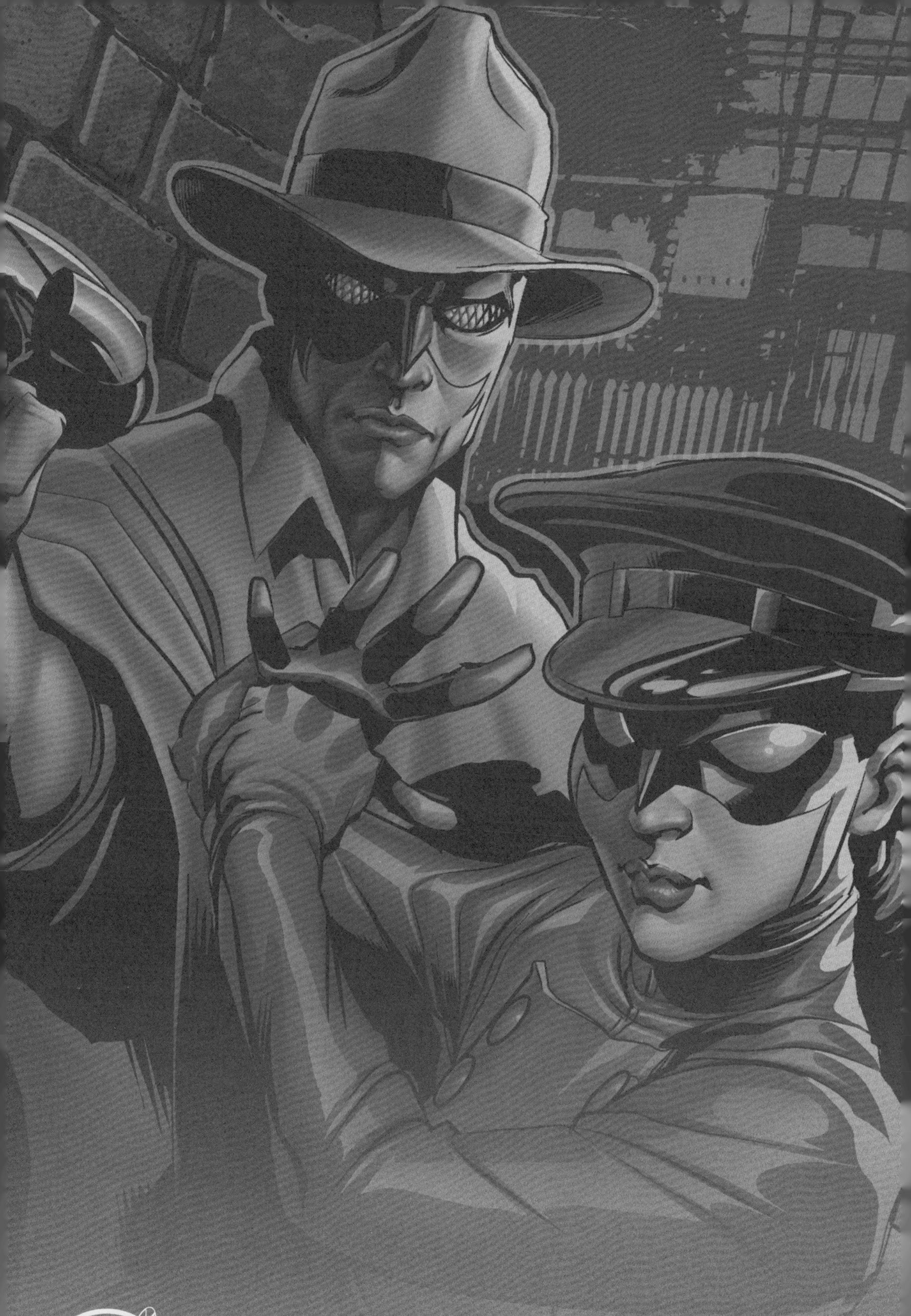

EPISODE TWENTY-ONE: THE OTHER SIDE OF THE COIN

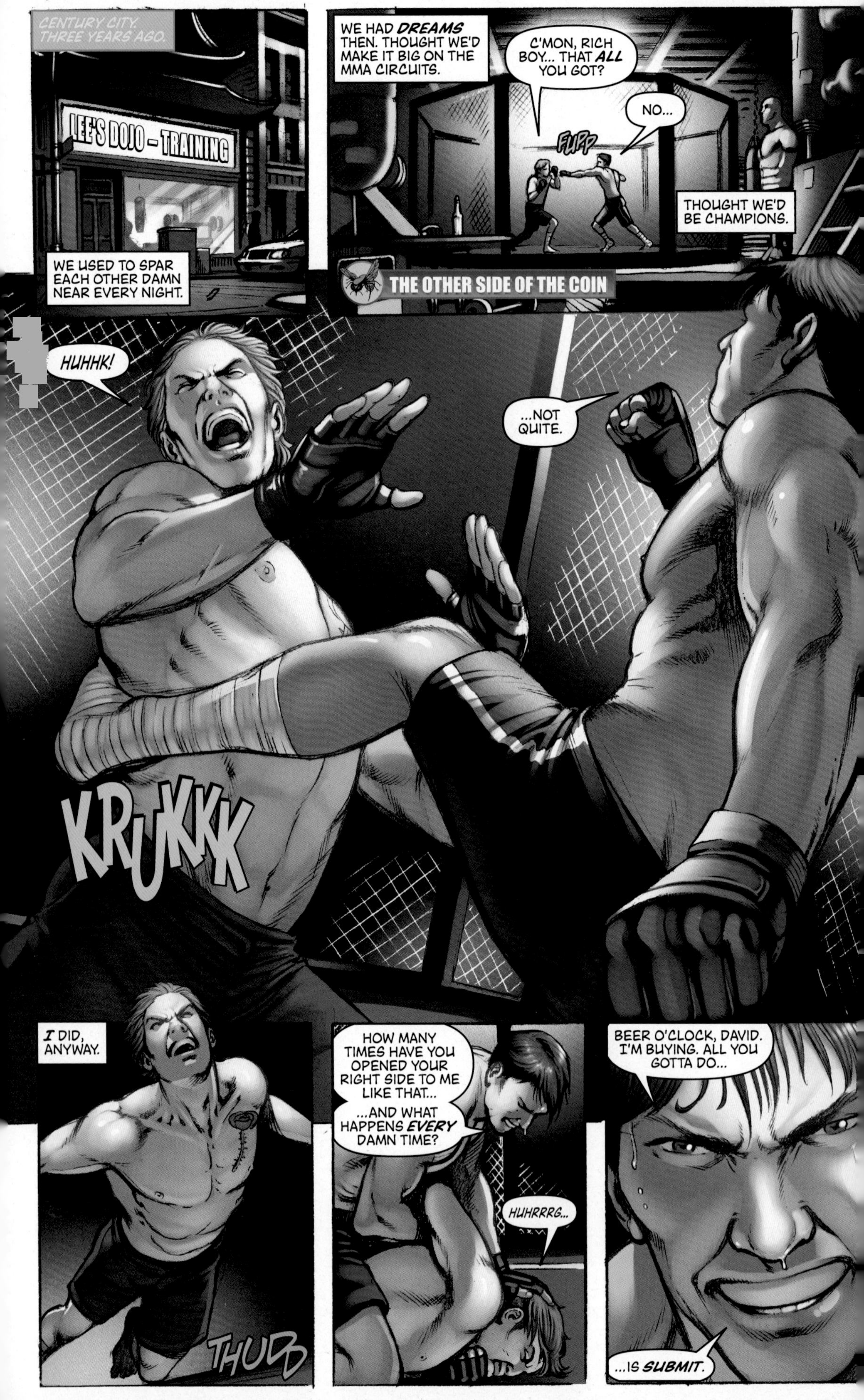
CENTURY CITY. THREE YEARS AGO.
LEE'S DOJO – TRAINING
WE USED TO SPAR EACH OTHER DAMN NEAR EVERY NIGHT.
WE HAD DREAMS THEN. THOUGHT WE'D MAKE IT BIG ON THE MMA CIRCUITS.
C'MON, RICH BOY... THAT ALL YOU GOT?
FUPP
NO...
THOUGHT WE'D BE CHAMPIONS.
THE OTHER SIDE OF THE COIN
HUHHK!
...NOT QUITE.
KRUKKK
I DID, ANYWAY.
THUDD
HOW MANY TIMES HAVE YOU OPENED YOUR RIGHT SIDE TO ME LIKE THAT...
...AND WHAT HAPPENS EVERY DAMN TIME?
HUHRRRG...
BEER O'CLOCK, DAVID. I'M BUYING. ALL YOU GOTTA DO...
...IS SUBMIT.

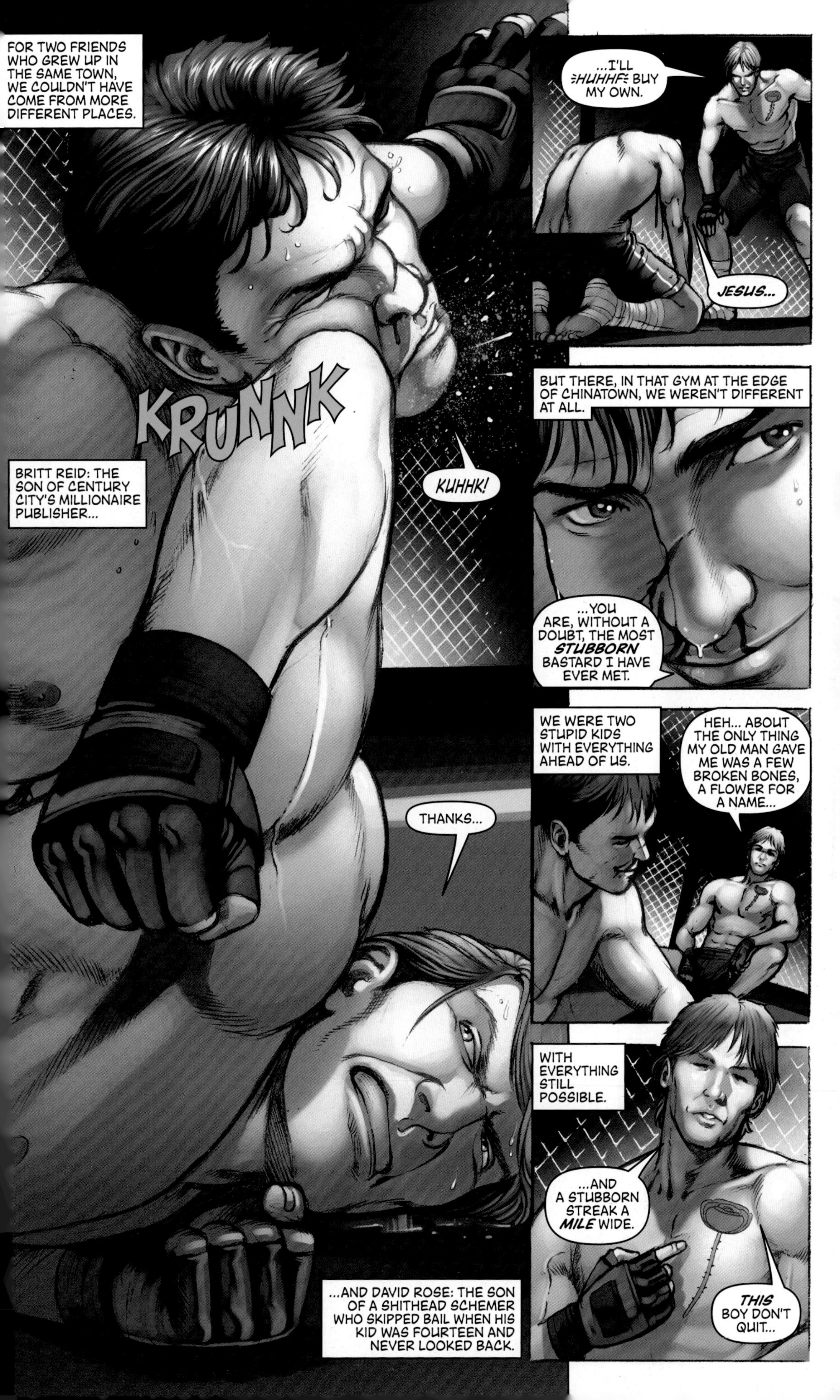
FOR TWO FRIENDS WHO GREW UP IN THE SAME TOWN, WE COULDN'T HAVE COME FROM MORE DIFFERENT PLACES.
KRUNNK
KUHHK!
BRITT REID: THE SON OF CENTURY CITY'S MILLIONAIRE PUBLISHER...
THANKS...
...AND DAVID ROSE: THE SON OF A SHITHEAD SCHEMER WHO SKIPPED BAIL WHEN HIS KID WAS FOURTEEN AND NEVER LOOKED BACK.
...I'LL =HUHHF= BUY MY OWN.
JESUS...
BUT THERE, IN THAT GYM AT THE EDGE OF CHINATOWN, WE WEREN'T DIFFERENT AT ALL.
...YOU ARE, WITHOUT A DOUBT, THE MOST STUBBORN BASTARD I HAVE EVER MET.
WE WERE TWO STUPID KIDS WITH EVERYTHING AHEAD OF US.
HEH... ABOUT THE ONLY THING MY OLD MAN GAVE ME WAS A FEW BROKEN BONES, A FLOWER FOR A NAME...
WITH EVERYTHING STILL POSSIBLE.
...AND A STUBBORN STREAK A MILE WIDE.
THIS BOY DON'T QUIT...

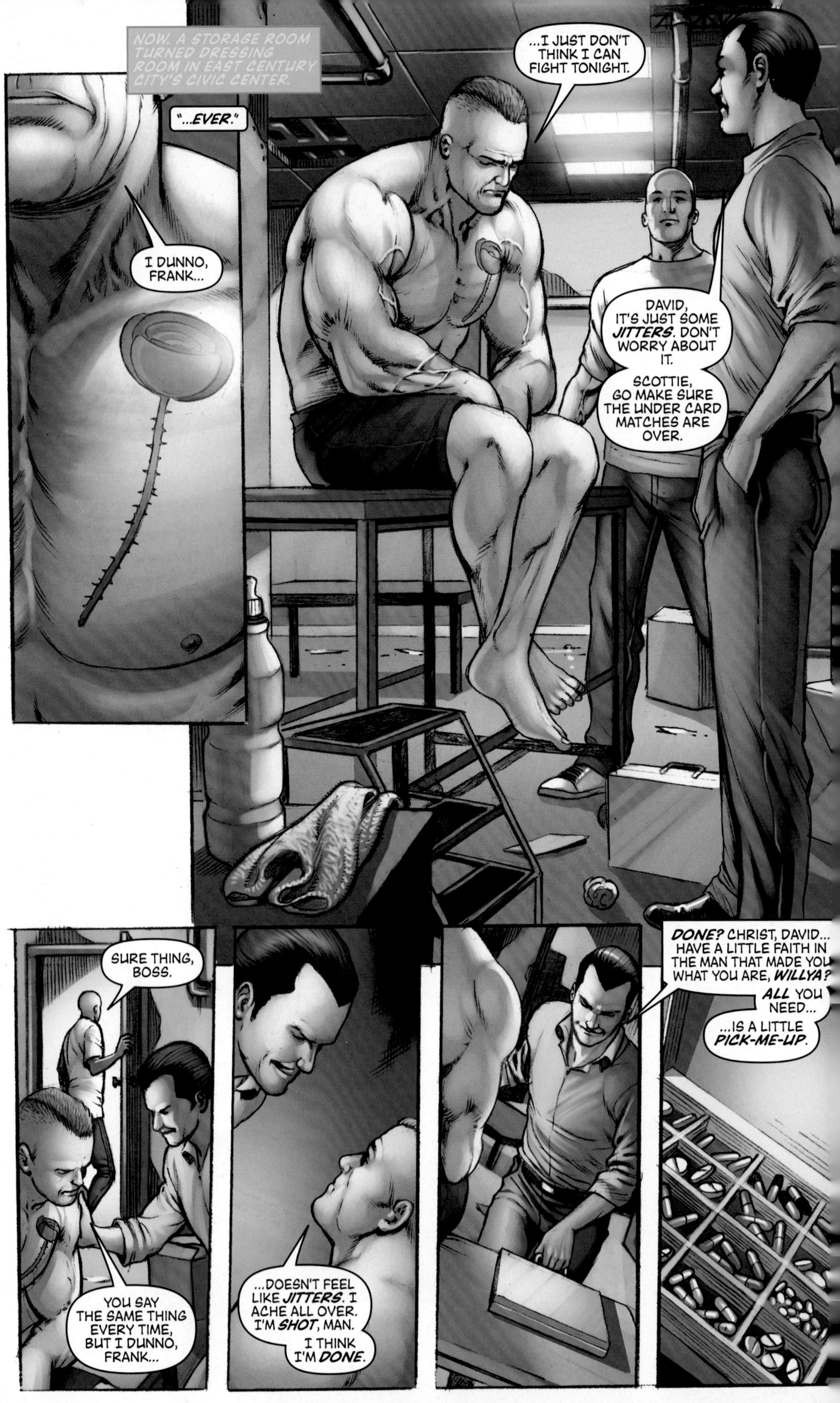
NOW. A STORAGE ROOM TURNED DRESSING ROOM IN EAST CENTURY CITY'S CIVIC CENTER.
"...EVER."
I DUNNO, FRANK...
...I JUST DON'T THINK I CAN FIGHT TONIGHT.
DAVID, IT'S JUST SOME JITTERS. DON'T WORRY ABOUT IT.
SCOTTIE, GO MAKE SURE THE UNDER CARD MATCHES ARE OVER.
SURE THING, BOSS.
YOU SAY THE SAME THING EVERY TIME, BUT I DUNNO, FRANK...
...DOESN'T FEEL LIKE JITTERS. I ACHE ALL OVER. I'M SHOT, MAN.
I THINK I'M DONE.
DONE? CHRIST, DAVID... HAVE A LITTLE FAITH IN THE MAN THAT MADE YOU WHAT YOU ARE, WILLYA?
ALL YOU NEED...
...IS A LITTLE PICK-ME-UP.

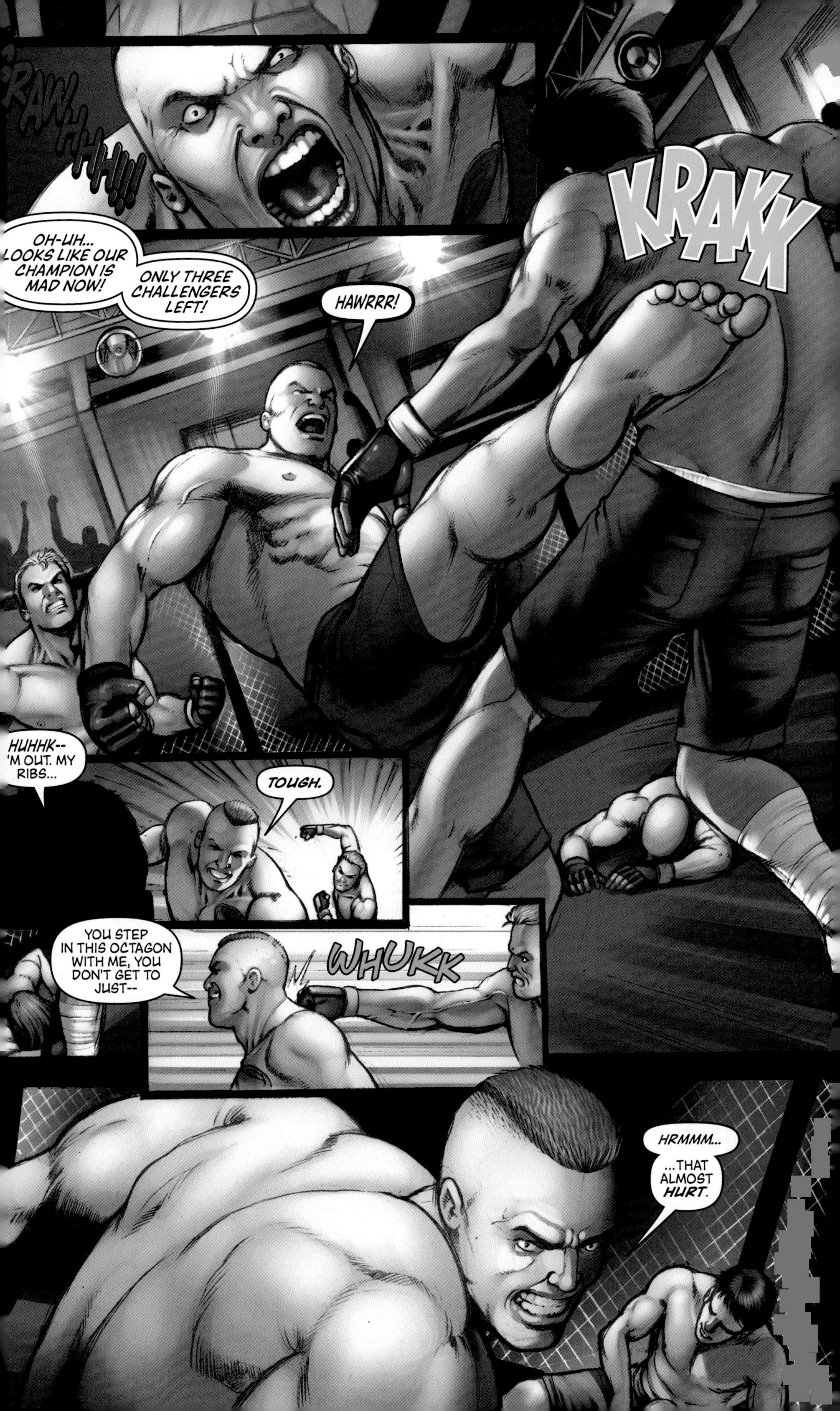

RAWHHH!!!
KRAKK
OH-UH... LOOKS LIKE OUR CHAMPION IS MAD NOW!
ONLY THREE CHALLENGERS LEFT!
HAWRRR!
HUHHK-- 'M OUT. MY RIBS...
TOUGH.
YOU STEP IN THIS OCTAGON WITH ME, YOU DON'T GET TO JUST--
WHUKK
HRMMM...
...THAT ALMOST HURT.

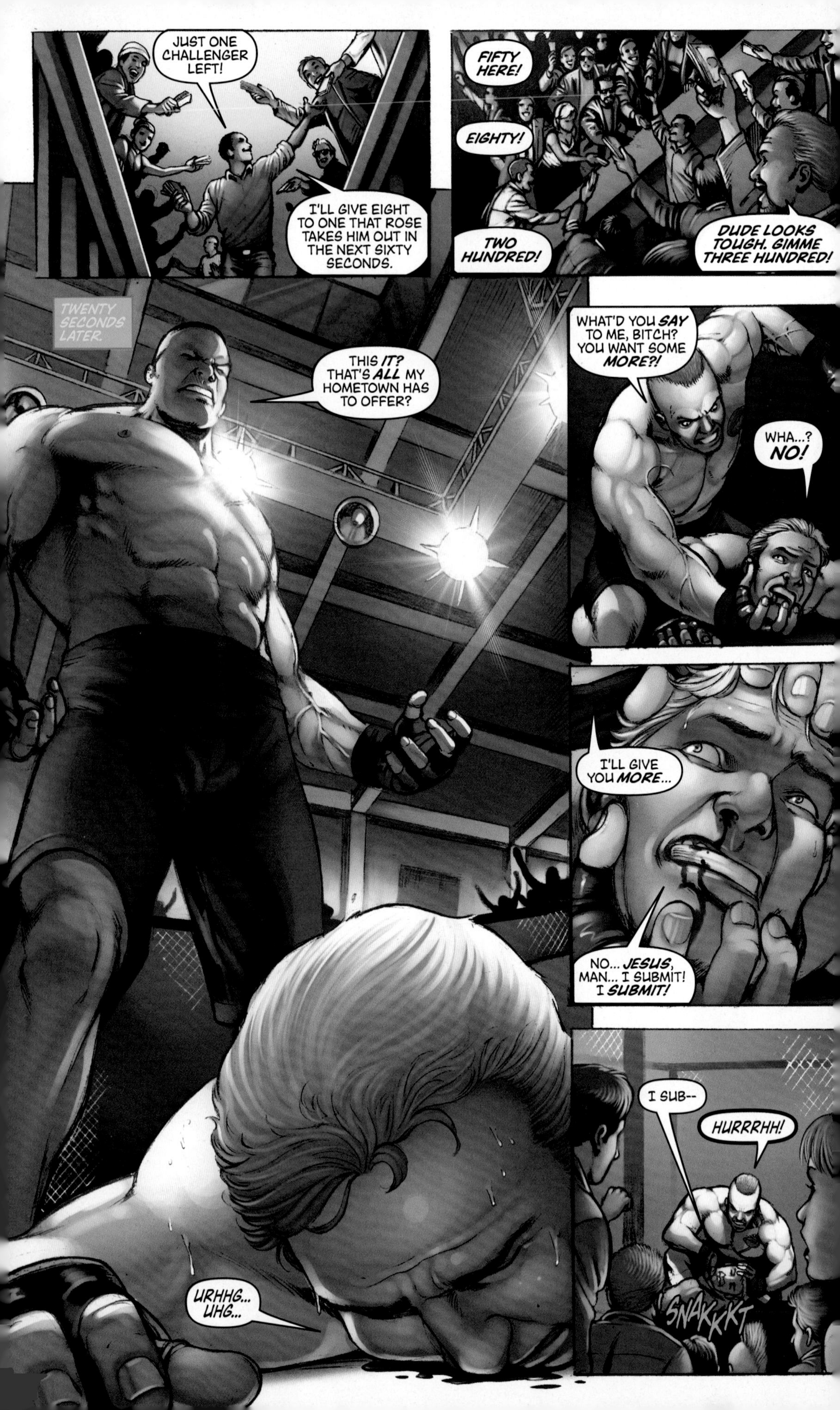

JUST ONE CHALLENGER LEFT!
I'LL GIVE EIGHT TO ONE THAT ROSE TAKES HIM OUT IN THE NEXT SIXTY SECONDS.
FIFTY HERE!
EIGHTY!
TWO HUNDRED!
DUDE LOOKS TOUGH. GIMME THREE HUNDRED!
TWENTY SECONDS LATER.
THIS IT? THAT'S ALL MY HOMETOWN HAS TO OFFER?
URHHG... UHG...
WHAT'D YOU SAY TO ME, BITCH? YOU WANT SOME MORE?!
WHA...? NO!
I'LL GIVE YOU MORE...
NO... JESUS, MAN... I SUBMIT! I SUBMIT!
I SUB--
HURRRHH!
SNAKKKT

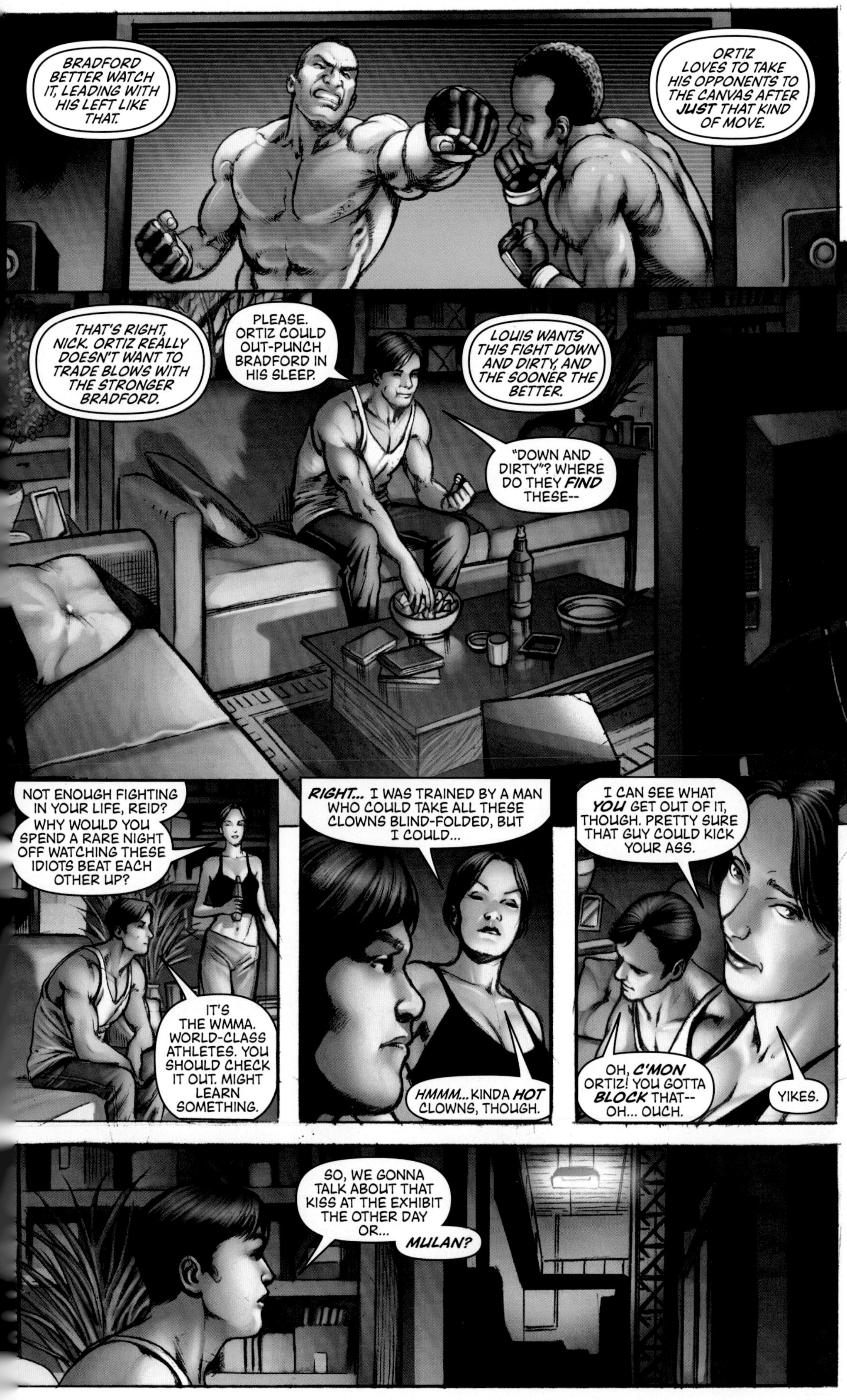
BRADFORD BETTER WATCH IT, LEADING WITH HIS LEFT LIKE THAT.
ORTIZ LOVES TO TAKE HIS OPPONENTS TO THE CANVAS AFTER JUST THAT KIND OF MOVE.
THAT'S RIGHT, NICK. ORTIZ REALLY DOESN'T WANT TO TRADE BLOWS WITH THE STRONGER BRADFORD.
PLEASE. ORTIZ COULD OUT-PUNCH BRADFORD IN HIS SLEEP.
LOUIS WANTS THIS FIGHT DOWN AND DIRTY, AND THE SOONER THE BETTER.
"DOWN AND DIRTY"? WHERE DO THEY FIND THESE--
NOT ENOUGH FIGHTING IN YOUR LIFE, REID? WHY WOULD YOU SPEND A RARE NIGHT OFF WATCHING THESE IDIOTS BEAT EACH OTHER UP?
IT'S THE WMMA. WORLD-CLASS ATHLETES. YOU SHOULD CHECK IT OUT. MIGHT LEARN SOMETHING.
RIGHT... I WAS TRAINED BY A MAN WHO COULD TAKE ALL THESE CLOWNS BLIND-FOLDED, BUT I COULD...
HMMM... KINDA HOT CLOWNS, THOUGH.
I CAN SEE WHAT YOU GET OUT OF IT, THOUGH. PRETTY SURE THAT GUY COULD KICK YOUR ASS.
OH, C'MON ORTIZ! YOU GOTTA BLOCK THAT-- OH... OUCH.
YIKES.
SO, WE GONNA TALK ABOUT THAT KISS AT THE EXHIBIT THE OTHER DAY OR... MULAN?

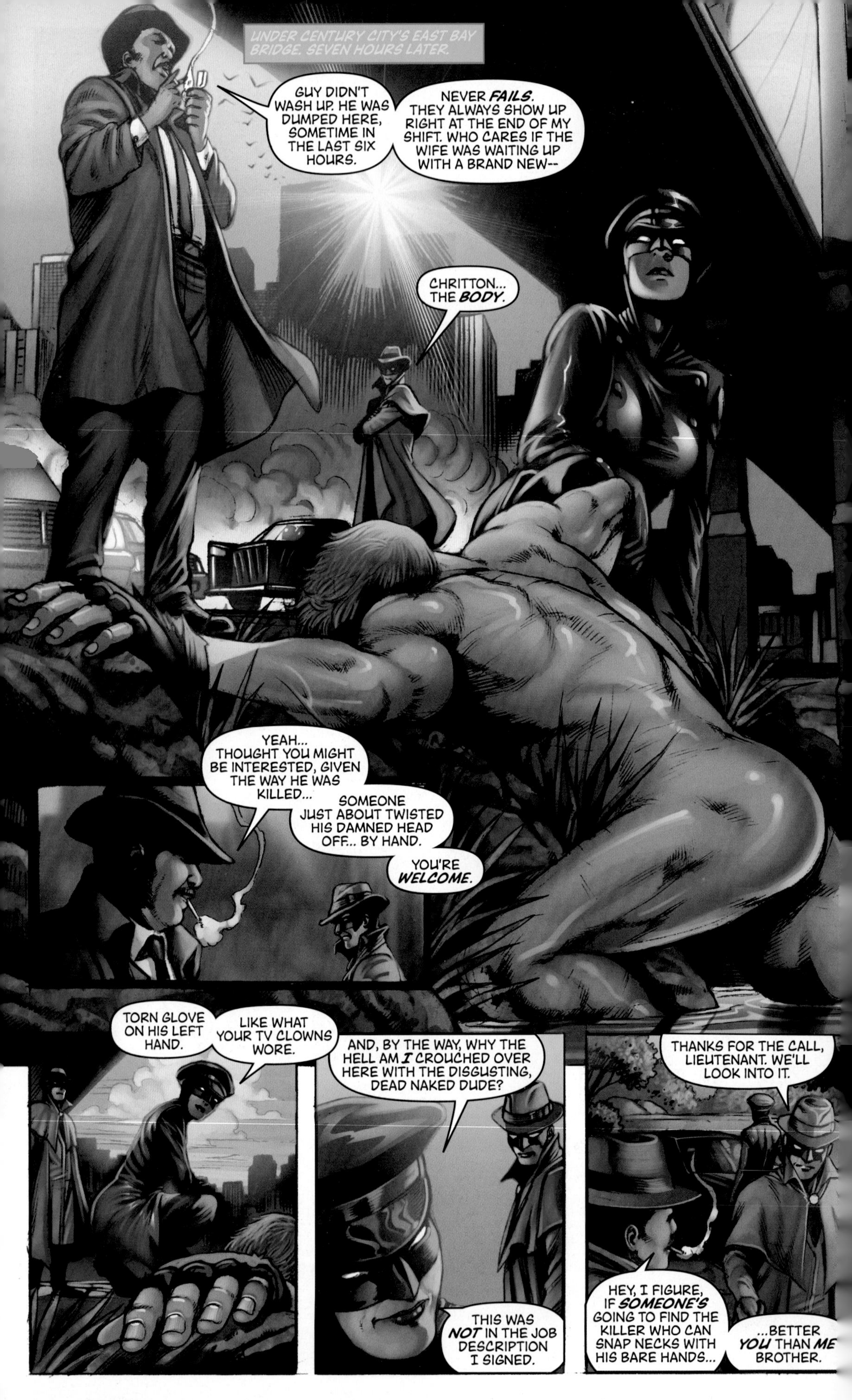
UNDER CENTURY CITY'S EAST BAY BRIDGE. SEVEN HOURS LATER.
GUY DIDN'T WASH UP. HE WAS DUMPED HERE, SOMETIME IN THE LAST SIX HOURS.
NEVER FAILS. THEY ALWAYS SHOW UP RIGHT AT THE END OF MY SHIFT. WHO CARES IF THE WIFE WAS WAITING UP WITH A BRAND NEW--
CHRITTON... THE BODY.
YEAH... THOUGHT YOU MIGHT BE INTERESTED, GIVEN THE WAY HE WAS KILLED...
SOMEONE JUST ABOUT TWISTED HIS DAMNED HEAD OFF... BY HAND.
YOU'RE WELCOME.
TORN GLOVE ON HIS LEFT HAND.
LIKE WHAT YOUR TV CLOWNS WORE.
AND, BY THE WAY, WHY THE HELL AM I CROUCHED OVER HERE WITH THE DISGUSTING, DEAD NAKED DUDE?
THIS WAS NOT IN THE JOB DESCRIPTION I SIGNED.
THANKS FOR THE CALL, LIEUTENANT. WE'LL LOOK INTO IT.
HEY, I FIGURE, IF SOMEONE'S GOING TO FIND THE KILLER WHO CAN SNAP NECKS WITH HIS BARE HANDS...
...BETTER YOU THAN ME BROTHER.

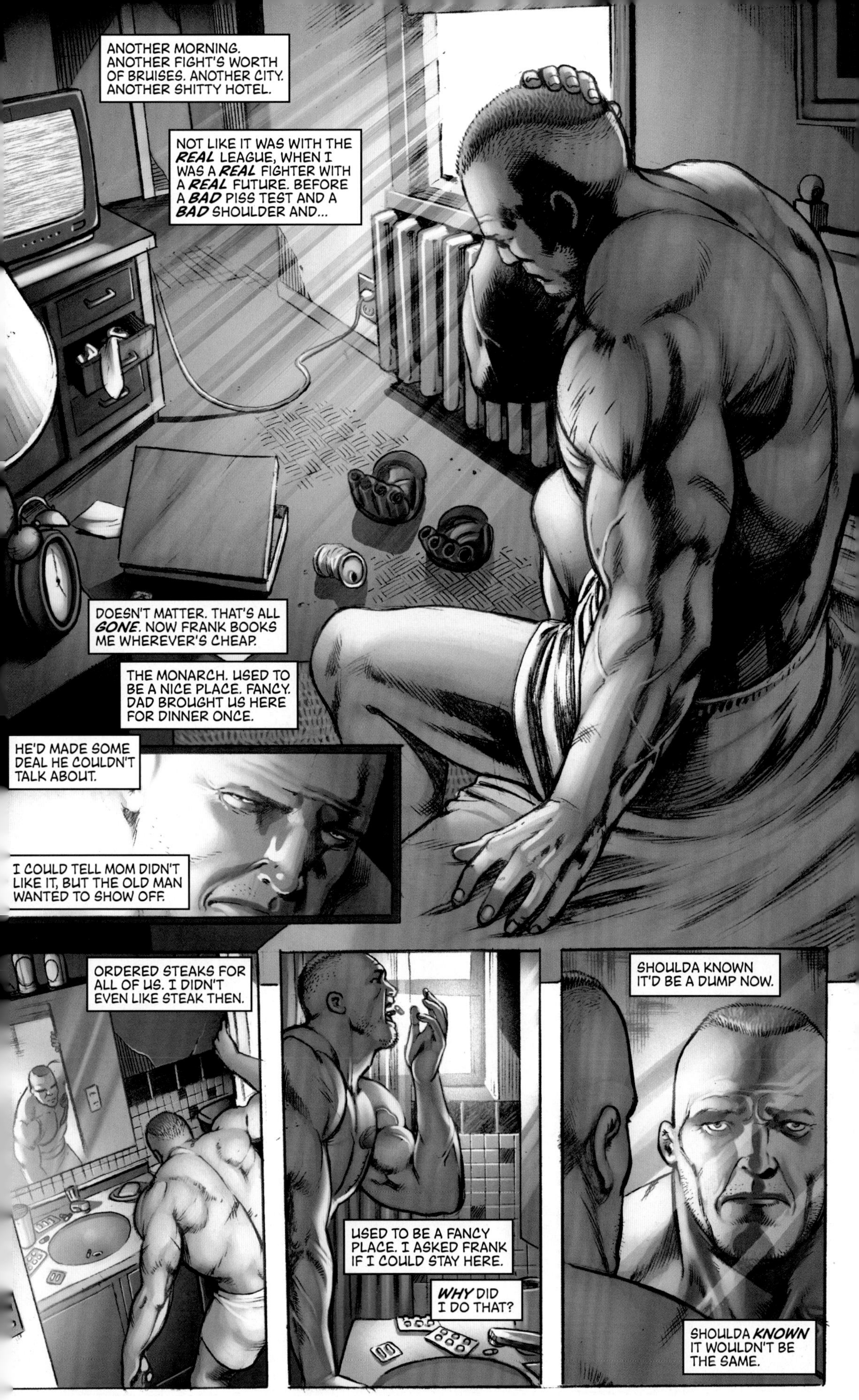
ANOTHER MORNING. ANOTHER FIGHT'S WORTH OF BRUISES. ANOTHER CITY. ANOTHER SHITTY HOTEL.
NOT LIKE IT WAS WITH THE *REAL* LEAGUE, WHEN I WAS A *REAL* FIGHTER WITH A *REAL* FUTURE. BEFORE A *BAD* PISS TEST AND A *BAD* SHOULDER AND...
DOESN'T MATTER. THAT'S ALL *GONE*. NOW FRANK BOOKS ME WHEREVER'S CHEAP.
THE MONARCH. USED TO BE A NICE PLACE. FANCY. DAD BROUGHT US HERE FOR DINNER ONCE.
HE'D MADE SOME DEAL HE COULDN'T TALK ABOUT.
I COULD TELL MOM DIDN'T LIKE IT, BUT THE OLD MAN WANTED TO SHOW OFF.
ORDERED STEAKS FOR ALL OF US. I DIDN'T EVEN LIKE STEAK THEN.
USED TO BE A FANCY PLACE. I ASKED FRANK IF I COULD STAY HERE.
WHY DID I DO THAT?
SHOULDA KNOWN IT'D BE A DUMP NOW.
SHOULDA *KNOWN* IT WOULDN'T BE THE SAME.

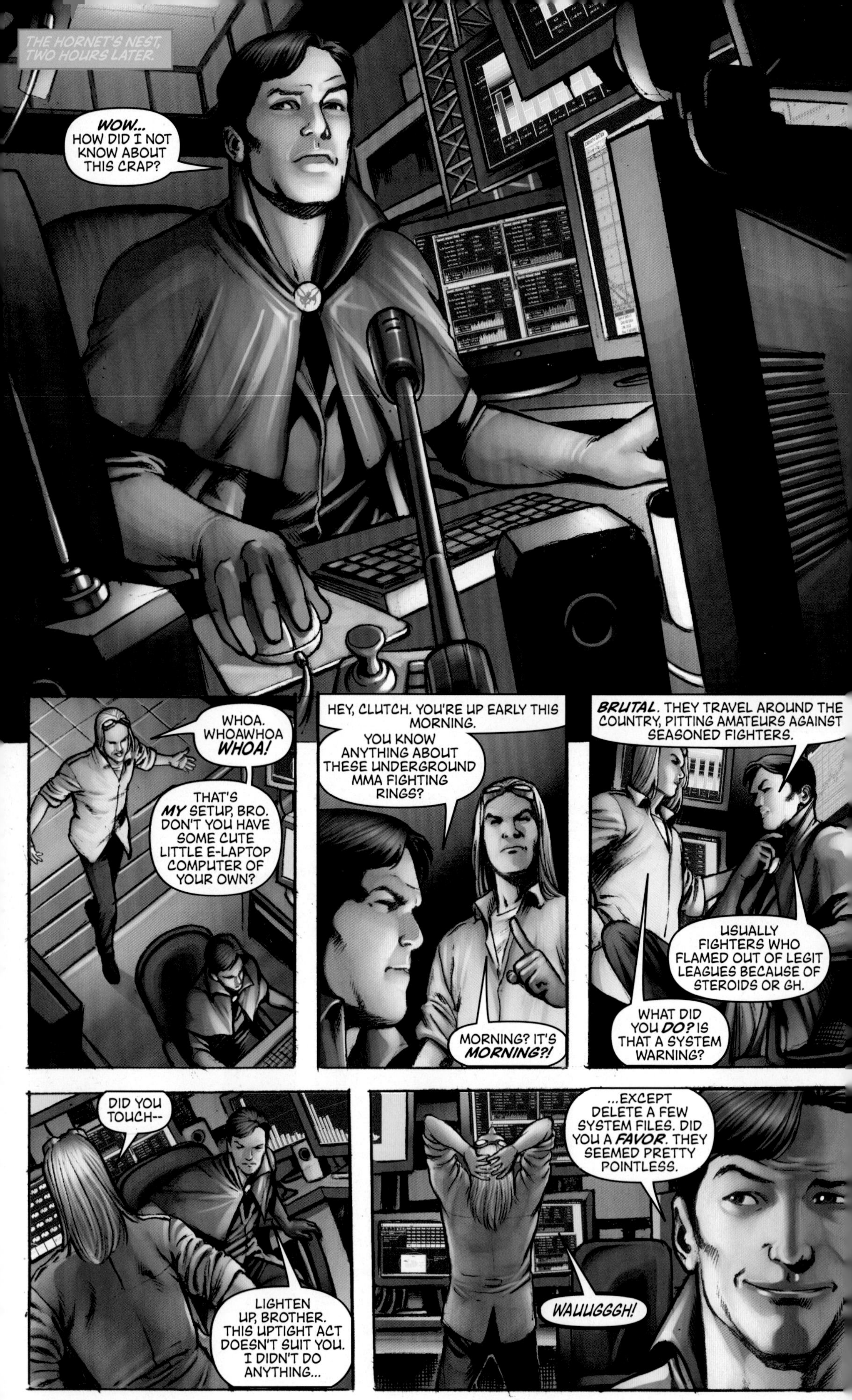

THE HORNET'S NEST, TWO HOURS LATER.
WOW... HOW DID I NOT KNOW ABOUT THIS CRAP?
WHOA. WHOAWHOA WHOA!
THAT'S MY SETUP, BRO. DON'T YOU HAVE SOME CUTE LITTLE E-LAPTOP COMPUTER OF YOUR OWN?
HEY, CLUTCH. YOU'RE UP EARLY THIS MORNING.
YOU KNOW ANYTHING ABOUT THESE UNDERGROUND MMA FIGHTING RINGS?
MORNING? IT'S MORNING?!
BRUTAL. THEY TRAVEL AROUND THE COUNTRY, PITTING AMATEURS AGAINST SEASONED FIGHTERS.
USUALLY FIGHTERS WHO FLAMED OUT OF LEGIT LEAGUES BECAUSE OF STEROIDS OR GH.
WHAT DID YOU DO? IS THAT A SYSTEM WARNING?
DID YOU TOUCH--
LIGHTEN UP, BROTHER. THIS UPTIGHT ACT DOESN'T SUIT YOU. I DIDN'T DO ANYTHING...
...EXCEPT DELETE A FEW SYSTEM FILES. DID YOU A FAVOR. THEY SEEMED PRETTY POINTLESS.
WAUUGGGH!

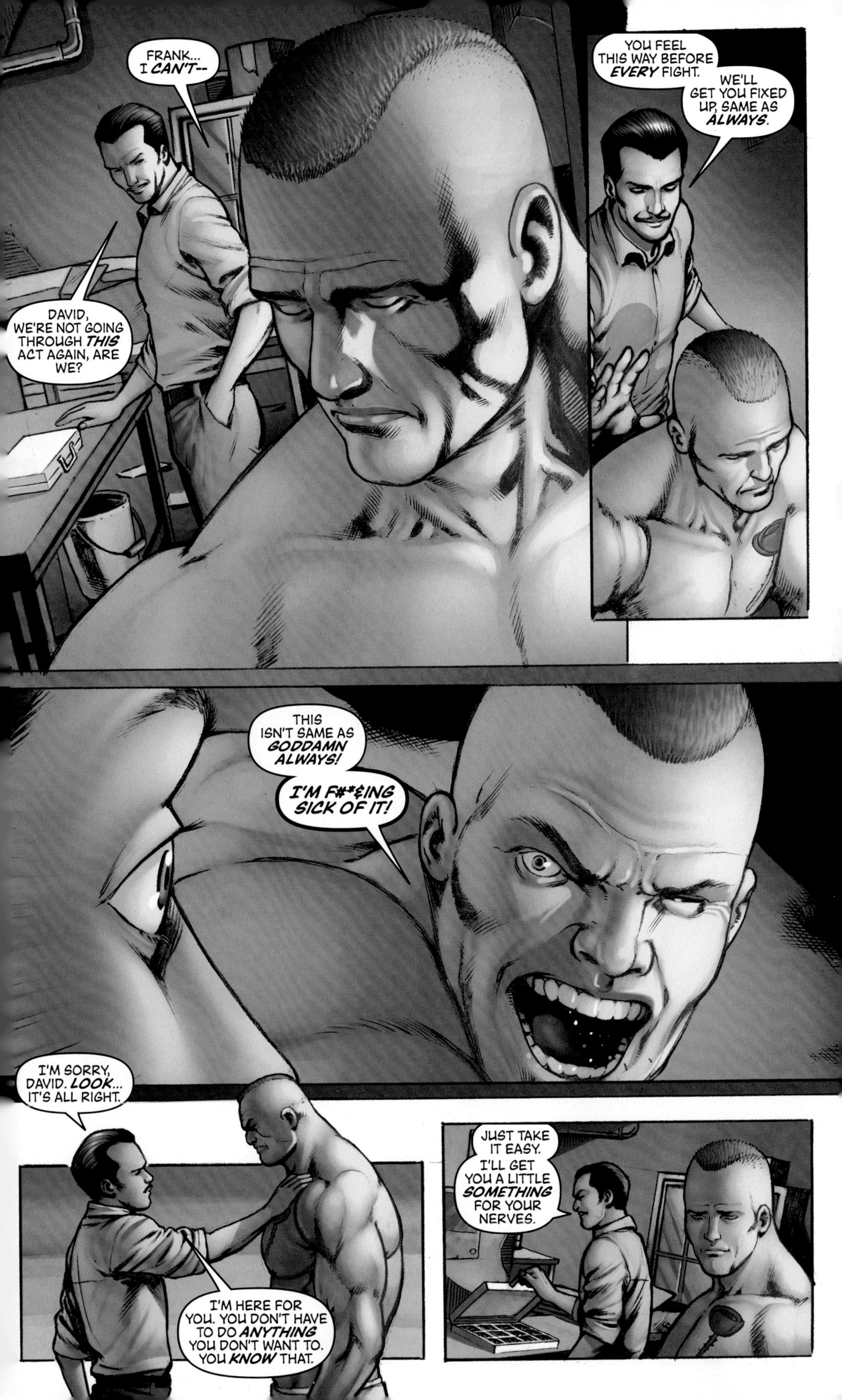
FRANK... I CAN'T--
DAVID, WE'RE NOT GOING THROUGH THIS ACT AGAIN, ARE WE?
YOU FEEL THIS WAY BEFORE EVERY FIGHT.
WE'LL GET YOU FIXED UP, SAME AS ALWAYS.
THIS ISN'T SAME AS GODDAMN ALWAYS!
I'M F#*$ING SICK OF IT!
I'M SORRY, DAVID. LOOK... IT'S ALL RIGHT.
I'M HERE FOR YOU. YOU DON'T HAVE TO DO ANYTHING YOU DON'T WANT TO. YOU KNOW THAT.
JUST TAKE IT EASY.
I'LL GET YOU A LITTLE SOMETHING FOR YOUR NERVES.

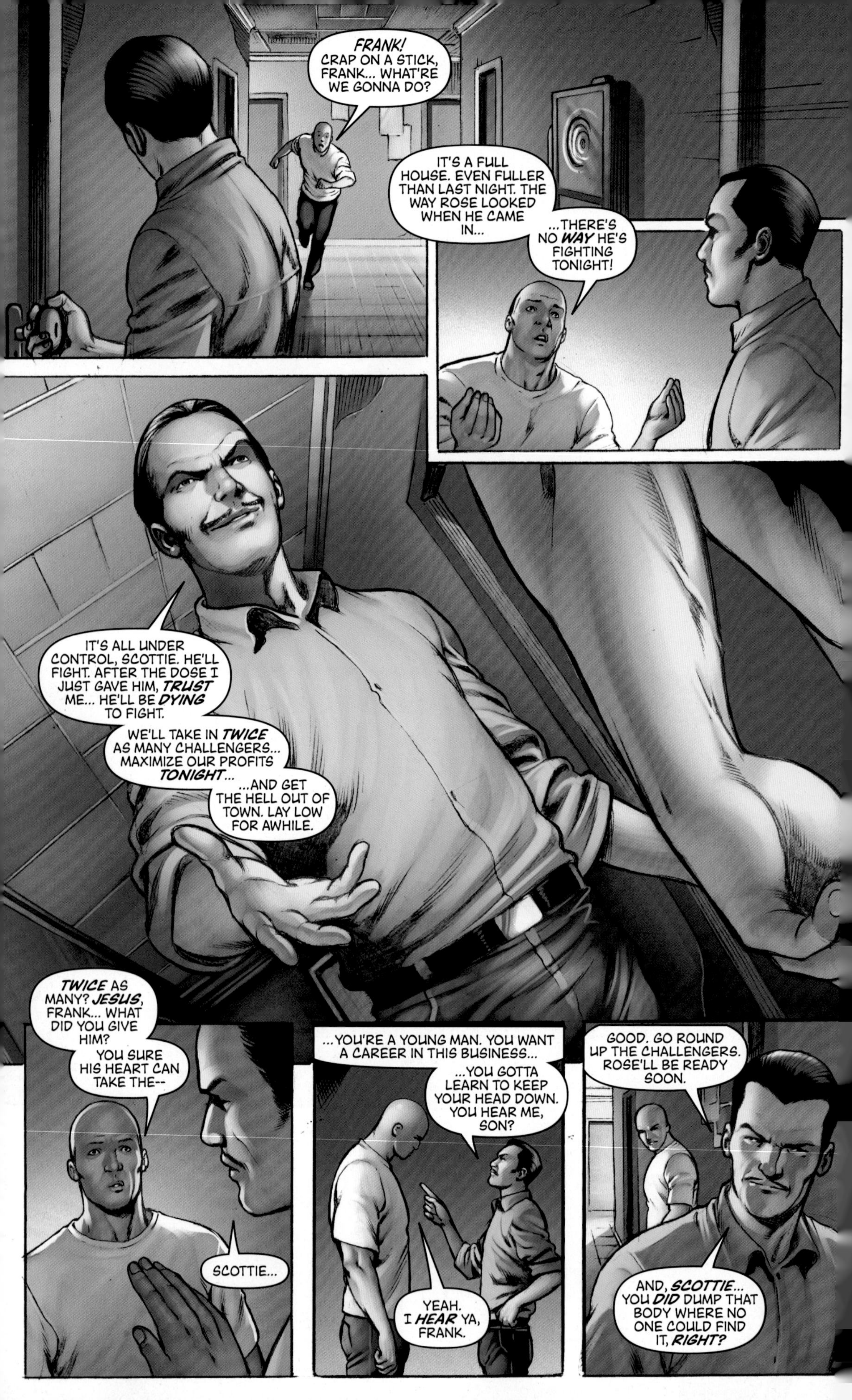
FRANK! CRAP ON A STICK, FRANK... WHAT'RE WE GONNA DO?
IT'S A FULL HOUSE. EVEN FULLER THAN LAST NIGHT. THE WAY ROSE LOOKED WHEN HE CAME IN...
...THERE'S NO WAY HE'S FIGHTING TONIGHT!
IT'S ALL UNDER CONTROL, SCOTTIE. HE'LL FIGHT. AFTER THE DOSE I JUST GAVE HIM, TRUST ME... HE'LL BE DYING TO FIGHT.
WE'LL TAKE IN TWICE AS MANY CHALLENGERS... MAXIMIZE OUR PROFITS TONIGHT...
...AND GET THE HELL OUT OF TOWN. LAY LOW FOR AWHILE.
TWICE AS MANY? JESUS, FRANK... WHAT DID YOU GIVE HIM?
YOU SURE HIS HEART CAN TAKE THE--
SCOTTIE...
...YOU'RE A YOUNG MAN. YOU WANT A CAREER IN THIS BUSINESS...
...YOU GOTTA LEARN TO KEEP YOUR HEAD DOWN. YOU HEAR ME, SON?
YEAH. I HEAR YA, FRANK.
GOOD. GO ROUND UP THE CHALLENGERS. ROSE'LL BE READY SOON.
AND, SCOTTIE... YOU DID DUMP THAT BODY WHERE NO ONE COULD FIND IT, RIGHT?

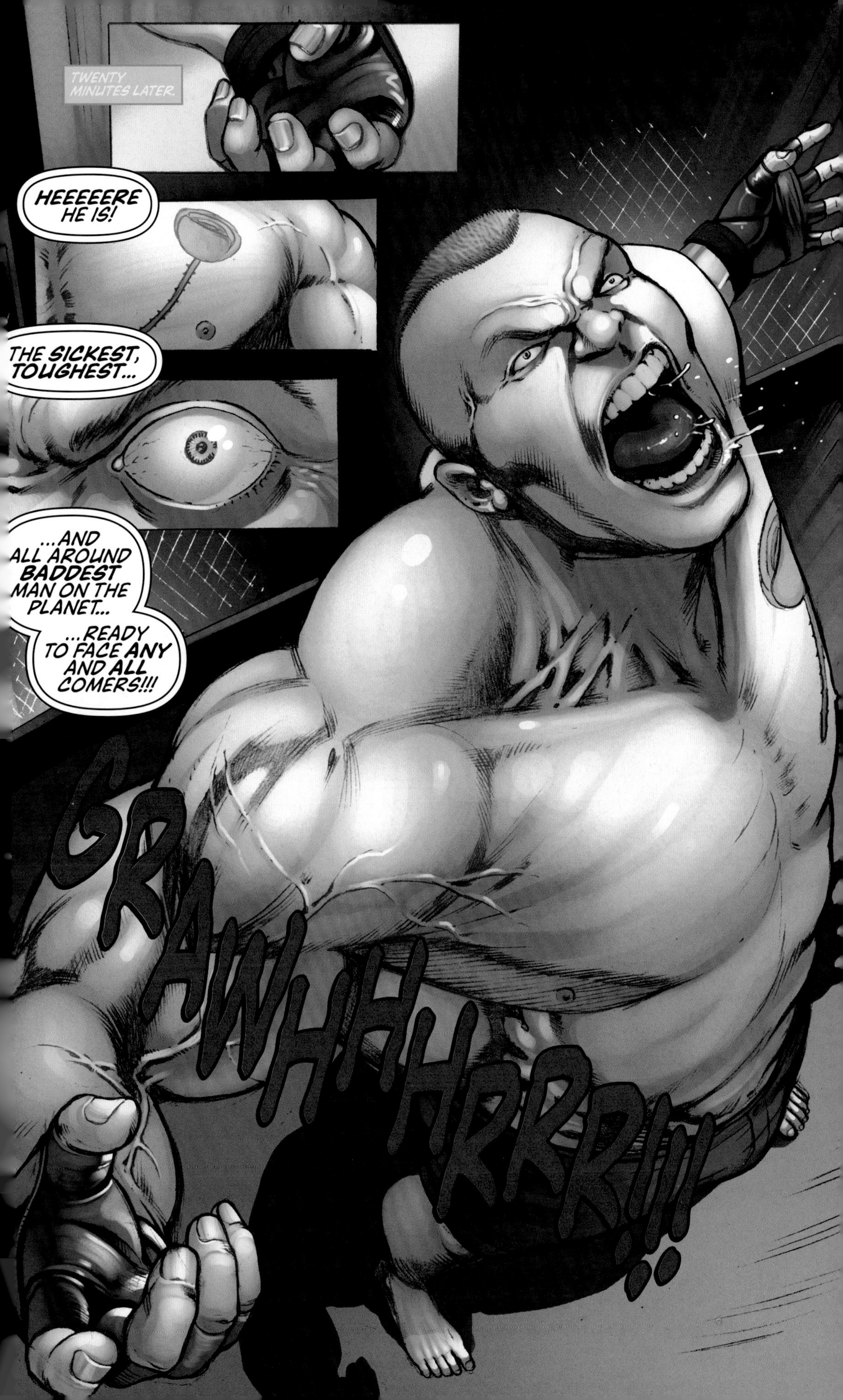

TWENTY MINUTES LATER.
HEEEEEERE HE IS!
THE SICKEST, TOUGHEST...
...AND ALL AROUND BADDEST MAN ON THE PLANET...
...READY TO FACE ANY AND ALL COMERS!!!
GRAWHHHHRRRR!!!!

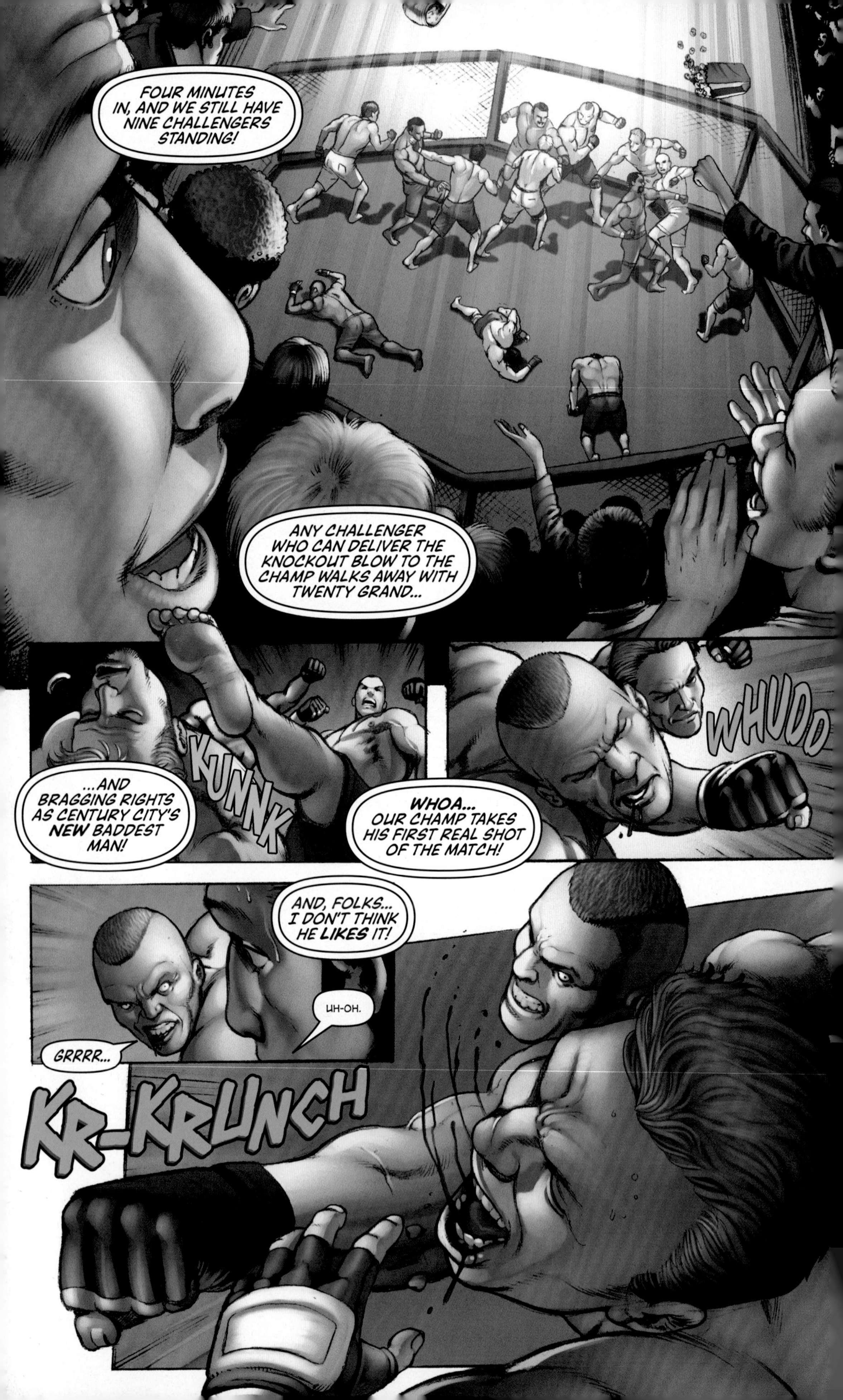
FOUR MINUTES IN, AND WE STILL HAVE NINE CHALLENGERS STANDING!
ANY CHALLENGER WHO CAN DELIVER THE KNOCKOUT BLOW TO THE CHAMP WALKS AWAY WITH TWENTY GRAND...
KUNNK
...AND BRAGGING RIGHTS AS CENTURY CITY'S **NEW** BADDEST MAN!
WHUDD
WHOA... OUR CHAMP TAKES HIS FIRST REAL SHOT OF THE MATCH!
AND, FOLKS... I DON'T THINK HE **LIKES** IT!
UH-OH.
GRRRR...
KR-KRUNCH

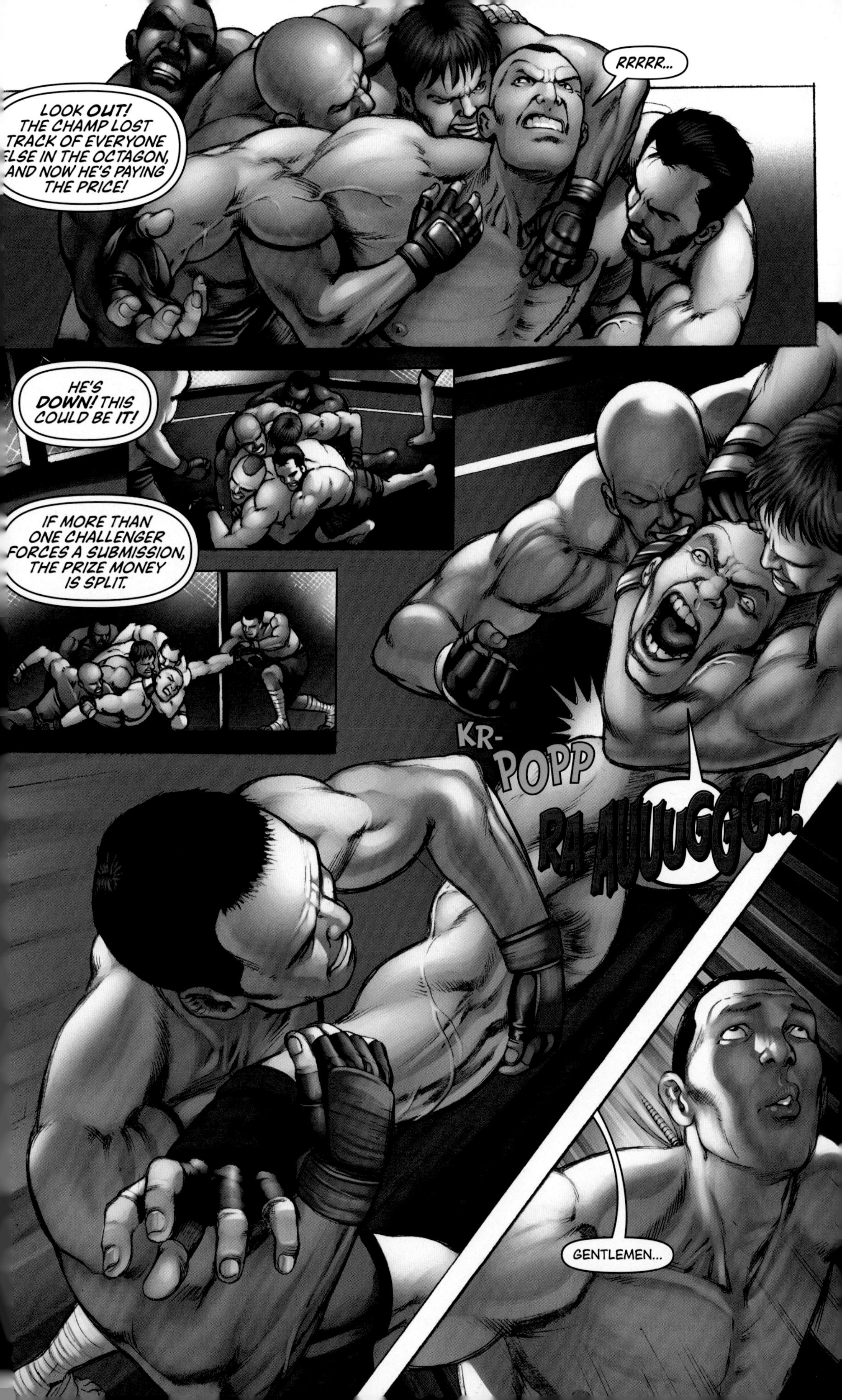
LOOK OUT! THE CHAMP LOST TRACK OF EVERYONE ELSE IN THE OCTAGON, AND NOW HE'S PAYING THE PRICE!
RRRRR...
HE'S DOWN! THIS COULD BE IT!
IF MORE THAN ONE CHALLENGER FORCES A SUBMISSION, THE PRIZE MONEY IS SPLIT.
KR-POPP
RA-AUUUGGGH!
GENTLEMEN...

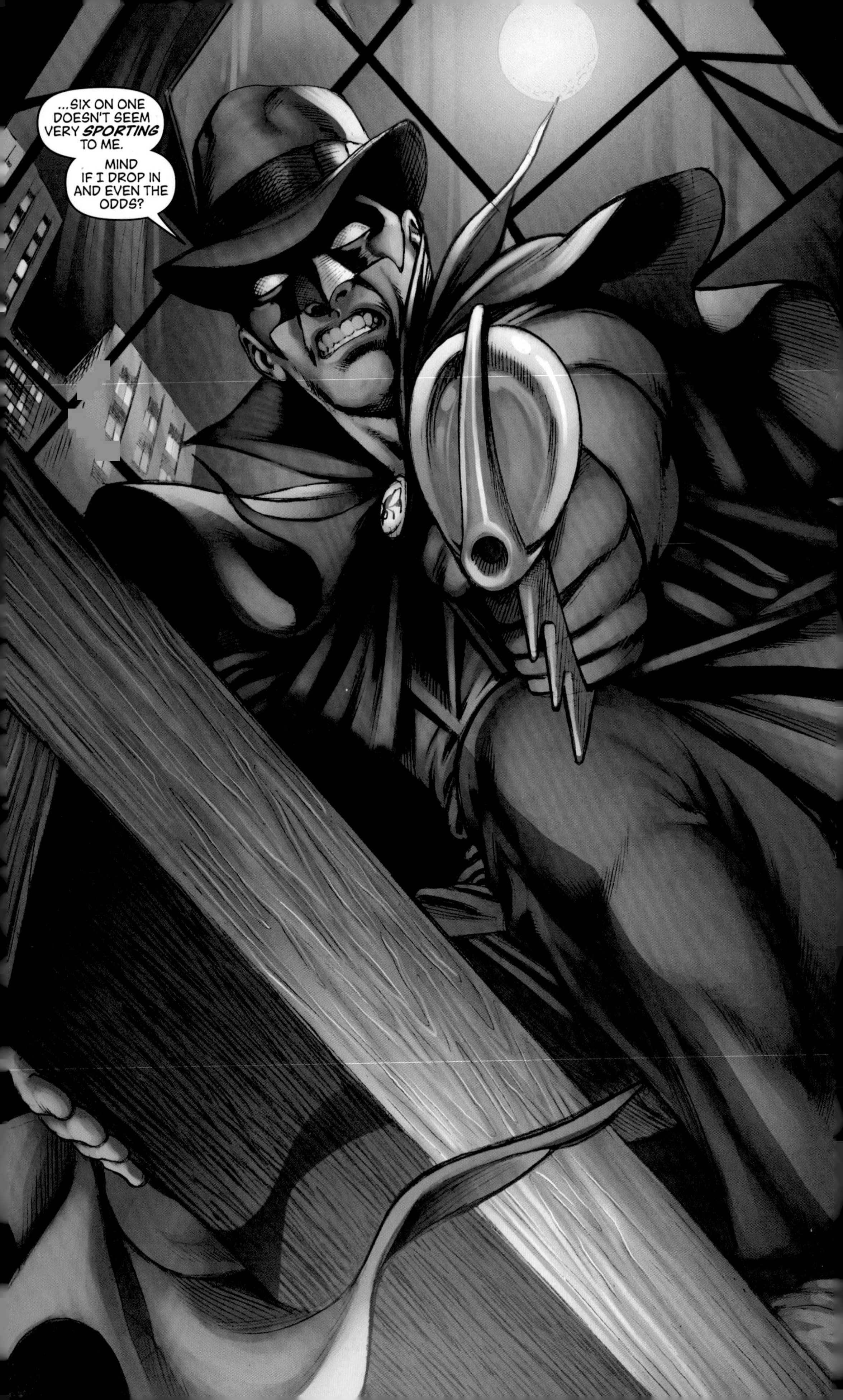
...SIX ON ONE DOESN'T SEEM VERY SPORTING TO ME.
MIND IF I DROP IN AND EVEN THE ODDS?

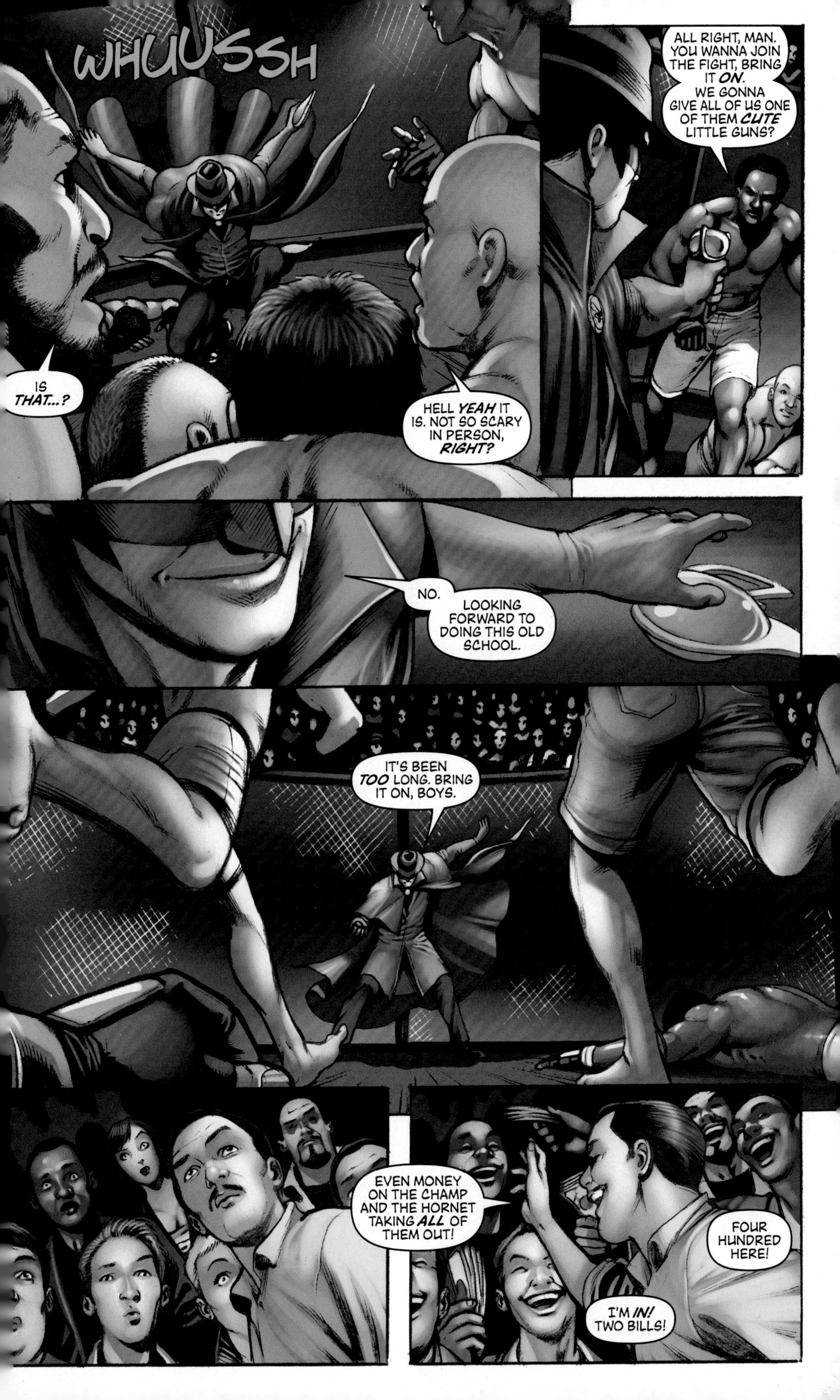
WHUUSSH
IS THAT...?
HELL YEAH IT IS. NOT SO SCARY IN PERSON, RIGHT?
ALL RIGHT, MAN. YOU WANNA JOIN THE FIGHT, BRING IT ON. WE GONNA GIVE ALL OF US ONE OF THEM CUTE LITTLE GUNS?
NO.
LOOKING FORWARD TO DOING THIS OLD SCHOOL.
IT'S BEEN TOO LONG. BRING IT ON, BOYS.
EVEN MONEY ON THE CHAMP AND THE HORNET TAKING ALL OF THEM OUT!
FOUR HUNDRED HERE!
I'M IN! TWO BILLS!

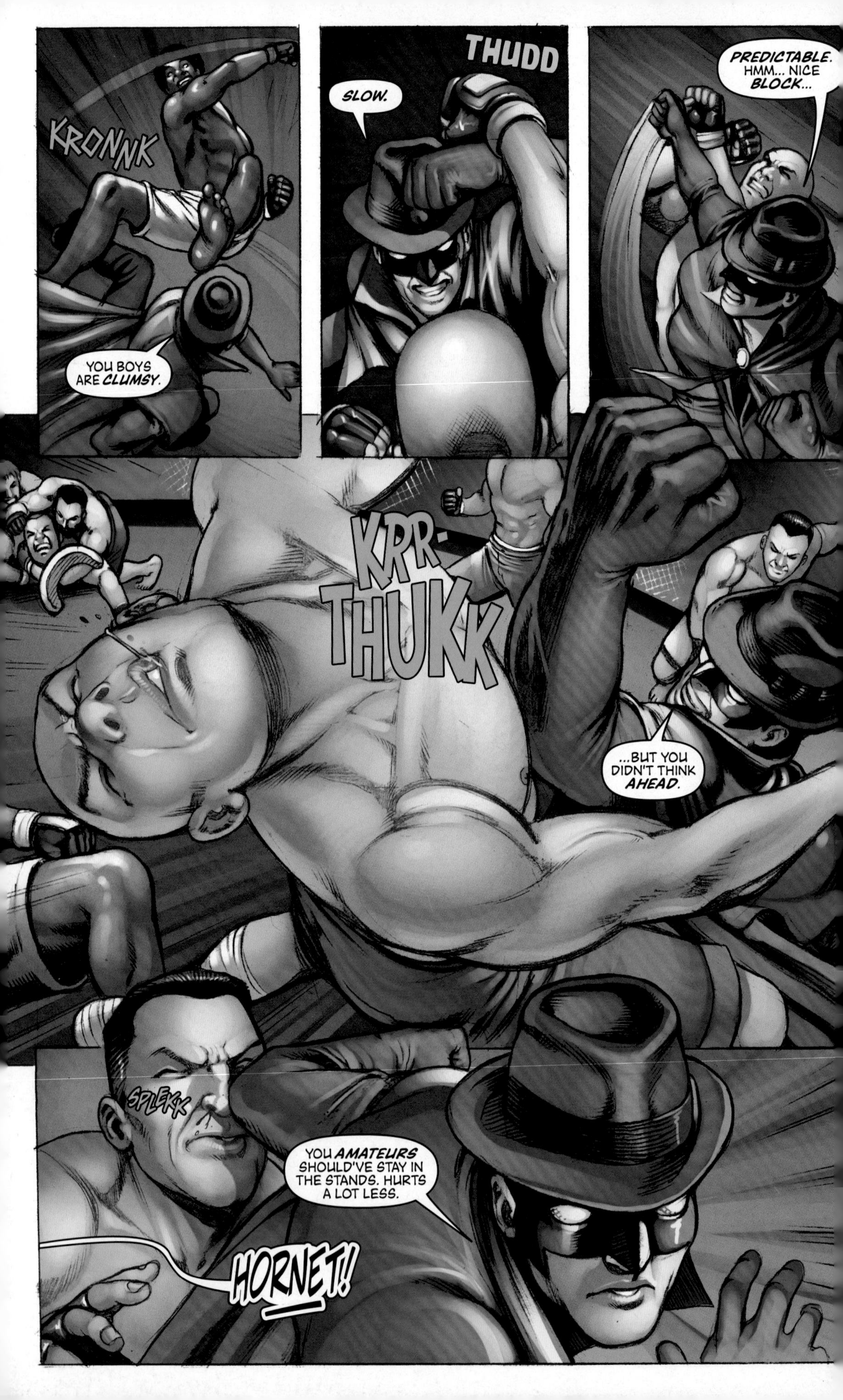
KRONNK
YOU BOYS ARE CLUMSY.
THUDD
SLOW.
PREDICTABLE. HMM... NICE BLOCK...
KRR-THUKK
...BUT YOU DIDN'T THINK AHEAD.
SPLEKK
YOU AMATEURS SHOULD'VE STAY IN THE STANDS. HURTS A LOT LESS.
HORNET!

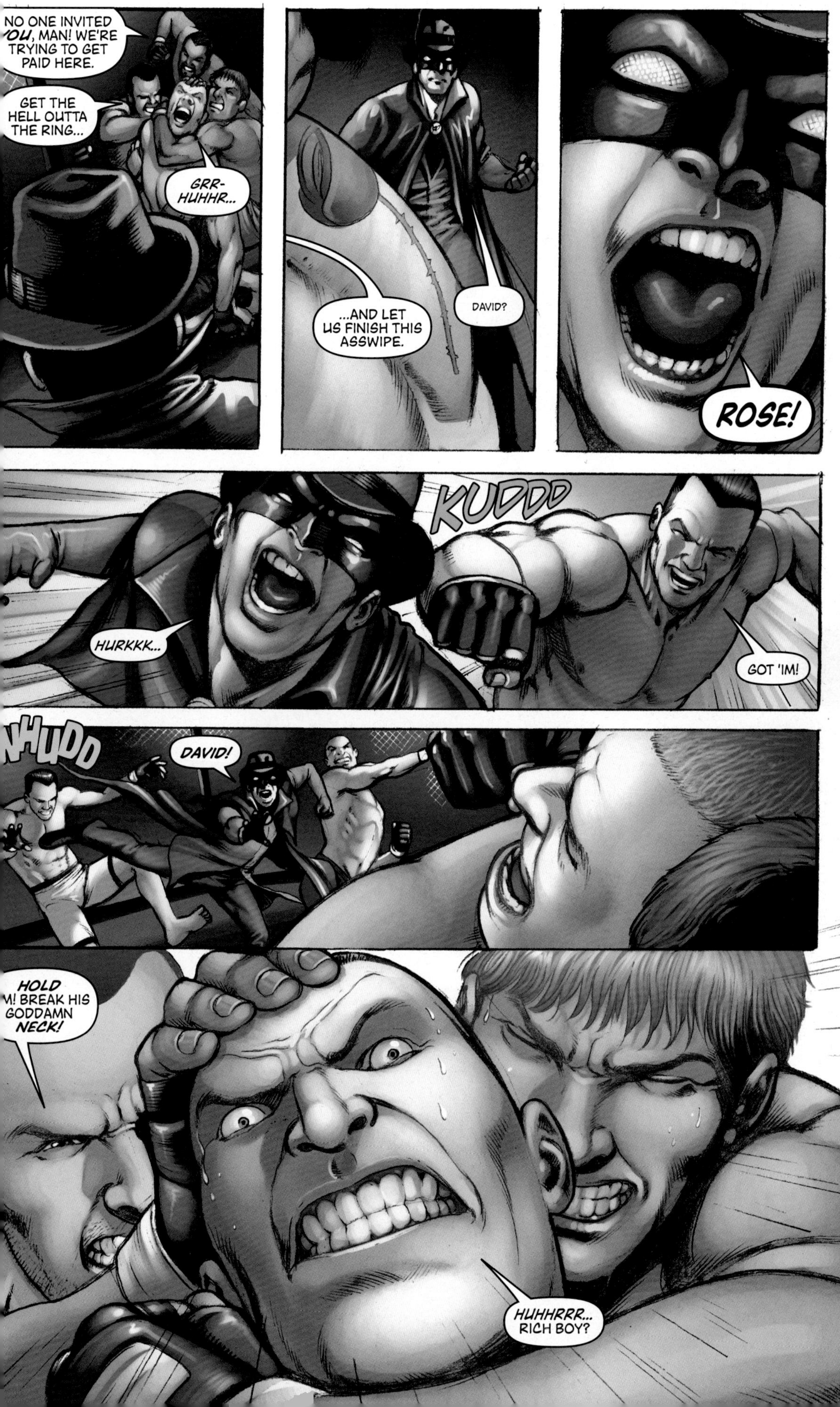
NO ONE INVITED YOU, MAN! WE'RE TRYING TO GET PAID HERE.
GET THE HELL OUTTA THE RING...
GRR-HUHHR...
...AND LET US FINISH THIS ASSWIPE.
DAVID?
ROSE!
KUDDD
HURKKK...
GOT 'IM!
DAVID!
HOLD 'M! BREAK HIS GODDAMN NECK!
HUHHRRR... RICH BOY?

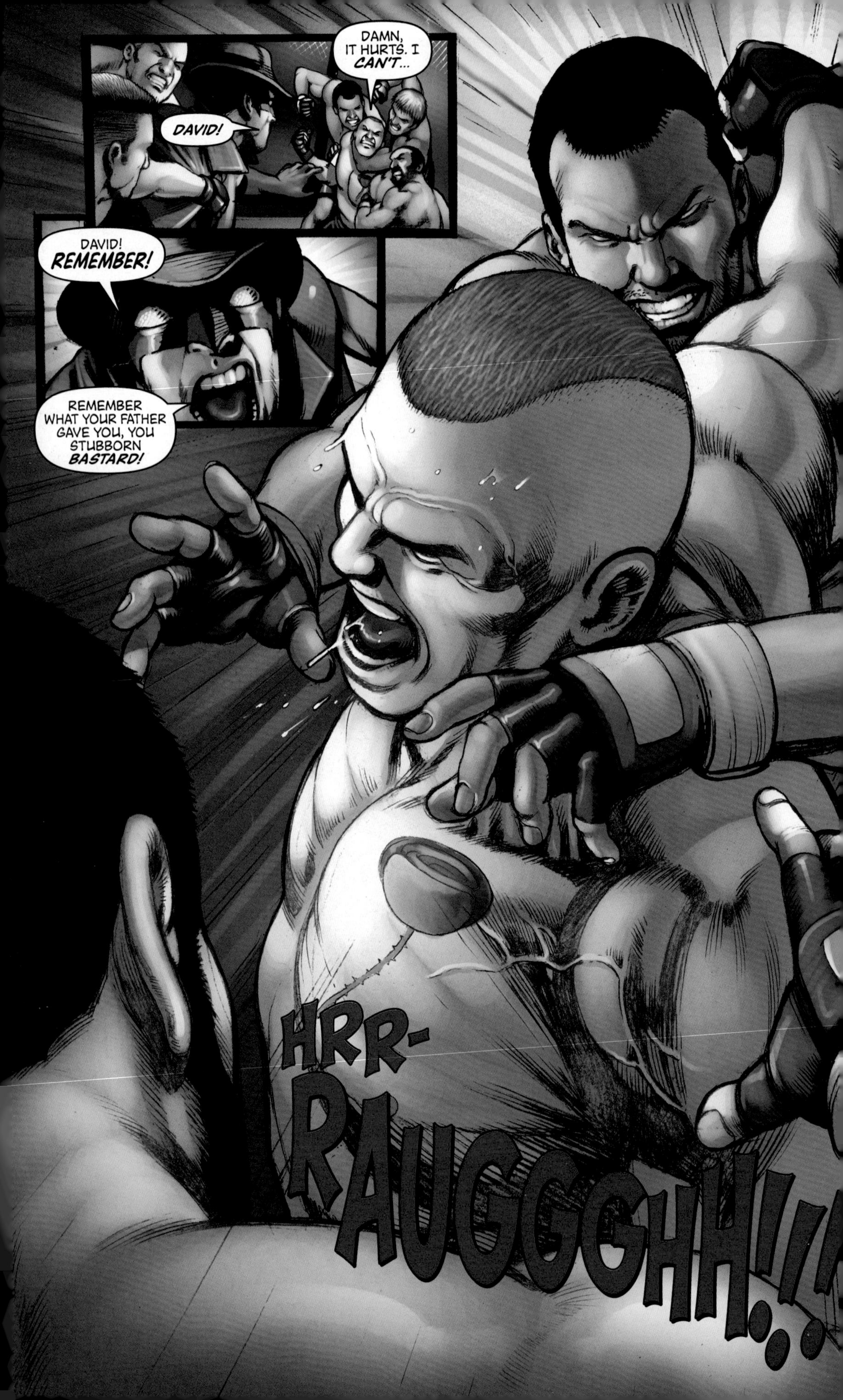

DAMN, IT HURTS. I *CAN'T*...
DAVID!
DAVID! **REMEMBER!**
REMEMBER WHAT YOUR FATHER GAVE YOU, YOU STUBBORN ***BASTARD!***
HRR-RAUGGGHH!!!

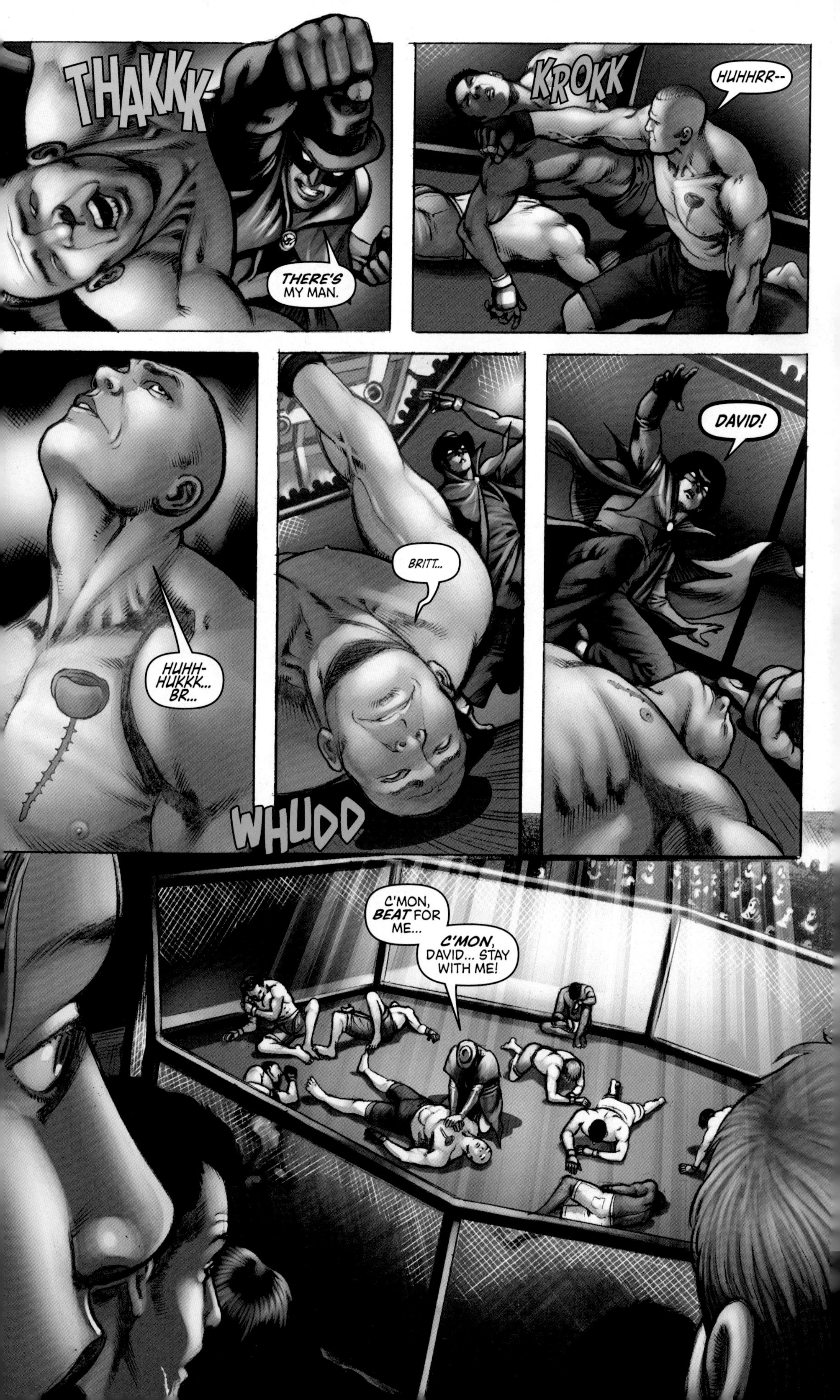

THAKKK
THERE'S MY MAN.
KROKK
HUHHRR--
HUHH-HUKKK... BR...
BRITT...
WHUDD
DAVID!
C'MON, BEAT FOR ME...
C'MON, DAVID... STAY WITH ME!

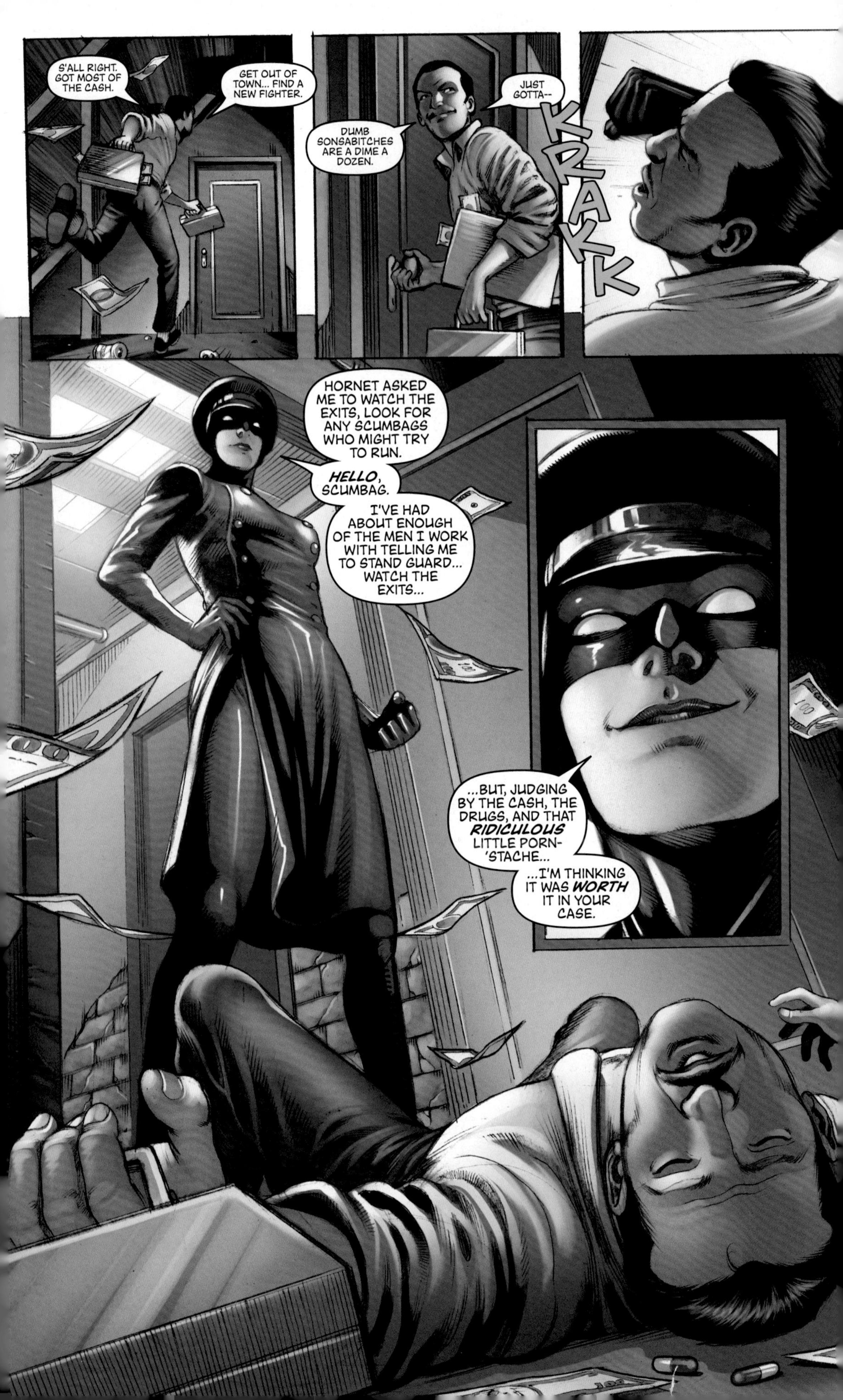
S'ALL RIGHT. GOT MOST OF THE CASH.
GET OUT OF TOWN... FIND A NEW FIGHTER.
DUMB SONSABITCHES ARE A DIME A DOZEN.
JUST GOTTA--
KRAKK
HORNET ASKED ME TO WATCH THE EXITS, LOOK FOR ANY SCUMBAGS WHO MIGHT TRY TO RUN.
HELLO, SCUMBAG.
I'VE HAD ABOUT ENOUGH OF THE MEN I WORK WITH TELLING ME TO STAND GUARD... WATCH THE EXITS...
...BUT, JUDGING BY THE CASH, THE DRUGS, AND THAT RIDICULOUS LITTLE PORN-'STACHE...
...I'M THINKING IT WAS WORTH IT IN YOUR CASE.

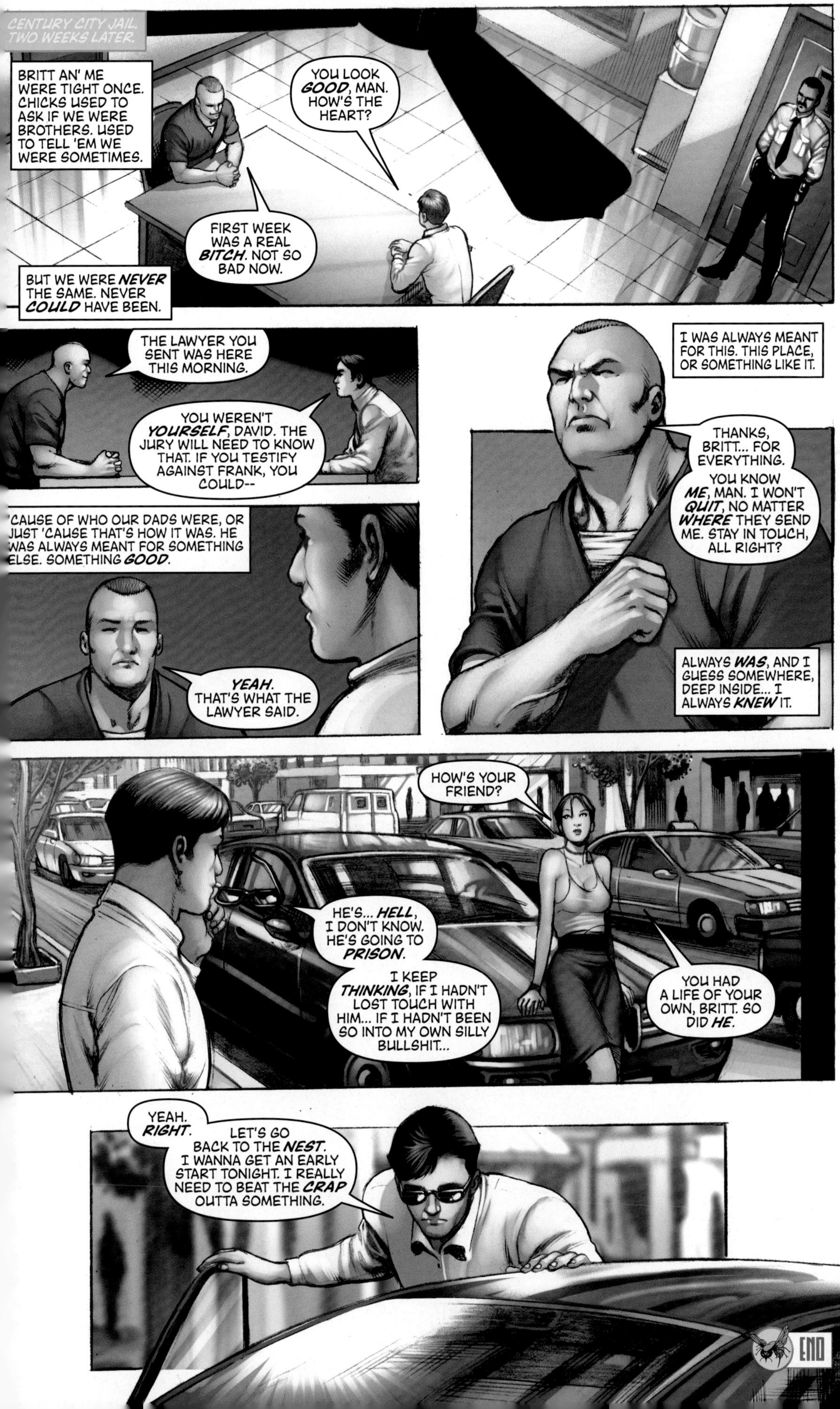

CENTURY CITY JAIL. TWO WEEKS LATER.
BRITT AN' ME WERE TIGHT ONCE. CHICKS USED TO ASK IF WE WERE BROTHERS. USED TO TELL 'EM WE WERE SOMETIMES.
YOU LOOK GOOD, MAN. HOW'S THE HEART?
FIRST WEEK WAS A REAL BITCH. NOT SO BAD NOW.
BUT WE WERE NEVER THE SAME. NEVER COULD HAVE BEEN.
THE LAWYER YOU SENT WAS HERE THIS MORNING.
YOU WEREN'T YOURSELF, DAVID. THE JURY WILL NEED TO KNOW THAT. IF YOU TESTIFY AGAINST FRANK, YOU COULD--
'CAUSE OF WHO OUR DADS WERE, OR JUST 'CAUSE THAT'S HOW IT WAS. HE WAS ALWAYS MEANT FOR SOMETHING ELSE. SOMETHING GOOD.
YEAH. THAT'S WHAT THE LAWYER SAID.
I WAS ALWAYS MEANT FOR THIS. THIS PLACE, OR SOMETHING LIKE IT.
THANKS, BRITT... FOR EVERYTHING.
YOU KNOW ME, MAN. I WON'T QUIT, NO MATTER WHERE THEY SEND ME. STAY IN TOUCH, ALL RIGHT?
ALWAYS WAS, AND I GUESS SOMEWHERE, DEEP INSIDE... I ALWAYS KNEW IT.
HOW'S YOUR FRIEND?
HE'S... HELL, I DON'T KNOW. HE'S GOING TO PRISON.
I KEEP THINKING, IF I HADN'T LOST TOUCH WITH HIM... IF I HADN'T BEEN SO INTO MY OWN SILLY BULLSHIT...
YOU HAD A LIFE OF YOUR OWN, BRITT. SO DID HE.
YEAH. RIGHT.
LET'S GO BACK TO THE NEST. I WANNA GET AN EARLY START TONIGHT. I REALLY NEED TO BEAT THE CRAP OUTTA SOMETHING.
END

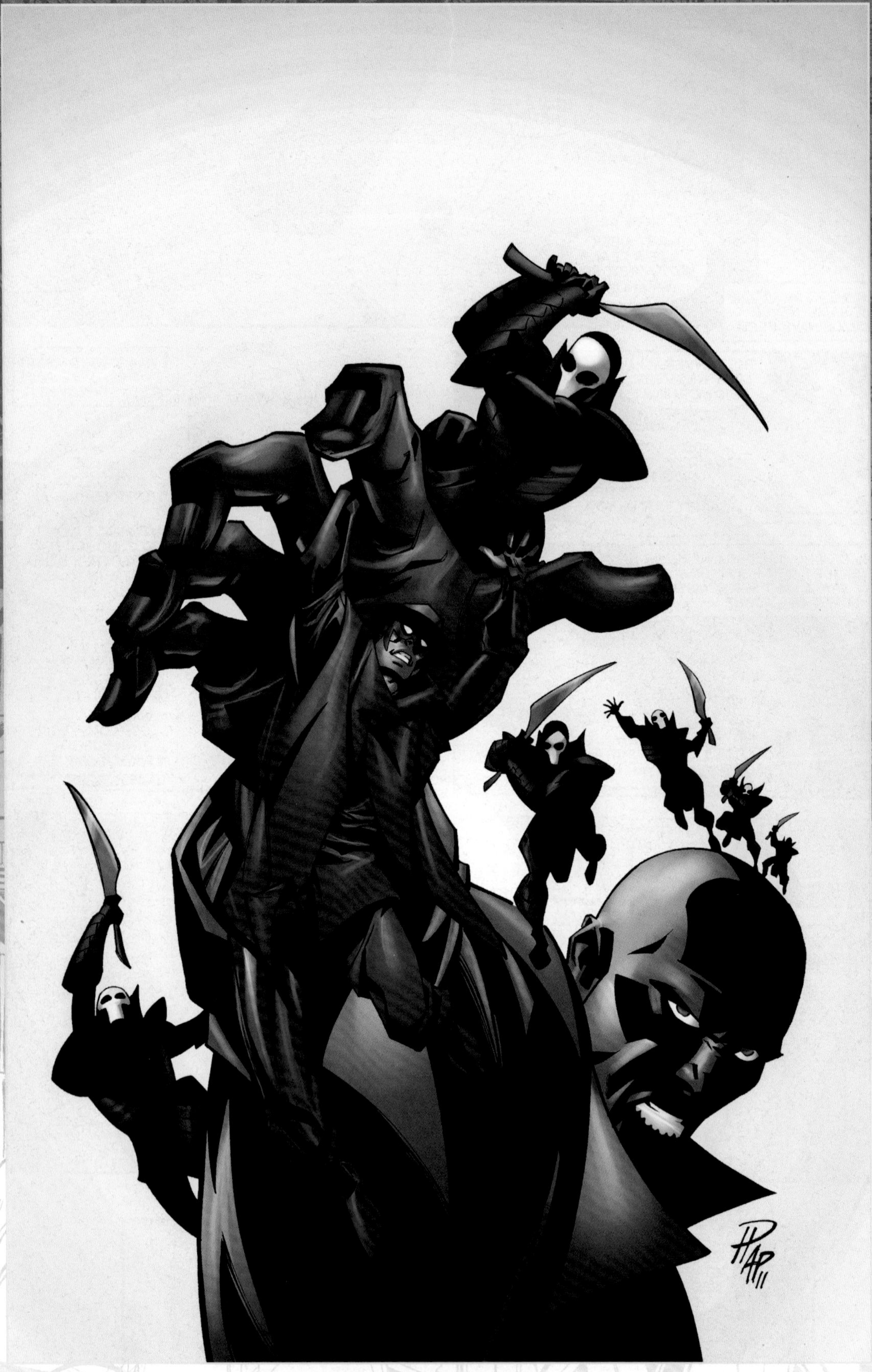

Cover to issue #16 by PHIL HESTER

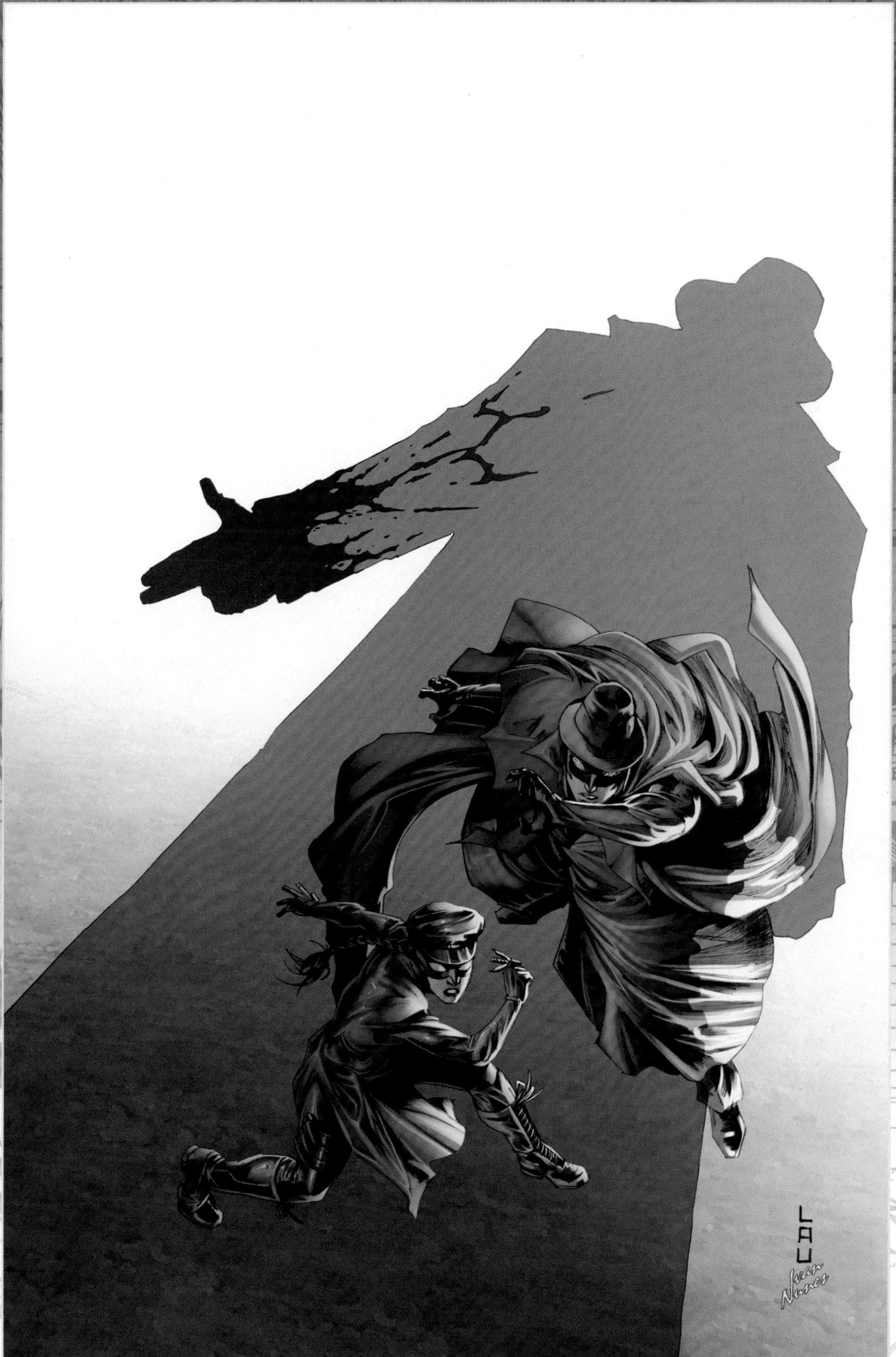
LAU

Cover to issue #16 by JONATHAN LAU

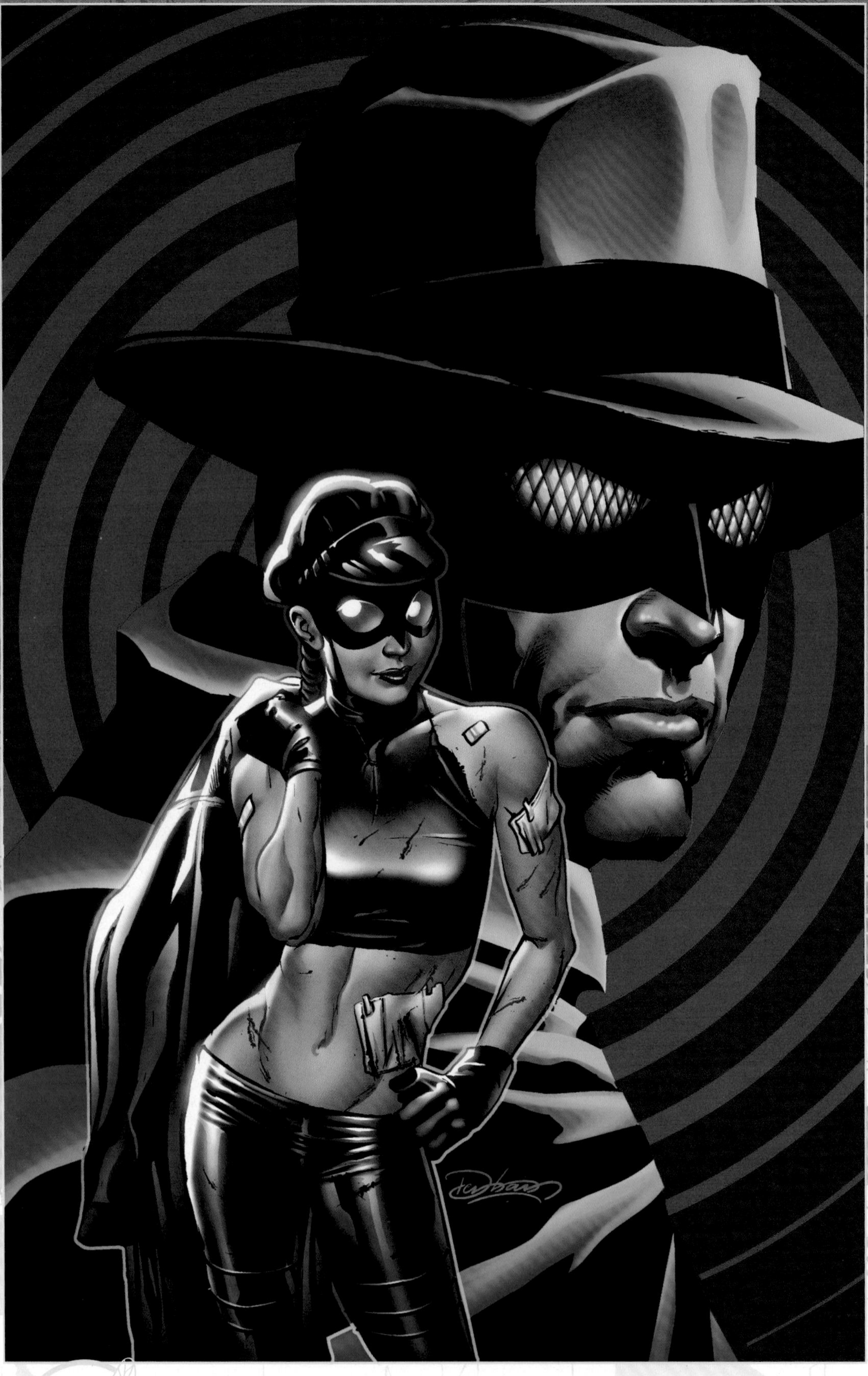

Cover to issue #16 by BRIAN DENHAM

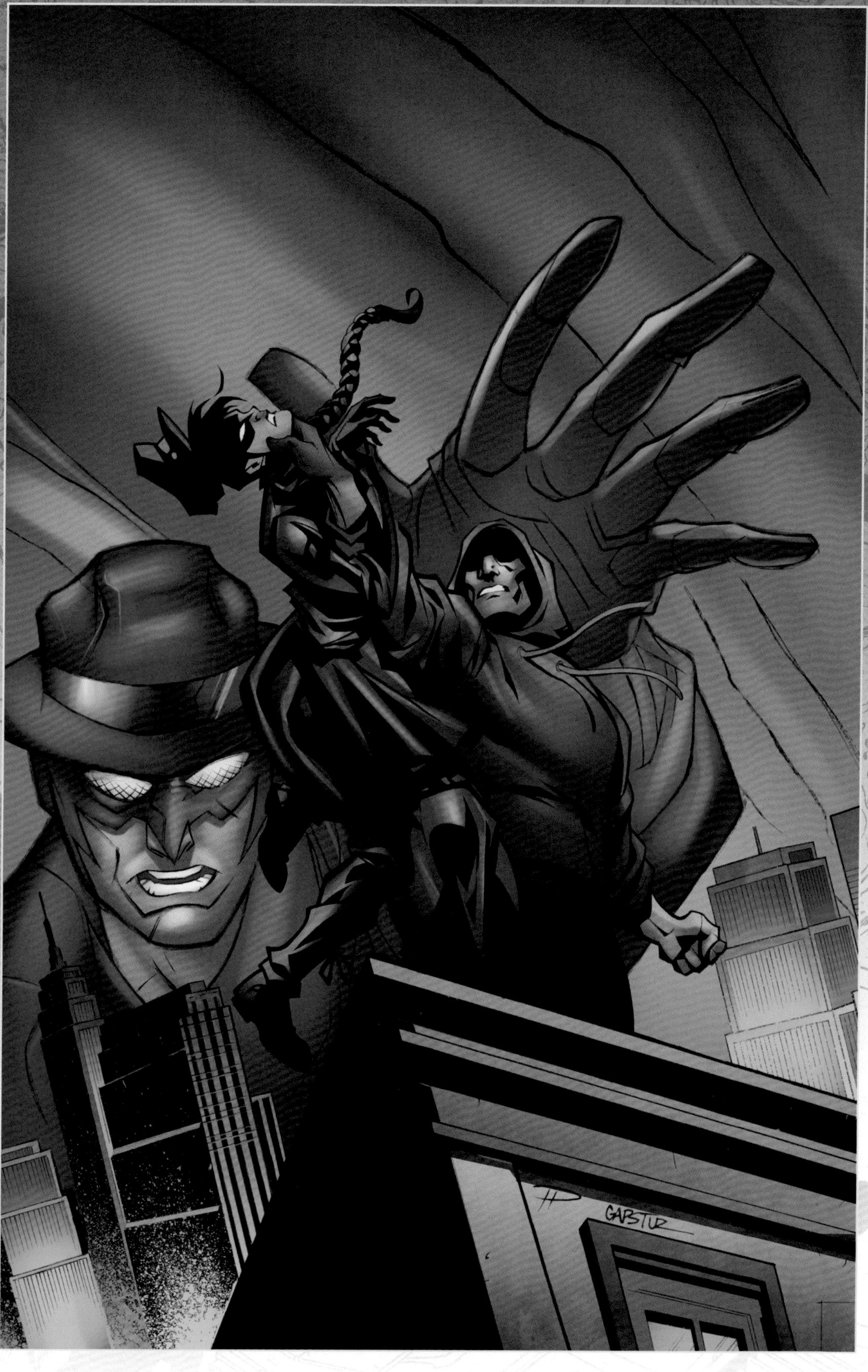
GABSTUR

Cover to issue #17 by PHIL HESTER

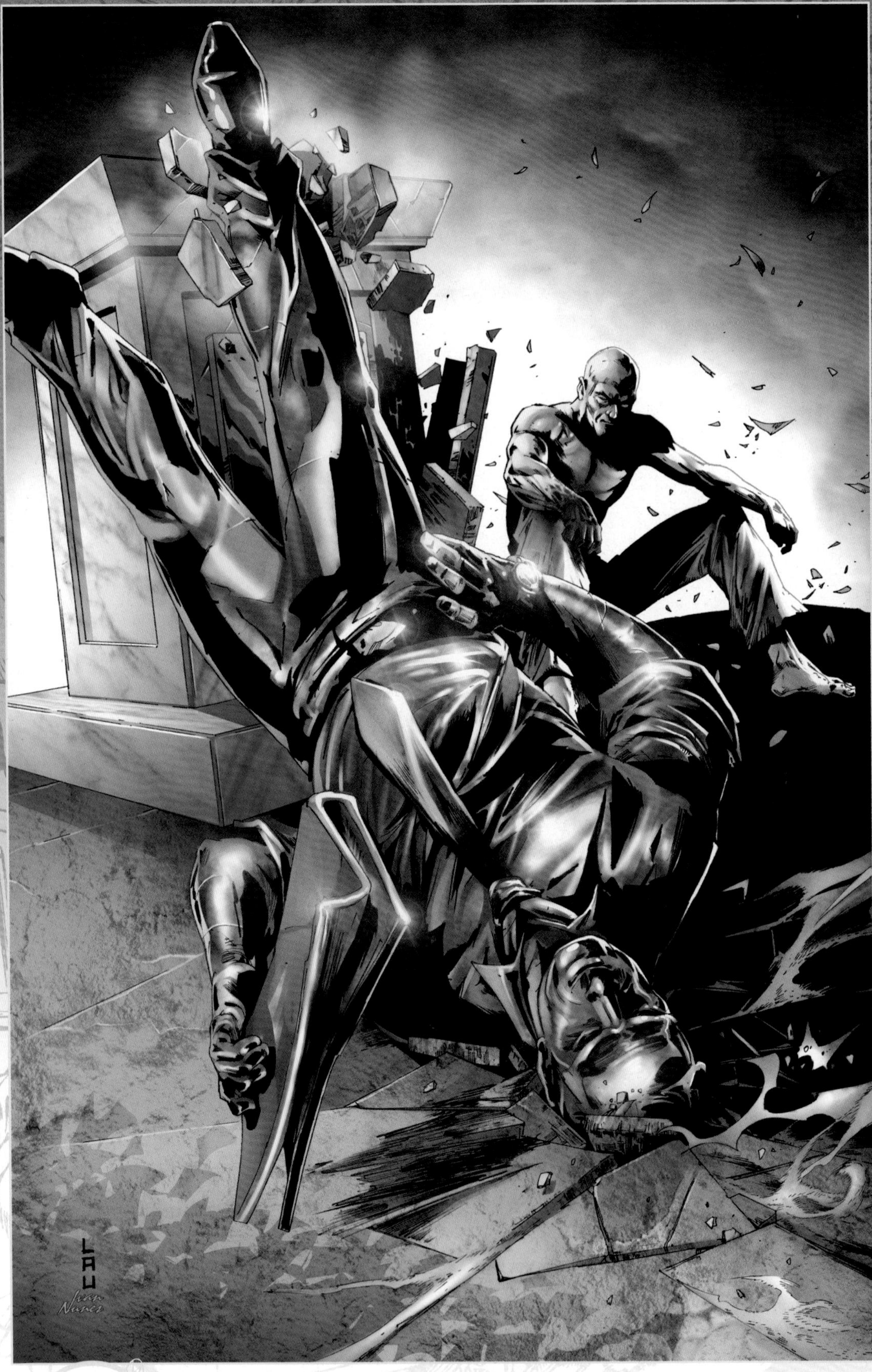
LAU

Cover to issue #17 by JONATHAN LAU

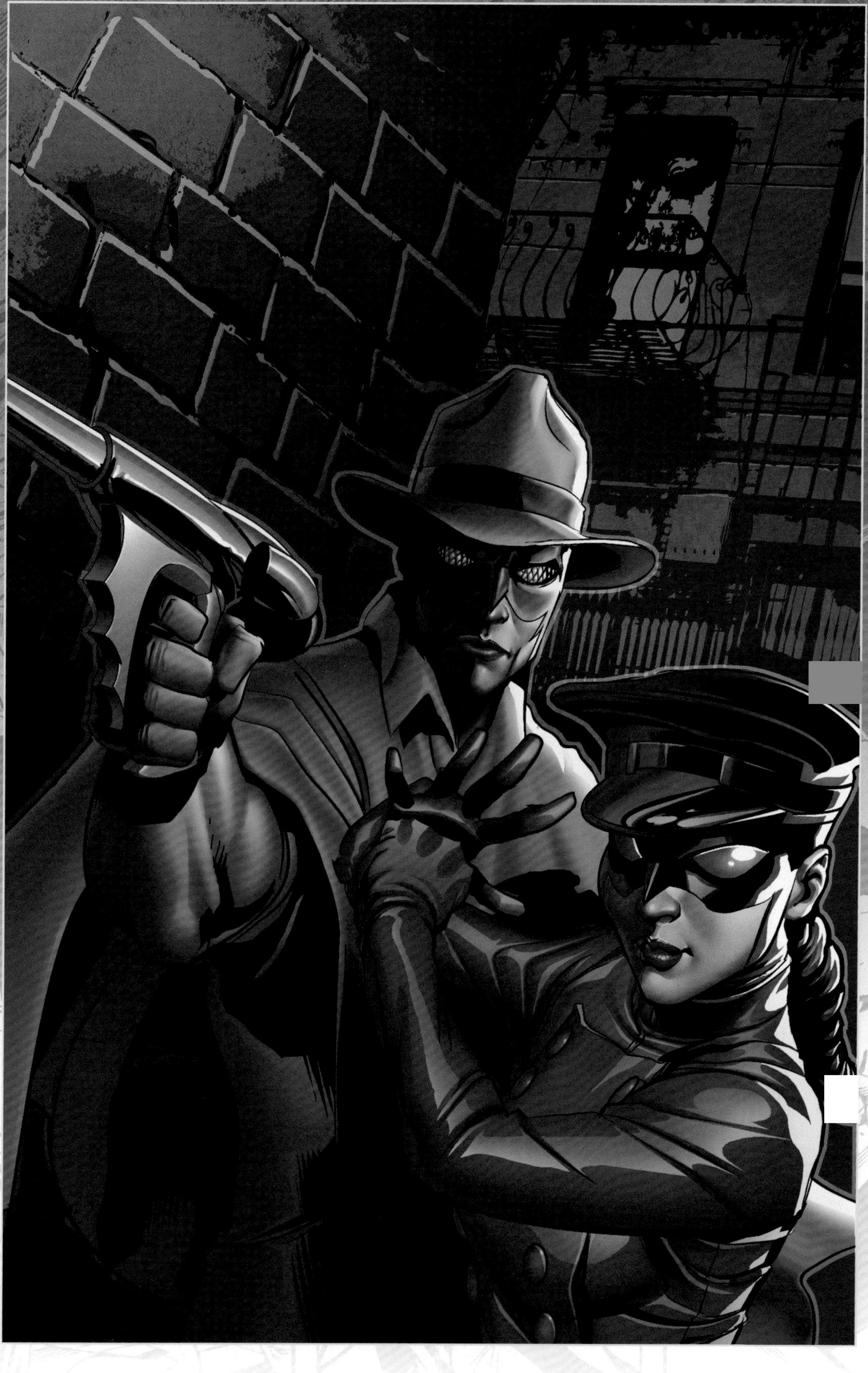

Cover to issue #17 by BRIAN DENHAM

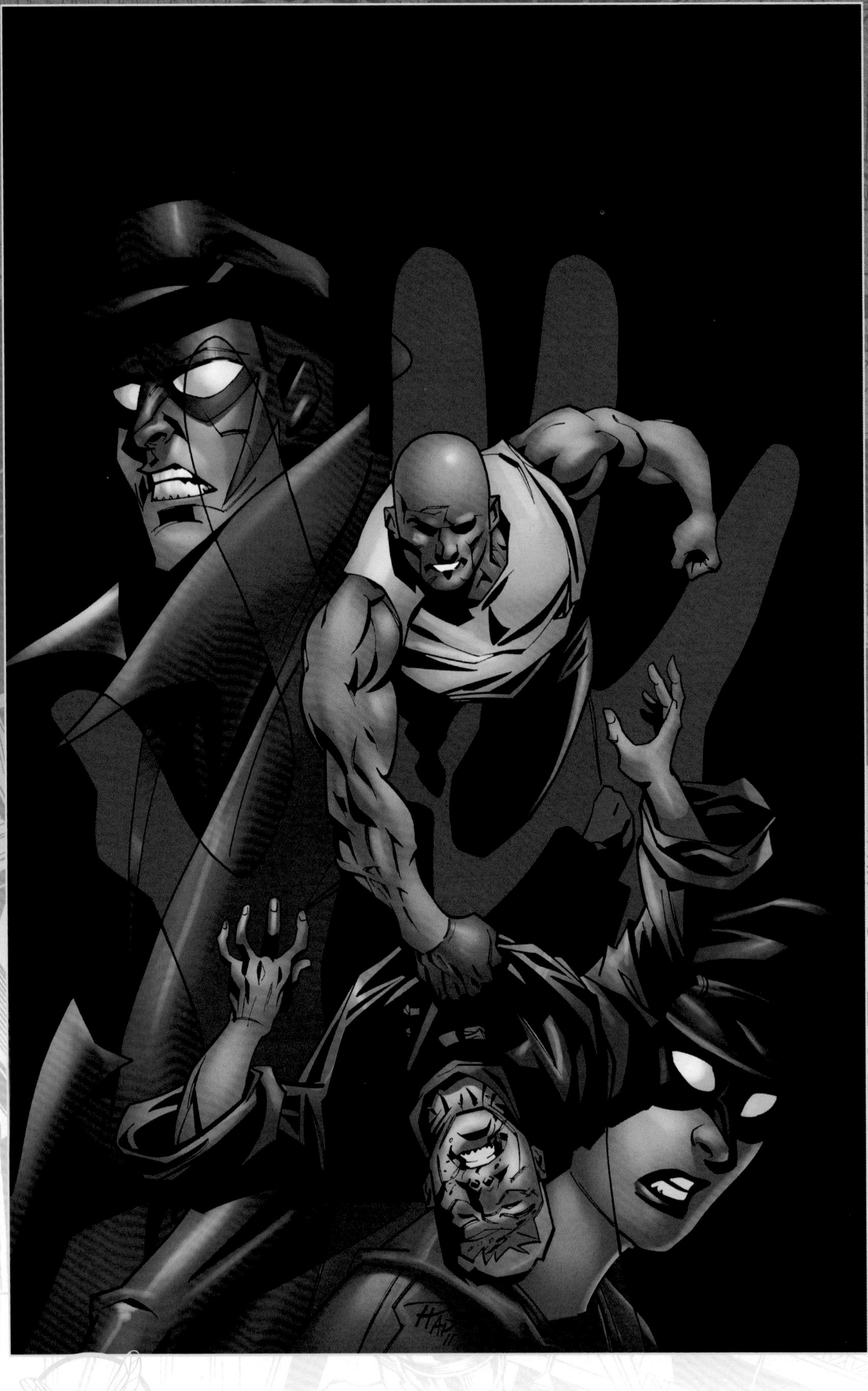

Cover to issue #18 by PHIL HESTER

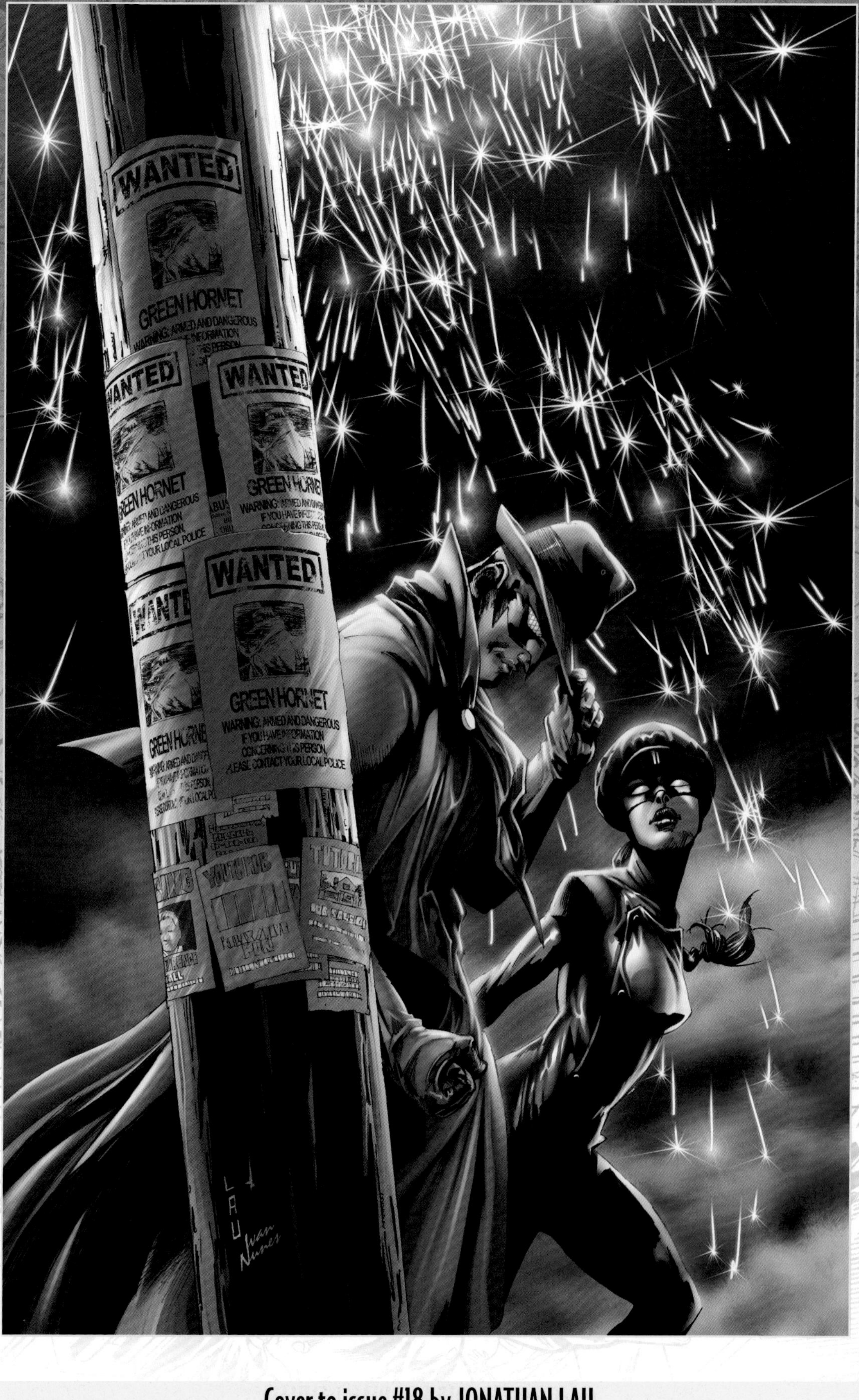
WANTED
GREEN HORNET
WARNING: ARMED AND DANGEROUS
IF YOU HAVE INFORMATION
CONCERNING THIS PERSON,
PLEASE CONTACT YOUR LOCAL POLICE
LAU

Cover to issue #18 by JONATHAN LAU

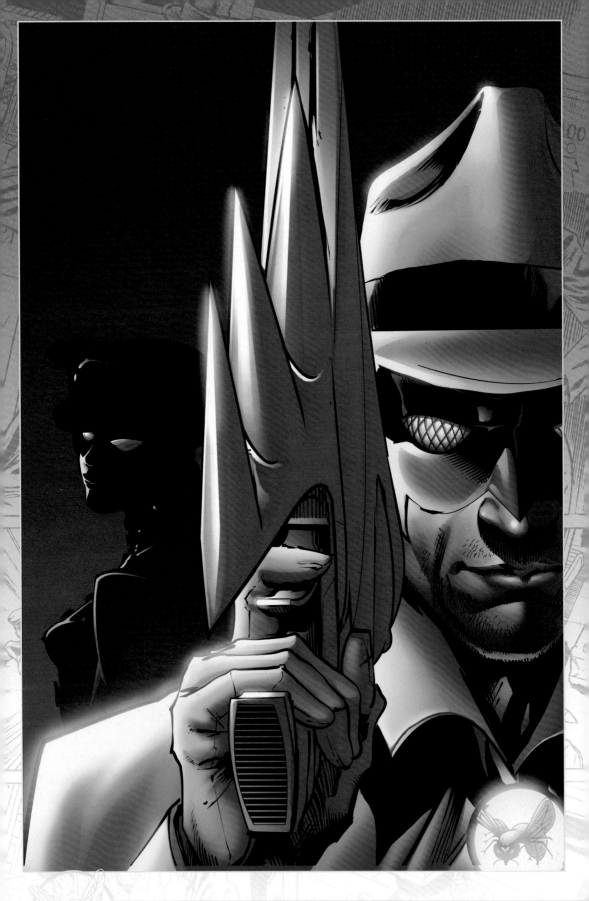

Cover to issue #18 by BRIAN DENHAM

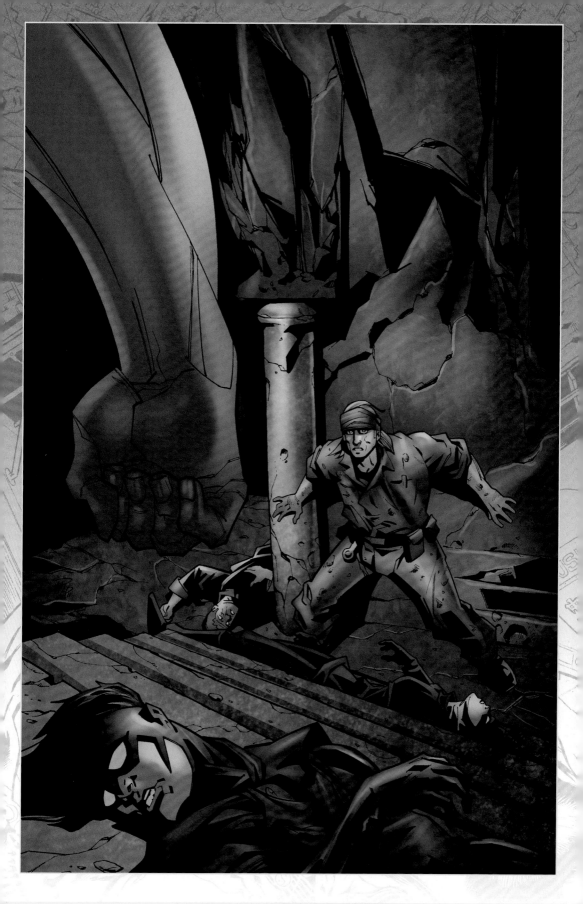

Cover to issue #19 by PHIL HESTER

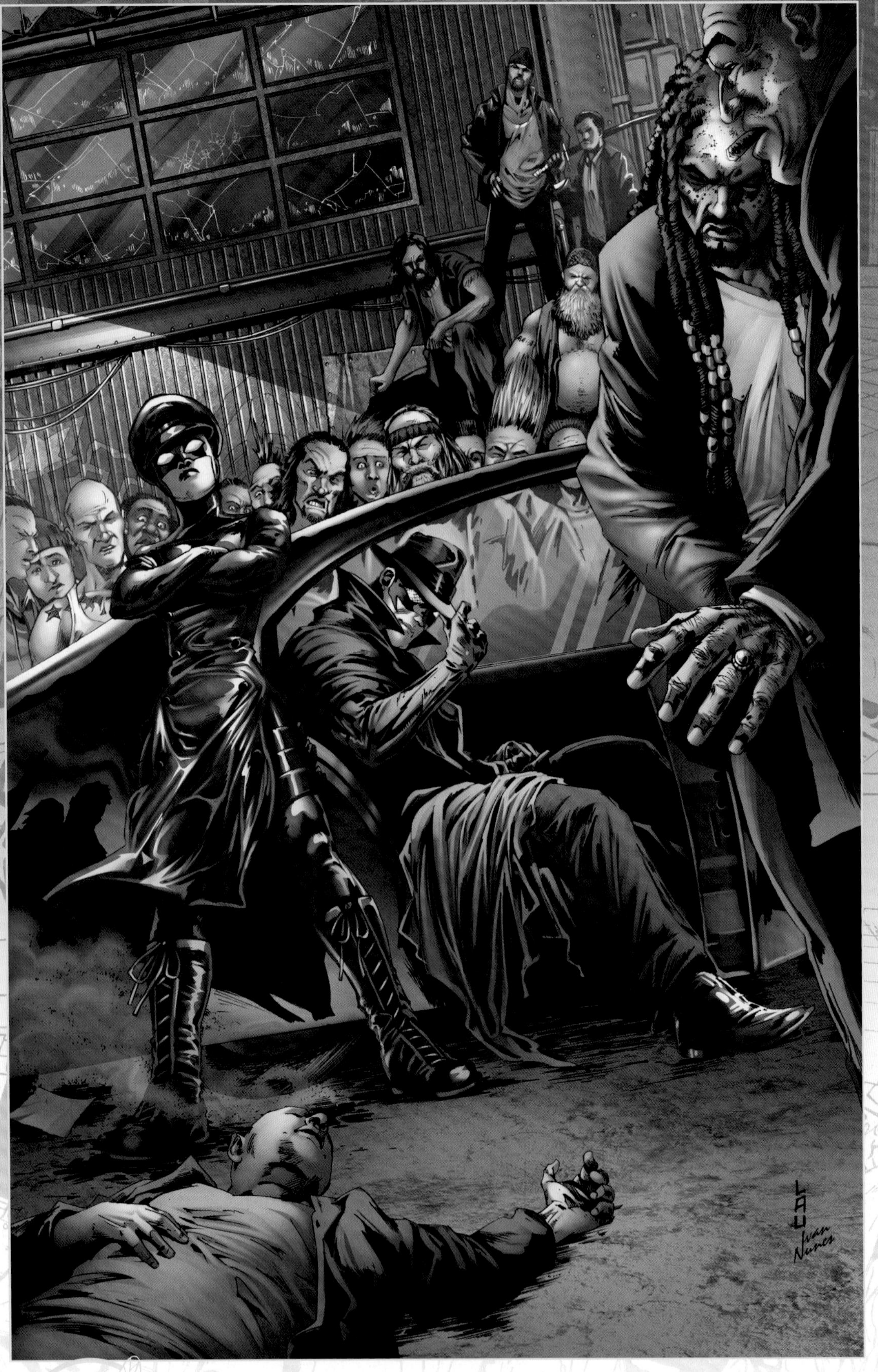
LAU
Ivan Nunes

Cover to issue #19 by JONATHAN LAU

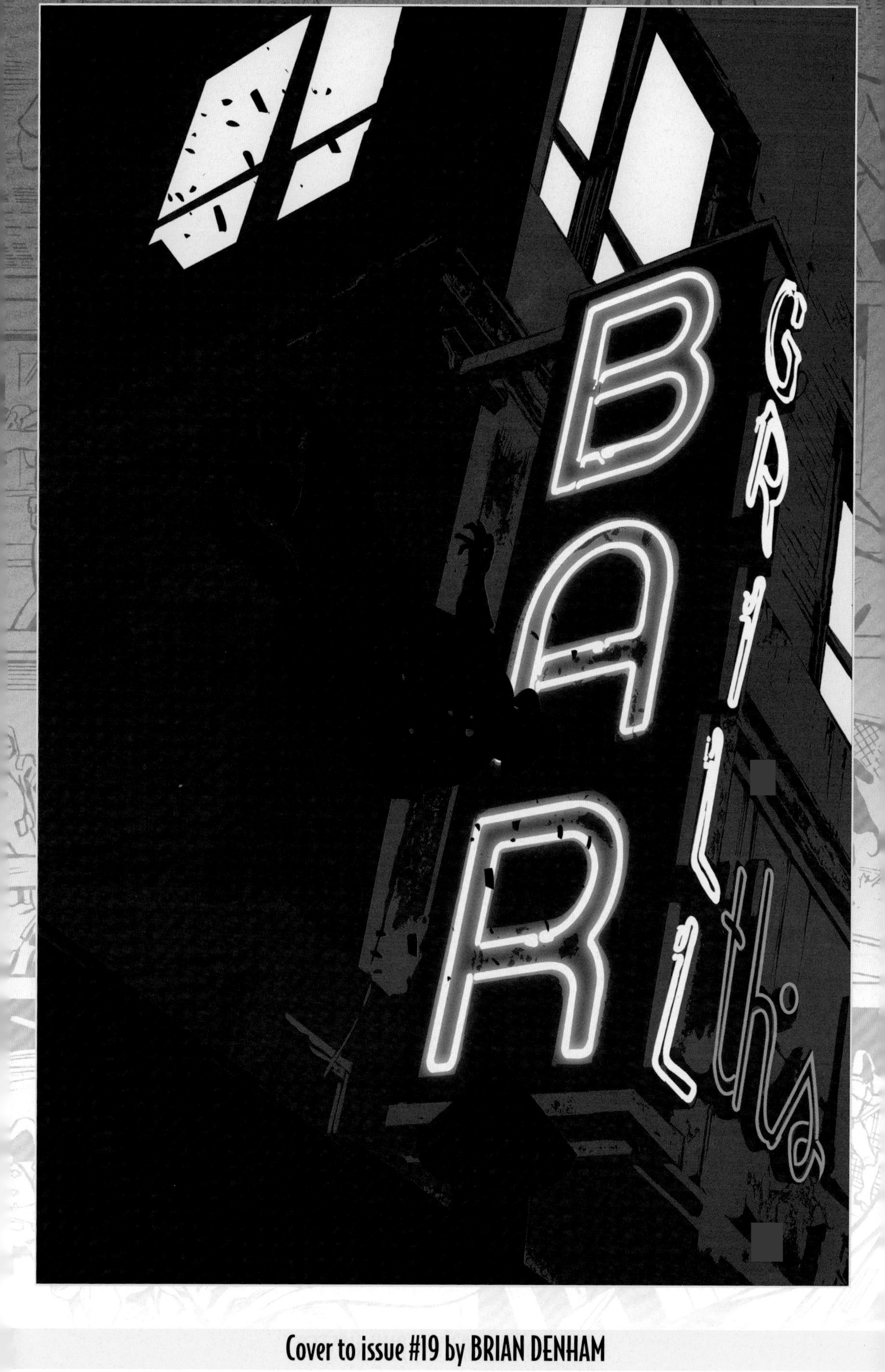
BAR

Cover to issue #19 by BRIAN DENHAM

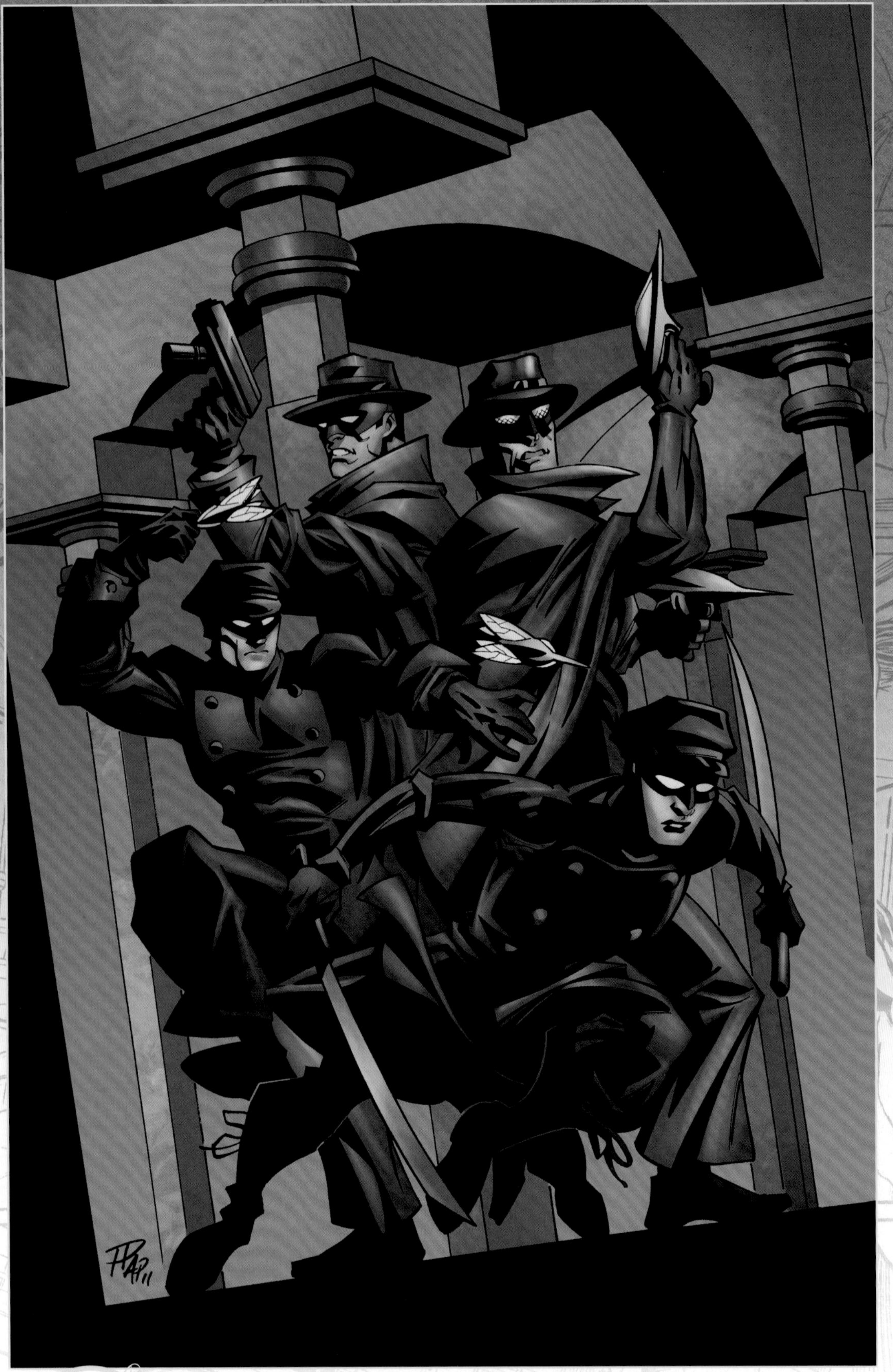

Cover to issue #20 by PHIL HESTER

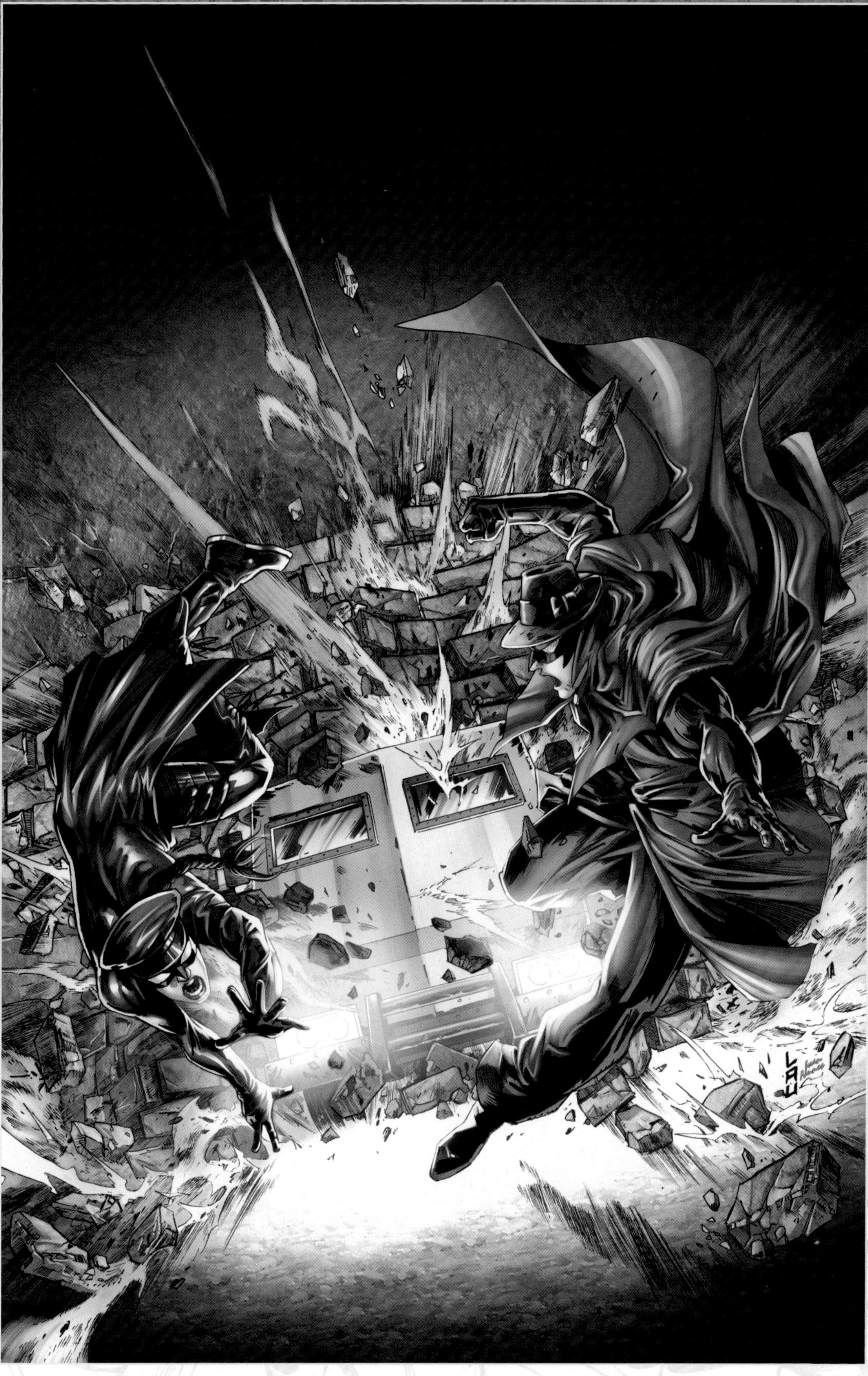
LAU

Cover to issue #20 by JONATHAN LAU

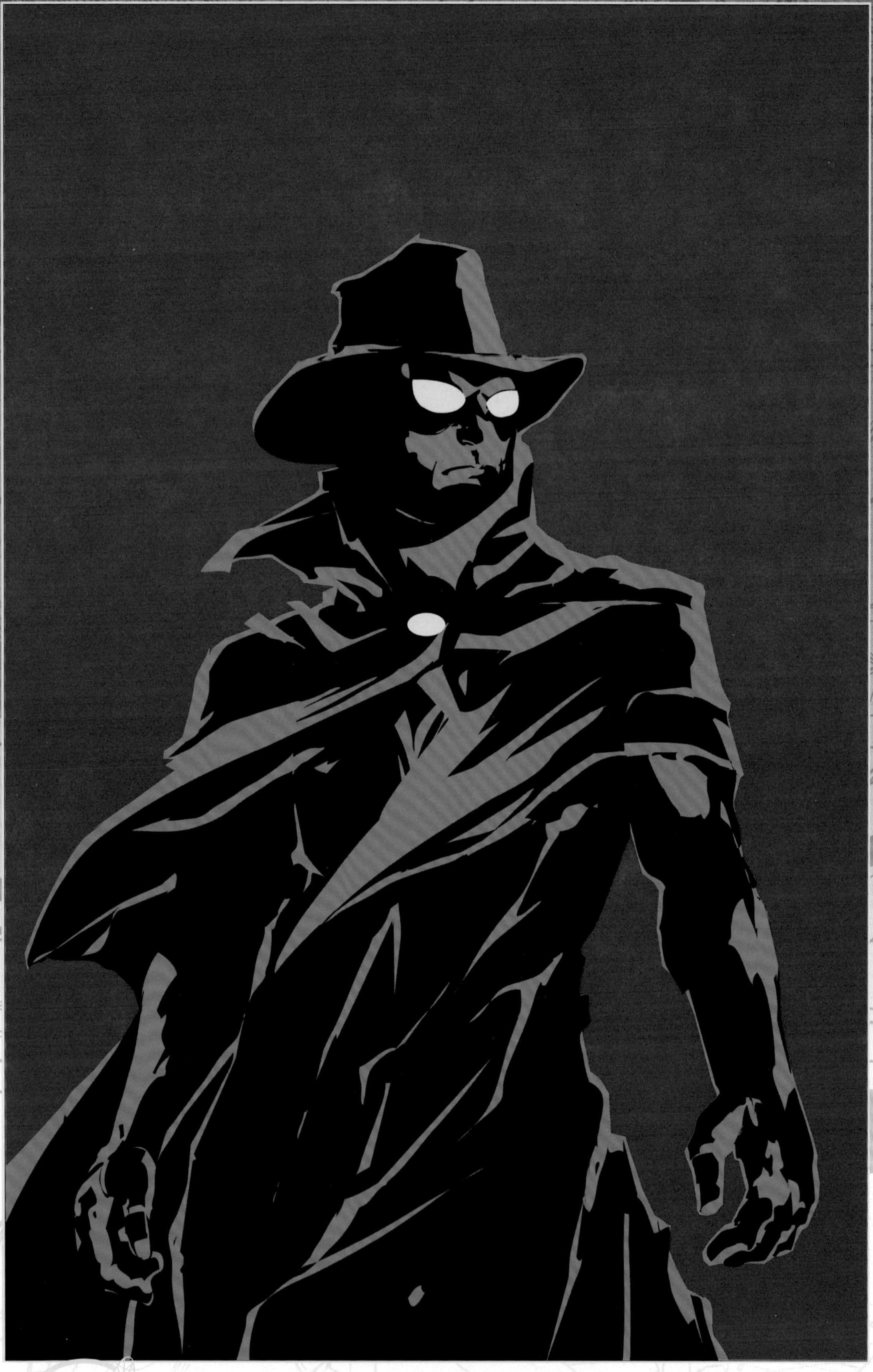

Cover to issue #20 by BRIAN DENHAM

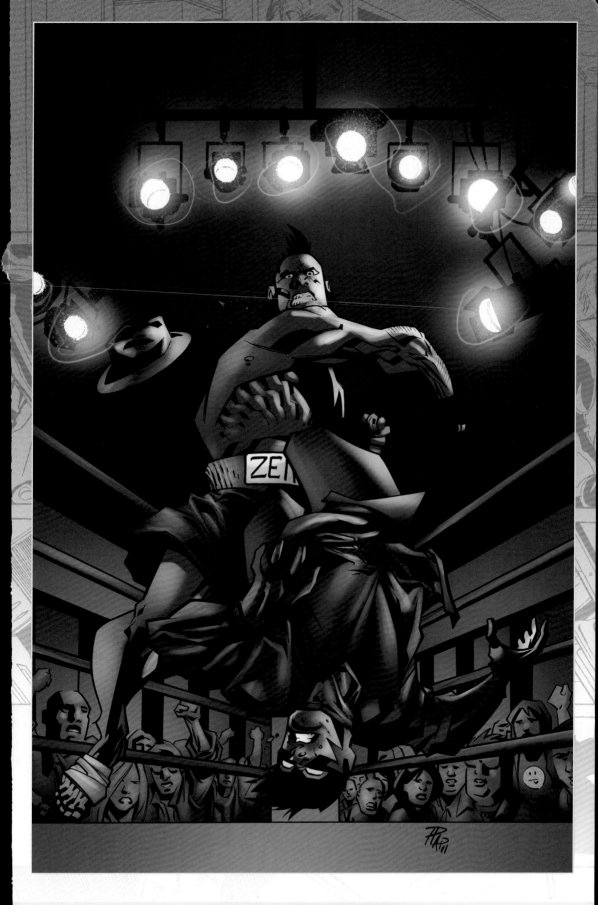

Cover to issue #21 by PHIL HESTER

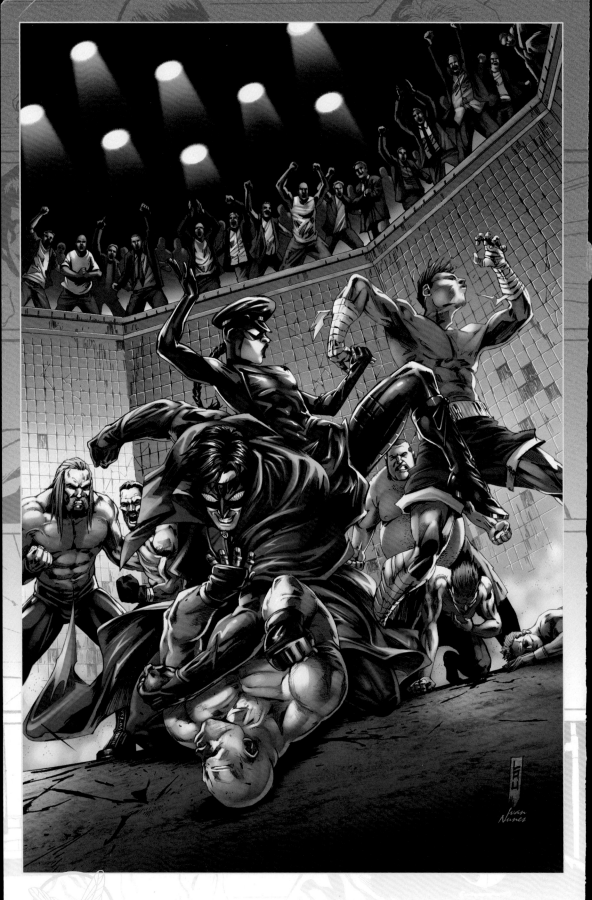

Cover to issue #21 by JONATHAN LAU

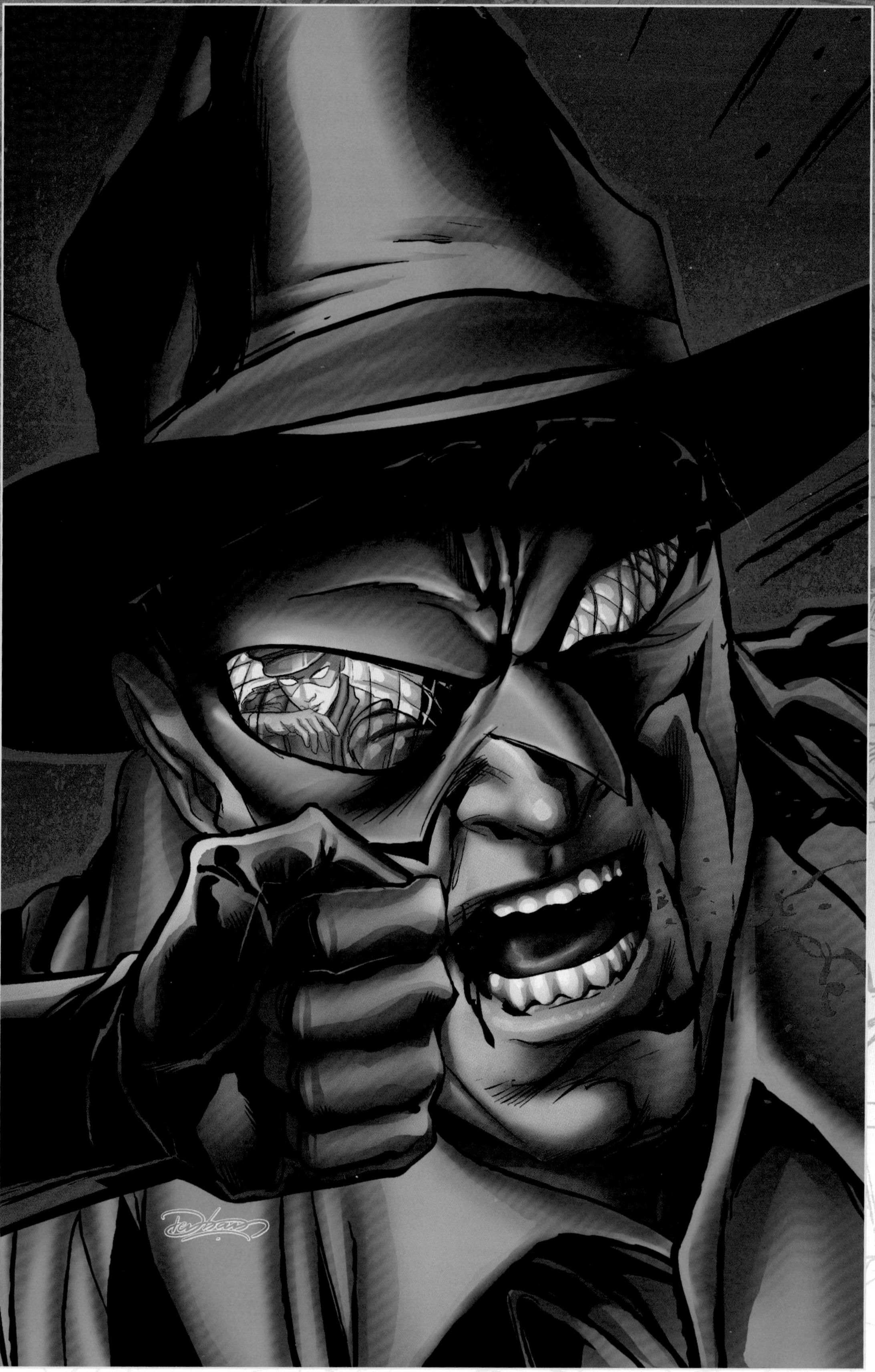

Cover to issue #21 by BRIAN DENHAM

CURRENTLY AVAILABLE AND UPCOMING COLLECTIONS FROM DYNAMITE
For a complete list, visit us online at www.dynamite.net

ARMY OF DARKNESS:
Army of Darkness:
Movie Adaptation
Raimi, Raimi, Bolton

Army of Darkness:
Ashes to Ashes
Hartnell, Bradshaw

Army of Darkness:
Shop 'Till You Drop Dead
Kuhoric, Bradshaw, Greene

Army of Darkness vs.
Re-Animator
Kuhoric, Bradshaw, Greene

Army of Darkness:
Old School & More
Kuhoric, Sharpe

Army of Darkness: Ash vs.
The Classic Monsters
Kuhoric, Sharpe, Blanco

Army of Darkness:
From The Ashes
Kuhoric, Blanco

Army of Darkness:
The Long Road Home
Kuhoric, Raicht, Blanco

Army of Darkness:
Home Sweet Hell
Kuhoric, Raicht, Perez

Army of Darkness:
Hellbillies & Deadnecks
Kuhoric, Raicht, Cohn

Army of Darkness:
League of Light Assemble!
Raicht, Cohn

Army of Darkness
Omnibus Vol. 1
Hartnell, Kuhoric, Kirkman, more

Army of Darkness
Omnibus Vol. 2
Kuhoric, Raicht, Perez, more

Army of Darkness:
Ash Saves Obama
Serrano, Padilla

Army of Darkness vs. Xena
Vol. 1: Why Not?
Layman, Jerwa, Montenegro

Xena vs. Army of Darkness
Vol. 2: What...Again?!
Jerwa, Serrano, Montenegro

Darkman vs. Army of Darkness
Busiek, Stern, Fry

BATTLESTAR GALACTICA
New Battlestar Galactica Vol. 1
Pak, Raynor

New Battlestar Galactica Vol. 2
Pak, Raynor

New Battlestar Galactica Vol. 3
Pak, Raynor, Lau

New Battlestar Galactica
Complete Omnibus V1
Pak, Raynor, Jerwa, Lau

New Battlestar Galactica: Zarek
Jerwa, Batista

New Battlestar Galactica:
Season Zero Vol. 1
Jerwa, Herbert

New Battlestar Galactica:
Season Zero Vol. 2
Jerwa, Herbert

New Battlestar Galactica
Origins: Baltar
Fahey, Lau

New Battlestar Galactica
Origins: Adama
Napton, Lau

New Battlestar Galactica
Origins: Starbuck & Helo
Fahey, Lau

New Battlestar Galactica:
Ghosts
Jerwa, Lau

New Battlestar Galactica:
Cylon War
Ortega, Nylund, Raynor

New Battlestar Galactica:
The Final Five
Fahey, Reed, Raynor

Classic Battlestar Galactica
Vol. 1
Remender, Rafael

Classic Battlestar Galactica
Vol. 2: Cylon Apocalypse
Grillo-Marxuach, Rafael

GALACTICA 1980
Guggenheim, Razek

THE BOYS
The Boys Vol. 1
The Name of the Game
Ennis, Robertson

The Boys Vol. 2
Get Some
Ennis, Robertson, Snejbjerg

The Boys Vol. 3
Good For The Soul
Ennis, Robertson

The Boys Vol. 4
We Gotta Go Now
Ennis, Robertson

The Boys Vol. 5
Herogasm
Ennis, McCrea

The Boys Vol. 6
The Self-Preservation Society
Ennis, Robertson, Ezquerra

The Boys Vol. 7
The Innocents
Ennis, Robertson, Braun

The Boys Vol. 8
Highland Laddie
Ennis, McCrea

The Boys Vol. 9
The Big Ride
Ennis, Braun

The Boys Vol. 10: Butcher,
Baker, Candlestickmaker
Ennis, Robertson

The Boys
Definitive Edition Vol. 1
Ennis, Robertson

The Boys
Definitive Edition Vol. 2
Ennis, Robertson

The Boys
Definitive Edition Vol. 3
Ennis, Robertson, McCrea, more

THE GREEN HORNET
Kevin Smith's Green Hornet
Vol. 1 Sins of the Father
Smith, Hester, Lau

Kevin Smith's Green Hornet
Vol. 2 Wearing 'o the Green
Smith, Hester, Lau

Green Hornet Vol. 3 Idols
Hester, Lau

Green Hornet Vol. 4 Red Hand
Hester, Smith, Vitorino, more

Kevin Smith's Kato Vol. 1
Not My Father's Daughter
Parks, Garza, Bernard

Kevin Smith's Kato Vol. 2
Living in America
Parks, Bernard

Green Hornet: Blood Ties
Parks, Desjardins

The Green Hornet: Year One
Vol. 1 The Sting of Justice
Wagner, Campbell, Francavilla

The Green Hornet: Year One
Vol. 2 The Biggest of All Game
Wagner, Campbell

Kato Origins Vol. 1
Way of the Ninja
Nitz, Worley

Kato Origins Vol. 2
The Hellfire Club
Nitz, Worley
The Green Hornet: Parallel
Lives
Nitz, Raynor

The Green Hornet Golden Age
Re-Mastered
Various

PROJECT SUPERPOWERS
Project Superpowers Chapter 1
Ross, Krueger, Paul, Sadowski

Project Superpowers Chapter 2
Vol. 1
Ross, Krueger, Salazar

Project Superpowers Chapter 2
Vol. 2
Ross, Krueger, Salazar

Project Superpowers: Meet The
Bad Guys
Ross, Casey, Lilly, Lau, Paul, Herbert

Black Terror Vol. 1
Ross, Krueger, Lilly

Black Terror Vol. 2
Ross, Hester, Lau

Black Terror Vol. 3
Inhuman Remains
Ross, Hester, Reis, Herbert

Death-Defying 'Devil Vol 1
Ross, Casey, Salazar

Masquerade Vol. 2
Ross, Hester, Laul

RED SONJA
Adventures of Red Sonja Vol. 1
Thomas, Thorne, More

Adventures of Red Sonja Vol. 2
Thomas, Thorne, More

Adventures of Red Sonja Vol. 3
Thomas, Thorne, More

Queen Sonja Vol. 1
Ortega, Rubi

Queen Sonja Vol. 2
The Red Queen
Nelson, Herbert

Red Sonja She-Devil With a
Sword Vol. 1
Oeming, Carey, Rubi

Red Sonja She-Devil With a
Sword Vol. 2: Arrowsmiths
Oeming, Rubi, more

Red Sonja She-Devil With a
Sword Vol. 3: The Rise of
Kulan Gath
Oeming, Rubi, more

Red Sonja She-Devil With a
Sword Vol. 4: Animals & More
Oeming, Homs, more

Red Sonja She-Devil With a
Sword Vol. 5: World On Fire
Oeming, Reed, Homs

Red Sonja She-Devil With a
Sword Vol. 6: Death
Marz, Ortega, Reed, more

Red Sonja She-Devil With a
Sword Vol. 7: Born Again
Reed, Geovani

Red Sonja She-Devil With a
Sword Vol. 8: Blood Dynasty
Reed, Geovani

Red Sonja She-Devil With a
Sword Vol. 9: War Season
Trautmann, Geovani, Berkenkotter

Red Sonja She-Devil With a
Sword Omnibus Vol. 1
Oeming, Carey, Rubi, more

Red Sonja vs. Thulsa Doom
Vol. 1
David, Lieberman, Conrad

Savage Red Sonja: Queen of
the Frozen Wastes
Cho, Murray, Homs

Red Sonja: Travels
Marz, Ortega, Thomas, more

Sword of Red Sonja: Doom
of the Gods (Red Sonja vs.
Thulsa Doom 2)
Lieberman, Antonio

Red Sonja: Wrath of the Gods
Lieberman, Geovani

Red Sonja: Revenge of the
Gods
Lieberman, Sampere

Savage Tales of Red Sonja
Marz, Gage, Ortega, more

VAMPIRELLA
Vampirella Masters Series Vol 1
Grant Morrison & Mark Millar
Morrison, Millar, more

Vampirella Masters Series Vol 2
Warren Ellis
Ellis, Conner Palmiotti, more

Vampirella Masters Series Vol 3
Mark Millar
Millar, Mayhew

Vampirella Masters Series Vol 4
Visionaries
Moore, Busiek, Loeb, more

Vampirella Masters Series Vol 5
Kurt Busiek
Busiek, Sniegoski, LaChanc, more

Vampirella Masters Series Vol 6
James Robinson
Robinson, Jusko, more

Vampirella Archives Vol 1
Various

Vampirella Archives Vol 2
Various

Vampirella Archives Vol 3
Various

Vampirella Archives Vol 4
Various

Vampirella Vol. 1
Crown of Worms
Trautman, Reis, Geovani

Vampirella Vol. 2
A Murder of Crows
Trautman, Jerwa, Neves, more

Vampirella And The
Scarlet Legion
Harris, Malaga

MORE FROM GARTH ENNIS
Dan Dare Omnibus
Ennis, Erskine

Garth Ennis' Battlefields
Vol. 1: The Night Witches
Ennis, Braun

Garth Ennis' Battlefields
Vol. 2: Dear Billy
Ennis, Snejbjerg

Garth Ennis' Battlefields
Vol. 3: The Tankies
Ennis, Ezquerra

Garth Ennis' The Complete
Battlefields Vol. 1
Ennis, Braun, Snejbjerg, Ezquerra

Garth Ennis' Battlefields
Vol. 4: Happy Valley
Ennis, Holden

Garth Ennis' Battlefields
Vol.5: The Firefly and His
Majesty
Ennis, Ezquerra

Garth Ennis' Battlefields
Vol.6: Motherland
Ennis, Braun

Garth Ennis' The Complete
Battlefields Vol. 2
Ennis, Braun, Holden, Ezquerra

Jennifer Blood Vol. 1: A
Woman's Work Is Never Done
Ennis, Batista, Baal, more

Just A Pilgrim
Ennis, Ezquerra

Seven Brothers Omnibus
Ennis, Woo, Kang, more

ART BOOKS
The Art of Howard Chaykin

The Art of Red Sonja

The Art of Vampirella

The Dynamite Art of Alex Ross

George Pérez, Storyteller

The Romita Legacy